CHANGING MOODS: THE PSYCHOLOGY OF MOOD AND MOOD REGULATION

Brian Parkinson
Peter Totterdell
Rob B. Briner
Shirley Reynolds

LONGMAN

London and New York

Addison Wesley Longman Limited,
Edinburgh Gate,
Harlow, Essex CM20 2JE, England
and Associated Companies throughout the world.

*Published in the United States of America
by Addison Wesley Longman Publishing Company, New York*

First published 1996

ISBN 0 582 278147 PPR

British Library Cataloguing-in-Publication Data
A catalogue record for this book is available from the British Library

Library of Congress Cataloging-in-Publication Data
Parkinson, Brian, 1958–
Changing moods: the psychology of mood and mood regulation/
Brian Parkinson . . . [et al.].
p. cm.
Includes bibliographical references and index.
ISBN 0–582–27814–7 (paper)
1. Mood (Psychology) 2. Affect (Psychology) I. Title.
BF521.P37 1996
152.4—dc20   96–17192
                                         CIP

Typeset by 35 in 10/12pt Times
Printed in Great Britain by Henry Ling Ltd., at the Dorset Press,
Dorchester, Dorset.

CONTENTS

Preface   vii

1 Introduction to the Psychology of Mood   1
   Overview   1
   Mood in Everyday Language   1
   Mood as a Psychological Concept   4
   Contextualizing Mood Research   10
   Structure of Book   14
   Summary   16

2 Mapping the Structure of Affect   17
   Overview   17
   Introduction   17
   Dimensions of Affect   19
   Circumplex Models of Affective Structure   25
   Independence of Positive and Negative Affect   32
   Measurement of Mood Dimensions   35
   Are Two Dimensions Enough?   39
   Summary   41

3 Predictors of Mood   43
   Overview   43
   Introduction   43
   External Predictors   44
   Experimental Manipulations of Mood   51
   Internal Predictors   55
   Transactions as 'Predictors' of Mood   63
   Summary   68

4 Mood Effects   70
   Overview   70
   Introduction   70
   Demarcation of Mood Effects   71

Explanations of Mood Effects 76
Effects of Mood on Different Aspects of Psychological Function 89
Summary 103

5 Mood Dynamics 105
Overview 105
Changes in Mood 105
Mood as Dynamic Equilibrium 106
Mood as Socially Entrained Rhythms 113
Mood as Nonlinear Dynamics 123
Investigating Mood Dynamics: The Process Approach 126
Summary 128

6 Mood Regulation 129
Overview 129
Introduction 129
Regulation in Relation to Other Aspects of the Mood Process 130
Evaluating Mood 132
Changing Mood 138
Key Issues 148
Towards a Model of Mood Regulation 152
Summary 154

7 Clinical Approaches to Mood and Mood Disorders 156
Overview 156
Introduction 156
Psychological Theories of Mood Disorders 160
Mood Disorders and Mood Regulation Processes 171
Psychological Interventions for Mood Disorders 177
Summary 185

8 Conclusions and Future Directions 187
Overview 187
Implications of a Process Approach to Mood 187
Aspects of Mood Regulation 191
Mood-Regulation Episodes 200
Sketch for a Theory of Mood Regulation 208
Future of Mood Research 211
Mood Across the Subdisciplines of Psychology 213
Reformulation of Mood 216

Appendix Methods for Implementing a Process Approach to Mood 218

References 222

Index 247

PREFACE

The four authors of this book first met while working at the Social and Applied Psychology Unit (SAPU) in Sheffield, a period in our research careers that perhaps seems rosier in retrospect, especially if the mood of the group is positive while we are reminiscing together. We were friends as well as colleagues, meaning that we took even academic arguments personally. At the time, each of us worked in quite separate research groups under the supervision of different team leaders. Brian Parkinson was managing and processing data for large-scale cross-national longitudinal studies relating to work socialization without finding any close identification with his own occupational role; Peter Totterdell was studying the effects of shiftwork on performance and well-being while maintaining his own idiosyncratic office hours; Rob Briner had recently completed his Ph.D which approached so-called occupational stress phenomena from a critical angle, just as he still approaches any of his own working problems or successes; and Shirley Reynolds was involved in an investigation of the effectiveness of different forms of psychotherapy, though in practice none of these proved of any particular use to the rest of us. Meanwhile all of us were also pursuing our "personal" research interests in whatever X percent of working hours was permitted for such activities as a result of the continuing negotiations with management. Happily there was some convergence and overlap of these interests which led to the first (and almost the last) completely cross-team research collaboration in the Unit's history.

Although many origin myths have arisen since then, most of us would agree that a key initial impetus for the research group came from Peter and Rob's discussions about adopting dynamic rather than static approaches to psychological variables. Both had wrestled with time-series diary data concerning well-being and affect and wanted to develop ways of analysing them and to generate bold new theories capable of dealing with the findings. At some point, Shirley and Brian also became involved in these "talks about talks", bringing complementary research interests relating to affect and emotion in real-life social settings. Although our disagreements are still many, there has always been some fertile common ground.

Our discussions eventually led to a diary study known affectionately as SAM (Study of Activity and Mood) which used a methodology whereby participants entered self-report and performance data into hand-held computers every two of their waking hours for two weeks. The four of us piloted this procedure on ourselves with mixed results. Unwitting onlookers must have been more than slightly puzzled on those occasions when team members were out together of an evening and, on the cue of four nearly simultaneous electronic bleeps, each produced a grey object (looking rather like a calculator designed for the slightly larger pocket) and proceeded intently to press buttons for the next couple of minutes. Strangely, our list of reported hassles programmed into the rating battery failed to include any that related to the answering of persistent and repeated questions about how we felt and what we were doing (what we were doing, that is, apart from answering the same persistent repeated questions again and again). Fortunately, the 30 participants in our study took on the experimental task with better grace. Our continued gratitude goes to them for the data mountain they left for us, which we still sometimes explore simply because it is there.

One benefit of piloting SAM ourselves, in addition to generating empathy with the real participants, is that we began to appreciate the variety of ways in which we as respondents approached the task of rating our mood. Sometimes particular adjectives seemed either supremely apt or clearly inappropriate; yet at other times, the same adjectives made little sense and apparently had no bearing on how we felt. Nonetheless, ratings were duly made. Similarly, we became aware of how particular events or situations sometimes seemed to dominate our mood completely, making the rating task both easy and obvious, and yet at other times we didn't really seem to be in any particular mood at all.

There was also considerable discussion of how each of us had interpreted particular mood adjectives. From the research team's data archive maintained meticulously by our honorary curator Rob, we have been able to unearth a rare tape recording of a team meeting that took place soon after completion of the pilot study. The following is a brief transcript of part of our conversation concerning the mood-rating task:

S: This . . . goes back to a conversation we had with Bryn the other day about whether tenseness and anxiety were the same thing. And doing this actually made me realize that they weren't. And this is tenseness and not anxiety we're after, isn't it?
R: Not really. So what does "anxious" mean and what does "tense" mean?
S: "Anxious" is to do with fear and anticipation and threat and "tenseness" is to do with . . .
B: Edginess.
S: Yes, yes, edginess.
R: And what's edginess?
S: Or wound-upness?
B: Uptight.
R: So it's kind of like a high state of arousal that's quite unpleasant but it's not necessarily because of a threat. If that's so, then that means that we haven't really been getting at anxiety thus far, doesn't it? We could just say "here are some words that describe moods. Rate them". The end.

The experience of being guinea pigs *and* researchers was, in many ways, a sobering one. While ratings of mood are relatively easy to obtain, we soon realized that we knew virtually nothing about the processes whereby respondents actually answer the relevant questions, and very little about their specific understanding of the mood adjectives specified in these questions. This realization may go some way to explaining our apparent equanimity regarding debates about the "underlying" structure derivable from these self-reports, or about selection of the "correct" adjectives to use for mood-rating.

SAM might have reached an untimely end were it not for the interest of an ex-colleague and friend Steve Evans, who was commissioning research for Unilever at around this time. His input to the development of our approach from the earliest stages should not be underestimated, quite aside from the practical assistance and guidance arising from our subsequent dealings with the company.

Steve was responsible for initiating our current research contract with Unilever which we generally refer to as project ARIEL because of its focus on Affect Regulation In Everyday Life. Now may be the time to offer our official apologies to this multinational company for semi-accidentally arriving at such an objection-able acronym, which could be interpreted as referring to a brand leader in the washing-powder market that is produced by one of Unilever's chief competitors. We toyed, of course, with investigating instead Personal Effectiveness in Responding to Small Irritants and Lapses, but sadly it didn't have quite the same ring to it.

The ideas reported here would not be what they are without the input of Steve and other subsequent contacts at Unilever. Of course, this does not mean that the opinions expressed in this book necessarily correspond to those of Unilever, and we are happy to make all the usual disclaimers in this regard. Indeed, the views contained here do not even match up with those of any of the individual authors but rather reflect something approximating to our transactionally defined social identity as a team.

Although the overall shape of the book arose from group discussions and more than one of us had some input into each of its chapters, chief responsibility for their content was as follows: Chapters 1 and 2 were written mainly by Brian. Rob wrote most of Chapter 3. Chapter 4 was again mainly Brian's work. Peter wrote most of Chapters 5 and 6. Shirley wrote most of Chapter 7. All of us made some contribution to the final Chapter 8, but most of it was written by Brian.

Several people merit an acknowledgement. First, we would like to thank Steve Evans for summoning us to expensive hotels, sitting us down at expensive restaurants, and generally encouraging us to do our affect-regulation thing. Steve's idiosyncratic style of chairing ARIEL meetings was a pleasure to witness and demonstrated a rare skill (though exactly what that skill was, we still haven't been able to figure out). We are also specifically grateful to Steve for the landscape metaphor which makes a cameo appearance in the final chapter of this book.

Thanks too go to Professor Peter Warr, the Director of SAPU, for making resources available for the conduct of the first SAM diary study and for support-ing our collaboration at this early stage. Finally, we would like to acknowledge the assistance, both conceptual and financial, of Unilever Research. Without their

1

INTRODUCTION TO THE PSYCHOLOGY OF MOOD

OVERVIEW

This book is about people's moods and the ways in which they change over time. Our approach to this topic draws mainly on social psychology and personality theory and focuses specifically on mood as it occurs in the context of everyday life. In this first chapter, we introduce the concept of mood as it is used in ordinary language and in psychological research. We develop a working definition of the phenomenon in question and compare and contrast its meaning with that of related concepts such as "emotion" and "affect". Next we provide some historical context for the recent upsurge of psychological interest in mood and affect. Research into these topics has only begun to advance over the last few decades and we consider some of the factors that have contributed to this development. Currently, a number of alternative angles are available for approaching the psychology of mood and we consider these briefly before introducing in general terms our own perspective, which emphasizes mood variation over time, and the regulatory processes that control and underlie this variation. Finally, we present a basic outline of the content of subsequent chapters.

MOOD IN EVERYDAY LANGUAGE

"Mood" is one of those familiar words which people use constantly in everyday life without ever really paying too much attention to what it means. This happens partly because we assume that we understand what mood is directly on the basis of our own experience, so that no further specification of the underlying idea seems necessary. What we feel inside already makes perfect sense to us, so we believe. We *just know* when we are in a mood of a certain kind, or in a mood at all, without needing to work it out, and so the application of the word seems straightforward and obvious.

In fact, though, things may not be quite so simple. For example, if mood is directly experienced, how is it that we occasionally come to the conclusion that we have been in a certain mood all day without really noticing it? Similarly, why is it that we are sometimes in a "funny kind of mood" that we cannot exactly put

1

our finger on? Furthermore, how are we able to tell that *someone else* is in a particular mood with any degree of confidence? Consideration of these questions suggests that mood means something apart from an immediate internal registration of how we feel. In this chapter, and the rest of the book, we hope to develop a psychological concept of mood which should help to clarify some of these superficially puzzling facts about mood.

We can start to get a handle on the real meaning of mood by examining how people use the concept in everyday conversation. Common expressions including the word in question include: "I'm just not in the mood" (e.g. for celebrating, dancing, talking etc.); "You're in a good/bad/peculiar mood today"; "I'm just trying to create the right mood"; "She's a moody kind of person", and so on. Two core aspects of the concept seem immediately apparent: first, moods usually relate to feelings, good or bad; and second, moods put you in the right or wrong frame of mind for doing certain kinds of things. The commonsense idea seems to be that moods are states of mind that feel good or bad and dispose people towards acting in certain kinds of ways (and against acting in others).

Similarly, the *Concise Oxford English Dictionary* defines mood as follows:

> **mood** *n.* state of mind or feeling; (in *pl.*) fits of melancholy or bad temper; (*attrib.*) inducing a particular mood (*mood music*); **in the** ~, **in no** ~, inclined, disinclined, (*for* thing, *to* do).

Further understanding of what mood means in everyday conversation is facilitated by considering the kinds of words people use to describe the different types of mood that are possible. First and most obviously, moods are said to be good or bad. Additionally, it seems possible to be in an irritable mood, an anxious mood, a distracted mood and so on. In other words, in addition to the basic dimension of pleasantness–unpleasantness, moods seem to differ according to the particular forms of action and reaction that they encourage. Being in a distractible mood is thought to mean that attention is easily diverted by irrelevant happenings, and being in an irritable mood implies that even a mild provocation may produce an exaggerated aggressive response, for example. Psychological investigations of the possible distinctions between different kinds of mood are reviewed in the following chapter.

As well as differing in their particular quality, moods also seem to vary in strength. People can be in a slightly bad or an extremely bad mood, for example. This fact seems to suggest that the intensity of mood states might potentially be measurable along a simple dimension of degree. The usual idea is that mood strength directly reflects the extent of the underlying feeling, but some researchers have questioned whether such a simple interpretation of the intensity dimension is viable. For example, it is possible to argue that a person can be in a pronounced mood without necessarily being directly aware of the fact: You might be exhibiting all the signs of intense anger, say, but explicitly deny that you are angry at all. Cases like this suggest that mood intensity is not just based on a direct readout of an internal signal in all circumstances. Despite these potential complexities, however, psychologists have capitalized on the fact that people usually seem to

2

make consistent distinctions between moods of different strength by developing self-report scales which assess the extent of mood for different people or for the same person on different occasions (see Chapters 2 and 3).

When people describe their own mood or someone else's as good or bad, strong or weak, they also often qualify their statement with reference to a time period. For example, someone might say "I'm just not in the mood *right now*", "You're in a really bad mood *this morning*" and so on. Implicit in the everyday idea of mood is the assumption that it reflects a more or less temporary condition: people just don't stay in the same mood for extended periods under normal circumstances. Indeed, moods often seem to pass of their own accord without the person actually having to do anything about them. For example, many people feel tired and down in the period after lunch in a working day, but pick up again naturally later on. These patterns of spontaneous mood change over time are thought to be caused by a combination of biological and cultural processes which impose rhythm on our psychological experiences. In this book, we will be paying particular attention to the ways in which moods change over time in quality and intensity, and in the processes underlying variations in mood (see Chapter 5).

Because moods can apparently come and go against our will, people frequently assume that they are simply conditions to which people fall victim, which explains why apologies of the form "Sorry, I'm just not in the mood" have any force. However, it is also true that people often do things that are explicitly intended to change their moods, whether or not these activities actually turn out to be effective. For example, we may decide that we are not going to put up with being in a depressed mood any longer and go out and do something active in order to pull ourselves out of it. Sometimes it seems possible to bounce back to happiness with just a simple effort of will. Popular wisdom suggests a range of different strategies that may be implemented for changing moods including "getting it out of your system", "counting to ten", "putting a brave face on things" and so on. There are even popular self-help books providing specific instructions for taking control of our feelings (e.g. Carlson, 1992; Burns, 1980; Hart, 1957; Wilson, 1995). In Chapter 6, we will discuss some commonly used mood-regulation techniques and how successful they might be for different kinds of mood in different circumstances.

Just as one person might vary from one hour to the next or from day to day in the quality and intensity of mood and in what he or she does to try to control it, it also seems to be the case that different people show characteristic patterns of mood. Mood as represented in everyday language seems to be closely associated with temperament and personality, with some people being described as dispositionally moody, as gloomy in outlook, or as excitable. To call someone moody usually suggests that that person is prone to bad temper or depression, but may also imply simple unpredictability in reaction from one day to the next. This discussion brings us to the conclusion that the ways in which mood changes over time may be different for different people. Individual differences in dispositions to experience particular moods, and in variability in mood over time are specifically considered in Chapters 3 and 5 of this book.

In this section, we have developed a preliminary idea of what mood is and how it changes based on commonsense ideas contained in everyday language. However, it is worth noting that the concepts that we use in normal conversation are not always perfectly precise, and that words relating to mood in particular may be used in inconsistent and variable ways. Although the ordinary-language concept of mood seems to pick out a range of phenomena that have relevance for psychology, allowing the possibility of a more specific and well-defined scientific notion of "mood", it is also conceivable that many of our everyday ideas about mood may be based more on myth than reality. For example, we have already argued that moods are not purely private experiences as is commonly assumed, nor are they necessarily always passive states outside the person's control. Psychological research into mood can help to determine when and how commonly accepted observations about mood apply or do not apply.

MOOD AS A PSYCHOLOGICAL CONCEPT

The concept of "mood" as used in psychology derives fairly directly from the commonsense understanding of the phenomenon as discussed in the previous section. However, while the usage of the word in everyday conversation allows multiple meanings and implies a range of contingent connotations, psychologists typically attempt to be more precise and specific about the concept. For example, the definition of mood has been clarified by positioning the phenomenon within broader categories of psychological function, distinguishing it from similar phenomena, characterizing the processes it might involve, and delineating the various instances of the category. In this section, we develop a conceptualization of mood based on these considerations.

What kind of psychological phenomenon is mood? On the broadest level, human mental function is commonly divided into three basic faculties: cognition (thinking), conation (willing), and affect (feeling, e.g. Hilgard, 1980). Mood falls mainly inside the last of these categories, although there is some overlap too with other functions, because mood affects and is affected by thinking, and may also have fairly direct consequences for motivation and action.

The first and most inclusive term that we need to define, then, is *affect*. Affect generally refers to mental states involving *evaluative feelings*, in other words psychological conditions when the person feels good or bad, and either likes or dislikes what is happening. Thus, the category of affect covers a wide variety of phenomena including mood and emotion, ranging from vague discomfort to intense fury, from a nagging toothache to a general state of boredom.

Distinguishing emotions and moods

One of the easiest ways of understanding the subcategory of affect which we call mood is to consider how it contrasts with and relates to another subcategory,

4

namely emotion: a number of distinguishing characteristics of these two similar concepts help us to get a handle on both of them. Different theorists have emphasized different distinctions, some of which seem to reflect descriptive and extrinsic aspects of the two kinds of state, while others seem to suggest more intrinsic differences in the underlying processes that are involved (see Batson, Shaw, & Oleson, 1992; Ekman & Davidson, 1994).

1. *Duration*

On a simple descriptive level, it is often argued that moods tend to last longer than emotions (e.g. Ekman, 1994; Nowlis & Nowlis, 1956; Watson & Clark, 1994). Emotions often seem to be over in a matter of seconds or minutes, whereas moods can last for hours, days, or even weeks. However, when people are questioned about the duration of emotional experiences, many claim that they persist for protracted periods. For example, in a study by Sonnemans (see Frijda, Mesquita, Sonnemans, & van Goozen, 1991) in which participants were asked to describe one of their emotional experiences from the previous week, 50 percent of the recalled emotions were reported to have lasted for more than an hour, with several examples persisting for a day or longer. Indeed, when we think of emotions such as grief, it seems unrealistic to suggest that they always dissipate rapidly. One possible interpretation of these observations would be to suggest that the people experiencing such prolonged emotional episodes are in fact getting *repeatedly* emotional about the same concern but each particular emotional event actually lasts only for a short time. In other words, the emotion may wax and wane over the course of an extended period. In any case, even if emotions usually tend to be relatively brief and moods more enduring, there are certainly exceptions to this general rule.

2. *Time pattern*

A further problem with the notion that moods are by definition longer lasting than emotions arises from the idea that mood may be something that is always with us but that continually fluctuates over time. In this case, mood episodes do not have any definite start or finish, just gradual changes in felt quality and intensity. Thus, another possible distinction between emotion and mood based on temporal characteristics relates to their typical pattern of variation. Emotions usually seem to have a clear moment of onset then dissipate fairly rapidly, whereas moods often change more slowly and continue to linger somewhere in the background of consciousness (cf. Watson & Clark, 1994). In more technical terms, emotions are said to be *acute* or *phasic* whereas moods are more *chronic* or *tonic* (see Figure 1.1). Although this observation seems to provide a reasonable descriptive distinction between emotions and moods, it still does not tell us about the underlying processes that determine the observed differences.

5

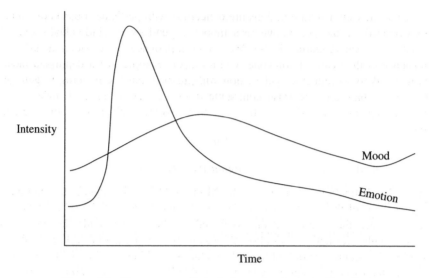

Figure 1.1 Time-course of a typical mood and a typical emotion

3. *Relative intensity*

A third possible difference is that emotions are often assumed to be more intense and involving than moods (e.g. Isen, 1984; Nowlis & Nowlis, 1956). Combining this observation with the previous distinctions, it seems that emotions are powerful but burn out quickly whereas moods are weaker and more persistently nagging. Here again, however, there are exceptions. Clinical states of depression and anxiety may involve intense mood states that persist for long periods, for example (Morris, 1989). Nevertheless, generally speaking, it seems true to say that moods tend to be weaker in intensity than emotions.

4. *Specificity of cause*

All of the above distinctions have some validity, but in each case there are exceptions, and none of them actually specifies a difference that is central to characterizing either of the phenomena in question. A less descriptive approach has been adopted by investigators who have attempted to distinguish mood and emotion by calling attention to differences in their origins. According to this view, emotions are caused by specific events localized in time, whereas moods build up as a consequence of either a concatenation of minor incidents, persistent conditions in the environment, and/or internal metabolic or cognitive processes (e.g. Ekman, 1994; Watson & Clark, 1994). Some theorists define emotion even more specifically in terms of its causation by the *appraisal* or personal evaluation and interpretation of a specific event (e.g. Ortony, Clore, & Collins, 1988; Reisenzein, 1994, see Chapter 3).

6

A related view is that emotions are concerned with particular objects or events experienced by the person whereas moods depend on the individual's overall existential state (Lazarus, 1994). We might experience the emotion of grief in response to the death of someone we know, for example, but a depressed mood is more likely to reflect dissatisfaction with the way our life is going in general. Of course, bad news can also contribute to our pervasive sense of malaise and lead to unpleasant moods as well as emotions, so the distinction is not hard and fast.

5. *Signal function*

A similar distinction was proposed by Morris (1992), who argued that emotions signal states of the environment while moods signal states of the self. According to this view, the experience of mood and emotion can provide the conscious system with information about how things are proceeding in our dealings with the world. The occurrence of emotion tells us that something is going wrong or going well in the external situation, whereas mood tells us that our *personal* resources are insufficient for dealing with current demands or exceed what is required of us. Although there may be some degree of truth in Morris's position, it also seems that certain emotions, such as shame and embarrassment, are crucially related to aspects of self rather than situation and can therefore tell us that some facet of our competence is lacking. More generally, it is often difficult to make a distinction between self-related or situation-related events or resources because most important concerns reflect both personal and environmental considerations. When someone insults us, for example, it is the relevance of the affront to our personal well-being that is upsetting rather than anything specific in the objective event itself. As Lazarus (1991) has argued, what has affective significance for us always depends to some extent on a *transaction* between the individual and situation, and on an assessment of internal as well as external coping potential with respect to this transaction (see Chapter 3).

6. *Directedness*

As suggested in an earlier section, a common claim is that emotions are caused by specific events but moods are not. We believe that this is an oversimplification and that a more accurate characterization of the two conditions relates to what they are *about* rather than what determines them (see also Frijda, 1994; Schwarz & Clore, 1988). It is important in this regard to draw a distinction between the *cause* of an emotion and its *object* (e.g. Kenny, 1963; Wittgenstein, 1953). For example, although you may become angry as a consequence of repeated provocation, the object of your emotion is the specific insult that you are currently focusing on. More generally, a range of personal and situational factors interact in emotion causation, but emotions are always *directed* at, or focused on, a specific intentional object which may overlap with the set of causes but is rarely entirely identical

7

Table 1.1 Proposed distinctions between mood and emotion

	Mood	Emotion
Duration	Relatively long-term	Relatively short-term
Time pattern	Gradual onset, continuous, tonic	Rapid onset, episodic, phasic
Intensity	Relatively weak	Relatively strong
Causation	Not caused by specific event	Caused by specific event
Function	Provides information about current state of self	Provides information about current state of situation
Directedness	Unfocused	Takes specific object

with them. In our view, emotions are directed at specific objects rather than necessarily *determined* by specific events (see Parkinson, 1995).

Moods, on the other hand, are not about anything in particular. Rather they reflect more general and diffuse states of mind. In other words, moods reflect general conditions of feeling good or bad which pervade our reactions to a wide variety of situations, but emotions tend to be about something in particular. Whereas emotions are evaluative states focused on a particular intentional object (for example, something that one is angry about), moods are unfocused evaluative states that affect a wide range of objects (e.g. Clark & Isen, 1982). When we are in an irritable mood, for instance, almost anything that happens can seem a frustration or hindrance to us.

A related point is that emotion tends to imply a specific *action tendency* directed towards the object of the emotion (Frijda, 1986). Moods, on the other hand, have a less direct connection with action. Restless moods may lead to general tendencies towards any kind of active behaviour and depressed moods may tend to inhibit responsivity non-specifically but there are no *particular* classes of action triggered by most mood states.

This underlying distinction between emotion and mood based on their directedness helps to explain the contingent descriptive differences observed between the two kinds of affective condition. Because emotions are focused on a particular object, their duration is usually dependent on the presence of that object, which is intrusive and upsetting: when the object is removed or becomes familiar, the emotion dissipates. Thus emotions do not usually last very long. Similarly, the directedness of emotion is related to the urgency of dealing with the object, which usually means that emotions are experienced as interrupting and intense. Moods, on the other hand, have more of a life of their own, not focusing on any specific aspect of the life situation but ebbing and flowing with the general tenor of personal concerns over time. A summary of the various proposed distinctions between mood and emotion is presented in Table 1.1.

8

Connections between emotions and moods

Although we have suggested that it is possible to make some relatively consistent distinctions between emotion and mood, it is also worth remembering that emotion and mood are related concepts. Both refer to affective states that feel pleasant or unpleasant, both reflect and affect evaluations of what is happening, and both have a limited duration (although the duration of emotion is likely to be more limited than that of mood). More specifically, particular emotional states are often similar in many respects to corresponding moods. For example, the emotion of terror could easily be seen as an intense kind of anxious mood that happens to be focused on a particular object. In fact, some of the words we use to describe our moods can also be used to describe corresponding emotions, such as "happy", "sad", "depressed" and so on. According to the present analysis, being happy, sad, or depressed *about* something would represent an emotional state, whereas just feeling generally happy, sad, or depressed but not in connection with anything in particular would constitute a mood.

Connections between moods and emotions reflect their empirical interactions as well as their conceptual overlap. For instance, some theorists have suggested that mood-states often arise as a result of emotional experiences: you can still feel generally good or bad long after the direct cause of the reaction has ceased to affect you directly (Isen, 1984; Ruckmick, 1936). Relatedly, a number of repeated minor emotional experiences can combine into a general mood on days when everything seems to go right or wrong (see Chapter 3).

The reverse relationship between emotion and mood may also apply when being in a certain kind of mood seems to make it more likely that a relevant emotion arises. For example, irritability can easily transform itself into anger when the last straw finally breaks the camel's back. Thus, moods may be seen to some extent as temporary predispositions to experience specific kinds of emotion.

Finally, note that mood and emotion share common components and are controlled to some extent by similar processes. Indeed much of the psychology of emotion (e.g. see Frijda, 1986; Oatley, 1992; Parkinson, 1995) has relevance to the understanding of mood, and many of the theories and findings discussed later in this book will apply equally to both kinds of phenomenon.

Conclusion

To summarize the similarities and differences between mood and emotion: both are affective conditions involving good or bad feelings. Emotion is focused on a particular object or event and implies a readiness for action with respect to that object or event, whereas mood is more diffuse and generalized. In descriptive terms, moods tend to be weaker and more long-lasting than emotions but there are exceptions to this general rule.

This preceding discussion puts us in a position where we are able to offer a preliminary definition of mood as follows: *Mood is an undirected evaluative*

9

mental state which temporarily predisposes a person to interpret and act towards a wide variety of events in ways according with its affective content.

In other words, mood is a non-permanent, cognitive-motivational disposition with evaluative characteristics. The phenomenon of mood can also be specified on a more descriptive level as follows: *Mood is experienced as either pleasant or unpleasant, typically lasts longer than a matter of seconds, and usually changes gradually rather than having any definite moment of onset.*

By the end of this book, we should be in a position to add further specification to this definition.

CONTEXTUALIZING MOOD RESEARCH

In the previous section we considered how psychologists have characterized and defined mood. We now turn to the question of how they have investigated phenomena relating to mood. Our aim is to set out in a general way some of the many possible approaches to mood research and delineate what we believe are the most promising angles of attack. In the rest of the book we will review research arising from these traditions in a more thorough and substantive way; in the present section our aim is simply to give some background context for these perspectives.

A brief history of mood research

Given that mood is such a recognizable and pervasive feature of our everyday experience and seems to have definite and obvious effects on what we do, think, and feel, it might be imagined that psychologists have paid a great deal of attention to mood phenomena and that a substantial and well-developed body of relevant knowledge is available. In fact, however, psychological research into mood has only started to get off the ground in a serious way over the last few decades. For example, the number of articles with "mood" in the title in a widely used social science citation index has doubled over the last ten years. Although early psychologists were clearly interested in the subjective aspects of feelings (e.g. Wundt, 1897), their conclusions were questioned and largely abandoned by a later more objectively inclined generation of behaviourist investigators, who tended to argue that moods were internal experiences which were unobservable and therefore not amenable to proper scientific investigation (e.g. Watson, 1929).

The cognitive approach to psychology which started to emerge in the 1950s (e.g. Broadbent, 1954; Bruner, Goodnow, & Austin, 1956; Miller, 1956; see Gardner, 1985) placed more emphasis on mental processes which could not be directly measured or observed but tended to restrict its focus to the more formal structures that controlled thinking, reasoning, and memory rather than acknowledging the importance of affect (e.g. Miller & Johnson-Laird, 1976). Seeing the mind as analogous to a computer was not usually conducive for the modelling of mood and emotion. More recently, however, cognitive theory has tried to encompass affect within a more general information-processing framework (e.g. Teasdale & Barnard, 1993; Mandler, 1984), often with the unintended consequence that some of its most distinctive features are left out of the analysis.

Away from mainstream experimental psychology, of course, various subdisciplines developed their own independent accounts of affect, but there was no real integration of theories or findings. Thus, there have been psychoanalytic theories of affect (e.g. Jacobsen, 1957), comparative investigations of emotional behaviour in different species (e.g. Harlow, 1958; Hebb, 1946), accounts of the development of affect and knowledge about affect during cognitive maturation (e.g. Flapan, 1968; Jersild & Holmes, 1935), attempts to implement techniques for mood measurement (Nowlis & Nowlis, 1956), and studies of the impact of affect on social relations (e.g. Schachter, 1959), without any serious attempt at drawing together the various strands.

A renaissance in mood and emotion research has occurred in recent years for a number of reasons. The first (and perhaps the most important) stems from the inevitable historical reaction against any purportedly inclusive system of ideas. As knowledge develops within a particular perspective or paradigm there is often increasing awareness of the limitations of the outlook it provides and growing sensitivity to the phenomena that it leaves out of consideration (cf. Kuhn, 1962). Thus, the very sophistication of cognitive theory in psychology has ironically drawn attention to its own weaknesses and blind spots, including the area of affect. Among cognitive researchers, there are those who have become disillusioned with the failed promise of the initial attempt to build a grand theory of human psychological function and now seek to extend the perspective to incorporate new phenomena (e.g. Neisser, 1976).

Correspondingly, researchers outside the cognitive tradition have become more critical about its limitations and the specific exclusion of important topics like mood and emotion (e.g. Zajonc, 1980). At one level, the renewed interest in affect partly results from the repeated pendulum swing between classicist and romanticist ideologies, and there is a fair chance that the movement will some day rebound once more. However, in many ways the promise and successes of recent affect research suggest strongly that this time round, affect may be here to stay.

There are also broader cultural forces that have provided a context that is particularly amenable for the development of research in affect. For example, the emphasis on personal growth in Western society that developed in the late 1960s together with a more general anti-materialist outlook may have contributed to the current emphasis on personal experience, including mood and emotion. Many psychologists working in mood grew up as part of the "me generation" (Wolfe, 1983), for example. Relatedly, the self-help industry has generally encouraged people to view the pursuit of happiness not only as one of the basic rights of the individual but also as an interesting hobby with obvious and direct affective pay-offs (e.g. Kaminer, 1993). On a more practical level, the growth of the counselling movement has required usable knowledge relating to feelings and well-being to support its continuing development. Similarly, political and institutional pressures

11

for improved occupational health and work satisfaction have helped to facilitate mood research in recent years.

Although affect has now started to attract psychological attention, knowledge is still fragmentary and there is as yet no overarching framework within which research in this area can progress. We hope that this book will make some contribution to the development of theory and research approaches in this area.

Delineating the present approach

There are a number of possible approaches to the psychological investigation of mood, not all of which are directly relevant to the themes of the present volume. For example, there will be little discussion in what follows of the physiological aspects of mood. This might seem surprising. Many people take it for granted that feelings are things that happen inside our bodies and can be investigated almost exclusively in those terms. However, in fact there is little evidence that different mood-states are characterized by distinctive patterns of bodily response (e.g. Johnston & Anastasiades, 1990). Although moods are clearly related to physiological changes in tension and arousal as well as fluctuating hormonal levels in many circumstances, we believe that it is wrong to assume that these factors are the only important determinants of mood. Indeed, it seems that the affective impact of physiology often depends on the way the associated experiential changes are interpreted and dealt with by the individual, and that physiological and cognitive factors interact in mood-related phenomena (cf. Schachter, 1964, and see Chapter 3).

For example, expectations and cultural beliefs about how the menstrual cycle influences mood make a clear difference to the experiences that are reported by women over the course of the month (e.g. Dan & Monagle, 1994; Snowden & Christian, 1983). Thinking that mood depends on hormones can sometimes lead to self-fulfilling prophesies partly because when a person expects to feel bad this also tends to distort interpretation of what is happening in a negative way. Similarly, effects of various drugs on affect depend crucially on the social context as well as on cognitive interpretations of what is normative among the subculture concerned (Becker, 1953). Furthermore, in addition to seeing drugs simply as exerting reactive effects on the mind or body, it is important to acknowledge that people's use of psychoactive substances is often part of a deliberate strategy to attain desired mental states or to alleviate unwanted feelings (e.g. Cooper, Frone, Russell, & Mudar, 1995). Physiological analysis of the conventional kind is incapable in principle of providing a comprehensive analysis of this kind of active control and regulation of mood, which will be a central topic addressed by the present approach in subsequent chapters. In short, although physiology naturally makes an important difference to experienced affect, its impact needs to be contextualized within a broader psychological framework in order to get the complete picture of the operation of mood.

In this book, we will also place little emphasis on the brain mechanisms that are implicated in mood phenomena. Again, it is obviously important for many purposes to understand how the central nervous system contributes to mood processes, but we believe that this understanding in turn will depend on a more precise and developed psychological description and explanation of the relevant effects. Until we are clear about how mood works at the psychological and experiential level, it is hard to map these functions onto corresponding brain systems, and there is a danger of reifying commonsense prejudices about mood by postulating neuronal structures that supposedly underlie affective mechanisms before we are really certain about the nature of the phenomena to be explained.

Instead of focusing on physiological aspects of mood and affect, in this book we draw mainly on personality psychology, cognitive psychology, social psychology, health psychology, and clinical psychology. In the next section, we introduce the specific topics that are covered, but for now it is worth saying a little about our general approach. We are interested in mood as it is represented in experience and as it influences and is controlled by cognition within a wider social context. Furthermore, we believe that this perspective allows us to address practical issues relating to mood in a clinical context (see Chapter 7).

Mood, in our view, not only reflects and affects our experience of the world, but is also recognized as serving these functions by people who are undergoing affective reactions. People not only experience moods but they are also often aware that they are experiencing them and this latter fact allows some degree of anticipation and control of affect. In this book, we will pay particular attention to the ways in which moods change over time, and the ways in which people try to modulate and modify these changes. For example, knowing that having a big lunch will make us lethargic in the early afternoon allows us to schedule tasks around this anticipated lowering of alertness, or to refrain from eating to alleviate these effects in advance. We are interested in the processes underlying the moment-to-moment, hour-to-hour, and day-to-day variations in mood as well as the processes whereby people seek to exert deliberate control over these changes and their expected impact on our behaviour and experience.

Knowledge relating to some of these issues has been given added impetus by a recent methodological development in mood research. Previous studies tended to treat mood as a simple independent or dependent variable in a before-and-after style experimental design. For example, factors influencing mood (see Chapter 3), and factors influenced by mood (see Chapter 4) were investigated separately with little integration of the findings from the two paradigms. In contrast to this restricted methodological focus on input–output relations, Epstein (1983) suggested that a whole range of important psychological phenomena crucially depend on ongoing time-based processes and therefore need to be tracked continuously or measured repeatedly to be captured accurately. This process approach (Larsen, 1989) is particularly amenable to researching mood, which as we have argued is a phenomenon which changes over time and which is in continual interaction with other dynamic aspects of psychological functioning. The time-based perspective is one which we endorse in this book and we will discuss its practice and implications in more detail in much of what follows.

STRUCTURE OF BOOK

In this book, we present an approach to mood which acknowledges its dynamic interrelations with other aspects of psychological function, emphasizes its temporal basis, and draws specific attention to the various kinds of regulatory process that influence the extent, quality, and variability of mood. We start out by reviewing more conventional research which examines the nature of momentary mood experience and looks at the factors which lead to, and result from, mood. Following this coverage, we broaden the analysis by seeing mood as a process that develops over time rather than an input to, or output from, other temporally delimited processes. Rather than seeing mood as something with definite and distinct causes and effects, we consider the continuous interaction of mood with other processes. In particular, we emphasize the regulatory processes that underlie and control real-time variations in mood. This approach is specifically applied to clinical disorders of affect which are seen partly as arising from failures of regulation. Finally, we attempt to draw together the strands of our argument and map out some future directions for mood research.

The specific content of the chapters is as follows:

Chapter 2 reviews theory and research into the relations and distinctions between different mood states, and the dimensions underlying the variety of affective experience. Moods are commonly agreed to differ according to the extent to which they are pleasant or unpleasant, and the degree of associated activation or arousal. A two-dimensional mapping can therefore be applied to mood experiences on the basis of these independent continua. Although further dimensions of affective meaning are clearly possible, there is little consistent evidence for them or agreement about their nature. In Chapter 2, we evaluate the conclusions of this research into structural models of mood and examine its implications for self-report measurement of mood and for the general theory of affect.

Chapter 3 considers what factors influence mood. The relevant variables may be classified into three categories: *external events*, *personal dispositions* (transient or enduring), and *transactional encounters*. In short, mood depends on what goes on out in the world, on what goes on in people's minds (and bodies), or on some combination of these two sets of factor. Research into external influences on mood has focused on the impact of major life events and daily hassles on well-being. In this chapter, we will review this research and consider the role of so-called stress-related phenomena. Secondly, we will develop Lazarus's approach (e.g. Lazarus, 1991) which considers affect as a response to the way situational events are appraised and evaluated by the person. Finally, we will consider the personality and emotional variables that may predispose people to experience particular kinds or levels of mood. Our view is that it is unrealistic to see mood simply as a response to stimuli with inherent affective power. Rather we feel that

14

it is important to look at the coordination over time between affective, personal, and interpersonal variables. This dynamic approach to mood will be developed further in later chapters.

In Chapter 4, we move from a consideration of the antecedents and causes of mood to a discussion of its effects. Most of the relevant research concerns how pleasant and unpleasant moods have contrasting influences on cognition and behaviour. For example, being in a good mood often inclines people to help others, to be more easily persuaded, to look on the bright side of things, and to remember positive events more readily than negative events. These mood-congruence effects are intuitively predictable on the basis of everyday experience, but psychological research has demonstrated that sometimes they fail to apply and are occasionally even reversed. In general, it turns out that the effects of unpleasant moods are less consistent than those of pleasant mood. In this chapter, we will attempt to account for the variability in the effects of any given mood in terms of underlying processes and the impact of regulation attempts. One of the reasons why unpleasant moods do not always make our perceptions and interpretations more negative is because we deliberately look on the bright side to try and counteract our bad feelings.

In Chapter 5, we turn our focus more directly to one of the central themes of the book: how moods change and develop from one moment to the next. Rather than seeing mood simply as either a cause or effect in a sequence of events, Chapter 5 develops an account of moods as developing over time as a function of various dynamic processes. This chapter reviews evidence relating to the different patterns and rhythms of mood change that are observed in people's everyday lives, and examines the cultural and biological processes that might control and influence these temporal variations. For example, we consider how mood variations may be linked over time with rhythmic physiological variations, such as those relating to the menstrual cycle or circadian changes in autonomic activation, in interaction with the time structure of the sociocultural environment.

Chapter 6 extends the dynamic perspective developed in Chapter 5 by examining moods as unfolding events which may be operated upon by the person experiencing them at every stage of their development. In this chapter, we review theory and research into the different kinds of affect regulation that can occur. The traditional psychological approach to affective phenomena tends to assume that people are passive victims or beneficiaries of these states. In contrast, we believe that moods are worked upon actively by those who experience them, or anticipate experiencing them. For example, not everyone resigns themselves to being in a bad mood. Rather, many people engage in deliberate techniques that are specifically designed to alleviate their unpleasant feelings, such as treating themselves to something nice, or distracting themselves from their problems. We consider recent research into people's strategies for dealing with mood and mood-related events, and their relative effectiveness for different people.

Chapter 7 on clinical aspects of mood applies the dynamic regulational perspective to the moods experienced by people suffering from the affective disorders of depression and anxiety. Psychodynamic and cognitive-behavioural approaches to the understanding and treatment of these clinical conditions are considered. We propose that the development and maintenance of some affective disorders may often depend on failure to implement appropriate affect-regulation strategies, or the continued use of maladaptive forms of coping. Correspondingly, successful psychotherapeutic treatment for affective disorders generally depends on learning to use more appropriate ways of dealing with situations and the feelings associated with them. For example, clients suffering from specific phobias may go to great lengths to avoid the object of their fear in order to avert its unpleasant affective consequences, but this avoidance stops them from ever learning whether they are capable of confronting what frightens them. Treatment of such disorders thus focuses on controlled exposure to the phobic object under conditions where resources are available for coping with the experienced affect. In this chapter, the general implications of this kind of regulation-based account for theory and therapy relating to affective disorders are discussed.

Chapter 8 summarizes the conclusions of the book and suggests future directions for research based on the dynamic regulational perspective developed in the preceding chapters. We will review the theory and research reviewed in the earlier chapters of the book in the light of our conclusions from later chapters about variation and regulation and the viability of a process approach to mood. Our general recommendation is that researchers focus on mood in its everyday dynamic context as the central phenomenon of interest, and pay particular attention to the interacting control processes underlying real-time mood variation. In Chapter 8, we sketch out a provisional model of mood regulation which is sensitive to the requirements of such an approach, and consider some of its theoretical and practical implications. Finally, we will conclude the book with a revised definition of mood that explicitly incorporates the notions of change and regulation over time.

SUMMARY

Mood represents an important area of our lives which until relatively recently has been underresearched by psychologists. Working from ordinary language, we can provisionally define the phenomenon as a temporally variable mental condition involving evaluation which is not directed at any specific object or event. At different times and for different people, mood may be pleasant or unpleasant, and more or less intense. Psychological research into mood has taken a number of separate tracks, but in this book we place particular emphasis on how moods change over time and how people try to control their own mood. In the following chapters, we will review the available psychological research relating to these issues and develop our own model of mood and mood change.

2

MAPPING THE STRUCTURE
OF AFFECT

OVERVIEW

In the previous chapter, we introduced the general concepts of mood and affect. Now we turn to a discussion of the variety of particular mood states that are possible. In particular, we review research that has attempted to map out the psychological domain of affect either by exploring the similarities and differences between the meanings of words and expressions describing moods and emotions, or by investigating what kinds of affective feelings tend to go together in everyday experience. On the basis of this research, it is now commonly accepted that differences in affective states can validly be reduced to their respective values on two basic dimensions of meaning commonly considered to reflect pleasantness (evaluation) and activation (arousal). In other words moods may be more or less pleasant or unpleasant, and characterized by varying degrees of excitation or activity. This chapter reviews the evidence for these and alternative dimensions, and draws attention to some of the potential limitations of thinking about mood solely in terms of simple values along abstract continua.

INTRODUCTION

How many different kinds of mood are possible and how do they relate to one another? These are some of the first questions that needs to be considered when trying to develop a psychology of mood. The answers are important for a number of reasons. First, knowing which particular psychological phenomena are contained in the mood category helps to clarify what the general concept means, as discussed in Chapter 1. Second, the relations and distinctions between different affective states may contribute to our understanding of the processes underlying the production and operation of mood. For example, if evaluation is a basic component of all moods, then evaluative processes are likely to be implicated in a wide range of mood processes. Third, finding structure in the mood category enables prediction of what kinds of moods are likely to have similar causes and functions. If subsets of moods are related to one another then it is no longer necessary to investigate them as completely separate and distinct states. For instance, if depression and sadness are similar conditions, we would expect them to be experienced in similar situations and to have similar effects on thought, action, and feeling. Fourth and finally, any structure that is uncovered in the mood category has methodological implications for the way that mood is measured. In other words, a structural representation enables researchers to determine which aspects of experience should be considered when trying to provide a valid and accurate representation of the quality of affect. For example, if the main important differences between mood states reflect their degree of pleasantness, then pleasantness values are what investigators should focus on when trying to characterize people's moods in laboratory and real-life situations.

A number of techniques have been employed to uncover affective structure, including introspection, investigation of facial expressions, direct comparisons of meanings of affective terms, and sampling everyday experience. Each of these methods brings its own advantages and drawbacks but the overall convergence of findings suggests that their results reflect something more fundamental than the specifics of the particular comparisons or judgements elicited in the respective procedures. For example, just about every study of affective meaning ever conducted has confirmed the relevance of the distinction between pleasant and unpleasant or good and bad moods, implying that affective conditions certainly and consistently differ from one another according to criteria relating to evaluation. The evaluative meaning of mood was also emphasized in our definition of the phenomenon presented in Chapter 1.

There is also some consensus that moods are characterized by different levels of activation or arousal, suggesting that they are more or less excitable states which may be associated with increases or decreases in behavioural activities of various kinds (and with general levels of physiological responding). This second common dimension bears some relation to our contention in Chapter 1 that moods involve predispositions of varying strength to engage in, or refrain from, certain kinds of action and reaction. Of course, the specific *nature* of the behaviour that is encouraged or discouraged by mood remains unspecified by this activation dimension.

Beyond the two basic dimensions of pleasantness and activation, there is less agreement about how differences between particular mood states should be characterized, and about whether further distinctions are necessary or even possible. In this chapter, we will review the evidence for two-dimensional models of mood structure, consider what additional dimensions might be important, and assess the general validity of a simple dimensional approach to affective experience.

Although the general topic of this book relates to mood, most of the structural models of mood experience that have been developed concern affect more generally and apply to emotions and moods equally. One of the reasons for this is that many of the words that people use to describe mood, such as "happy", "angry", and "sad" can also be applied to emotions. Similarly, facial expressions and other observable effects may sometimes be similar in the case of both emotion and mood. These considerations mean that it is quite difficult to develop a specific

18

mapping of mood as opposed to a mapping of affective experience as a whole. Consequently, much of the research reviewed below does not make the distinction between emotion and mood explicitly but works instead towards a general-purpose structural model of affect. In what follows, we will be more concerned with the implications of this research for mood research than for emotion research but it is worth bearing in mind that more general conclusions may often also be implied.

DIMENSIONS OF AFFECT

In this section we will review psychological studies that have attempted to uncover basic dimensions that can account for the most important differences between affective states. This research tradition has a long history and has employed a variety of techniques including introspective examination of conscious experience, comparisons of facial expressions, psychometric investigation of word meanings, and analyses of consistencies in self-reports of affect between people, each of which we will consider in turn. Reassuringly, these different methodologies have often tended to yield similar conclusions. The remaining issues of debate concern interpretation of the significance of the agreed dimensions and how they might relate to each other. These considerations are addressed in the subsequent section of this chapter.

Introspective analysis of affect

One of the earliest psychological accounts of the dimensional structure of affect was provided by Wundt (1897), who based his model on introspections about the feelings that accompanied simple perceptual experiences such as listening to auditory rhythms produced by a metronome. On the basis of repeated observations, Wundt claimed that regular rhythmic patterns produced more agreeable feelings than irregular ones (and that at the end of a group of clicks there was a satisfying sense of completion), and so concluded that affect could vary along a dimension of *pleasure–displeasure*. He also noted that the expectation of the arrival of the next click during the interval between clicks produced a noticeable feeling of tension, and then there was a sense of relief after the click arrived. This subjective distinction led to the postulation of a dimension of feeling corresponding to *strain–relaxation*. Finally, Wundt observed that faster rhythms tended to cause excitement whereas slower rhythms had a more calming effect, leading to a third affective dimension (*excitement–calm*). According to Wundt, these three dimensions exhausted the possible kinds of conscious distinctions between feelings, and all affective experiences were completely definable in terms of their location along these three continua.

Wundt's exclusive emphasis on experiential aspects of affect is restrictive because it fails to address the informational attunements and behavioural orientations also accompanying mood-states as defined in the previous chapter. Despite these limitations, however, subsequent research using quite different techniques has yielded findings that are broadly consistent with Wundt's early conclusions about the dimensional structure of affect.

Studies of facial expression

Schlosberg (1952) devised a more rigorous and quantitative technique for mapping the dimensional structure of affect. His procedure involved inferring similarity of affective states from data concerning how often people confused one affect with a related one. In other words, Schlosberg reasoned that moods and emotions that are more often mistaken for one another are also more likely to be similar in meaning. In his research, participants were asked to sort photographs of facial expressions of emotion into six affective categories labelled: happiness/love; surprise; fear/suffering; anger/determination; disgust; and contempt. Although some pictures were allocated to these categories consistently by participants, there was some disagreement about the proper label for others. Schlosberg found that these classification "errors" were systematic and that certain affect categories were far more likely than others to be confused with each other. For example, a facial expression that was usually classified as anger might also be labelled as disgust or fear but was almost never put into the happiness category. The implication of this finding is that some facial expressions of affect (e.g. anger and disgust) are judged to be more similar than others (e.g. anger and happiness).

By looking at the relative frequencies of categorization errors, Schlosberg was able to chart the relations between the different emotion categories and found that an almost circular arrangement represented the conceptual space most accurately (see Figure 2.1). According to this mapping, two dimensions of affective meaning can be used to account for all possible differences between facial expressions of affect: these two dimensions were specified as *pleasantness–unpleasantness* and *attention–rejection* by Schlosberg. In short, Schlosberg concluded that expressions differed according to their judged pleasantness (with love, mirth, and happiness considered to be highly pleasant and anger as highly unpleasant), and according to whether they were seen as indicating attention or rejection (surprise reflecting high attention and disgust and contempt reflecting high rejection). In a later related study, Schlosberg (1954) suggested that a third dimension of *sleep–tension* should be added to the representation. The resulting structural model shares some obvious similarities with Wundt's earlier proposals for a tridimensional theory of affect.

Abelson and Sermat (1962) asked respondents to rate the similarity of pairs of facial expressions directly, and used the statistical procedure of *multidimensional scaling* to determine the structure underlying these judgements. Again, these investigators found evidence for a pleasantness–unpleasantness dimension, as well as a second dimension relating to sleep–tension combined with attention–rejection. Other studies of similarities and differences between facial as well as vocal expression (e.g. Dittman, 1972) have also consistently yielded the dimension of

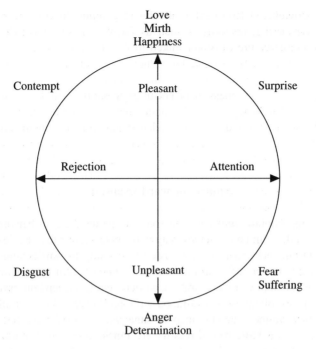

Figure 2.1 Schlosberg's (1952) proposed circular arrangement of affective expressions

pleasantness–unpleasantness in addition to one or more other dimensions usually including one relating to activation (e.g. Gladstones, 1962; see Russell, 1978, for a review).

One problem with the interpretation of these findings concerning facial expressions of affect is that we cannot be certain whether experimental participants make their judgements of similarity or classifications purely on the basis of the expressed affective state as opposed to the visual characteristics of the expression itself. For example, it may be that a smile is rather similar in appearance to a startled expression but that the corresponding affective states are quite different. However, Russell and Bullock (1985) addressed this issue by asking participants to sort photographs of expressions specifically according to the feelings they conveyed. The categorization pattern could again be explained using the two dimensions of pleasantness and activation, suggesting that the associated distinctions depend on the *meaning* of expressions rather than their observable features. Furthermore, because the participants in this study were preschool children, it seems unlikely that the dimensions depended on complex verbal representations of different affective states rather than the experiences themselves.

Research that focuses on similarities and differences between facial expressions, though clearly relevant to affective structure, also brings limitations. For example, any affective condition not associated with any distinctive facial display would obviously be excluded from any structural representation derived from such a procedure. Given that researchers such as Ekman (1994) have suggested that moods in general are typically not linked to facial expressions, this could mean that structures derived from these procedures are applicable to emotion but not mood. A corresponding problem is that some mental states that manifest themselves on the face, such as sleepiness, may not be very good examples of affect (Izard, 1972), meaning that the dimensional structure may not even be specific to emotion. Clearly, other kinds of evidence are needed to support the conclusions from this research.

Studies of word meanings

In the previous chapter, we considered some of the distinctions between different kinds of mood as formulated in everyday conversation. For example, some words describing mood seem to represent directly opposing meanings (e.g. happiness and sadness, excitement and calmness) whereas others seem semantically close to each other (e.g. calmness and relaxation, anxiety and fear). This observation opens up the possibility of investigating mood structure by examining similarities and differences in word meanings in much the same way as similarities and differences in facial expression have been investigated. Furthermore, such studies of word meaning may be more capable of producing a comprehensive representation of the structure of affect because it seems more likely that all the relevant distinctions are coded in language than that they always show up clearly on people's faces.

Studies of the meaning of affect words rely on a psychometric methodology pioneered by Osgood, Suci, and Tannenbaum (1957) known as the *semantic differential*. In this procedure, participants rate various concepts (e.g. *modern art*, *my mother*, *tornado*) according to their position along a comprehensive series of semantic dimensions anchored by opposing adjectives such as good–bad, light–dark, empty–full, and so on. Intercorrelations between the ratings are then computed in order to determine the commonalities of meaning. In the early studies by Osgood and colleagues, three basic dimensions emerged consistently for a wide variety of concepts. These dimensions were *evaluation* (the extent to which the object denoted by the concept was thought to be good or bad), *potency* (how powerful or strong the object was judged to be), and *activity* (how active the object was). Whatever linguistic domain was sampled, evaluation turned out to be the most important dimension for differentiating the meanings of the concepts in question. These findings bear obvious relations to the results of studies of structure of affect considered above, since evaluation is very close in meaning to pleasantness, and both potency and activity overlap to some degree with activation. Indeed, Osgood (1962) explicitly argued that the semantic differential dimensions reflected the basic *affective* connotations of concepts.

Averill (1975) conducted a semantic differential study of 558 emotion words and again found evidence for dimensions of evaluation, activity, and potency, but the last of these factors broke down into the two separate subcomponents of *control* and *depth of experience*, suggesting that the structure of affect itself may be more complex than the general structure of affective meaning uncovered by Osgood. However, Russell (1978) suggested that these two potency factors referred to aspects of the emotional situation rather than aspects of the affective experience itself, and that the two dimensions of pleasantness (evaluation) and activation (activity) may fully account for *intrinsic* affective quality (see below). On the basis of the arguments presented in the previous chapter that moods are less tightly linked to specific situations than emotions, the additional situationally based dimensions are likely to have less relevance to mood than emotion.

Russell (1978) reviewed research employing multidimensional scaling and semantic differential procedures (e.g. Averill, 1975; Block, 1957; Russell & Mehrabian, 1977) and concluded that there was consistent and strong evidence for pleasantness and activation dimensions and weaker evidence for a third dimension variously labelled control, dominance, or depth of experience. By intercorrelating ratings on the scales used by several different investigators, Russell was also able to demonstrate empirically that pleasantness and activation were the main sources of the variance in ratings of affective meaning across studies.

A basic ambiguity still remains concerning the precise implications of these studies of the meanings of words used to describe affect: On the one hand, they might tell us what affective experience itself is really like (e.g. Reisenzein, 1994); on the other hand they might only give information about how people understand and represent affect. In other words, it is difficult to know whether judged similarities and differences in word meanings reflect the objects (affective states) referred to by the words, or depend simply on the way people conceive of, or think about, those objects (or some combination of the two). Fortunately, the fact that other kinds of evidence produce similar conclusions suggests that something more than mere beliefs about affect are being tapped by these studies. According to Russell (1979), pleasantness and activation are primarily features of the way in which affect is represented by people, but affective experience is necessarily mediated by these same representations anyway. In other words, feeling affect always involves first representing it cognitively in terms relating to the two dimensions of meaning, so that pleasantness and activation have equal relevance to representation and experience.

In terms of the application of the affective circumplex for self-report measurement of mood (see below), it makes little difference which of these interpretations of affect dimensions is accepted, because even if affective experience does not necessarily require prior representation, affective self-report certainly does. The fact that respondents are able to make consistent quantitative distinctions between affective states along two basic dimensions implies that rating scales conforming to these dimensions may be used in characterizing affective experience. Of course, this does not mean that dimensional ratings necessarily capture the essence of affective experience itself, only that they encapsulate affective information that is meaningful for respondents.

Studies of self-reported affect

While most of the studies considered so far have asked for abstract comparisons of affective states represented by facial expressions or by common words, it is also possible to investigate the structure of people's judgements about their own actual affect. Instead of focusing on conceptual relations between affective states, these studies provide data relevant to the composition of affect in ongoing experience. However, it would not be surprising if the results of these investigations produced results similar to those produced by studies of affective word meaning, simply because semantic similarities between affect terms will also be reflected in judgements about whether the words characterize experience itself. For example, your self-report of happiness at any given moment is likely to correspond substantially to your rating of joy simply because the words seem to mean similar things, and therefore have similar relevance to what you are feeling. Conversely, a high rating of happiness or joy will usually be associated with a low rating of sadness or depression and vice versa.

Another consideration that might influence relations between ratings of actual affective experience concerns the co-occurrence of different kinds of affect. For example, if we assume that people in our society generally believe that anger is often a morally unacceptable thing to feel (e.g. Stearns & Stearns, 1986), then it is likely that when people experience this emotion, they will also feel some level of guilt about experiencing it. This means that when people's affective experiences are sampled there is likely to be a discernible positive correlation between anger ratings and guilt ratings. However, this correlation does not arise from any similarity between the experiences of anger and guilt, but rather because these affective states often tends to occur in conjunction with each other.

On the basis of these arguments, it seems that studies of the intercorrelations of self-ratings of affect may depend jointly on semantic similarities between scale items (as also assessed in studies of word meaning) and the co-occurrence of different kinds of affective experience. This joint determination makes the results of these studies at least as hard to interpret as those of direct investigations of semantic structure.

Perhaps partly for this reason, studies of intercorrelations of self-reported mood-ratings have generally produced less consistent results than those directly addressing affective meaning of words or facial expressions (e.g. Izard, 1972). Nevertheless, here too it is apparent that two dimensions account for most of the variance (e.g. Russell, 1980; Watson & Tellegen, 1985). For example, Russell (1980) asked respondents to rate the extent to which a series of affective adjectives described the affect they had experienced so far that day and found that pleasantness and activation accounted for most of the obtained variance along 28 representative scales. Other studies (e.g. Russell, 1979; Watson & Tellegen, 1985) point to similar conclusions but as we shall see in the next section, there is still some dispute about the precise nature of the underlying dimensions of self-reported affect.

CIRCUMPLEX MODELS OF AFFECTIVE STRUCTURE

The previous section reviewed evidence for the existence of basic common dimensions of affective experience. In this section, we consider models which have explicitly tried to map out the structure of affect based on these observations and find the coordinates of particular affective states in the conceptual space implied by these dimensions. The two influential models reviewed here both propose that the established dimensions have a particular relationship to one another so that affect space is seen to have a particular shape rather than simply existing in two or three dimensions. This shape is generally claimed to be a circular one (cf. Schlosberg, 1952, described above).

The pleasantness–activation circumplex

All of the evidence considered so far suggests that affective states differ from one another on the basis of two or more dimensions, with pleasantness (or the related dimension of evaluation) typically being the most important. Russell (1980) has also made additional assumptions about the structure of affective meaning by arguing that not all combinations of values on these two dimensions are possible, and that affect terms should be arranged in a *circumplex* representation with axes corresponding to pleasantness and activation. According to this account, words having similar affective meaning may be arranged close to each other on the circumference of the circle, while words with contrasting meanings fall opposite one another. In more precise terms, a circumplex is defined as a two-dimensional circular structure in which items correlate highly with items close to them on the circumference of the circle, have zero correlations ($r = 0.0$) with items at 90 degrees on the circumplex, and have perfect negative correlations ($r = -1.0$) with items opposite them (and separated by the circle's full diameter).

Russell (1980) provided evidence that people's implicit representations of emotion corresponded to the circumplex by asking participants to group 28 emotion words into eight basic categories that were predicted to characterize the 45-degree sectors (octants) of the circumplex (*arousal, excitement, pleasure, contentment, sleepiness, depression, misery,* and *distress*). These eight categories then had to be arranged into a circle by respondents so that words placed directly opposite each other referred to "opposite feelings" and words put close to each other on the circle described feelings that were similar.

The predicted arrangement was that axes corresponding to pleasure–misery and arousal–sleep would be at right angles from each other and that at 45 degrees from these axes would be secondary axes corresponding to excitement–depression and contentment–distress (see Figure 2.2). Ten of the 36 participants produced exactly this circular arrangement of terms, and most of the others tended to differ only slightly. The median correlation between predicted and obtained orderings was 0.80.

Some of the individual emotion words fell consistently into one of the eight

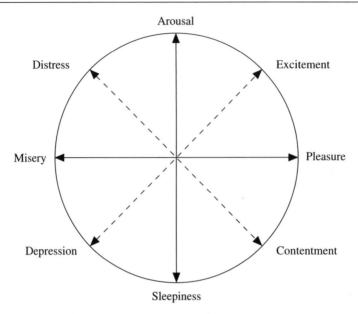

Figure 2.2 Russell's (1980) predicted circular arrangement of eight basic affect categories

categories, while for others there was disagreement between participants concerning to which of two or three categories the word best belonged. From data concerning frequency of inclusion in categories, Russell (like Schlosberg, 1952, in his investigation of facial expressions considered above) was able to construct statistically a model of the conceptual arrangement of the individual emotion words. Specifically, the number of participants who put a particular word in a category was used to determine how close that word was to the central point in the relevant sector of semantic space. For example, the word "happy" was put into the *pleasure* category by a substantial majority of respondents and therefore was positioned close to the centre of the relevant sector of the circumplex. On the other hand, the word "delighted" was judged to be an example of pleasure by roughly half the participants and judged to be an example of "excitement" by most of the other half. Therefore, "delighted" was positioned close to the boundary between *pleasure* and *excitement*. Using these basic principles, an arrangement of all 28 words was mapped out and its shape, as predicted, corresponded closely to the circumplex. Finally, self-reports of affect along the 28 dimensions were found to depend on approximately the combinations of pleasantness and activation predicted by the circumplex model.

The pleasantness–activation circumplex model also appears to apply in different cultural groups. For example, bilingual Chinese, Croatian, Gujarati, and Japanese speakers living in an English-speaking area of Canada showed comparable circular structuring in their ratings (Russell, 1983). Furthermore, Russell, Lewicka, and Niit (1989) found supportive results when native Estonian, Greek, and Polish speakers judged the similarity of the same basic set of translated affect adjectives. Finally, judgements based on standard photographs of emotional facial expressions by these same national groups yielded similarity ratings that conformed to the original circumplex, confirming that it has a reasonable level of cross-cultural generality. Semantic differential studies of non-affective concepts similarly reveal that the general evaluation-potency-activity structure applies cross-culturally too (e.g. Osgood, May, & Miron, 1975).

It should be noted that these findings do not mean that people in different cultures necessarily experience or conceptualize affect in exactly the same way as Anglo-Americans do. In fact, anthropological studies suggest that affective concepts may be used very differently in different cultures, especially those that have had little contact with Western civilization (e.g. Lutz, 1988; Rosaldo, 1984). However, the data do imply that a basic set of affect adjectives can be translated successfully into different languages, and that people from different cultures have similar ideas about how these particular terms and associated facial expressions relate to, and contrast with, each other. This finding has relevance to cross-cultural measurement of pleasantness and activation even if its implications for general cultural differences in affective experience are uncertain.

To summarize Russell's results from a series of studies, he found that affective concepts can be reliably arranged in a circumplex with axes labelled pleasantness and activation. The pleasantness dimension reflects the fact that affective states are thought to range in quality from highly unpleasant to highly pleasant. Activation refers to the contrast between states such as tranquillity which are associated with low levels of activity or arousal, and conditions like astonishment or anger which are thought to involve high degrees of arousal. In Russell's circumplex, a state such as fear is characterized by high activation and low pleasantness and is thus the direct opposite of calmness or relaxation, which are judged to be highly pleasant states associated with a low degree of activation. In general, terms which imply similar levels of pleasantness and activation are near to one another on the edge of the circle, and terms that have opposite meanings are separated by the circle's full diameter (see Figure 2.3). According to Russell, all words describing affective states can be arranged at some point around the edge of the circumplex, or, to put this another way, all affective meanings can be precisely located and characterized according to their combined values of activation and pleasantness.

Despite the consistent findings in support of the pleasantness–activation circumplex, it also faces certain empirical and conceptual problems: first, there is some question concerning whether the mapping specifies only genuinely affective meanings. This problem arises because terms that seem to refer to non-affective states seem to be included on the circumplex. For example, "sleepy" does not seem to be a word that typically describes an evaluative state of mind (cf. Ortony, Clore, & Collins, 1988). More generally, if we take evaluation to be a central feature of affect as suggested in Chapter 1, then points on the circumplex that have a zero value on the pleasant–unpleasant dimension are not really affective at all. Similarly, if we assume that moods and affective states more generally have

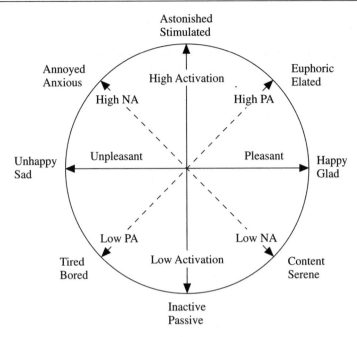

Figure 2.4 Mapping of Watson and Tellegen's (1985) positive and negative affect dimensions on Russell's (1980) affective circumplex

moderate activation, and maximal activation or deactivation is automatically associated with evaluative neutrality (Larsen & Diener, 1992). In fact it seems possible for some affective states to have high values on both dimensions. For example, terror and panic seem to be highly unpleasant and highly activated affective states, and conversely delirious excitement and mania can be highly pleasant and highly activated.

The positive affect–negative affect circumplex

An alternative circular mapping of affect has been suggested by Watson and Tellegen (1985) among others (e.g. Meyer & Shack, 1989), who argued that it is more productive to see Russell's arrangement from a different angle, and draw the axes at 45 degrees from the vertical (see Figure 2.4). Watson and Tellegen suggested that moods and emotions are judged to differ along the two separate dimensions of *positive affect* (PA) and *negative affect* (NA). In their view, high PA reflects pleasurable engagement with the environment and is characterized by words such as *euphoric*, *peppy*, and *elated*, which imply a combination of pleasantness and activation, whereas low positive affect is marked by depression and lethargy and described in terms such as *drowsy* and *dull* which indicate a lack of pleasantness and activation. Correspondingly, high NA includes distressing and unpleasant affective states such as anxiety and anger, suggesting high activation and high unpleasantness, while low NA implies calm and relaxation.

It has usually been found that PA and NA dimensions tend to emerge from factor analysis of self-reported affect (as opposed to judgements of word meanings) when dimensions are rotated, whereas pleasantness and arousal are often the simple unrotated dimensions that are obtained (Watson & Tellegen, 1985). The rotation procedure works by turning the axes of the circumplex to the point where they both come closest to the largest possible number of variables (affects). In other words, Watson and Tellegen's representation maximizes the distinctiveness of the two dimensions by making sure that as many of the rated affect terms as possible correlate strongly with only one of them. This procedure has obvious advantages when the aim is to construct self-report measures of affect dimensions based on ratings of words which relate very directly to one or other of the factors (see below).

Choosing between the circumplexes

Essentially, Russell's and Watson and Tellegen's schemes may be seen as intertranslatable, with high PA combining pleasantness and activation, low PA involving unpleasantness and deactivation, high NA definable in terms of unpleasantness and activation, and low NA implying pleasantness and deactivation. Correspondingly, high pleasantness can be viewed as a combination of high PA and low NA and so on (see Figure 2.4). To the extent that the two schemes of classification can both be mapped onto the same circumplex, the choice of dimensions may be seen as an arbitrary decision based on preferred procedures for factor analysis and data sampling (Larsen & Diener, 1992).

One justification of the argument that the dimensions are arbitrary rests on the assumption that affective experiences or meanings are evenly distributed around the circumplex (i.e. that it really is a circumplex as mathematically defined). In this connection, Russell (1980) argued as follows: "Rather than clusters of synonyms falling near the axes, terms spread out more or less continuously around the perimeter of the space" (p. 1167). However, as we have already mentioned, there may be sections of the circumplex where the terms included do not imply strong affective meaning such as the regions near to the zero point on the pleasantness dimension or close to the activation mid-point. In fact, Russell may have included terms like "sleepy" in his studies with the specific intention of covering all points on the circumplex rather than because they necessarily referred to good and representative examples of affect (Ortony, Clore, & Collins, 1988).

Watson and Tellegen (1985) contended that commonly used affect words tend to be more densely spaced around the poles of the NA and PA axes (i.e. between the poles of pleasantness and activation), making these dimensions more basic (and explaining why rotation of factors in factor analysis tends to arrive at this particular two-dimensional solution). Of course, one implication of this argument is that Watson and Tellegen's model is not strictly a perfect circumplex. The difference in conclusions may depend on the fact that Watson and Tellegen paid more attention to self-reports than word-meaning tasks, and their data may therefore reflect commonness of different kinds of affective experience, rather than (or in addition to) the underlying dimensions of affective meaning. In other words, it is possible to conceive of pleasantness and activation as basic *semantic* dimensions of affective experience, and PA and NA as *descriptive* factors which account for commonly experienced affective reactions. For example, it may be that the affect we experience tends to fall into the four loose categories of pleasant-activated, pleasant-deactivated, unpleasant-activated, and unpleasant-deactivated states. Indeed, according to the commonsense definition developed in Chapter 1, we would not call our experience affective unless it belonged in one of these groupings, because affect implies evaluation and motivational impact. However, our perception and understanding of affective states may depend on basic concepts and representations relating to pleasantness and arousal, rather than positive and negative affect.

Intuitive consideration also seems to support the idea that pleasantness and activation are the fundamental components of affective meaning. In particular, it seems possible to break down the semantic content of PA or NA into more basic terms relating to pleasantness and activation, whereas it is not so easy to conceive of pleasantness or activation as being reducible to particular combinations of PA and NA (cf. Reisenzein, 1994).

Feldman (1995a) showed specifically that there were structural differences between the representations of affect derived respectively from word-meaning tasks and self-reported affect. In particular, she showed that the activation dimension was less important when considering ratings of actual experience than when semantic judgements were being made. Her interpretation of this finding was that people are generally more attentive to aspects of their experience relating to pleasantness than aspects relating to activation and therefore give the former aspects more weight when characterizing their affective state. However, when considering word meanings, activational implications of the relevant terms may be more obvious and salient. Further, Feldman (1995b) found that individual differences in the extent to which participants characteristically focused on their activation when representing affective experience were related to how strongly PA and NA emerged as independent dimensions. These findings suggest once more that the PA–NA circumplex depends to some extent on *interpretations* of experience as well as any structure inherent in the experiences themselves (see above). In other words, the emergence of PA and NA as basic factors may partly reflect the ways in which people generally make sense of their feelings rather than directly arising from the actual nature of these feelings.

None of the preceding discussion should be taken to imply that the constructs of positive and negative affect have little value in mood research. For example, measurement of these factors may be the best strategy for characterizing everyday experiences of affect in many circumstances, since they clearly reflect common patterns of response to many important psychological processes as they are characterized by those experiencing them. For example, assessment of the relative values of PA and NA may help in diagnosis of certain clinical conditions (e.g. Clark & Watson, 1991). Thus, the PA–NA circumplex may prove to be of considerable practical value to psychologists.

INDEPENDENCE OF POSITIVE AND NEGATIVE AFFECT

Intuitively, it seems obvious that the more happy we feel the less likely we are to be sad, and that pleasantness of experience is by definition incompatible with unpleasantness. Even ambivalence, which might be seen as a state during which we feel good and bad simultaneously, in fact usually implies either rapid alternation between opposing evaluations or uncertainty about what our feelings really are. At first blush, similar considerations might seem to apply to our experience of positive and negative affect, which also sound like incompatible opposites. However, Watson and Tellegen's (1985) model specifies these factors as statistically independent, implying that it is just as possible to feel strong positive and negative affect simultaneously as it is for them to have directly opposite values. Other psychologists too have made similar claims about possible relationships between positive and negative feelings (e.g. Bradburn, 1969).

A substantial amount of empirical and theoretical effort has been devoted to this issue of the supposed independence of positive and negative affect, partly because of the apparently counterintuitive implications of the hypothesis. Unfortunately, there are problems in integrating the conclusions of these studies because different investigators have interpreted the research questions differently and used similar terminologies in a variety of different ways. In this section, we try to clarify what independence of this kind might actually mean, and determine whether there is convincing evidence for it.

One of the earliest versions of the independence hypothesis arose from Bradburn's (1969) work on psychological well-being. Bradburn found that self-reports of positive and negative experiences over the few weeks preceding the time of questioning were uncorrelated. In other words, respondents who said that they had experienced negative feelings did not necessarily also report not having experienced positive feelings and vice versa. Although Bradburn labelled his two scales positive and negative affect, this usage predated Watson and Tellegen's more technical definitions of these terms and actually referred more directly to the *pleasantness* of the experiences in question.

Bradburn's superficially counterintuitive findings seem less surprising when the *time-frame* of the analysed affect assessments is taken into account. Specifically, nothing in Bradburn's data suggests that pleasant and unpleasant feelings are experienced *simultaneously* at any given moment; rather, they imply that over a few weeks both unpleasant and pleasant experiences may occur without having any influence on the probability of occurrence of the opposite kind of experience (e.g. Warr, Barter, & Brownbridge, 1983). Warr and colleagues found that when respondents explicitly reported the *number* of unpleasant and pleasant episodes they had experienced over the designated period, ratings were uncorrelated, but when they reported the *proportion of time* occupied by pleasant and unpleasant experiences, the expected negative relationship emerged. In other words, the more time participants spent in a bad mood, the less time they spent in a good mood, but good things happening did not necessarily either remove the possibility of bad things happening, or counteract their effects.

A related analysis was offered by Diener and colleagues (Diener, Larsen, Levine, & Emmons, 1985) who introduced a useful distinction between *intensity* and *frequency* influences on reports of affect generalized over extended time periods. Working from the assumption that pleasant and unpleasant feelings are incompatible at any given moment, they reasoned that the more often a person experiences either pleasant or unpleasant affect, the less time remains available for experiencing the other kind of affect. This means that measures of *frequency* of pleasant and unpleasant affect should be inversely correlated. However, with regard to *intensity*, there are people who characteristically experience stronger affect of both the pleasant and unpleasant variety (e.g. Larsen & Diener, 1987) so that measures of this factor tend to correlate positively over time.

According to Diener and colleagues, a basic problem with many measures of mood is that they include both frequency and intensity components on the same scales. For example, when participants are asked to report how much they have experienced pleasant and unpleasant affect over the course of a day or a week, their ratings probably depend not only on how strongly pleasant or unpleasant their mood has been at any particular time, but also on how much of the time they have spent in a pleasant or unpleasant mood. Combined intensity-frequency ratings of this kind might show statistical independence because the positive correlation between the intensity components of positive and negative affect ratings tends to cancel out the negative correlation of their frequency components.

Diener and colleagues provided data in support of their argument by deriving *separate* indices of affect frequency and intensity from repeated self-reports of affect. They were able to confirm that pleasant affect frequency and unpleasant affect frequency showed a strong inverse correlation but that pleasant affect intensity was positively correlated with unpleasant affect intensity in general.

According to Diener and colleagues, intensity and frequency of affect should replace activation and pleasantness as the basic dimensions of affective structure. However, this suggestion is problematic for the study of ongoing mood because it is impossible to apply the concept of frequency to a single moment of experience. The proposal may, however, have more relevance to the study of subjective well-being over time (see also Chapter 6).

A basic conclusion of these findings from Diener, Warr, and their respective co-workers is that the more one's time is occupied with pleasant or unpleasant feelings, the less the remaining opportunity for feelings of the opposing kind to arise. At any given moment, then, one may feel good, affectively intermediate, or bad, but never simultaneously good and bad. However, over a more extended time period, there are more likely to be episodes of both pleasant and unpleasant affect. Diener and Emmons (1984) explicitly tested this conclusion by asking respondents to report their levels of pleasant and unpleasant affect over several different time-frames ranging from the present moment, through the preceding day or week, to the last year. The investigators found that when current *momentary* mood was rated, pleasant and unpleasant affect were negatively correlated, especially when strong emotion was being experienced, but as the time-frame widened, the lower this correlation tended to become. In other words, it is quite conceivable that someone could correctly characterize their mood over an extended time period as high in both positive and negative affect, if there were separate episodes of each.

Diener and Iran-Nejad (1986) qualified Diener and Emmons's earlier findings about the concurrence of contrasting feelings. They showed that although low levels of pleasant or unpleasant affect do not prevent the simultaneous occurrence of the other kind of affect, high levels of momentary pleasant or unpleasant feelings are mutually exclusive. In other words, *intense* pleasant feelings are incompatible with unpleasant feelings of any strength, and intense unpleasant feelings are incompatible with any pleasant feelings. At lower rated levels of affect, it may be that feelings are ill-defined and thus more likely to be characterized in terms of mixtures of slight anxiety and mild excitement and so on.

Watson (1988a) questioned Diener and colleagues' finding that the independence of positive and negative affect only applied to extended time-frames. In his study, participants rated their affective experience across several different time-frames using standardized scales of PA and NA in addition to the pleasant and unpleasant affect measures originally used by Diener and Emmons. Scores on Diener and Emmons's scales were generally more negatively intercorrelated than PA and NA values, but there was little evidence that this intercorrelation depended on the time-frame under consideration. However, Watson failed to report the results of any analysis that corresponded precisely to that used by Diener and Emmons in which each individual's momentary report of pleasant feelings at times of strong emotion were correlated (within subjects) with the same person's momentary report of unpleasant feelings. A similar analysis conducted on PA and NA scores showed that when scale values on PA or NA were higher, there did tend to be a stronger negative correlation. It is hard to draw firm conclusions from these apparently inconsistent studies given their subtle differences in methodology and statistical analysis, but it certainly does seem to be the case that high levels of emotion reduce the independence of momentary positive and negative affect.

Feldman (1995b) showed that within-subject correlations between PA and NA depended on the levels of *arousal focus* and *valence focus* of the individual making the ratings. Specifically, those participants who generally paid more attention to the activation aspects of their moods and emotions showed more positive correlations between PA and NA, and those who attached more weight to their pleasantness showed more negative correlations. Thus, as argued above, the independence of positive and negative affect seems partly to depend on people's interpretations of their affective experiences rather than necessarily reflecting anything basic to those experiences themselves. More generally, these findings again confirm that PA and NA are not necessarily independent under all circumstances.

Another factor extrinsic to mood experience itself which may contribute to apparent PA–NA independence relates to people's responses to the characteristics of the self-report items used to measure these factors. For example, the *acquiescence response bias* often results in respondents tending to agree with any statement they are rating regardless of its content (e.g. Bentler, 1969). When rating their affect, therefore, people may show a tendency to say that both positively and negatively valenced adjectives characterize their moods to a greater extent than is really the case, thus reducing any negative correlation between the two kinds of rating. Green, Goldman, and Salovey (1993) demonstrated that after allowances were made for measurement errors including those arising from acquiescence, PA and NA scales showed substantial negative intercorrelations, regardless of the time-frame assessed.

The general conclusion of this section is that PA–NA independence may depend on a number of factors other than the intrinsic qualities of the relevant affective experiences themselves, including those relating to time-sampling, individual differences in attentional focus, and response biases. However, there still remains at least one sense in which positive and negative affect as defined by Watson and Tellegen seem to be genuinely independent arising from the observation that the scale values are influenced by quite separate kinds of variable. A range of evidence supports the conclusion that PA is related to the personality trait of extraversion (Eysenck, 1967) and is responsive to the frequency of pleasant events and social engagement as well as time of day and season of the year (see Chapter 5). NA on the other hand is related to characteristic levels of neuroticism and varies in connection with perceived stress and health complaints but not so much with time *per se*. If these generalizations are broadly correct, then any lack of concordance in the variation of these two factors of affect over time would be unsurprising.

MEASUREMENT OF MOOD DIMENSIONS

In addition to their theoretical significance for understanding the structure of affect, the circumplex models also carry implications for how mood should be measured. For example, if most of the meaning of affect can be captured in terms of values along two simple dimensions, then for many research purposes assessment of values along these dimensions will give sufficient specification of the phenomenon. Further, mappings of specific affect terms around the circumplex allow investigators to choose the adjectives that best represent the dimensions for inclusion in self-report scales designed to measure affect. For example, measurement of PA apparently requires asking participants to what extent adjectives such as "excited", "peppy", and "enthusiastic" characterize their current state, and assessment of pleasantness involves questioning people about their level of happiness, pleasure, and satisfaction.

35

Table 2.1 The Positive And Negative Affect Scale (PANAS; Watson, Clark, & Tellegen, 1988)

This scale consists of a number of words that describe different feelings and emotions. Read each item and then mark the appropriate answer in the space next to that word. Indicate *to what extent you feel this way right now, that is, at the present moment* [OR: *to what extent you have felt this way today, to what extent you have felt this way during the past few days* etc]. Use the following scale to record your answers:

Very slightly or not at all	A little	Moderately	Quite a bit	Extremely
1	2	3	4	5

..... interested*	..... hostile	..... nervous
..... distressed	..... enthusiastic*	..... determined*
..... excited*	..... proud*	..... attentive*
..... upset	..... irritable	..... jittery
..... strong*	..... alert*	..... active*
..... guilty	..... ashamed	..... afraid
..... scared	..... inspired*	

* All asterisked items relate to PA. All non-asterisked items relate to NA.

Self-report measurement of affect

The most common way of measuring mood follows exactly this strategy of self-report along various rating scales anchored with affect adjectives. A number of response formats are used, most of which require participants to rate the extent to which the adjective characterizes their current or recent experience along a numerical dimension. For example, a popular questionnaire assessing PA and NA (PANAS: the Positive And Negative Affect Scale, Watson, Clark, & Tellegen, 1988, see Table 2.1) lists 20 affect adjectives including "interested", "distressed", "excited", "upset", and "irritable", and asks respondents to rate to what extent each adjective applies to the way they feel (or have recently felt) on a five-point scale. A number of almost interchangeable questionnaires have been constructed to measure the basic dimensions of positive and negative affect and, in practice, it may not make much difference which one is used. Watson (1988b) presented evidence that all but one of twelve short scales for assessing PA and NA were sufficiently reliable for most research purposes, and that each of them showed strong positive correlations with the others.

An even quicker and simpler way of indexing affect was suggested by Russell, Weiss, and Mendelsohn (1989). As the name suggests, their *affect grid* provides participants with a two-dimensional nine cell by nine cell square grid, with sides representing pleasantness and activation, in which respondents must mark a cell in a place that corresponds to their current level on both of these dimensions (see Figure 2.5). Russell and colleagues found that scores derived from this procedure were highly correlated with scores obtained using longer and more time-consuming

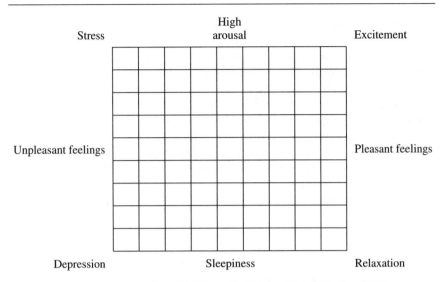

Figure 2.5 The Affect Grid (Russell, Weiss, and Mendelsohn, 1989)

verbal self-report scales, suggesting that the grid may prove useful when ratings of affect are required under time pressure or processing constraints.

For many studies investigating the general impact of various personal and environmental factors on mood (see Chapter 3), assessment of the dependent variable in terms of two basic dimensions is sufficient. Indeed, the standardization of scales along these dimensions makes them seem the proper target of investigation anyway. However, more specific hypotheses about the role of mood in psychological functioning may require distinctions over and above those allowed by these scales. For example, current scales assessing pleasantness and activation or PA and NA would fail to detect the substantive difference between an anxious and an irritable mood of subjectively equivalent intensity. It therefore seems necessary to construct more focused measures of mood to suit the purposes of different studies. In the final section of this chapter, we will return to the question of whether two dimensions are sufficient to capture all the important variations and differences in mood.

Limitations of self-report measures of affect

There are a number of obvious problems with using self-reports to measure mood states. The first is that the procedure assumes a degree of mood awareness (e.g. Swinkels & Giuliano, 1995) which may not always be present. For example, we have argued in Chapter 1 that it is possible to be in a particular mood without being explicitly conscious of it, as happens when other people have to draw our attention to the fact that we have been in a bad mood all day. Obviously, it is unlikely that moods which we do not know are there will be represented in our self-ratings. However, it is possible that the administration of a self-report scale containing explicit questions about current affective state sensitizes respondents to affective information, and makes them more conscious of their previously unnoticed moods. Unfortunately, if this kind of induced mood consciousness occurs during self-report, then the measurement procedure is potentially influencing the very phenomenon it is supposed to be assessing. For example, some investigators have suggested that conscious mood experiences have quite different effects to non-conscious moods (e.g. Morris, 1992). Relatedly, introspective examination may lead to deliberate attempts to modify mood (see Chapter 6), or to additional feelings about finding oneself in such an affective state (e.g. a person might be unhappy to discover how bored he or she is). Thus, if one of the purposes of a study is to assess consequences of mood, there is a danger that imposition of self-report may interfere with the direct effects of mood on the dependent variable.

Another set of potentially contaminating factors relate to the social meaning of mood-related statements. Checking a response on a questionnaire is not simply a neutral descriptive act but also part of a communicative process addressed to the person who will use the supplied data. In other words, people may make their mood ratings in accordance with what they want to tell the other person about how they are feeling rather than directly reading off information from their actual affective experience itself. For example, in contemporary Western culture there are generally accepted norms of politeness which encourage the expression of pleasant feelings and discourage the expression of unpleasant feelings and these may contribute to the common finding that most people report themselves as feeling mildly happy most of the time (e.g. Diener, 1984). On the other hand, there may also be circumstances where expression of unpleasant affect is more appropriate to the social situation, such as when you want to make a complaint to someone, or share their apparent disapproval. Finally, you might report a particular affective state if you believe that the person to whom the communication is addressed wants or expects you to feel it, for example, if they have gone to the trouble of showing you films or playing you music that seems designed to induce that reaction, as often happens in experimental studies of mood (see Chapter 3). In practice, it is extremely difficult to factor out the contribution of these com-municative aspects of self-rating in order to get at what the respondent is really feeling. Of course, it may also be true that presenting oneself to someone else in a certain way influences mood itself in addition to its representation on rating scales.

Although self-report may not always be the most accurate or precise way of assessing affect, it is certainly one of the most convenient. At present none of the obvious alternatives is capable of providing sensitive or discriminating enough measurement. For example, it is possible to derive affective information from non-verbal indices based on facial expression (e.g. Ekman & Friesen, 1975), psychophysiological responses such as skin conductance and heart-rate (e.g. Cacioppo, Klein, Berntson, & Hatfield, 1993), or performance characteristics (e.g.

38

Mayer & Bremer, 1985), but none of these has been found to show a perfect or consistent relationship with other affective assessment procedures (see Chapter 4). However, it is often a good idea to use non-verbal measures such as these as a partial validity check on self-reports. Another useful procedure is to ask observers such as spouses who might be expected to have accurate information about a person's mood-state to give supplementary ratings (e.g. Marangoni, Garcia, Ickes, & Teng, 1995). For the foreseeable future, however, the most viable and discriminative way of assessing mood is by using self-report of some kind, despite the limitations of such procedures.

ARE TWO DIMENSIONS ENOUGH?

Most of the research reported so far in this chapter suggests that differences between the qualities of affective states mainly depend on pleasantness and activation or positive and negative affect. However, many studies have also found evidence for additional dimensions of affective meaning relating, for example, to levels of control, depth of experience (Averill, 1975), intensity (Daly, Lancee, & Polivy, 1983), and locus of causation (Parkinson & Lea, 1991). Further, although pleasantness and activation seem to account for a large amount of variance in affective judgements, they still do not account for it all, and it is unlikely that what remains is entirely due to methodological artefacts and experimental error (e.g. Russell, 1978).

On an intuitive level too, it seems implausible that all affect consists of is a particular mixture of pleasantness and arousal. There seems to be more to restlessness, exuberance, or dismay, for example, than a simple combination of values of these two variables. Relatedly, a basic problem with the two-dimensional representation of affective meaning is that it puts affective states which apparently have quite distinct meanings close to each other in semantic space (Larsen & Diener, 1992). For instance, both anxious and irritable moods score similarly high on activation and low on pleasantness (or high on negative affect and low on positive affect), making it difficult to differentiate these quite dissimilar conditions using only the two dimensions of the circumplex. This reasoning suggests that the postulated affect dimensions do not completely account for the representational content of mood or emotion terms.

In Russell's (1979) view, the experiential core of affect may be fully represented in terms of pleasantness and activation, but ordinary-language words and everyday expressions representing affect may also carry additional information relating to the *causes* and *consequences* of what is felt. Thus, dimensions such as control and locus of causation depend on interpretations of the psychological situation surrounding the affect rather than the feeling itself. Further, Russell (1979) implied that these extra components of meaning conveyed by affective concepts should be treated separately as extrinsic to the structure of *bona fide* affect. However, even if this point is accepted, it remains an open question whether the specific conceptual geography of mood (as opposed to affect in general) should exclude or include these additional components of meaning.

In Chapter 1, we argued that moods predispose people to interpret situations in particular ways and to act in certain patterned ways as well as implying evaluative feelings. From this point of view, extra dimensions of affective meaning relating to consequences for cognition and motivation have clear relevance to how different mood states should be defined. In particular, we would expect further specification of moods on the basis of their interpretational and action-directing aspects. For example, irritability seems to be an unpleasant activated state that involves a tendency to interpret events as annoyances and react to them accordingly, while an anxious mood is apparently an unpleasant activated condition in which the world is seen in a threatening light and there is an urge to escape or hide. Thus, attention to additional components of meaning clarifies the distinction between two moods that are relatively undifferentiated in the circumplex models. Unfortunately, there have been no studies that have specifically focused on these aspects of the structural meaning of moods, but related investigations of emotional appraisals and action tendencies allow some more general conclusions.

Smith and Ellsworth (1985) advanced the study of emotional meaning by suggesting that a limited number of dimensions of cognitive *appraisal* may account for all possible differences between different emotions (appraisal refers to the interpretative-evaluative process which leads to a recognition that the situation has personal significance). In their study, participants reported the situational evaluations and interpretations associated with the recalled experiences of fifteen different emotions. It was found that each emotion had a relatively distinctive profile along six independent appraisal dimensions relating to pleasantness, anticipated effort, certainty, personal responsibility/control, and situational control. For example, anger was closely associated with judgements that someone else was responsible for what was happening whereas fear was associated with uncertainty about how the situation would turn out. Both fear and anger (but not happiness or pride) were associated with an expectation that effort would be required for dealing with the situation. Subsequent studies have extended and tightened the appraisal definitions of specific emotional terms (e.g. Manstead & Tetlock, 1989; Roseman, 1991; Smith, Haynes, Lazarus, & Pope, 1993).

A basic conclusion from this research is that different emotional meanings are related to particular patterns of interpretation and evaluation of the present or impending situation. In Chapter 1, we suggested that moods are more diffuse and unfocused states than emotions, so it seems unlikely that all of the identified appraisal dimensions have equal relevance for all mood states. However, it does seem plausible that moods are related to more general patterns of appraisal in some cases. For example, the tendency to interpret events as being caused by other people rather than impersonal agencies may be a defining characteristic of irritable moods (cf. Keltner, Ellsworth, & Edwards, 1993).

Related studies have also investigated the modes of *action readiness* associated with different emotions and different appraisal patterns. For example, participants in Frijda, Kuipers, and ter Schure's (1989) experiment reported that anger involved wanting to engage in behaviour directed against someone or something (antagonism) together with excitement, and love involved general excitement along with a desire to approach or make contact with someone. Again, moods are probably less tightly connected with action readiness modes than emotions but some specification of general approach–avoidance, or attention–rejection, tendencies may still be possible. It is probably also true that there is a more limited range of possible mood states than of possible emotion states, reinforcing this point that a more limited number of generalized modes may be applicable in the former case.

In summary, mood states may be defined partly according to their evaluative implications and partly according to the attunements they imply towards affectively relevant information and the predispositions towards action associated with these attunements. Moods, from this perspective, are always more than simple feelings. The quality of judged pleasantness emerging from dimensional studies clearly reflects the evaluative aspects of mood, and the activation component relates to the fact that moods generally lead to energizing or inhibiting effects on action. However, neither of these components are simply qualities of feeling. Rather they reflect dynamic aspects of ongoing mood states. Further specification of the meaning of mood states requires attention to the particular appraisal and action readiness modes engendered by the mood (cf. Frijda, 1986). For example, being in an anxious mood involves a watchfulness directed to threatening objects and events and a general tendency to react quickly and vigorously to them. An irritable mood, on the other hand, involves attunement to potential attack and a tendency towards aggressive response. The fundamental intrinsic quality of each of these moods is not reducible to unpleasantness and activation even though these are common aspects of both states. In order to define each state fully it is necessary to specify where the activation (in terms of attention and the disposition to action) is directed.

Despite this general conclusion that mood implies more than simple pleasantness and activation, most of the research into the operation of mood and its relationship with other psychological factors has focused specifically on these dimensions, especially the pleasantness dimension. The basic distinction between pleasant and unpleasant or good and bad moods is one that will frequently recur in the research reviewed later in this book. Consideration of more specific mood qualities currently awaits further conceptual and methodological development.

SUMMARY

Psychometric investigation has uncovered two consistent dimensions of affective meaning relating to pleasantness and activation. In everyday experience, mood states tend to involve particular combinations of these factors with activation often going together with pleasantness to give high "positive affect" or excitement, and deactivation combining with unpleasantness to give low "positive affect" or depression. Similarly, unpleasantness and activation often co-occur to produce

3

PREDICTORS OF MOOD

OVERVIEW

Having discussed the nature of mood in general (Chapter 1) and of particular kinds of mood (Chapter 2), we now move on to a consideration of the factors that determine and predict mood's level and quality. Three general classes of mood predictor will be specifically considered: events and situations that can be regarded as *external* to the person; factors seen as *internal* to the person, such as personality; and most importantly, predictors that are neither internal nor external to the person but rather are the consequence of *transactions* between the person and the environment. We will suggest that the present book's *process approach* calls into question the idea that mood has simple or straightforward predictors. In this connection, we show how application of Lazarus and colleagues' transactional model (e.g. Lazarus & Folkman, 1984) implies that mood predictors can best be understood in the context of an unfolding relationship between people and their environment.

INTRODUCTION

Why do we feel the way we do at any particular moment or over any particular time period? To some extent the causes of our moods seem obvious. For example, when we are in a good mood, it is frequently because we are doing something we enjoy, or because something good has happened to us. Similarly, if we are in a bad mood, we may often find it easy to fix upon something that is going wrong in our lives to explain our feelings. However, the cause of our moods can also sometimes be difficult to fathom. For instance, we may feel depressed when we are doing something we usually enjoy or when nothing particularly bad has happened to us. Likewise, we may feel inexplicably happy when things are not actually going particularly well. On the one hand, then, our moods may be predictable responses to favourable or unfavourable circumstances; on the other, their origins are sometimes more of a mystery.

In most cases our moods are unlikely to have a single cause and will depend on the combination of a large number of different and often interacting factors. This fact provides a second reason why our ability to clearly identify the causes of our mood may be quite limited in many circumstances. Indeed, as suggested in Chapter 1, moods, in contrast with emotions, are not focused on any specific event or situation. The diversity and range of potential influences on mood means that each particular predictor is unlikely in itself to explain much of the observed variance in mood. Despite this limitation, many of the studies described in this chapter tend to focus on just one or perhaps a few of these possible mood predictors.

A further complication in predicting mood is that people often attempt to regulate their own mood. For example, we may actively seek out situations that we expect to improve our mood, such as when we go to see a film to take our minds off our problems. Hence, in addition to the factors discussed in this chapter, an important influence on mood is the process of *mood regulation*, which is the specific topic of Chapter 6.

Although predicting mood and mood change is clearly complex, a number of relevant variables can be identified. Three categories of such predictors will be discussed here: "external" or situational factors, "internal" or personal factors, and interactional and transactional factors which involve some combination of internal and external influences. It would be impossible to provide an exhaustive characterization of the entire range of potential mood predictors in the present chapter, so instead we will present illustrative examples from each of the three listed categories to give a general flavour of the factors that influence mood.

EXTERNAL PREDICTORS

One of the most obvious categories of mood predictor includes events that seem to be external to the person and to take place in the outside world. For example, things that "happen to us", such as a late train or a complimentary remark, or situational characteristics such as the pressure of overwhelming demands at work, are often readily identified as important causes of mood change. In this section, we will consider a number of such external or situational predictors, although as we shall see later when discussing transactions between individuals and their environment, it may not always be meaningful to locate such events as wholly outside the person. The specific external predictors of mood considered in the following sections come under the general headings of hassles and uplifts, "stress", and activities and situations.

Hassles and uplifts

Work on *hassles* developed from research on major life events (such as divorce, bereavement or job loss) in which scores on life events inventories were used to attempt to predict illness (e.g. Dohrenwend & Dohrenwend, 1981; Holmes & Rahe, 1967). Hassles have also been termed *daily life events* (e.g. Clark & Watson, 1988; Larsen, Diener & Emmons, 1986; Neale, Hooley, Jandorf, & Stone, 1987) or *daily stressors* (e.g. Bolger & Schilling, 1991; Caspi, Bolger & Eckenrode, 1987). In order to clarify the meaning of the concept to study participants, researchers have described hassles as "minor irritants that can range from minor annoyances to fairly major pressures, problems, or difficulties" (Kanner, Coyne, Schaefer, & Lazarus, 1981, p. 24) and as "things that annoy or bother you; they can make you upset or angry" (DeLongis, Folkman, & Lazarus, 1988, p. 495). In more general terms, Lazarus (1984) defined hassles as "experiences and conditions of daily living that have been appraised as salient and harmful or threatening to the endorser's well-being" (p. 376). On the basis of these descriptions, it is clear that the theoretical basis for links between hassles and mood has more than a ring of common sense: things we do not like will make us feel bad.

Much of the research on daily hassles and moods asks participants to provide ratings of hassles, mood and other variables on a daily or more frequent basis for around fourteen days or more. Mood is usually assessed by self-report using affect adjective measures of the type described in Chapter 2, and hassles are typically measured using checklists where participants are asked to indicate the extent to which each of a number of hassles has affected them during that day. In accordance with the rather broad definitions of hassles provided above, hassles checklists often include a great many different kinds of items relating to such experiences as arguments, work demands, financial worries, physical symptoms, domestic responsibilities and the health of others (see also, e.g. Bolger, DeLongis, Kessler & Schilling, 1989; DeLongis, Folkman, & Lazarus, 1988; Kanner et al., 1981). Some researchers use an open-response format (e.g. Caspi et al., 1987; Clark & Watson, 1988) where participants describe negative experiences or events which are subsequently coded by the researchers.

The general and rather unsurprising findings from such studies are that daily hassles have negative effects on, or are at least associated with, general mood. Where researchers have measured different dimensions of mood, there is also some indication that they are associated more with increases in negative affect than decreases in positive affect (e.g. Clark & Watson, 1988; Kanner et al., 1981; Neale et al., 1987; Watson, 1988b).

There is also some evidence that while hassles have a negative impact on mood the same day, they have a positive impact on mood the following day. For example, according to findings from a study by DeLongis and colleagues (1988) a high level of hassles today is associated with worse mood today but better mood tomorrow. There are a number of possible explanations for this "rebound effect". One is that some kind of regulative mechanism operates to make sure that mood stays within certain preset boundaries of pleasantness. When mood moves outside these boundaries, homeostatic processes come into operation in an attempt to pull mood back to within its specified range of equilibrium, but this attempt may sometimes result in overcompensation and hence rebound (see Chapter 5 for further discussion of dynamic equilibrium models). Another possible explanation is that subsequent experiences merely *seem* less unpleasant in comparison to the really bad things that have recently happened, producing a kind of contrast effect, ". . . like that described in the old adage about how good it feels when one stops hitting one's head against a wall" (DeLongis et al., 1988, p. 492).

45

More recently, investigators have suggested that it is the broader *relevance* of hassles rather than simply their intensity or number that is likely to lead to changes in mood. For example, Lavallee and Campbell (1995) found that daily negative events that were related to participants' personal goals produced more unpleasant mood than those that were not related to these goals. More generally, it seems likely that a wide range of personal and contextual factors will influence the relationship between hassles and mood.

A central problem in interpreting the effect of hassles on mood was identified by Dohrenwend and colleagues (Dohrenwend, Dohrenwend, Dodson, & Shrout, 1984; Dohrenwend & Shrout, 1985). They argued that measures of hassles, in particular the hassles scale developed by Kanner and his co-workers (Kanner et al., 1981), are often confounded with psychological distress or unpleasant mood. In other words, some of the items in the scale are *measures* or *indicators* of unpleasant mood rather than independent *predictors* of unpleasant mood. For example, items on this scale include "trouble relaxing" and "job dissatisfactions" which seem to refer to people's affective reactions to events rather than to the events themselves. Such items are highly likely to correlate with mood measures simply by virtue of the fact that they are measuring the same or a similar phenom- enon. Thus, although hassles are usually conceptualized as causes of unpleasant mood, the way they are measured sometimes makes it seem more likely that unpleasant mood is the cause of hassles (or at least of the reporting of hassles).

This analysis implies that checklists or questionnaires designed as measures of hassles (and uplifts) should contain only items that are as independent from mood as possible, so that respondents do not endorse these items as a simple and direct consequence of being in a particular mood. However, in defence of their approach, Lazarus and his colleagues (Lazarus, DeLongis, Folkman, & Gruen, 1985) argued that hassles are not in fact theoretically or empirically separate from mood. Their approach emphasizes that mood comes about as a consequence of *transactions* over time between people and their environment and not as a result of simple cause–effect processes. This transactional perspective will be discussed in more detail later in this chapter but it is worth noting here that any attempt to use participants' subjective ratings to examine predictors of mood is likely to encounter similar problems: it is always difficult to know whether the participant's mood was caused by the predictor or if their rating of the predictor was caused by their mood.

Relatively little research has examined the effects of *uplifts* and almost all of it has been conducted by Lazarus and his colleagues (e.g. DeLongis, Coyne, Dakof, Folkman, & Lazarus, 1982; Kanner et al., 1981; Lazarus, 1984). Mirroring the definition of hassles provided above, Lazarus (1984, p. 376) described uplifts as "experiences and conditions of daily living that have been appraised as salient and positive or favourable to the endorser's well-being". The theoretical basis of links between uplifts and mood is somewhat more interesting in that they are considered by Lazarus and his colleagues to act in such a way as to *buffer* the effects of hassles on mood. In other words, uplifts serve to soften or alleviate the negative affective impact of hassles in addition to any more direct positive effects they may have. However, subsequent studies failed to find any strong buffering role for uplifts.

Studies that have examined the *direct* effects of positive daily events or uplifts on mood have shown that their occurrence is associated with mood and, more specifically, with increased positive rather than reduced negative affect (e.g. Kanner et al., 1981; Zautra, Guarnaccia, Reich, & Dohrenwend, 1988). In general, however, researchers have paid far less attention to the effects of pleasant than unpleasant events on mood. Like hassles, the effects of uplifts on mood is likely to depend on many other variables. For example, a study by Langston (1994) indicates that taking advantage of or *capitalizing* on positive events (for example, through making expressive responses) enhances their effects on positive mood. This finding parallels the common observation that people's *coping* responses may be important in determining the affective impact of negative events (e.g. Folkman & Lazarus, 1985). The question of how people "deal with" and schedule positive events as well as negative events is likely to become of increasing interest to mood researchers (e.g. Hsee & Abelson, 1991; Hsee, Salovey, & Abelson, 1994).

The past decade has witnessed increasing interest in the role of hassles and uplifts in predicting daily mood. While such events clearly represent an important influence on affect, the theoretical and methodological problems outlined in the present section suggest that the precise nature of this influence is still far from clear.

A note about stress

Within contemporary psychology, one of the most common ways of thinking about negative external events that predict mood is in terms of *stress* and *stressors*. Indeed, as discussed above, hassles have also been referred to as "daily stressors". Despite the apparent popularity of the stress concept, there are a number of reasons why we do not consider it to be useful in the present context. First, models of stress tend to focus only on negative and extreme outcomes, such as illness or clinical depression, whereas our main concern here is with predictors of less extreme outcomes (affect) which may be either positive or negative. Second, there are numerous definitional and conceptual problems (e.g. Appley & Trumbull, 1986; Pollock, 1988) which limit the explanatory power of stress models. For instance, many models go little further than stating that stressors (the stimulus) cause strain (the response) and that this relationship may be moderated or mediated by other variables (e.g. social support, coping). They do not, like theories of mood or theories of well-being for example, attempt to *explain* why and how affective states are produced. Rather, these models simply suggest that stressors are a cause of strain and strain is caused by stressors in an almost circular fashion. Lastly, the transactional approach (which is described in more detail below) rejects the stimulus–response or cause–effect implications of stress models and the notion that stress is a specific and delimited phenomenon or variable. In this connection,

Lazarus and Folkman (1984, pp. 11–12) write that stress "is not a variable but a rubric consisting of many variables and processes" and go on to define stress as "a particular relationship between the person and the environment that is appraised by the person as taxing his or her resources and endangering his or her well-being" (p. 19). For these reasons, we believe that traditional stress models may be unhelpful and even misleading in the attempt to increase our understanding of the causes of mood.

Activities and situations

Activities may be differentiated from hassles and uplifts according to two basic criteria. First, while the conceptualization of hassles and uplifts already implies some evaluative content (i.e. hassles are bad and uplifts are good), activities do not have any *necessary* affective impact (although obviously they too can also be pleasant or unpleasant). Second, hassles and uplifts typically refer to relatively brief and temporally localized events whereas activities often take place over more extended time-periods. Many descriptions of activities also make reference to the situation in which the activity is conducted: for example, both "being with other people" or "being at work" may be activities as well as "external" situations. However, as we shall discuss below, it may often prove difficult to draw this distinction in a hard and fast way.

Given people's general level of interest in feeling good and having a good time in our culture, there is remarkably little evidence about what kinds of activities and situations actually do make us feel pleasant or unpleasant. One of the reasons for this may be that the answer already seems obvious to us: we like doing things and being in situations that we like, and we don't like doing things or being in situations that we don't like. On the other hand, it also seems obvious that activities or situations that we believe we will, or ought to, enjoy do not always produce the anticipated pleasant mood, and that activities or situations that we expect to find unpleasant are not necessarily as bad as we anticipate. In other words, there may be few simple links between activities, situations, and mood.

One of the few attempts to find out the ways in which mood and emotion differ across activities and situations was undertaken by Brandstätter (1991). In this study, participants were asked about their momentary mood and activity four times a day for 30 days. This procedure is also known as *experience-sampling methodology* and differs from the daily diary studies described above because participants are asked to answer questions about how they feel *at that moment* instead of giving retrospective reports of how they have felt during the day or during the previous few hours (see Chapter 5 for further details of these procedures).

The results of this study present a complex picture of the links between activities/ situations and moods, partly because Brandstätter's affective self-report measure used four combinations of individual emotion words (e.g. joy/activation, relaxation/ satiation) rather than the usual two dimensions of positive and negative affect.

48

However, many of the findings still have obvious relevance to the present concerns. Some illustrative examples will be given here. First, with respect to the social situation, more joy/activation was reported when participants were with relatives or friends than when they were with other categories of people or were on their own, and more anger/fear was reported when they were with acquaintances or strangers. In relation to work and leisure, as might be expected, more fatigue, anger, and fear were reported during work activities whether or not these activities were undertaken at home or away from home. People reported more relaxation at home than outside the home irrespective of whether they were engaging in work or leisure activities, and most joy was experienced during leisure activities outside the home.

In a related daily diary study conducted by Watson (1988b), participants made estimates of how long they had spent with friends, reported whether or not they had taken exercise, and rated their general mood in terms of positive and negative affect at the end of each day. The results indicated that social activity and exercise were related only to increases in PA and not to decreases in NA.

One of our own studies (Briner, Reynolds, Totterdell, & Parkinson, 1994) employed two-hourly and daily ratings of mood together with activity logs which were completed at the end of the day. This procedure allowed us to examine both the effects of activities on momentary mood, and the effects of time spent in different activities on daily mood. Preliminary results indicated that levels of pleasant affect were lower during paid and unpaid work than in passive and active leisure activities, but there were no differences in unpleasant affect across the four activity categories. Daily mood (rated at the end of the day) was not found to be associated with daily activities with the exception that time spent in unpaid work (such as domestic work) predicted higher levels of unpleasant affect.

Though clearly an important area of research, there are a number of reasons why exploring causal relationships between activities and mood is far from simple. First, many activities and situations are habitually time-dependent. We get up, we may go to work, we usually eat at particular times of the day. It is very hard therefore to separate out empirically the effect of an activity or situation on mood from the effect of the time of day at which it occurred, and from the effect of any preceding situation or activity. For example, if we almost always watch television in the evenings after work it is difficult to establish if any associations between television-watching and mood are a consequence of the time of day and/or a delayed effect of the day's work activities (see Chapter 5 for a discussion of the effects of temporal variables on mood and mood variation).

A second interpretational problem arises from the recognition that we may choose to engage in an activity or place ourselves in a situation as a *consequence* of our being in a particular mood. Again, this potential mood-dependency of activities and situations makes it more difficult to establish causal relationships between mood and activity without using very fine-grained sampling of activities and mood. In general, activities and situations are not always imposed on people from outside but rather may be actively chosen and selected by them. This observation also reinforces our earlier point that many activities or situations are not really "external" to the person in any strict sense.

Research in this area is hampered further by the fact that it turns out to be surprisingly difficult to categorize activities and situations in a psychologically meaningful way. For example, many apparently straightforward categories of activities or situations, such as "being with one's partner", "working", or "at home", may tell us where the person is or who the person is with but are nevertheless relatively uninformative about the specific quality or nature of what is happening. What is lacking in these descriptions is any indication of the *psychological* quality of activities and situations. In this regard, Csikszentmihalyi and colleagues (e.g. Csikszentmihalyi, 1992; Csikszentmihalyi & Csikszentmihalyi, 1988; Csikszentmihalyi & LeFevre, 1989) have at least examined one relevant aspect of activities and situations which they describe as *flow*. Flow occurs when the skill levels of the person are closely matched to the demands of the activity, and when skills and demands are both at a relatively high level. Because this particular quality of experience is clearly not entirely external to the person, we will return to the topic of flow in our later section concerning transactional approaches to mood. For the moment, however, we should make the general observation that it is necessary to develop a meaningful and theoretically grounded way of classifying activities and situations before the relationships between mood and activities can be adequately assessed.

One aspect of the situation that we have not discussed so far but which is popularly believed to affect mood is the *weather*. Seasonal effects on mood, such as *seasonal affective disorder*, will be discussed in Chapter 5 along with other temporal influences, but what about day-to-day changes in weather? Do these predict mood? Indirect evidence generally supports such a connection. For example, some kinds of social behaviours such as helping and tipping which are thought to be more common in pleasant moods have also been found to increase in frequency during good weather (e.g. Cunningham, 1979). In addition, there is evidence that specific aspects of weather phenomena (e.g. temperature, negative ions, air pressure) may have some impact on affect (Thayer, 1989).

Some of the effects of the weather on mood may depend on people's beliefs and expectations about weather–affect relationships. For example, we may believe that hot sunny weather generally puts us in a good mood, or that very hot humid weather will irritate us. Likewise, a warm sunny day may have associations with holidays and relaxation, while a wet Sunday afternoon may remind us of being unable to go out to play as a child (cf. Schnurr, 1989). It seems possible that these ideas about the differential affective impact of different kinds of weather may influence our actual reactions with the result that we often end up feeling the way we had anticipated feeling, or at least report our affect in accordance with what the current weather implies for us.

In a study where people were asked to report daily hassles using an open-response format rather than a precoded checklist, Clark and Watson (1988) found that some participants spontaneously reported bad weather as a hassle. On days when rain was reported as a hassle, negative affect was actually lower and positive affect was unchanged. The investigators then retrospectively collected weather reports for the diary-keeping period in order to examine whether objective weather conditions would show relationships with mood. Despite extensive analyses they found no significant relationships between actual weather reports and daily mood. These results suggest that it may be the context in which particular weather conditions occur (e.g. while on holiday), rather than the weather conditions themselves, which influence mood.

Clearly, many other kinds of activities and situations in addition to those discussed in this section are likely to influence mood. Equally clearly, we need to know far more about the specific psychological characteristics of those activities and situations before their effects on mood can be accurately examined and adequately explained.

EXPERIMENTAL MANIPULATIONS OF MOOD

Indirect evidence relating to external predictors of mood is also available from less naturalistic studies than those considered in the previous section. In this section, we will examine the various techniques that have been used specifically to manipulate mood in laboratory experiments designed to assess the effects of mood (see Chapter 4 for a review of mood effects research more generally). To the extent that these techniques produce reliable effects on mood, they provide relatively incontrovertible evidence that the factors manipulated are genuinely *causes*, rather than merely correlates or effects, of mood. However, the fact that an independent variable influences mood in a social psychology experiment does not necessarily mean that comparable effects would be observed in other less contrived settings. In short, the relevance of the findings of this research is generally limited by its low level of *ecological validity*. Nevertheless, the experimental approach does provide a unique opportunity to control both the setting and the participant's behaviour in a systematic way and to assess the impact of any implemented changes on mood.

In this section, we will discuss three general types of experimental mood manipulation in turn. These are: *instructional techniques*, *stimulus-based manipulations*, and *event-staging*.

Instructional techniques

Instructional mood-manipulation techniques, as the name suggests, simply involve asking participants to effect a specified change in their mood. Although it may appear somewhat improbable that simply asking someone to feel differently will produce the desired effect, such techniques have in fact been found to be generally effective. A good example of a direct instructional technique is the *Velten Procedure* (Velten, 1968) which asks participants to read out a series of 60 self-descriptive statements and try to feel the mood suggested by these statements. The initial statements are fairly neutral but then become increasingly emotionally laden as the series progresses. Examples of the statements used to induce unpleasant affect include: "Every now and then I feel so tired and gloomy that I'd rather just sit than do anything"; "Things have been going really badly for me lately"; "I'm feeling very lonely, isolated, and depressed"; and "I've too many bad things in my life". Statements used to induce pleasant mood include: "If your attitude is good, then things are good, and my attitude is good"; and "This is great – I really do feel good – I *am* elated about things".

Rather than read aloud statements, participants can be asked to remember or imagine events or situations which are emotionally relevant. For example, in a study of mood and self-focused attention, Salovey (1992) used taped instructions lasting about five minutes to induce mood. The tape first asked participants to relax and to pay attention to what they were about to hear. Participants were then encouraged to imagine a real or hypothetical situation which, depending on the condition, would leave them feeling either sad, happy, or neither sad nor happy (neutral). The tape continued as follows:

> I would like for you to begin imagining a situation that would make you feel [happy, sad or neutral]. Imagine the situation as vividly as you can. Picture the events happening to you. See all the details of the situation. Picture in your "mind's eye" the surroundings as clearly as possible. See the people or objects; hear the sounds; experience the event happening to you. Think the thoughts you would actually think in the situation. Feel the same [happy, sad or neutral] feelings you would feel. Let yourself react as if you were actually there. (p. 702)

Another example of an instructional mood-manipulation technique that asks participants to recall or imagine events was described by Sedikides (1994) who asked participants first to imagine (for two minutes), then to write about (for three minutes), a sad, happy, or neutral event. In this case, however, the events (a friend being burned and dying in a fire, a friend winning a free cruise and a lottery, and a friend watching news on the television and riding on a bus) were specified by the experimenter. Other similar techniques that involve the structured recall or imagining of events include the *autobiographical recollections method* and *self-generated imagery* (see Salovey, 1992).

Another type of instructional mood-manipulation technique also asks participants to recall an emotionally laden experience, but does this after the participant has been hypnotized. The advantage of such a procedure is that it apparently allows for the intensity of the mood to be adjusted, at least for the minority of participants who are highly suggestible. Bower, Monteiro, and Gilligan (1978), for example, hypnotized participants and then asked them to recall an event or situation that would make them feel sad, happy, or neutral. Participants were then asked to adjust the strength of their mood so that it became "intense but not unbearable" and to maintain that mood for the remainder of the study.

The demonstrated effectiveness of instructional techniques not only confirms that the social situation can have a powerful impact on mood (external predictor), but also that people can exert some level of personal control over the affective states that they experience (mood regulation, see Chapter 6). The practical disadvantage of using instructional techniques to manipulate mood in experiments, however, is that participants are bound to be explicitly aware of the mood that they have managed to conjure up, and this awareness may itself make a difference to mood effects (see Chapter 4).

Stimulus-based manipulations

A second type of mood-manipulation technique involves exposing participants to various affect-inducing stimuli such as smells (e.g. Ehrlichman & Halpern, 1988; Kraut, 1982), music (e.g. Clark & Teasdale, 1985; Pignatiello, Camp, & Rasar, 1986; Wood, Saltzberg, & Goldsamt, 1990), stories (e.g. Kuykendall & Keating, 1990; Nisbett & Wilson, 1977, Smith & Petty, 1995), slides (e.g. Wagner, MacDonald, & Manstead, 1986), or videotaped material (e.g. Forgas, Bower, & Moylan, 1990). While such techniques are generally effective, and have methodological advantages over instructional techniques in that participants are likely to be less aware of the purposes of the manipulation, the strength of induced affective response can be unpredictable and variable. Some specific examples of some of these stimulus-based techniques will now be described to give a clearer picture of their use in experimental settings.

In a study conducted by Wegener and Petty (1994), twelve-minute-long video-taped clips of television programmes were presented in order to induce a happy, sad, or neutral mood, though participants were told that the purpose of the study was to examine "media preferences". The happy clip included a news item featuring good things about a city in the summertime and scenes from a programme showing people attempting to do silly or stupid tasks. The neutral videotaped material was taken from a natural history programme about the social organization of lions. The sad clip contained material about the diagnosis and treatment of a child with cancer.

Mayer and his colleagues (Mayer, Gayle, Meehan, & Haarman, 1990) used a combination of self-generated imagery (see above) and music in order to induce mood. While imagining the different moods induced by vignettes (e.g. "You pass a demonstration commemorating the victims of Hiroshima. You think of atomic bombs destroying your hometown"), mood-congruent music was played in order to enhance their effects.

Event-staging techniques

A third kind of mood manipulation involves the staging of personally involving events for participants. As discussed above, naturally occurring positive and negative events have been shown to influence daily mood. In a similar way, it seems that staging certain kinds of events can also produce changes in mood. While many specific kinds of event-staging are possible, two commonly used categories involve *rewards* and *false performance feedback*. Each of these will be discussed in turn.

Even small rewards can produce measurable changes in mood. In a well-known study, Isen and Levin (1972) left a dime in the coin-return tray of a public telephone and found that simply finding the coin had an effect on mood. Other kinds of rewards that have been found to produce effects include giving refreshments to students in a library (Isen & Levin, 1972) and presenting free gifts or samples (Isen, Clark & Schwarz, 1976).

While rewards are used to enhance the pleasantness of mood, false performance feedback can be used to increase either pleasant or unpleasant affect. It is also possible to manipulate the personal relevance of the feedback to alter the specific quality of the induced mood-state. For example, feedback about performance on a perceptual-motor task is likely to be perceived as less important to one's self-image than feedback about one's social competence. Forgas and Bower (1987) asked participants to complete a questionnaire measure of social adjustment that was then scored by the experimenter in their presence. Participants were either told that they had obtained a high score and were obviously skilled in social situations, or that they had obtained a low score and clearly had problems in dealing with people. The positive and negative feedback had the predicted effects on mood.

In a study of affect regulation and self-esteem, Baumgardner and her colleagues (Baumgardner, Kaufman, & Levy, 1989) used a number of different kinds of false performance feedback in a series of studies. In one, participants were asked to complete a series of questions administered via computer. After completion, responses were "scored" by the computer, and feedback appeared on the screen. In the positive feedback condition, participants (who were students) read that "they were of above average to superior intelligence, were quite popular and were perceived by others as very sincere, sensitive and insightful" while in the negative feedback condition, they read that "they were most likely of average intelligence with little or no college education and that they were not particularly popular" (p. 909). In another study, participants were given bogus feedback from a partner with whom they had interacted for fifteen minutes. The feedback consisted of personality ratings on a scale containing adjectives such as "friendly", "sincere", and "smart" (p. 914). In the negative feedback condition the partner's ratings were at the lower end of the scale, while in the positive feedback condition ratings were consistently favourable. For obvious ethical reasons, it is important to debrief all participants thoroughly after the use of false performance feedback, paying particular attention, perhaps, to those who have been given negative feedback.

What do mood manipulation techniques tell us about predictors of mood?

Despite the obvious limitations of the research reviewed in the present section, the findings obtained using mood-manipulation techniques may help us to think about everyday mood more generally in at least three ways. First, one possible criticism of these manipulations is that they mostly induce emotion rather than mood, because the induced affective state is usually focused on a particular object of attention (see Chapter 1). Nevertheless, it still appears that such manipulations may in some circumstances also bring longer-term consequences for mood. Extrapolating to more naturalistic settings, one can imagine that a series of naturally occurring emotional incidents might similarly exert a cumulative effect on daily mood. For example, one could wake in the morning from a dream that recalled some deeply upsetting event, then read in the newspaper about a horrific accident, and then receive a bank statement containing some rather depressing performance feedback about your personal financial management skills. After all this, it is unlikely that your mood would be a good one. In short, moods may arise from the accumulation of specific emotional reactions (cf. Ruckmick, 1936). Experimental mood manipulations may therefore give us some clues about the ways in which emotion-eliciting events and situations, such as daily hassles and uplifts, actually affect mood in everyday life.

A second relevant feature of the work on mood manipulations concerns the large number and variety of mood-manipulation techniques and the ways in which these can be used and contextualized. It sometimes seems as though almost *anything* can be used to manipulate mood that falls within the limits of researchers' ingenuity and ethical standards. As emphasized throughout this chapter, there are a vast number of mood predictors, and some of the work on mood manipulation may help to explain this fact. The mood manipulation techniques described here seem to work through a diverse range of psychological systems such as memory, imagery, self-esteem, performance, punishment and reward, and so on. This provides us with further evidence that mood does not operate through a single or even a few different processes, but can be brought about in many ways.

A third and final lesson that can be drawn from the work on experimental mood manipulations is that people are *active* in bringing about mood. Nearly all the techniques discussed here do not simply expose people to a stimulus which then produces a mood response. Rather, participants have to take part actively in the procedures for them to be effective. For example, the instructional procedures discussed here require participants to work through the instructions and attempt to remember or imagine the details of emotionally significant events. Similarly, responding to emotional material such as music and film is not simply a passive process. Although there may be less conscious effort involved for participants in stimulus-based procedures than in instructional mood-manipulation techniques, they must still be prepared to become involved with the material in the former case. Event-staging techniques clearly require the least effort and participation of all, but even here the staged event needs to be treated as important by participants before they can affect their response. The issue of the extent to which people are active in the production of their moods is one to which we will return when we consider the role of transactional processes later in this chapter.

INTERNAL PREDICTORS

In the previous sections, we discussed mood predictors that may be seen as "external" to the person; now we turn to more "internal" predictors of mood.

What do we mean by an internal predictor? Again, we encounter many of the same problems as we did when attempting to define an external predictor. However, to the extent that external predictors are things that seem to be "out there" in the environment, it makes sense to see internal predictors as "in here" and as residing inside the person. One of the most obvious things that is "in here" is our physiology: put crudely, our internal organs and the fluids that surround and move between them. The relationship between physiological parameters and mood will therefore be discussed first (further discussion of physiological aspects of mood *rhythms* will appear in Chapter 5). Moving away from physiology and back to psychology, another important category of "internal" predictors concerns the relatively stable and endogenous factors that somehow define us as a person, or describe our typical ways of thinking, feeling, and behaving: in other words, our personalities. The role of personality variables as mood predictors will be discussed in the second part of this section.

Physiological precursors

People hold a range of common-sense beliefs about the links between physiological states and mood. The most general of these beliefs is that there *are* links between the two. More specifically, we may believe that when we are anxious we are also "wound up", that our muscles are tense, that our heart beats faster, and our blood pressure increases. We may also believe that when we become tired, a snack or drink containing sugar will "perk us up". Unfortunately, anyone hoping to find evidence for direct relationships between mood and physiological activity of this simple kind will be disappointed.

The first problem that arises when thinking about the role of physiology in mood concerns the extent to which physiological changes can be considered to operate as predictors as opposed to consequences of mood. Indeed, a similar debate has become a perennial chestnut within the emotion literature (e.g. see Parkinson, 1995) where the precise nature of the causal links between physiological changes, cognitive appraisal, and emotion still remains unclear. With respect to emotion, some theorists have concluded that perception of the symptoms of activation in the autonomic nervous system (ANS) may lead to people interpreting their reaction as emotional and acting accordingly (e.g. Schachter & Singer, 1962). Similarly, Teasdale and Barnard (1993) suggested that registration of internal bodily changes by central processing systems may be one of the factors that contributes to the activation of mood-generating schemata (see Chapter 4). In other words, when we feel our bodies reacting this may make it more likely that we appraise the current situation in affective terms. Autonomic activation may also exert more direct effects on affective and cognitive function (e.g. Duffy, 1962).

In this chapter, we will focus on physiological changes as causes of mood change, even though the available evidence does not always allow us to make any definite distinction between causes, correlates, or effects. For example, much of

56

the non-experimental research in this area relies on cross-sectional, correlational designs which are incapable of untangling the direction of causation. In general, it is worth remembering that, like other predictors of mood, physiological variables are unlikely to operate as simple causes (or effects) in one-way cause–effect sequences, or as mere stimuli (or responses) in distinct stimulus–response connections. Hence, while we may be able to examine how physiological changes cause mood changes (and vice versa) for some purposes and in some circumstances, in practice these two "systems" probably operate in constant interaction.

A second problem is that there are very many physiological parameters and physiological systems that also interact with *each other*. This means that isolating and identifying those specific physiological variables that are likely to influence specific mood states may prove very difficult: the influence of one particular parameter or system on mood is likely to depend on the state of other parameters and systems, as well as the many other psychological factors that can influence mood.

A third issue concerns interpretation of experimental results relating to physiological predictors of mood. Because physiology is often only manipulated indirectly by altering variables such as exercise or eating, any demonstrated links between physiological parameters and mood depend on the *inferred* effects of these manipulations. There are two general problems with such a research strategy. First, the variables manipulated may have psychological as well as physiological effects which also have the potential of influencing mood. Second, the effects of the manipulated variables on physiological state itself may often be inconsistent from person to person or situation to situation (cf. Lacey & Lacey, 1958). For both these reasons, it is hard to establish definitively that physiological factors function as predictors of mood in experiments that do not manipulate physiology directly.

Having drawn attention to these general problems faced by research into physiological mood predictors, it is now time to look at the evidence itself, such as it is. The few studies that have been conducted have tended to show somewhat weak and inconsistent associations between physiological responses and mood (e.g. Matthews, 1992; Schnurr, 1989; Thayer, 1989). Of course, this does not mean that no causal relationships exist between physiological states and mood but rather that more data of a higher quality need to be collected using more sophisticated methodology before we can begin to spell out the precise nature of such relationships.

The most common way of examining the effects of physiological variables on mood is to ask participants to do something that would be expected to influence their physiological state and then assess what happens to mood. Thayer (1989) has extensively investigated the effects of two kinds of manipulations: exercise and food. He found that a brisk ten-minute walk reliably increases levels of *energetic arousal* (which is similar to positive affect), although exactly how and why exercise has such effects remains unclear (see also Thayer, Peters, Takahashi, & Birkhead-Flight, 1993).

Foods such as carbohydrates and sugar have been found to have different patterns of effects over time on different dimensions of mood. For example, studies by Thayer (1989) have shown that sugar ingestion increases energetic arousal after 20 minutes followed by reductions in energetic arousal after one and two hours. *Tense arousal* (similar to negative affect) on the other hand showed no change until one hour after sugar ingestion when it increased, but then decreased again after two hours. Other studies indicate differing acute effects of carbohydrate and protein on arousal or vigour (rather than positive or negative affect *per se*) with the former reducing arousal more than the latter (e.g. Young, 1989).

Similarly there are few simple relationships between drugs and mood. First, drugs appear to affect more than one dimension of mood simultaneously (e.g. Matthews, 1992) which means that a neat correspondence between a particular drug and a particular mood will not be found. Second, the dosage and the time elapsed since ingestion are important influences on the effects of drugs on mood. For example, many people know that alcohol is supposed to "depress" the nervous system, yet in small doses and in the shorter term it may produce pleasant mood and euphoria (Thayer, 1989).

Although experimentally manipulating a physiological parameter and then measuring the effects of that change on mood might seem an ideal way of investigating physiological mood predictors, Thayer (1989) suggests that ". . . in the study of subtle, long-term mood states, the value of these procedures may be limited" (p. 140). This is partly because the experimental conditions impose demands on participants that may themselves strongly affect mood, and partly because of a more general lack of ecological validity. For example, the way in which people respond to controlled ingestion of substances in a laboratory setting may not correspond to the way they would normally react after deliberately choosing to consume food or take drugs in their everyday lives outside the laboratory. Indeed, the fact that people sometimes use food and drugs specifically as means of altering or maintaining mood (see Chapter 6) suggests that their effects may normally depend on the specific psychological context of their use.

Given the general difficulty of controlling physiological parameters, Gold and colleagues (Gold, MacLeod, Frier, & Deary, 1995) considered that "mood research may benefit from the addition of a controllable biological manipulation in which the physiological mechanisms are relatively well understood" (p. 499). In their study, participants' blood-glucose levels were carefully controlled and monitored over a four-hour period during which mood was also measured on seven occasions. The procedure specifically involved the induction of acute hypoglycaemia by a systematic reduction of glucose level, followed by a restoration of glucose to its previous level. Significant increases in tense arousal and decreases in energetic arousal were observed during periods of lowered blood-glucose levels. The investigators concluded that induced hypoglycaemia "represents one of the few available techniques for inducing the theoretically important mood state of tense tiredness" (p. 504) and that it could also be used to study other aspects of mood. Gold and colleagues' study represents one of the few definitive demonstrations that physiological parameters exert some relatively direct influence on mood.

What about more naturalistic studies of the physiological precursors of mood? Unfortunately there have been even fewer of these, not least because of the obvious technical problems in obtaining regular physiological measures from people who are moving about and engaging in daily activities. A further problem with such studies is that both the key independent variables (i.e. physiological parameters) and key dependent variables (i.e. mood) are likely to be influenced by the person's activities.

One study of this kind was conducted by Johnston and Anastiades (1990) who examined the underresearched relationship between heart rate and mood. The procedure involved fitting participants with a device that enabled continuous monitoring of heart rate without interfering with their activities. Participants were also asked to complete mood scales every 30 minutes and describe their current activity. The results indicated that heart rate was related to mood in only two out of the 32 participants. This general lack of association strongly suggests that heart rate is neither a reliable precursor nor a consistent effect of mood states.

To summarize, surprisingly little is known about physiological precursors of mood. The limited experimental results may have little validity outside the laboratory, and the field studies are too few and far between to allow many definitive conclusions. In very general terms, it seems likely that any relationships between physiological states will be subtle and complex. What this means is that such relationships are methodologically difficult to study, and that significant effects are both difficult to find and difficult to interpret.

Personality

Perhaps the most studied of all "internal" predictors of mood is personality. In this section, we will consider personality variables that might specifically predict mood's level and quality (see Chapter 5 for discussion of relations between personality and mood variation over time, and Chapter 6 for discussion of personality variables relevant to mood monitoring and mood regulation). Personality and affect are often assumed to be closely associated at a theoretical level (e.g. Arnold, 1960; Eysenck, 1967), so it is perhaps not surprising that personality variables are widely considered to be one of the strongest predictors of mood. The notion of "happy and unhappy people" (Costa & McCrae, 1980), for example, is firmly embedded within psychological thinking.

One problem we immediately encounter when discussing personality factors as predictors concerns the theoretical status of these variables. If we take personality to refer simply to certain stabilities or consistencies in behaviour and experience, then the concept does not really *explain* behaviour in any causal sense but instead merely *describes* or summarizes what people usually do and how they typically react. According to this interpretation, any correlation obtained between personality measures and indices of mood states only confirms that the tendency to experience

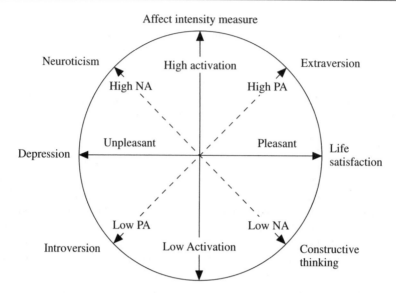

Figure 3.1 Relationships between personality predictors and affective states (adapted from Larsen & Diener, 1992)

the mood has sufficient generality and consistency to show up on the questionnaire assessing the individual difference in question. For example, positive associations between scores on trait negative affect (TNA) and self-reports of momentary negative affect do not necessarily imply that the feelings are *caused* by a corresponding internal predisposition, because an equally viable interpretation is that answers to personality questions (e.g. "I am generally an unhappy person") simply reflect the respondent's summary evaluation of commonly experienced affective states. Of course, if we can additionally specify what factors *underlie* or determine any observed consistencies in affective experience, then this brings us closer to specifying a genuine *explanation* of the phenomenon in question.

The empirical links between personality variables and mood states were examined in a study reported by Larsen and Diener (1992). In this study, participants completed self-report measures of mood along with a wide range of personality questionnaires. The measured personality variables were then plotted with reference to the circumplex representation of affective states described in Chapter 4 according to how closely they correlated with ratings of positive and negative affect. The resultant mapping of relationships between affect and personality is shown in Figure 3.1. In general, personality variables that are highly correlated with affective states appear near to the position of those states on the circumplex. For example, in the top right quadrant, we can see that *extraversion* is placed next to the PA (activated pleasant affect) diagonal axis. This shows that people scoring highly on extraversion also reported high levels of PA and varying levels of NA (i.e. extraversion is uncorrelated with NA). Another personality variable, the *Affect Intensity*

Measure (AIM, Larsen & Diener, 1987) can be seen at the top of the vertical (activation) axis. This indicates that it was found to be positively correlated with both NA and PA. Larsen and Diener's circumplex clearly provides a useful summary of some of the possible relationships between personality and mood.

In the rest of this section, we will consider two general classes of personality variable. The first includes variables that can be regarded as operating at a rather general or basic level, and that are thought to relate to a wide range of other factors in addition to mood. For example, the so-called *Big Five* personality dimensions of *extraversion, neuroticism, agreeableness, conscientiousness*, and *openness* seem to have relevance to many different aspects of psychological function (e.g. Block, 1995; Goldberg, 1990; McCrae & Costa, 1987). The second category of personality variables to be considered contains those that have been conceptualized and operationalized with particular reference to mood. For example, positive and negative affectivity (Watson & Clark, 1984; Watson & Pennebaker, 1989), and affect intensity (Larsen & Diener, 1987) measures have obvious and direct connections with mood, and indeed were originally devised with the specific intention of investigating these connections. Both of these types of personality variable will be considered in turn.

Two of the Big Five personality variables, neuroticism and extraversion, have been found in many studies to be associated with NA and PA respectively. Larsen and Diener (1992) conclude that "the list of independent researchers who have similarly demonstrated a link between extraversion and activated pleasant affect and/or a link between neuroticism and activated unpleasant affect is long enough to conclude that replicability is firmly established" (p. 37, see also Meyer & Shack, 1989). There is little relevant evidence concerning relations of other three of the Big Five variables with affect, and on theoretical grounds we have no particular reason to assume such relations should exist.

Two personality variables regarded as similar to (or identical with) neuroticism and extraversion, *negative affectivity* and *positive affectivity* (Watson & Clark, 1984; Watson & Pennebaker, 1989), have also been found to predict NA and PA respectively. According to Watson and Pennebaker (1989), individuals who obtain high scores on measures of negative affectivity or trait negative affect (TNA) are more likely to: (a) experience higher levels of distress at all times in any situation; (b) be more introspective and dwell on their failures and shortcomings; (c) focus on the negative aspects of others and the world more generally; and, (d) have a less positive self-view and be less satisfied with their lives. Low TNA individuals "tend to be content, secure and self-satisfied" (p. 235) while people who are high in trait positive affect (TPA) are more likely to "lead a full, happy, and interesting life, and maintain a generally high activity level" (p. 235).

Moving away from the merely descriptive interpretations of links between personality and mood outlined above, McCrae and Costa (1991) have made a potentially important distinction between *temperamental* and *instrumental* approaches to explaining such links. The temperamental approach suggests that personality variables are endogenous dispositions that determine how *sensitive* we are to negative emotional situations, thus mediating the extent of our negative reaction to them. For example, parts of the description of TNA above would seem to fit with this approach: high TNA individuals tend to perceive or even actively seek out the negative aspects of the situation, themselves, and others. In this regard, an experimental mood manipulation study conducted by Larsen and Ketelaar (1991) showed that a positive-affect induction technique was more effective when used on participants scoring high on a measure of TPA, while a negative-affect induction technique worked better on participants with high scores on TNA. This seems to offer some support for the temperamental view.

The instrumental view, on the other hand, suggests that personality influences our more objective life circumstances, which in turn result in our exposure to more negative or positive situations and events. For example, high TPA individuals are likely to engage in more activities which may lead to them having a larger social network of friends and acquaintances, who help to keep them in a state of positive affect. This latter view provides a good example of the way in which an internal mood predictor operates by influencing external predictors of mood, such as the situation. There are some indications that in practice both the temperamental and instrumental view may operate together. For example, a study examining reactivity and exposure to daily negative life events found that participants scoring higher on a measure related to TNA (neuroticism) had more experience of, and reacted more strongly to, negative events (Bolger & Schilling, 1991).

More recent work on associations between TNA and NA and TPA and PA have attempted to look at interactions between TNA and TPA in predicting mood. In other words, does the link between, say, TNA and mood also depend on the level of TPA? One study by McFatter (1994) showed that TPA (or in this case extraversion) was linked to both positive and negative affect but only among participants who had high scores on a measure of TNA (neuroticism). This suggests that the nature of the relationships between trait and state affect is likely to be more complex than initially suggested.

While TNA and TPA are thought to be related to either NA or PA, some researchers have suggested that there may also be a disposition to experience greater levels of affect in general. This disposition has been referred to as *affect intensity* (Diener, Larsen, Levine, & Emmons, 1985). Two studies conducted by Larsen and his colleagues (Larsen, Diener, & Emmons, 1986) provided some evidence for such an individual difference. In the first study, participants recorded daily life events and their affective reactions to them. These events were subsequently coded in order to obtain more objective ratings of how positive or negative each event was. In the second study, participants were asked how they would react to a range of life events. Both studies showed that participants with higher scores on the Affect Intensity Measure (AIM) reacted more strongly to both positive and negative events.

As indicated above, a large number of personality variables are likely to be predictors of mood. In this section, we have considered some of those that relate to the level or quality of mood; other important personality variables that are relevant to mood variability and mood regulation will be discussed in Chapters 5 and 6 respectively.

An intriguing question arising from the discussion so far concerns the extent to which internal or external factors can generally be considered to be the stronger predictors of mood. As Thayer (1989) puts it, ". . . what is not clear is the *relative* importance of external events versus natural internal processes and cognitive constructions in determining and maintaining mood" (p. 167). Such a question is difficult to answer on the basis of the currently available evidence. Indeed, the conceptual difficulties involved in making clear distinctions between internal and external predictors of mood mentioned above can only exacerbate any practical problems in making a determination either way. We now turn to transactional approaches, which attempt to address some of these conceptual difficulties.

TRANSACTIONS AS 'PREDICTORS' OF MOOD

Thus far, we have discussed the role of external factors, such as daily hassles, and internal factors, such as personality, in predicting mood. A point made repeatedly in the preceding discussion is that the distinction between external and internal factors is very difficult to draw in a clear and definitive way. Similarly, we have also emphasized that the predictors of mood are unlikely to take the form of a straightforward cause leading to mood as a separate response.

A different way of thinking about mood can be found within *transactional approaches* which attempt to characterize mood as a more dynamic and complex process or set of processes. Such approaches represent a relatively recent theoretical development, and are, by their very nature, difficult to conceptualize and research. In psychology (as well as common-sense reasoning), we are used to considering phenomena within the person, and those in the situation, as separate (e.g. Heider, 1958; Ross & Nisbett, 1991). Correspondingly, many of our studies work from the experimental logic of independent and dependent variables, and are largely based on cause–effect reasoning. Transactional approaches, with their emphasis on process, do not draw on, and in some cases even reject, these distinctions or such reasoning.

In this section, we will first consider transactional theory and then go on to examine some examples of the kind of research that has been conducted within a transactional framework or approach. Finally, some of the strengths and weaknesses of this approach will be discussed.

Transactional theory

What is a transaction? One way of describing it is to consider how it contrasts with the notion of an *interaction* between the person and the environment. An interaction suggests that a property (or properties) of the person and a property (or properties) of the environment come together to produce some particular effect or outcome. For example, we might say that there is an interaction between an

63

event in the environment (e.g. a daily hassle) and an individual's personality (e.g. neuroticism) which produces a response (e.g. negative affect). Without the hassle or without the internal predisposition to react to the hassle, there would be little affective reaction, so the effect depends on the combined effect of the internal and external factors in interaction. The idea of an interaction therefore incorporates the notion of cause and effect (but includes the interacting properties of both the environment and the person as causes), focuses on a particular effect at a particular point in time (rather than a process unfolding over time), and assumes that causality is unidirectional (usually with the environment affecting the person).

This can be contrasted with transactional approaches which "view the person and the environment in a dynamic, mutually reciprocal, bidirectional relationship. What is a consequence at Time 1 can become an antecedent at Time 2; and the cause can either be in the person or the environment" (Lazarus & Folkman, 1984, p. 293). Although Lazarus and Folkman developed this transactional model with specific reference to "stress" phenomena, the same principles also apply more generally. Indeed, Lazarus (1991) has more recently applied a transactional or *relational* approach to emotion.

Lazarus and Folkman (1984) continue their description of a transaction as follows:

> Another distinguishing feature of transactional thought . . . is that transaction implies a newly created level of abstraction in which the separate person and environment elements are joined together to form a new relational meaning. In interaction, particularly in statistical analyses that fractionate the variances of a cause-and-effect-sequence (as in analysis of variance), the interacting variables retain their separate identities. From a transactional perspective, the characteristics of the separate variables are subsumed. (p. 294)

In other words, a transaction refers to a description of the *reciprocal relationship* between the person and the environment rather than a simple interaction between the two. Instead of considering variables as existing entirely independently of each other or as separate stages in a causal sequence, the transactional approach suggests that they combine and overlap to produce structure at a higher level. The whole, in short, is greater than the sum of its parts (cf. Wertheimer, 1925).

Last, transactional approaches emphasize processes rather than outcomes or effects, particularly processes in which both the environment and the person are constantly changing, and in which the transaction between the person and the environment is constantly changing.

In general terms, much psychological theory and research does not attempt to understand processes but rather attempts to look for the causes and effects of certain phenomena. For this reason, transactional approaches can be somewhat difficult to understand. It is important to emphasize that a transactional approach is not a theory as such. Rather it is a general way of thinking about the nature of the relationship between the person and the environment in producing a range of psychological phenomena.

Some examples of transactional approaches

No researchers have thus far studied mood from a purely transactional perspective. In the studies described below, independent and dependent variables are still measured, a particular direction of causality is usually assumed, and mood is not assessed as a process unfolding over time. However, the studies are transactional in that they attempt to assess the relationship between the person and the environment (albeit at one point in time) and examine how this relationship may be associated with mood. We will also discuss a model of affect which specifically emphasizes process and the relationship between the person and the environment.

Lazarus and colleagues' research on hassles (e.g. DeLongis et al., 1988; Kanner et al., 1981) cannot be considered to be especially transactional in its approach, because it simply involves measurement of hassles and assessment of their effects on affect. However, in defence of their approach to measuring hassles, briefly mentioned above, these investigators explicitly claimed they were studying transactions. This debate provides a good illustration of how a transactional approach differs from a more traditional approach.

Following criticism that their hassles scale was confounded with mood and the use of such measures "almost guarantees positive correlations" between hassles and mood (Dohrenwend et al., 1984, p. 772), Lazarus et al. (1985) argued that such measures were not only justifiable but essential:

> Some of the confounding . . . reflects the fusion of variables in nature, rather than being merely the measurement errors of researchers. If we try to delete the overlap in variables of genuine importance, we will be distorting nature to fit a simpler, mythical metatheory of separable antecedent and consequent variables. We urge researchers to be very wary of throwing out the baby with the bathwater in their efforts to objectify stress as an event in the environment. The positivist position has, over the past fifteen years, repeatedly failed to demonstrate its usefulness in stress and coping research. (p. 778)

In other words, Lazarus and colleagues suggest that from a transactional perspective what happens to people and how they feel cannot be separated and hence research methods and theories which attempt to make such a distinction will be unable fully to capture or understand people's experiences.

While this debate was specifically about the measurement of stress (or stressors), the same point could be made, from a transactional perspective, about any attempt to measure external subjectively rated predictors of mood. However, Dohrenwend and Shrout (1985) continued their criticism of Lazarus and colleagues' approach by suggesting that "they need, we believe, to break down hassles into events and reactions to events" (p. 785). The transactional approach would maintain that such a distinction does not make sense in the unfolding flow of events and encounters in daily life.

A very good example of research that has attempted to characterize one particular aspect of the transactional relationship between the person and the environment has been conducted by Csikszentmihalyi and his colleagues (e.g. Csikszentmihalyi, 1992; Csikszentmihalyi & Csikszentmihalyi, 1988; Csikszentmihalyi & LeFevre,

1989). They have argued that optimal experience, or *flow*, occurs when individuals perceive that their skills are matched with the challenges or demands of the current activity and, most importantly, when both skills and challenges are at a high level for those individuals. Studies of flow use experience-sampling methodology (see above) in which participants are interrupted by a signal from a bleeper or pager and asked to make a number of ratings of variables including those relating to skills, challenges, and mood.

In conditions of flow, it has been found that people feel "more active, alert, concentrated, happy, satisfied, and creative – but not necessarily more cheerful or sociable" (Csikszentmihalyi & LeFevre, 1989, p. 816). While flow can occur during any activity in which skills and challenges are high, if the person is exercising a skill that is well within his or her ability, or the activity is one in which the challenges are simple or repetitive, flow will not be experienced. Typical flow activities are games, sports, and artistic performances. Some aspects of work can also produce flow experiences. In a study comparing flow in work and leisure activities, for example, Csikszentmihalyi and LeFevre (1989) found that the vast majority of flow experiences occurred during work rather than leisure.

Another example of research that attempts to characterize the relationship between the person and environment is found in work by Williams and colleagues (Williams, Suls, Alliger, Learner, & Wan, 1991; Williams & Alliger, 1994) who also use experience-sampling methodology to examine *multiple role juggling*. This occurs when a person is monitoring performance on several tasks relating to different roles simultaneously. For example, in their study of working mothers, Williams and colleagues (1991) suggested that "when roles are juggled, goal-oriented behaviour in one domain (e.g. work) is interrupted by demands from another domain (e.g. family). Interruption of behaviour is associated with anxiety and negative affect" (p. 665). Further, it may be that high levels of interruption actually impede the attainment of goals in any domain, so that in addition to the effects of interruption itself, the consequent non-attainment of goals may also produce negative affect. In general, Williams and colleagues found that at those times when multiple role juggling was reported, participants also rated their task enjoyment and overall pleasant mood as lower.

Carver and Scheier (1990) have developed what they call a "control process" model which again suggests that it is the particular relationship between the person and the environment that determines affect. While many other theories assume that goal attainment produces pleasant affect (e.g. Oatley & Johnson-Laird, 1987; Weiner, 1986), they generally face difficulties in accounting for changes in pleasant affect arising in situations where goals have not actually been reached. Carver and Scheier (1990) offered a solution to this problem by proposing that it is the *rate of progress* towards goals rather than their actual attainment that determines affective reactions. In their view, moving towards goals at a higher rate than expected produces pleasant affect, and progressing more slowly than anticipated results in unpleasant affect. Like other transactional approaches, then, Carver and Scheier's model suggests that it is not simply a property of either the person or the environment, or a simple interaction between the two that causes affect, but rather the way in which the person's activities are related to what is happening in the environment over time.

Lazarus's (1991; 1994) influential *appraisal theory* suggests a more general transactional account of how different kinds of mood and emotion might be caused. In his view, the *intensity* of affect is determined by a mainly cognitive process of *primary appraisal* which assesses the extent to which recent, current, or impending transactions are relevant to the individual's current life concerns. In other words, only external factors that impinge on active goals and intentions in some way are interpreted in affective terms (Lavallee & Campbell, 1995, and see above). Primary appraisal further determines whether affective state is pleasant or unpleasant by evaluating whether the situation accords or conflicts with motivational processes. In effect, people feel good when their goals are being approached or attained, and feel bad when progress toward their goals is impeded in some way. In addition, Lazarus argued that the specific quality of experienced pleasant or unpleasant affect depends on *secondary appraisal* of the available options for *coping* with the situation. Individuals are thought to weigh up the personal and situational resources that they may draw on either to remove the goal impediment during unpleasant affect or to take full advantage of goal progress during pleasant affect. The outcome of this process then determines precisely what kind of affect is experienced. For example, if events are generally interfering with a range of goals but there seems little chance of being able to do anything about this interference, the person will feel helpless and experience a sad or depressed mood. Further, Lazarus assumes that when options for correcting an unpleasant transaction are appraised as limited (low *problem-focused coping potential*), individuals may try to make themselves feel better by working on their feelings themselves (*emotion-focused coping*). Thus, Lazarus's theory not only provides an account of how transactions can produce different affective outcomes, it also predicts when affect regulation is more likely (see Chapters 6 and 8).

Strengths and weaknesses of transactional approaches

One strength of transactional approaches is that they attempt to characterize and understand processes that are both causes and effects of mood. In this sense, they recognize that mood is intricately bound up with, and part of, what we do, not merely the response to some internal or external stimulus. Relatedly, transactional approaches portray mood as being in a constant state of flux. These are only strengths, of course, if the basic premise of transactional approaches is accepted: namely that it is the nature of the *relationship* between people and their environment that is key to understanding mood. If mood actually depends more on separate effects of individual personal and environmental variables, then equally clearly the transactional approach falls down.

A second potential strength of the transactional approach is that it emphasizes people's active contribution to the way in which their own experiences are constructed and shaped. In most circumstances, people do not passively wait for the next stimulus to come along and elicit some response in them. Rather, they play a more active role in producing, making sense of, and engaging with, their experiences. Mood regulation (see Chapter 6) is a good example of how people may actively attempt to influence and change their own experience.

One weakness of transactional approaches is that they can appear somewhat vague and inadequately specified. A number of questions are raised by the adoption of such an approach, such as: Exactly when and how do transactions occur? What is meant precisely by a "relationship" between the person and the environment? How can cause and effect be thought about within a transactional approach? Clearly, much theoretical development is required before these questions can be adequately answered.

A second, and related point, is that transactions are very difficult to research. The examples of studies provided above do not actually examine processes as such but rather interrupt a person's activities to take a snapshot of them at one particular moment: whether or not these cross-sectional images could ever be spliced together to delineate a transactional process is far from clear. In general terms, it is only possible to make inferences about a process from the available data and, because of the difficulty of studying processes, these data are still rather limited at the present time.

Last, it seems plausible that both transactional theories and more traditional cause–effect theories of mood operate at different times. In some situations, trans-actional theories may provide the best account of what is happening, whereas in others, a relatively straightforward cause and effect may apply. A final weakness of transactional theories, then, is that they should ideally be able to specify both when and where transactional rather than cause–effect processes are likely to operate, and what determines the shift between these two modes of operation.

In summary, while transactional approaches to understanding mood seem intuitively appealing and plausible, much theoretical, methodological, and empirical work clearly still needs to be done before their contribution can be adequately evaluated.

SUMMARY

Mood has many predictors and any individual one of these is unlikely to explain much of the variance in mood. This chapter has considered three basic categories of mood predictors: those external to the person (hassles, activities and situations, and experimental manipulations), those internal to the person (physiological pre-cursors and personality), and transactions between the person and the environment. It is not known whether internal or external influences have a greater influence on mood, and the difficulty of maintaining distinctions between external and internal predictors may make such a question practically unanswerable. In general, pre-dictors of mood have not been clearly specified. Instead of viewing predictors of mood as external or internal to the person, we have placed great emphasis on the role of the relationship or transaction between the person and the environment as a predictor of mood. In this sense, mood is neither simply a dependent or independent variable but rather a process.

4

MOOD EFFECTS

OVERVIEW

Following our consideration of determinants of mood in Chapter 3, we now turn to mood's *effects* on other aspects of psychological functioning. When people are in a pleasant or an unpleasant mood, their judgement, behaviour, cognitive processing, and memory often seem to be affected in ways that are consistent with the evaluative tone of the mood (*mood congruence*). For example, the world may seem a nicer place when we are happy and we tend to think more pleasant thoughts and remember more pleasant things. However, moods also sometimes have effects that are the opposite of those that might be predicted on the basis of their pleasantness or unpleasantness (*mood incongruence*). Finally, some of the effects of mood are not related to its evaluative aspects in any direct way, but rather seem to depend on mood's more general consequences for thinking, feeling, and acting. In this chapter, we review the evidence for each of these varieties of mood effect and discuss some of the processes that might underlie them. In general, it turns out that unpleasant mood does not always have directly contrasting effects to pleasant mood, suggesting that different kinds or combinations of processes may operate in the two cases. Furthermore, the diversity of research findings in this area strongly suggests that not all mood effects can be attributed to a single explanatory mechanism. Therefore, our aim in this chapter is not to put forward an all-purpose theory to account for the effects of mood but rather to show how and why different kinds of mood in different kinds of situation might have different effects on different people.

INTRODUCTION

It is commonly believed that moods alter a person's mode of evaluative relationship to the experienced environment (see Chapter 1). Popular wisdom holds that affective state is reflected in the way the world is perceived and the way we respond to it. For example, in a good mood, the outlook seems brighter, and chores can seem less onerous, whereas bad moods may make us picky and intolerant even of minor impediments. From the perspective of any particular affective state of mind, certain kinds of activity seem appealing while we resist or recoil from others because we are "just not in the mood". Correspondingly, other people are thought to be friendlier and more cooperative when they are feeling happier. We know, for example, not to ask for favours when our potential benefactor is grumpy or irritable. From experience of our own and other people's moods, we are familiar with a number of obvious and relatively direct effects of being in particular kinds of mood.

Psychological research extends this common-sense knowledge by attempting to characterize the range of effects of mood on cognition and action and to specify exactly when and how these effects might occur. In this chapter, we give an overview of the range of mood effects that have been demonstrated in psychological research and evaluate the most influential theories that have been put forward to explain these effects. Our conclusion will be that moods exert a range of direct as well as indirect effects on thinking, feeling, and behaviour which depend on a variety of processes. The aim of this chapter is to move towards an integrative analysis which might allow us to predict which kinds of process are more likely in particular situations. In subsequent chapters, we will extend this analysis by reconceptualizing mood as part of a dynamic process over time, rather than simply an independent variable with one-way effects.

We will begin the present chapter by providing a general overview of the kinds of mood effects that have been investigated. Next, we will consider the theories that have been used to account for these various effects. Finally, we will discuss when and how different aspects of psychological function are influenced by affect and describe representative studies that have demonstrated mood effects on perception and encoding, reasoning and judgement, memory, and behaviour. The chapter does not aim to provide a comprehensive and exhaustive review of this extensive research area, but rather to emphasize the most important processes whereby moods might exert an influence on different kinds of psychological operation.

DEMARCATION OF MOOD EFFECTS

Because the literature on mood effects is so diverse, it is helpful to give some general orientation to the area before beginning to discuss possible explanations for the various findings. In this section, we try to delineate the many kinds of mood effect that have been demonstrated. Mood effects may be distinguished according to the psychological processes that are influenced (ranging from perception and encoding, through reasoning and judgement, to memory and behaviour), and according to the direction and kind of influence that operates (e.g. whether mood-congruence or mood-incongruence operates). In a later section of the chapter, we will consider separately mood's various effects on different aspects of functioning and different stages of processing. In the present section, we explicitly address the distinction between direct and indirect effects of mood, between its conscious and unconscious influences, and between effects that are mainly evaluative in nature (i.e. either mood-congruent or mood-incongruent) and those that are not.

71

Direct effects

Many of the effects of mood depend directly on the nature of the phenomenon itself rather than on secondary factors accompanying or resulting from mood. In this section, we will focus specifically on these direct effects. In Chapter 1, we described moods as relatively temporary dispositions to evaluate and act towards events in particular ways. On the basis of this provisional definition, what kinds of influence would mood be expected to have? First of all, we can distinguish effects based on different aspects of the mood state: its affective quality, its attentional attunements, and its characteristic behavioural orientation. Because moods are evaluative states they necessarily impact on evaluative processes; because moods imply modes of differential attunement to particular classes of information, they tend to facilitate the registration and processing of that information to the detriment of alternative information; and because moods involve modes of action readiness, they frequently motivate people to perform certain kinds of behaviour.

The evaluative aspect is central to most current formulations of mood, so it is not surprising that investigations of mood effects have mostly focused on the impact of affective quality (usually operationalized in terms of feelings of pleasantness or unpleasantness) on various psychological functions. The most common and predictable finding is that pleasant moods tend to bias perception, thinking, judgement, memory, and action towards evaluatively positive content, while unpleasant moods often (but less consistently) show effects in the opposite direction. For example, when presented with an ambiguous personality description containing both positive and negative features, participants in a bad mood attach more weight to, and spend more time thinking about, the listed bad points, whereas participants in a good mood accentuate the positive aspects (e.g. Forgas & Bower, 1987). Similarly, people experiencing depressed mood seem more inclined to remember negative events from their lives and less able to call to mind good things that have happened to them (e.g. Teasdale & Fogarty, 1979). Finally, people in a good mood are usually more inclined to act in a beneficent manner, for example, by helping other people (e.g. Isen & Levin, 1972). This general tendency of mood to push psychological operations into line with its evaluative implications is known as the *mood-congruence effect*.

The first important point to make about mood congruence is that it does not always work, especially in the case of unpleasant mood. For example, although bad moods usually decrease the likelihood of helping, they sometimes have the opposite effect (Isen & Levin, 1972). Further, although people in a bad mood are often inclined to remember more bad things than good things, under certain circumstances they seem instead to exhibit *mood incongruence* and show a positive recall bias (e.g. Parrott & Sabini, 1990). Some reasons for these and other inconsistencies (depending on indirect rather than direct effects of mood) will be discussed below. For now, it is worth remembering that mood congruence is by no means a pervasive phenomenon. Like other mood effects, it seems to depend crucially on a range of sometimes subtle personal and environmental factors.

Theories explaining mood congruence and incongruence will be explicitly considered later in this chapter.

Indirect effects

Although the most obvious explanation for mood congruence depends on the direct impact of the evaluative content of mood, some accounts suggest that it is not necessarily mood itself that exerts the effect, but rather extrinsic factors that happen to be associated with mood. For example, Schwarz and Clore (1983) suggested that mood influences judgement only to the extent that it provides the individual with relevant and consciously available information relating to the judgement (see also below). Thus, effects of mood are seen as mediated by its cognitive representation rather than operating directly. Several other possible mediators of mood effects relating to its impact on cognition or its motivational significance have been proposed which we will discuss in more detail in later sections of this chapter.

Most explanations of mood incongruence emphasize indirect influences for the obvious reason that it would seem self-contradictory to claim that mood led *directly* to effects implying evaluations opposite to those inherent in the affective state itself. For example, it is often argued that people react against their bad moods by trying to think pleasant thoughts, thus counteracting mood congruence (see below).

Conscious and unconscious effects of mood

One of the most important mediating factors in determining indirect mood effects concerns mood awareness (cf. Morris, 1989). In other words, the degree to which we are conscious of our present mood makes a difference to the way it influences our thought, feelings, and action. Although it can be argued that the presence of mood always colours conscious experience, we are not always explicitly aware that we are in a particular kind of mood (cf. Frijda, 1986, and see Chapter 6). For example, some of our own recent research suggests that mood often only becomes salient at relatively high levels of intensity. When mood enters reflective consciousness then it begins to exert cognitive effects that may be superimposed upon its direct influences. These effects are indirect because they depend on the way mood is represented, and not simply on mood itself.

One of the reasons why consciousness may lead to different mood effects is that it changes the way the relevant information is processed. A useful distinction in this regard is between *controlled* and *automatic* processing (Shiffrin & Schneider, 1977). Direct and unconscious effects of mood are likely to be *automatic*, meaning that they require little cognitive capacity, are relatively unresponsive to alternative demands on resources, and are more difficult to control deliberately. Indirect effects of mood mediated by conscious awareness, on the other hand, presumably depend on *controlled* deliberate processing, which involves relatively high levels of attention and draws heavily on cognitive resources. When people are aware of their moods, then, mood information is more likely to play an explicit role in reasoning processes, but the controlled use of this information will also decrease the cognitive capacity that remains for use on other subsidiary tasks. Thus, there are both benefits and costs associated with controlled processing of mood information.

An example of how mood may exert both conscious/controlled/indirect and unconscious/automatic/direct effects is provided by considering how people react to unpleasant moods (see also Chapter 6). In this regard, Isen (e.g., 1984) has argued that people often make concerted attempts to dispel any unpleasant mood that enters awareness, using *mood-repair* strategies of various kinds. The result of this may be that any automatic mood-congruence effects are counteracted by controlled processing that is selectively directed at positive aspects of the situation and intended to alleviate unpleasant feelings. Thus, when in a bad mood, people may automatically become attuned to unpleasant features of what is happening but may also simultaneously try to look on the bright side of events with the explicit intention of getting themselves out of the bad mood.

Of course, not all indirect effects of mood depend on controlled processing of this kind. For example, being in a pleasant mood may automatically attune you to pleasant aspects of the situation and your positive response to these features may affect other people's interpretations and reactions to you, which in turn influence your subsequent action and so on. When mood is considered in its everyday interpersonal context its indirect effects may stretch out almost indefinitely over time. However, most of the research considered in the present chapter focuses on shorter term and laboratory-based effects of mood.

Non-evaluative effects of mood

Most of the kinds of mood effects considered so far have related specifically to evaluative aspects of behaviour and experience. Indeed, the kind of congruence implied in mood congruence is evaluative congruence. However, moods can also influence non-evaluative aspects of other processes, suggesting a third possible category of mood effects in addition to mood congruence and mood incongruence.

Perhaps the most commonly studied non-evaluative effects of mood concern the nature and extent of cognitive processing. For example, Schwarz and Bless (1991) argued that unpleasant affect tends to produce an *analytic* (effortful, detail-oriented, and systematic) style of thinking, whereas pleasant affect usually leads to *heuristic* (relaxed, unfocused, and divergent) processing. Much of the evidence for these commonly accepted differences in processing styles associated with good and bad moods is indirect. However, Bless, Mackie, and Schwarz (1992) were able to confirm that the thoughts reported by participants who had processed a persuasive communication in a pleasant mood were generally less detail-oriented than those reported by participants who had processed the same message while in an unpleasant mood.

Mood-contingent processing-style differences may depend on direct or indirect, and automatic or controlled, effects of mood. For example, an indirect and controlled explanation of processing-style effects was suggested by Schwarz and Bless (1991). In their view, the conscious recognition that one is in an unpleasant mood leads to the desire to sort out whatever is wrong in the current situation, which in turn tends to activate an analytic, problem-oriented processing style.

It is also possible to explain processing differences as direct and automatic effects of being in particular mood states. For example, we have argued above that different mood states imply different patterns of attunement to environmental and personal information (see Chapter 1). If this assumption is correct, then moods imply distinctive processing modes by their very nature, regardless of whether mood information is registered consciously or unconsciously. Being in an irritable mood, for instance, involves a readiness to interpret unpleasant events as personal insults, and thus draws specific attention to relevant aspects of the situation. More generally, unpleasant moods of various kinds tend to be associated with the allocation of processing resources to potential concerns in a problem-oriented manner.

In our view, then, many processing differences depend on how attention is directed during different moods. Relatedly, many investigators have argued that moods can determine the extent to which attention is focused on the self. For example, Tomkins (1962; 1963) suggested that pleasant affect tends to direct attention towards other people whereas unpleasant mood turns attention inwards. More recent studies too have supported specific self-attention-enhancing effects of unpleasant moods (e.g. Ingram & Smith, 1984; Watson & Pennebaker, 1989; Wood, Saltzberg, & Goldsant, 1990; see Ingram, 1990 for a review). A common explanation of these effects is based on the idea that unpleasant affect is usually an indication of some problem or negative mismatch between expectation and reality which requires specific attention. Attention is turned inwards in order to understand the feelings and what they imply for well-being. Such an effect is clearly compatible with the analytic style implicated during unpleasant mood described above.

A final non-evaluative consequence of different moods concerns the affect-regulation strategies that they may tend to induce. Isen (e.g., 1984) suggested that unpleasant moods tend to trigger *mood-repair strategies* intended to make the person feel better, while pleasant moods generally result in attempts to maintain mood in its current state (*mood-maintenance strategies*). The differential use of such strategies is most likely to depend on controlled and indirect effects of mood, with people deciding whether or not to do anything about their current affect after having consciously recognized that they are in a particular mood. However, it is also possible that moods or mood changes of certain kinds may also directly lead to automatic self-regulatory processes designed to restore affective equilibrium (see Chapters 3 and 5).

Mood regulation helps to explain why pleasant and unpleasant moods do not always have symmetrical effects on encoding and judgement. For example, people may deliberately divert their attention from unpleasant aspects of the situation in order to get themselves out of their bad mood. Mood maintenance and mood repair may also provide a partial account of effects on processing style. For example, we may explicitly adopt an analytic processing style during unpleasant moods in order to search for a way of dispelling the present affect. The specific topic of mood regulation will be addressed in greater detail in Chapter 6.

EXPLANATIONS OF MOOD EFFECTS

Having delineated some of the kinds of mood effect that are possible, we now turn more explicitly to the question of how they might be explained. In this section, we specifically review and summarize theoretical models of mood and its consequences. Although there are obviously problems relating to the precise details of some of these theories, our conclusion will be that many of them have at least a degree of validity with respect to some areas of affective functioning. Rather than assuming that any single model represents the one true account, we will suggest that several of them pick out mood processes carrying potential applicability in specific situations. Researchers should therefore aim to map out the boundary conditions for particular theoretical principles rather than pitting one general-purpose model against another (cf. Forgas, 1995).

Range of explanations for mood effects

Early theories of mood effects emphasized psychodynamic or learning principles. For example, approaching the phenomenon from a psychoanalytic perspective, Jacobsen (1957) argued that moods reflected affect whose true causes were too threatening for people to acknowledge, forcing them to discharge the associated energy onto a wide range of displacement objects. In other words, mood influences evaluation and behaviour towards various aspects of the environment because the individual requires a safe way of releasing the associated energy. (See Chapter 7 for a detailed account of psychodynamic theories of mood disorder.)

From a learning theory perspective, Byrne (1971) suggested that the evaluative tone of a mood tended to become associated with aspects of the situations in which it occurred according to simple principles of classical conditioning (e.g. Pavlov, 1927; Watson & Rayner, 1920), so that a bad mood experienced frequently in the presence of a certain person would result in a negative attitude towards that person, for example.

Current theories share many similarities with these psychoanalytic and associationist accounts but usually put more emphasis on cognitive principles. It is generally assumed that mood influences other psychological processes either because of its informational value (*informational theories*), or by changing the way in which incoming (or internally generated) data are registered or processed (*schematic theories*). However, some schematic theories also assume that different patterns of attention and processing styles are specifically activated by the *informational* content of different moods (e.g. Schwarz & Bless, 1991, and see above), so not all cognitive models fall neatly into either one of the above categories.

Further, some theories also incorporate *motivational* principles by arguing that registration of mood information may activate goal-directed patterns of processing or action.

In general, then, the main differences between the various cognitive theories of mood effects concern how affective information is thought to be registered, and what consequences its registration is supposed to have. As suggested above, some theories assume that mood *automatically* triggers particular processes (e.g. Bower, 1981), whereas others contend that it is the *conscious* perception of mood that is important (Schwarz & Clore, 1983). Some theories take the notion of conscious involvement still further and suggest that mood's impact additionally depends on its specific meaning for the person experiencing it, and what that person decides to do about it (e.g. Wegener & Petty, 1994). Thus it is possible to categorize cognitive theories according to the level and kind of processing that is assumed to mediate mood effects. In the remainder of this section, we consider theories that emphasize implicit and automatic effects of mood, as well as those that focus more on explicit and controlled processes.

Affect priming

One of the most influential automatic mood effects models is the *affect-priming* model (e.g. Bower, 1981; Isen, 1984) which suggests that mood states selectively activate information that is stored in memory. For example, Bower argued that concepts are represented in the cognitive system as link-points or nodes in a lattice of interconnections, with similar or associated concepts lying close to each other in semantic space (see Figure 4.1). When any concept is activated, some of its activation is also transferred to nodes that are connected to it. Increases in activation make the concept generally more accessible to retrieval processes and more likely to surface into consciousness.

According to Bower, there are nodes in this semantic network that specifically represent pleasant and unpleasant affect, and presence of either kind of mood involves activation of the relevant node. This activation in turn spreads to associated nodes making evaluatively congruent information more available for processing. Thus, pleasant mood is thought to selectively trigger chains of images and thoughts connected with positive experiences in the past or with pleasant meanings, which in turn may affect the way current information from the situation is processed. In other words, mood sets an evaluatively congruent cognitive context for information processing and thereby influences the way the world is perceived.

Support for the affect-priming theory comes from a variety of sources. For example, Forgas and Bower (1987) investigated the processes underlying mood effects on the formation of personality impressions. In their study, participants were put into a pleasant or unpleasant mood and then asked to form an impression of a person described by a series of positive and negative statements presented on a computer. Participants in a pleasant mood subsequently described the target's personality in more favourable terms than participants in an unpleasant mood.

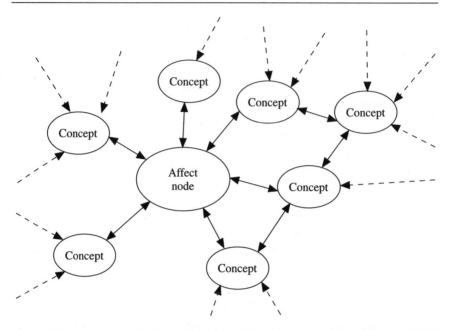

Figure 4.1 Association of affect node with related concepts according to Bower's (1981) affect-priming model

Evidence concerning the processes underlying this mood-congruence effect was provided by participants' speed of response to the computer-presented information about the target. It was found that participants who were in a pleasant mood spent longer reading positive than negative statements before making their judgements, suggesting that the material was being linked to material primed in memory by the pleasant mood. However, when it came to the decision task, pleasant-mood participants made their mood-consistent judgements quicker, suggesting that they were able to access the relevant mood-congruent information more easily when in a corresponding affective state.

The affect-priming model offers an explanation for processing differences between pleasant and unpleasant moods as well as mood-congruence effects. Several theorists (e.g. Isen, 1987; Mackie & Worth, 1991) have argued that, because we are more familiar with pleasant affective experiences (e.g. Diener, 1984), the associated semantic nodes have more extensive interconnections with other concepts (cf. Matlin & Stang, 1979). According to this view, pleasant mood primes a wider network of associations than unpleasant mood, leaving less remaining capacity for other cognitive tasks. Because of capacity limitations, then, people in a good mood may have to take short cuts in their information processing, resulting in a more careless *heuristic* processing style. For example, Mackie and Worth (1989) found that when capacity limitations were eased, pleasant mood had less impact on judgement.

78

According to Mackie and Worth, the fact that the associations triggered by pleasant moods occupy more cognitive capacity forces the person to rely on less thorough processing strategies. However, recent evidence suggests that the same mood can exert different effects on processing depending on message content, making the capacity limitation account implausible as a complete explanation of mood effects on processing style (Wegener, Petty, & Smith, 1995). Furthermore, on an intuitive level it seems implausible that being in a good mood prevents people from giving *all* kinds of task their complete attention in every possible circumstance. Correspondingly, there may be some individuals, such as chronically depressed people, for whom unpleasant moods have more extensive and stronger interconnections with related concepts (cf. Teasdale & Barnard, 1993).

Although Bower's model seems to provide a relatively good account of many kinds of mood effects, it is also clear that additional assumptions are required in order to explain others. For example, the theory predicts that moods will enhance the availability of evaluatively congruent information thus making people more sensitive to, and more able to detect, relevant stimuli. However, some of these predicted effects on perceptual thresholds for affect-related words do not always show up in the way predicted by the theory (e.g. Clark, Teasdale, Broadbent, & Martin, 1983). More seriously, it seems that the idea that activation spreads from particular locations in semantic space faces problems in practice. For example, quite specific mood manipulations seem usually to have relatively general effects on judgement, so that an unpleasant mood induced by imagining romantic problems, for example, influences judgements about coping with a stressful snake-handling task just as much as probability estimates related to enjoyment of future dates (Kavanagh & Bower, 1985). Assuming that snake-handling is less closely related semantically to romantic failure than enjoying romantic company, the associative network model would predict stronger effects on the latter judgements than the former.

A related technical problem is that spreading activation should distribute itself among all the associated concepts in the semantic network. However, if this occurred in the way suggested, then the amount of activation that spread would be divided between all the connected concepts and would diminish in strength rapidly as the connections fan out (Simon, 1982). In the case of the many possible associations of good and bad moods, this would result in a very rapid dilution of effects as activation spread outwards from the affect node itself (Teasdale & Barnard, 1993). Such predictions are hard to square with the relatively pervasive and relatively strong effects of mood on judgement that are obtained in studies.

Another difficulty concerns the ambiguity about the nature of affect nodes themselves. In one sense, these are simply representations of affect that would be triggered just as easily by thinking about the concept in question as by actually experiencing the mood itself. However, since the model argues that mood effects are entirely due to the activation of these affect nodes, then it would be predicted that simply thinking about mood should have exactly the same impact on judgement or memory as genuinely being in a mood state. Clearly, this is not the case.

In order to deal with this problem, Bower and Cohen (1982) suggested that separate nodes in the associative network correspond to affect itself (*hot* node) and its representation (*cold* node). This adjustment of the theory does not help us to understand how experience of affect might relate to its representation, however, nor does it specify what additional characteristics are carried by the hot node that give it a specific affective quality (see also Teasdale & Barnard, 1993). From the present perspective, only some of mood's effects are mediated by its representation, and others depend more directly on the evaluative and motivational properties of the state.

A final problem with the affect-priming theory is that it has difficulty explaining effects of mood that specifically depend on the way it is interpreted or registered by the person experiencing it. These effects are discussed in detail in the following section. For a thorough evaluation of the advantages and disadvantages of Bower's associative network theory of mood effects, see Teasdale and Barnard (1993).

Mood as conscious information

According to the affect-priming account, mood effects are mainly automatic and implicit. Mood does not function because its presence is explicitly recognized by the individual but because it directly activates internal representations. A second important theory of how the informational value of mood can influence other processes assumes that the conscious aspects of mood are important to its effects (Schwarz & Clore, 1983). According to this model, mood functions as conscious information that may be used when making judgements about the current situation.

Schwarz and Clore argued that a simple and commonly used way of evaluating situations is by considering how we are reacting to them affectively. For example, if we are asked as non-experts to assess the quality of someone's performance at a complex or ill-defined task (e.g. figure-skating, gymnastics, or public speaking), rather than going to the trouble of weighing up all the relevant information, we may simply rely on our global feelings at the time. Schwarz and Clore (1988) called this processing strategy the "how do I feel about it?" heuristic. According to their account, current mood may provide us with relevant information about the personal value of the prevailing situation. However, sometimes this information may be used inappropriately, when our mood is actually due to factors other than those that are the current object of our attention. Thus Schwarz and Clore (1983) suggested that we may occasionally *misattribute* current affect to objects, and thus draw conclusions about how we feel about them that are distorted in the direction of the evaluative tone of our mood.

According to Schwarz and Clore, then, a bad mood will make a person think negatively about the environment in general only when an alternative more specific explanation for the mood is unavailable. In other words, if we are perfectly aware that we are feeling bad about a particular stroke of misfortune, then we are less likely to generalize our negative attitude to other unrelated objects or events. Our specific disappointment at being rejected, for example, does not usually make us feel equally bad about all other aspects of our lives including having to do the washing up, the prospect of an evening out, the size of our pay-cheque and so on.

Dependence of mood-congruent evaluative effects on misattribution was demonstrated in two clever studies conducted by Schwarz and Clore (1983). In the first of these studies, Schwarz and Clore told participants that they were taking part in a study of memory for acoustic stimuli which would be presented in an unusual soundproof cubicle. One set of participants was warned that previous participants had found the room an unpleasant environment which made them feel tense and depressed, and another group was told that previous participants had reported feeling elated and "kind of high" in the room, perhaps because of the soundproofing. This instruction was intended to manipulate participants' explanations of any affect they experienced during the study. Next, participants were put in a pleasant or unpleasant mood by getting them to describe happy or sad incidents from their past. Finally, they were asked to rate their general level of satisfaction with their lives.

Schwarz and Clore found that participants in an unpleasant mood generally rated their life satisfaction as lower than those in a pleasant mood, unless they had been warned that the cubicle might make them feel bad. It seems then that when people can explain their current bad mood in terms of the situation, they will not use it as a basis for evaluation of other factors. However, the pattern of results was different for pleasant mood. In this case, judgements of life satisfaction were enhanced even when participants had been told the room might make them feel good. According to Schwarz and Clore this is because people are less motivated to construct explicit explanations for their good moods, being happy just to accept them on their own terms, whereas bad moods are more likely to require explaining partly because they are unexpected and partly because knowing how they are caused may help to deal with them.

In their second study, Schwarz and Clore found that people rated their life satisfaction as higher during a telephone interview when the weather was good than when it was bad. However, this difference disappeared when the interviewer drew attention to the possible influence of weather on mood, by prefacing her questions with the enquiry: "What's the weather like down there?", suggesting that making a specific attribution about mood removed its effect on judgement.

Schwarz and Clore's model seems to apply best to situations in which explicit judgements about multifaceted issues are made (Schwarz, Strack, Kommer, & Wagner, 1987), leading people to process information about mood in a controlled and conscious way. The theory apparently has less relevance to effects of mood on encoding and memory, which often seem to be mediated by more direct and automatic processes (Forgas, 1995, and see below). For example, it would be difficult to explain any non-conscious effects of mood on the basis of these principles. Thus the idea that mood may be used as conscious information does not really provide a comprehensive account capable of addressing all kinds of mood effects, but rather serves as a more specific explanation applicable only in certain contexts.

The conscious informational value of mood states does, however, suggest a plausible alternative explanation for the documented effects of mood on processing style to that offered by the affect-priming account. Specifically, if unpleasant mood tells us that we do not like our current situation, then this realization is likely to motivate us to locate the specific cause of our discontent and to try to do something about it. Finding and dealing with whatever is wrong, in turn, is likely to involve adoption of a more thorough and analytic style of processing information. Correspondingly, pleasant affect provides the message that we are generally doing OK and do not need to invest so much attention in the situation (Schwarz & Bless, 1991).

Schematic theories

The explanations considered so far attribute mood's effects to its informational content (whether that content is accessed automatically or in a controlled manner). Now we turn to explanations that emphasize the consequences of mood for modes of registering and processing information, and contend that differences in the ways information is dealt with by the cognitive system during different moods lead to different effects. These two kinds of explanations are not necessarily incompatible: as we have already argued, processing styles associated with different moods may depend either on the associations primed by the mood, or the explicit quality of the information it conveys to the person experiencing it, as suggested by Bower's and Schwarz and Clore's models respectively.

However, it is also true that some schematic models would reject the assumption that mood's effects depend on its informational content in any way. For example, Teasdale and Barnard (1993) see conscious awareness of mood as a by-product of certain kinds of processing, rather than as a determinant of these processing styles (see below). Similarly, the approach developed in this book assumes that many of mood's effects are consequences of its *direct* and nonconscious effects on attunement to specific aspects of the situation and therefore do not require any registration of the mood information itself.

Martin and colleagues (Martin, Ward, Achee, & Wyer, 1993) characterize the difference between the effects of pleasant and unpleasant moods on processing in terms of the requirements of the kinds of situation in which the respective mood states typically occur. Unpleasant affect is associated with avoidance situations where success depends on closing down all possible paths to the undesired outcome and thus necessitates vigilance and careful examination of the implications of any action. In contrast, pleasant mood tends to occur in approach situations in which any route to the desired outcome will suffice, so that a simple "anything goes" strategy becomes more appropriate.

In our view, mood-contingent processing styles do not result entirely from situational considerations, as Martin and colleagues' account implies. As we argued in the previous chapter, mood typically depends on transactions in which the person and situation play mutually interactive roles. Correspondingly, our moods may contribute to the way the situation is perceived and interpreted as well as the situation influencing our moods. Thus, the way information is processed during mood will be a combined function of the characteristics of the mood itself, the situation in which that mood occurs, and the way the mood influences the perception and interpretation of the situation over time. For example, an unpleasant mood may draw our attention to negative aspects of the present situation which we then try to work on behaviourally and cognitively. More generally, moods develop from the person's relation to the situation and involve the focusing of attention on concerns identified during this transactional process. In other words, moods always carry direct consequences for information uptake and processing. In addition, our conscious recognition that we are in a particular mood may also lead to more controlled processing concordant with the evaluative implications of what we are feeling, as suggested by Schwarz and Bless (1991).

Explicit affect regulation

Recognition that we are experiencing a certain mood does not only affect the way we interpret our current situation, but also influences the way we see our relation to that situation, including the nature of our affective reaction to it. In other words, conscious registration of mood information may lead to explicit evaluation of what we are feeling as well as where we are and what we are doing. In particular, we may evaluate the mood we are experiencing in favourable or unfavourable terms, and consequently decide to try to maintain or correct it, respectively.

Several theorists have suggested that some of the effects of mood depend on deliberate attempts to regulate or control our affect. For example, Isen (e.g., 1984) argued that pleasant moods are generally associated with the use of *mood-maintenance* strategies which attempt to keep the good feelings going. On the other hand, unpleasant moods tend to involve *mood-repair* strategies which involve deliberate attempts to correct or remove any bad feelings. Mood maintenance and repair strategies may be implemented in a number of different ways. For example, when in a bad mood, we might try to look as much as possible on the bright side of the situation to make ourselves feel better about what is happening, and when we want to maintain our good mood, we might decide to go out with friends who will reciprocate our positive attitude.

An experimental example of how mood-repair strategies might work in practice was provided by Forgas (1991). In this study, people in different mood states chose partners to work with on a decision-making task. Forgas found that participants who had watched a sad movie selected a socially rewarding partner for themselves in preference to a task-competent partner. However, a similar selection bias was not apparent in their choice of a partner for someone else, suggesting that the original choice was specifically motivated by the desire to improve their own mood.

Principles relating to mood maintenance and repair may go some way towards explaining the asymmetric effects of pleasant and unpleasant moods. If people are generally motivated to put or keep themselves in a good mood, then this means that they may *deliberately* focus on evaluatively positive aspects and act to maximize pleasant experiences whatever their current unpleasant affective state. In the case of good moods, these controlled processes would work in the same direction as any automatic mood-congruence effects, whereas in unpleasant moods the two kinds of processes would work in opposite directions. Thus the effects of unpleasant mood might be congruent, incongruent, or undetectable depending on the relative strengths of the opposing tendencies of direct evaluative effects and deliberate regulation attempts.

Recent accounts suggest that affect-regulation strategies are not necessarily associated with particular mood states, but rather that the kind of strategy used in any given situation will depend on relatively complex assessments of the utility and acceptability of the affective state in the current context. For example, in some circumstances, people may seek to maintain their unpleasant affect (e.g. Parrott, 1993; Parrott & Sabini, 1990). Indeed the very nature of controlled processes implies that they are flexible and implemented with sensitivity to what else is going on in the unfolding environment. Nevertheless, it is still possible that people automatically implement habitual regulatory responses in connection with particular moods. For example, in Western societies, people may have been taught at an early age to take a deep breath and count to ten when they get angry, and some may internalize this norm at a relatively deep level. Thus there are potential individual and cultural differences in automaticity of regulation strategies. In effect, some strategies in some people may be more or less automatic and uncontrollable in some situations and for some affective states. (The topic of mood regulation will be discussed in greater detail in Chapter 6.)

Integrative models of mood effects

Most of the models that have been considered so far were purpose-built to account for specific mood effects. For this reason, many of them simply cease to apply when effects outside their central range of application are considered. In the present section, we will discuss two more inclusive models which attempt to provide a relatively comprehensive analysis of how mood influences psychological functioning. The first of these models explicitly assumes that different kinds of process may be involved in different kinds of mood effect, and attempts to delineate the factors determining the particular influence that will operate in any specific case (Forgas, 1995). The second model, on the other hand, applies a set of principles developed to explain more general aspects of human cognitive function to the specific phenomenon of affect, and tries to apply these same principles to mood effects across the board (Teasdale & Barnard, 1993). We will consider these two approaches in turn.

The central assumption of Forgas's (1995) *affect infusion model* is that the influence of affect on judgement is likely to be greater when the individual is processing the relevant information in a more extensive and thorough manner.

Forgas distinguished four possible modes of information processing which may be used for different kinds of problem, ranging from the simplest, *direct-access* strategy (precomputed ready-made solutions are applied to familiar well-practised problems), through *motivated processing* (people are predisposed to arrive at a conclusion that satisfies their own purposes), *heuristic processing* (short cuts are taken to arrive at a substantive conclusion), to the highest level of *systematic processing* (thorough and articulated consideration of alternatives takes place).

According to Forgas, mood is unlikely to influence judgement in any way when a direct-access strategy is in operation, because the outcome of such a process is tightly specified in advance. Similarly, motivated processing will not normally be deflected by the presence of affect, because it involves a focused and directed information search which is unlikely to register mood data in memory. However, Forgas acknowledged that mood may set the agenda for motivated processing in the first place, whether by signalling that something in the current situation requires specific attention (Schwarz & Bless, 1991, and see above), or by encouraging the adoption of maintenance or repair strategies. Thus, although motivated processing is relatively unaffected by mood once it is set into motion, mood may be a factor in determining exactly when and how processing is motivated.

On the other hand, when data are being processed heuristically, mood may influence judgement by virtue of the general evaluative information it provides (Schwarz & Clore, 1983, and see above). In other words, when people are in need of a quick and easy solution to a judgement problem in which they have no particular personal stake, and for which there is no ready-made solution available, they may consult their current mood for guidance concerning how they feel about it (Schwarz & Clore, 1988).

Finally, when processing of information is systematic and involves a thorough memory search, then any material that has been primed by mood is more likely to be incorporated in the final judgement (which will therefore be more *infused* with affect). Thus, affect may produce a biased database from which conclusions are drawn. In a study concerning the influence of mood on judgements of relationship quality, Forgas (1993) tested this idea by presenting pictures of couples who were ill-matched in attractiveness. He found that the mood-congruence effect was greater for these atypical stimuli, presumably because they required more systematic processing. Other evidence too tends to support the view that pleasant mood distorts judgement more when the situation needs to be analysed more carefully by participants (see Forgas, 1995, for a review). In general, Forgas's approach seems to bring the potential of imposing some much-needed organization on the previously diverse and unstructured literature concerning mood effects. We must await further research findings to determine whether that potential is fulfilled.

Instead of seeking to combine and integrate mini-theories of how different mood effects operate, Teasdale and Barnard (1993) attempted to outline the general characteristics of the cognitive system and then apply these to the explanation of the various affective phenomena that have been observed. Their aim was to

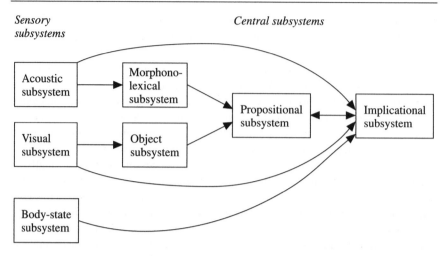

Sensory *Central subsystems*
subsystems

Figure 4.2 Schematic architecture of Interacting Cognitive Subsystems

develop an all-purpose model of human cognitive function which is also capable of accounting for affect. Naturally, any such inclusive theory is likely to have a high level of internal complexity in order to accommodate the range of flexible processes that characterize the phenomena in question. In this presentation, there-fore, we can only hope to give the general flavour of Teasdale and Barnard's sophisticated account. Further detail is available in the theorists' own comprehen-sive presentation of their model (Teasdale & Barnard, 1993).

The central assumption of Teasdale and Barnard's theory is that the cognitive system is modular, comprising a network of partially independent subsystems, each of which processes a particular kind of information. For example, separate sensory subsystems record and transform acoustic, visual, and body-state infor-mation and pass on processed output to higher-level subsystems which integrate this information in different ways. These more central subsystems also record and transform the input they receive from the peripheral subsystems and output to effector subsystems controlling speech and body movement, as well as sending messages to other central subsystems. In short, information processing is charac-terized by the operation of a set of *interacting cognitive subsystems* (ICS) sending messages back and forth to each other. (See Figure 4.2 for a schematic diagram of the ICS architecture.)

The ICS model attaches particular importance to two central subsystems whose interactions serve certain "executive" functions and integrate information from the rest of the system. The first of these is the *propositional* subsystem which deals with facts and beliefs about self and world. For example, the propositional subsystem might receive processed speech information and transform this to generate a representation of the meaning of the processed statement. Alternatively, visual information that has already been processed by the central object subsystems may then be passed on to the propositional subsystem which produces an internal description of the current state of affairs in the physical world. Either of these representations may in turn be output by the propositional subsystem to the speech-generating effector subsystem so that meanings can be communicated to someone else.

While the propositional subsystem only receives information that has already been processed either by the *morphonolexical* (speech-decoding) and object recognition subsystems, the *implicational* subsystem integrates information from sensory as well as central subsystems. Rather than simply dealing with factual knowledge about the world, the implicational subsystem is concerned with general existential state. Because the ICS model assumes that consciousness arises from the recording or *copying* of information in any subsystem, operation of the propositional subsystem results in awareness of meaning, whereas operation of the implicational subsystem produces an overall sense of being-in-the-world.

The ICS model explains affective experience in terms of implicational processing. When the implicational subsystem encounters a pattern of incoming information which matches earlier affective themes (based on learning or genetic inheritance), it generates affective schemas, which lead to specific patterned effects on information processing throughout the system. Thus, incoming data from body-state, visual, acoustic, and propositional subsystems can all contribute to affect. For example, if you are with someone whose appearance and voice remind you of a previous lover, in a situation which you interpret in similar terms to a previous assignation, and your bodily symptoms also correspond to those experienced in connection with love, then your affective reaction is obvious. On such an occasion, the implicational subsystem will generate a corresponding affective code which is not entirely translatable into a simple propositional description of what is happening, so that you may experience the situation in terms of an affective reaction coming over you.

The above account helps to explain momentary affective experience in *emotional* situations, but it is also necessary to specify what causes *mood* states in particular to persist. According to the ICS model, mood is maintained when the implicational subsystem's affective code is continually *regenerated* in one of two ways. First, mood may linger simply because the pattern of incoming information continues to activate affective themes. For example, when the weather is warm and we have some free time, then we may be repeatedly exposed to information that is integrated into representations of pleasantness. Thus, a stream of pleasant stimulation from the environment keeps the mood going.

The second main way in which mood is sustained is as a result of internal interactions between central subsystems. For example, it may be that a representation of the affective theme activated in the implicational subsystem is then passed on to the propositional subsystem which transforms the input to produce a meaning which in turn reactivates affect when fed back to the implicational subsystem. Thus, feeling bad may remind you of what a worthless person you are, which also makes you feel bad and so on.

What implications does all this have for the explanation of mood effects? In general, ICS suggests that it is the *schematic models* generated by the implicational subsystem during affect that influence processing. The specific nature of any effects not only depends on whether mood is pleasant or unpleasant, but also on the particular representation invoked in the implicational subsystem, and more generally on the processing configuration of the whole system. For example, Teasdale and Barnard (1993) argued that moods that are internally regenerated from interactions between central subsystems will be associated with effects on cognitive processing that are more pervasive than those of moods that are maintained by continuing external stimulation.

The ICS model thus contends that it is not moods themselves, or conscious representations of moods (cf. Schwarz & Clore, 1983), that influence other aspects of psychological function, but rather the specific modes of processing that are associated with their presence. In other words, the theory sees all mood effects as relatively indirect. Like Forgas (1995), Teasdale and Barnard (1993) argue that moods will have different effects on different kinds of processing, and suggest in particular that processing that involves the implicational subsystem will be particularly influenced. However, the exact nature of mood effects will also depend on how the affective state was activated and how it is being maintained.

In specific contrast to Forgas's account, Teasdale and Barnard (1993) attempted to devise an inclusive model which is generally capable of explaining all kinds of affective influence on cognitive function rather than seeing different mood effects as reflecting different kinds of process. However, even within the integrative ICS model, a range of distinct principles are required in order to accommodate the diverse data. The general viability of this theory should be more apparent when some of its specific applications are considered in subsequent sections of this chapter.

Summary

Various theories of how moods might affect other psychological processes have been proposed, some of which depend on automatic processes and some of which assume that controlled processes are also implicated. Not all of the theories are necessarily mutually exclusive, and it is commonly assumed that different kinds of effect arise in different contexts (e.g. Forgas, 1992; 1995). Mood probably exerts direct congruence effects on encoding and interpretation of information which operate automatically and regardless of mood awareness. Another possible set of automatic effects concerns affect's role as a signal to the cognitive system about concerns with potential adaptational relevance. Mood may directly activate processing styles and modes of behavioural response that are attuned to ongoing transactional concerns (see Chapter 3). Correspondingly, the conscious recognition of mood may lead to controlled and deliberate attempts either to identify and deal with the relevant concern, or to do something about the affective state itself. Finally, people's conscious experience of mood may directly influence evaluative responses of various kinds to the extent that it appears to be relevant to the task at hand (Schwarz & Clore, 1983). Essentially, mood directly produces encoding, evaluative, and processing effects, while conscious registration of mood may also lead to indirect effects on each of these aspects of psychological functioning, which sometimes supplement and sometimes counteract the direct effects, depending on the specific nature of the appraised transaction concerned. Armed with these theoretical principles, we are now in a position to apply them specifically to the range of mood effects that have been reported.

EFFECTS OF MOOD ON DIFFERENT ASPECTS OF PSYCHOLOGICAL FUNCTION

So far, we have looked at the kinds of effects mood may have, and on possible explanations for these effects. Now we turn to an examination of how these different effects may influence different aspects of psychological function and different stages of information processing. The literature on these topics is extensive and rapidly expanding, making it impossible to provide comprehensive coverage here. Instead, we will discuss representative examples of relevant research in detail, and only summarize conclusions from other studies. In the following sections, we will specifically consider documented effects of mood on perception, reasoning, message processing, memory, and action, and discuss which of the available theories are capable of explaining these various effects.

Effects of mood on perception

Some of the most obvious and direct effects of mood are on the way the environment is perceived and interpreted. It is usually assumed that the world seems a more pleasant and welcoming place when one is in a happy mood: an insight formalized in the idea of mood-congruent perception. When we are feeling good, things are seen in a warm glow, through rose-tinted spectacles, but when our mood is bad, things tend to look cold and bleak. As might be expected, there is a great deal of psychological evidence supporting such mood-congruence effects on the way information is perceived.

The idea that interpretation of sensory information may be influenced by motivational and affective considerations was popularized as part of the "new look" in perception research (e.g. Bruner & Postman, 1947). For example, it was found that the physical size of higher-value objects (e.g. coins and stamps) is typically overestimated (e.g. Tajfel, 1957) suggesting that goal-relevance can partly determine perception. The usual interpretation of such findings was that people do not simply passively register stimuli but instead actively impose meaning on them in accordance with their current concerns.

To the extent that moods can reprioritize goals and set evaluative agendas (see Chapter 1), they too might play a role in the active perception of the environment, which in turn might impact on stimulus encoding. In other words, good moods may put us in a frame of mind which leads us to pick out, or even exaggerate, the positive aspects of things, and bad moods might similarly encourage more negative perceptions. For example, different features of an object may carry different evaluative implications, and mood may lead to differential focus on these aspects so that the overall evaluative impression is changed. Someone in a bad mood may see a glass as half empty, while someone in a good mood may see the same glass as half full. Thus, good moods may cause us selectively to filter out information that is evaluatively incongruent and focus on the positive features of an object or event. Correspondingly, people in an unpleasant mood may see the more negative side of what is happening.

An example of mood-congruent attentional selectivity is provided in a study by Izard and colleagues (Izard, Wehmer, Livsey, & Jennings, 1965). In this experiment, participants who had either been criticized or praised by the experimenter were shown two competing pictures in a stereoscopic viewer and asked to report what they saw. The alternative images depicted a friendly and a hostile interaction between the same two individuals. Participants who had been criticized were more likely to report perceiving the hostile interaction than participants who had been praised. An obvious problem in interpreting this result is that it is unclear whether the demonstrated effect was mediated by mood rather than simple exposure to hostility or friendliness. However, more recent studies have obtained similar effects using different and less confounded mood manipulations (e.g., Schiffenbauer, 1974).

Baron (1987) used a simulated interview task to evaluate the effects of mood on ongoing interpretation of information. Participants were put into a pleasant, neutral, or unpleasant mood before conducting a prescripted face-to-face interview on an accomplice of the experimenter posing as an applicant for a job vacancy. The interviewee gave the same rehearsed ambiguous answers in each condition, but participants in a good mood rated his personality in more favourable terms and were more likely to say they would hire him than participants in neutral or unpleasant moods.

Forgas, Bower, and Krantz (1984) investigated effects of mood on people's impressions of their own behaviour in comparison with those of other people's behaviour. Participants were videotaped conversing with other people and subsequently viewed the recording of their interactions after having been put in a pleasant or unpleasant mood through hypnosis. Participants in a good mood identified more positive socially skilled behaviours, and less negative and unskilled behaviours in both themselves and their interaction partners. A corresponding pattern emerged for unpleasant mood, except that in this case participants were disproportionately harsh in their judgements of *themselves* in comparison to their interaction partners. This may reflect a tendency of unpleasant mood states to direct attention specifically onto the self, in addition to evaluatively consistent items of information (see above).

One of the consequences of self-focus during unpleasant affect may be that people are more likely to report symptoms of various kinds. For example, there is a well-established relationship between the tendency to complain of aches, pains, and other internal problems among people who are predisposed to unpleasant affect (Larsen, 1992; Watson & Clark, 1984). Of course, it is possible that increased symptom reporting during unpleasant affect is not only a result of internal attunement but also reflects an interpersonal tendency to exaggerate one's problems. Other interpretations of the phenomenon based on mood effects on memory (see below) and physiological changes arising from stress have also been proposed (Salovey, O'Leary, Stretton, Fishkin, & Drake, 1991). Of course general mood-congruence effects on perception and interpretation would also suggest that people are likely to draw more negative conclusions about their health when in a bad mood (e.g. Stretton, 1990, cited in Salovey et al., 1992).

In addition to these mood-congruent effects on selective registration of stimulus features, there have been many demonstrations that people allocate more processing time to mood-congruent than mood-incongruent information when exposure to information is unconstrained. For example, Bower (1983) reported that students who had been put into a good or bad mood by writing about happy or sad life experiences spent longer looking at slides showing mood-congruent scenes. Similarly, Forgas and Bower (1987) found that participants given positive feedback about their performance on a personality test spent longer considering statements relating to positive personal information about a target individual during a subsequent impression-formation task. Comparable but weaker effects were also found for the unpleasant mood condition. In other words, people are not just differentially receptive to mood-consistent information, they also devote more attention to this kind of data over time.

A clear example of a deliberate choice of mood-consistent information is provided in an experiment by Swann and colleagues (Swann, Wenzlaff, Krull, & Pelham, 1992) who allowed mildly depressed and non-depressed students to read through three different evaluations of their personality that were supposedly based on responses to an earlier questionnaire. One evaluation was positive, one neutral, and the other negative. After reading these evaluations, participants reported which of the three evaluators they most wanted to meet up with. Non-depressed students were more likely to want to meet the evaluator who was most positive, while mildly depressed students expressed their preference to meet the most negative evaluator.

At first sight, the preference of depressed participants for critical company seems rather odd. Why would someone who is already feeling bad want to make themselves feel worse by exposing themselves to a potentially unpleasant situation? The answer depends on rejecting the simplistic notion that behaviour is always motivated solely by simple and short-term hedonistic goals. For example, it may be that the mildly depressed participants wanted to meet the person who found fault with them in order to learn what their problems were and how they might start to deal with them, which in turn might potentially lead to an eventual overcoming of the apparent causes of the depression.

Most of the results reviewed so far imply that many of mood's effects on perception depend on the perceiver taking a relatively active role and engaging in controlled processing of information. However, some automatic effects of mood on perception are also possible. For example, evidence suggesting that affect may lower detection thresholds for evaluatively consistent information is usually interpreted in terms of affect-priming (e.g. Niedenthal & Setterland, 1994), although explanations in terms of motivated selective attunement or even *perceptual defence* (Postman & Brown, 1952) are also possible. In fact, mood does not consistently affect perceptual thresholds for related material in the graded way implied by the spreading activation model (e.g. Clark, Teasdale, Broadbent, & Martin, 1983), and the effects that have been reported are often quite specific to the particular nature of the mood state that has been induced (e.g. Niedenthal & Setterland, 1994).

The conclusion of this section is that a number of controlled and automatic perceptual and interpretational processes may operate in parallel to determine how an object is perceived, and many of these may be affected by mood. Mood may operate on perception as a function of its cognitive representation and its associations or as a result of more motivated processing of affect-relevant information. Thus, mood can directly as well as indirectly attune attention to mood-congruent features of objects and consequently influence their evaluation and interpretation.

Effects of mood on reasoning and judgement

If mood influences perception of evaluatively consistent material, this might lead in turn to further consequences for subsequent processing of information. For example, more positive perception of prevailing arguments is likely to lead to more optimistic conclusions in decision-making. In this section, we consider some of the demonstrated effects of mood on various forms of reasoning and judgement.

Johnson and Tversky (1983) investigated the influence of mood on likelihood estimates. The rationale for their study was that events that are more accessible in memory are considered to be more common and thus more probable in accordance with the *availability heuristic* (Tversky & Kahneman, 1973). In other words, when estimating how likely something is to happen, people think about related instances from their own direct or vicarious experience and make their probability judgement on the basis of how easily these instances are retrieved. This strategy is a useful short cut when one's sampling of events is representative and when availability solely reflects frequency, but can produce biased conclusions when extraneous factors relating, for example, to salience of events, influences memory accessibility. One of these possibly distorting extraneous factors is affect. If mood-congruent episodes become more accessible, then their ease of retrieval is also likely to make them seem more probable.

Johnson and Tversky (1983) demonstrated such a mood-congruent effect on probability judgements. In their experiment, bad moods brought on by reading about various disasters left participants thinking that other kinds of disaster were more probable in general, and more likely to happen to them in particular. So,

92

after reading the latest upsetting news in the paper, you may be put into a generally unpleasant affective state which leads you to overestimate the chances of bad things happening, including accidents to yourself, or getting a serious illness.

Although one obvious explanation of Johnson and Tversky's findings is that the affective manipulations primed associated material in memory (e.g. Bower, 1981, and see above), in fact the generality of the obtained judgement effect works against a simple spreading-activation explanation. Specifically, the manipulated information had equal effects on probability judgements about semantically related and unrelated events as long as they were evaluatively congruent with the manipulation. Thus, it seems that the evaluative rather than informational content of the manipulation was more important in determining what happened in this study.

Mood's tendency to enhance attention towards evaluatively consistent events may also lead people in more pleasant affective states to overestimate the extent to which positive events are occurring in their own lives relative to people in unpleasant affective states. For example, a range of studies seem to demonstrate that depressed people have a less positive outlook than non-depressed people even when the situation is objectively similar. Some investigators have even suggested that depression is associated with a more realistic perspective on the world, and that psychological well-being involves seeing things in an inaccurately favourable light (e.g. Taylor & Brown, 1988). This latter conclusion is controversial (e.g. Campbell & Fehr, 1990; Colvin & Block, 1994; Colvin, Block, & Funder, 1995; Taylor & Brown, 1994) and probably depends partly on the degree to which the evaluated circumstances genuinely are unfavourable. Whatever the correspondence of impression to reality turns out to be, however, there is still substantial evidence that unpleasant affect (including the unpleasant affect accompanying clinical conditions of depression) leads to more negative conclusions about ongoing life events.

For example, in an experiment by Alloy, Abramson, and Viscusi (1981), participants tried to control the delivery of monetary rewards by pressing or not pressing a button which actually made no difference to the probability of reinforcement. Mildly depressed participants were found to give lower (and more accurate) estimates of their level of control in this situation. Non-depressed participants induced into a depressed mood using the Velten procedure were also more realistic in their judgements.

The most likely explanation for this effect depends on mood's biasing effects on perception of, and memory for, evaluatively consistent events. Specifically, people who are in a more pleasant mood are more likely to pay attention to, and subsequently to remember, positive outcomes such as successfully obtaining reward on a particular trial. When making their judgements about levels of control, then, happier participants are likely to attach undue weight to these recalled success events leading to an *illusion of control* (Langer, 1975).

Interestingly, depressed participants sometimes judge *someone else*'s control in an observed contingency task as unrealistically high (e.g. Martin, Abramson, &

Alloy, 1984), suggesting that their more negative assessment of contingency only applies when it is they themselves who are receiving the reward. Once more, this finding suggests that unpleasant affect has a differential impact on self-related information. In particular, it may be that depressed mood only enhances attention to failures of control when they are personally experienced as unpleasant. Alternatively, people in depressed moods may find other people's successes unpleasant because they serve as reminders of what they see as their own relative failure. In this case, attention may be drawn to these successes simply because they represent mood-congruent information.

Related to the idea that non-depressed people succumb to an illusion of control, the *self-serving attributional bias* (e.g. Johnson, Feigenbaum, & Weiby, 1964; Miller & Ross, 1975) suggests that people ordinarily overestimate the extent to which they have personally caused pleasant outcomes, but underestimate their personal responsibility for negative outcomes. In other words, people tend to take full credit for their successes but blame difficult circumstances, or other people, for their failures (see Tetlock & Levi, 1982, for a review). Research by Forgas, Bower, and Moylan (1990) has shown that pleasant affect increases these self-serving tendencies. In their study, participants were shown films to put them into a happy, sad, or neutral mood then asked to make judgements about the causes of their recent exam performance, as well as of the exam performance of an "average" typical student. As ever, some of the students had done well in this exam, and others not so well. It was found that participants in a neutral mood showed the usual self-serving bias, attributing their own success to internal factors to a greater extent than their own failure. In the pleasant-mood condition, not only did participants show this self-serving bias when explaining their own examination results, they also applied it to their explanation of the average student's performance. In other words, they assumed that someone else's success was internally caused, while the same person's failure was externally produced.

Turning to participants in an unpleasant mood, however, it was found that they blamed themselves for their failures, and failed to show the usual self-serving bias. When judging someone else's performance, however, success was again attributed to internal factors. It seems then that good mood can make judgements of one's own and other people's achievements more positive, but bad mood focuses negative conclusions on the self. The explanation for this self-directedness may be that depressed people are often oriented towards scrutinizing their own performance and its inadequacies in order to understand what is going wrong so that they can do something about it.

Mood has also been found to influence performance in a wide range of other judgement and reasoning tasks too numerous to detail here (e.g. Isen & Daubman, 1984; Murray, Sujan, Hirt, & Sujan, 1990, see Forgas, 1995, for a review). These various findings attest to the conclusion already suggested by the evidence reviewed above, that a number of different automatic and controlled processes may underlie the effects of mood on reasoning.

Effects of mood on processing of persuasive messages

In everyday life, people are often reluctant to request favours from other people when they appear to be in a bad mood. It seems then that there is a popular implicit belief that persuasion is aided by the presence of pleasant mood, and hindered by unpleasant affect. For example, Mackie and Worth (1991) found that 90 percent of college students specified that the target of communication should be happy in order to maximize the chances of successful persuasion. However, psychological research suggests that the effects of mood on persuasive communication are rather more complicated than this commonsense model implies.

Probably the most influential contemporary theory of the persuasion process is Petty and Cacioppo's (1986) *elaboration likelihood model* (ELM). According to Petty and Cacioppo, we do not always have the time or the inclination to think carefully about the content of a message and its many implications (*elaboration*), and therefore sometimes make impressionistic judgements based on superficial aspects of the situation. In short, Petty and Cacioppo suggest that there are two basic ways of processing persuasive information, a thorough and detailed one, and a quick and easy one that just depends on a global impression. If attitude change is achieved via paying close attention and giving careful consideration to the message itself, this is called the *central route* to persuasion, whereas if persuasion works simply by associating positive or negative evaluations with the attitudinal object directly, this is called the *peripheral route* to persuasion (see also Chaiken, 1980 for a related model).

Different factors affect the success of persuasion depending on which processing route is operative. In general, persuasion using the central route is achieved using powerful arguments, while persuasion along the peripheral route is more sensitive to cues extrinsic to message content such as the attractiveness of the communicator or the sound of their voice. Furthermore, the consequences of successful persuasion may be different in that attitude change achieved using the peripheral route may be less durable and shorter lived.

The main determinants of which processing route is adopted are thought to be *motivation* and *ability*: unless the person has some interest in thoroughly processing the information contained in the message and has the resources necessary to engage in this careful analysis, peripheral processing will occur. One possible determinant of motivation and ability to process a persuasive message along the central route is mood. For example, people in a pleasant mood may be so preoccupied with positive thoughts that they have little remaining capacity to allocate to processing of persuasive communications. Further, when in a good mood, your main motivational priority may not be to carefully analyse information you are receiving.

Worth and Mackie (1987) assessed the effects of pleasant and neutral mood on responses to a persuasive speech. They found that participants in a good mood were equally persuaded by strong and weak arguments, whereas neutral-mood participants were more powerfully influenced by the strong arguments. On the other hand, participants in a pleasant mood were more likely to change their attitudes if the speaker was described as an expert, whereas the expertise of the speaker made little difference to participants in a neutral mood. Thus, pleasant-mood participants seemed to adopt peripheral-route processing more than partici- pants who were in no particular mood state. This finding offers further support for the conclusion that pleasant moods are generally characterized by heuristic as opposed to analytic processing (see above). The practical implication of this seems to be that putting someone in a good mood may help you if your arguments are weak, or if you convey an air of expertise, but may prove a hindrance if your argu- ments are strong, because these arguments may not be processed as thoroughly by the listener.

The question of whether these differential effects on message processing arose from the motivational implications of mood as opposed to its informational value was specifically addressed in a follow-up study. In this experiment, Mackie and Worth (1989) found that participants who were given control over exposure to the persuasive message spent longer studying it when in a good mood than when in a neutral mood, suggesting that pleasant mood does not interfere with the *moti- vation* to process persuasive material (but see Martin, Ward, Achee, & Wyer, 1993). Furthermore, when participants in a good mood were given unlimited time to process the message, they came to be more persuaded by the strong arguments than the weak ones, and were less convinced simply by the apparent credibility of the source of the arguments. Thus, people in a good mood will process mes- sages thoroughly and analytically when they are allowed to take their time to do so. Correspondingly, when participants in an unpleasant mood are prevented from engaging in elaborative processing by the imposition of a distractor task, their responses to persuasion are identical to those of pleasant-mood participants (Bless, Bohner, Schwarz, & Strack, 1990).

Further evidence against the idea that the effects of good mood on persuasion are based on motivational factors was obtained by Worth, Mackie, and Asuncion (see Mackie & Worth, 1991). In their study, participants' motivation to process a persuasive communication was manipulated directly by providing monetary in- centives for accurate performance. Even under these conditions of high motiva- tion, participants in a good mood, who had limited time to process the message, still failed to differentiate strong and weak arguments, suggesting that motiva- tional deficits are not the cause of the effects of good mood on processing.

Wegener, Petty, and Smith (1995) questioned the conclusion that pleasant moods *always* result in more relaxed processing. According to their *hedonic contingency* view, the most important difference between pleasant and unpleasant moods con- cerns the available options for mood improvement. Specifically, they suggested that when you are in a pleasant mood, many of the actions you might undertake would result in deterioration of that mood, making it necessary to pay attention to the affective consequences of what you are about to do if you want to stay happy or get happier. On the other hand, if you are in an unpleasant mood, most of the things you might do will actually make things better, so it is less important to focus on the affective implications of the situation. The consequence of this analysis is that pleasant mood will only decrease systematic processing of information when that information is perceived as potentially depressing (e.g. if it is likely to conflict with the person's pre-existing attitudes). When the message has apparently uplifting content (e.g. if it agrees with the person's attitudes) it will be processed more carefully in a pleasant mood. In support of this conclusion, Wegener and colleagues (1995) found that pleasant moods increased relative responsiveness to strong arguments when the topic of the communication was agreeable rather than mood-threatening. This finding also suggests that at least some of the impact of mood on processing depends on motivational considerations under certain circumstances.

There are also other processes that might contribute to mood's effects on persuasion. For example, mood may be used as information pertaining to the evaluation of persuasive messages (e.g. Schwarz & Clore, 1983), or as a signal concerning whether it is time to stop processing material which continues to be, or is no longer, engaging (e.g. Martin, Ward, Achee, & Wyer, 1993). Further investigation is likely to reveal more complex interactive effects between mood quality, processing styles, and message content (cf. Forgas, 1995).

Mood and memory: Effects on encoding and retrieval

Probably the most investigated effects of mood concern memory in one way or another. In this section and the following one, we attempt to review this vast and often inconclusive literature. There are three obvious ways in which mood might influence memory: by making a difference to the *encoding* of material to be remembered; by interfering with, or improving, *storage* of remembered material; or by affecting *retrieval* of material at the time of recall. There is evidence for the first and last of these effects, mainly showing that mood-consistent information is usually better encoded and retrieved than mood-inconsistent material (Blaney, 1986). However, there are also some examples of mood-incongruent memory reported in the literature which we discuss below. Also, as with effects on judgement, unpleasant moods seem less consistent in their effects on memory than pleasant moods.

Encoding and retrieval congruence were investigated by Nasby and Yando (1982). In their study, children memorized a series of words that were positive, negative, or evaluatively neutral in semantic content after having been put into a pleasant, unpleasant, or neutral mood. Next, a similar or different mood was induced and the children were asked to recall as many words as possible. Memory for evaluatively positive words was found to be better when mood at the time of either encoding or retrieval was pleasant. Unpleasant mood, on the other hand, had no significant impact on memory for negatively toned words at either encoding or retrieval. However, Nasby and Yando found that unpleasant mood at encoding *interfered* with learning of positive words.

Although it is possible that children's moods have different characteristics and effects to those of adults (e.g. adults may be more able to engage in controlled processing of mood-related information), Nasby and Yando's results seem to show a similar pattern to the reported findings concerning adult mood and memory (see Blaney, 1986 for a review). In short, encoding and retrieval congruence effects are generally more common in the case of pleasant than unpleasant mood (e.g. Mayer, Gayle, Meehan, & Haarman, 1990). Even in the case of pleasant moods, however, mood-congruent memory seems to depend crucially on the material that is encoded and on the way in which it is encoded (Teasdale & Barnard, 1993).

One of the reasons for the inconsistency of mood-congruent memory seems to be that people often spontaneously adopt mood-repair strategies (Isen, 1984) to correct any bad mood they are experiencing. In other words, people may actively try to focus on positive stimuli rather than negative ones. Thus, unpleasant aspects of the situation and unpleasant memories may be deliberately ignored during bad moods, leading in both cases to poorer memory performance for evaluatively negative material, especially when that material seems to carry the potential for worsening mood (e.g. Blaney, 1986; Singer & Salovey, 1988).

However, mood-repair strategies of this kind may be circumvented when participants believe that they are required to stay in an unpleasant mood. For example, if participants are told to adopt an unpleasant mood under hypnosis they will often attempt to preserve this mood in order to follow the hypnotic suggestion. Similarly, some procedures explicitly ask participants to generate negative imagery and try to maintain the mood it suggests for the full duration of the experiment. In these cases, congruent effects of unpleasant mood are more likely.

Parrott and Sabini (1990) argued that the simple knowledge that an experiment is about mood may implicitly encourage participants to dwell on mood-congruent information. Consistent with this interpretation, Parrott and Sabini reported several examples of mood-*in*congruent memory when mood was not manipulated overtly, but found mood-congruent memory in a study where participants were explicitly instructed to adopt mood states. Mood incongruence seemed to apply to pleasant as well as unpleasant mood, with participants generally recalling initial autobiographical memories of contrasting evaluative tone to current mood. Parrott (1993) has suggested several reasons why people might want to remove or reduce pleasant as well as unpleasant mood, but the exact explanation for mood incongruence remains uncertain (see Teasdale & Barnard, 1993, and below).

Another factor that seems to increase the likelihood of mood-congruent memory effects is the relevance of the encoded information to the self. For example, in an experiment conducted by Ingram, Smith, and Brehm (1983), participants were put into a good or bad mood using success or failure feedback from a social perception test, and were then presented with a series of evaluatively positive or negative words. In the *self-referent* condition, the participants' task was to say to what extent these words applied to themselves, whereas another *semantic* condition simply involved judgement of the word's meaning. Subsequently, memory for the words was assessed in a recall test. Mood-congruent recall only occurred in the self-referent condition, suggesting that participants adopted an encoding bias in favour of mood-consistent material only when the personal implications of the information were made salient.

Teasdale and Barnard (1993) argued that mood-congruent encoding effects are more common when the material to be memorized activates implicational processing (i.e. when it involves high-level abstraction of various kinds of information, see above). This is because evaluatively relevant material for encoding can then be integrated with the ongoing implicational processes maintaining affect, leading to the wider distribution of memory records throughout the system. For example, when participants have to relate the meaning of material to the self, this is more likely to involve relatively deep processing involving schematic models within the implicational subsystem. Such processing will be particularly facilitated when the material is mood-congruent and can therefore be incorporated within presently active mood-regeneration processes.

According to the ICS model, mood-congruent *retrieval* depends on the current mood state being regenerated by interactions between the implicational subsystem and other central processing modules. Specifically, Teasdale and Barnard argue that repeated reworking of affective themes within the cognitive system produces a wide range of associations that are capable of accessing and activating evaluatively congruent memories. For example, if your unpleasant mood is being maintained by consciously ruminating about how worthless you are as a person then this may also send your train of thought around and around an evaluatively negative circuit, picking up unpleasant memories along the way. Because the implicational subsystem is widely interconnected with other subsystems, a relatively large number of unpleasant memories becomes accessible when it processes negative affective themes. However, if your bad feelings result simply from a series of continuing unpleasant events then the only negative associations will arise from the specific subsystems that are activated by this incoming data stream. In these circumstances, Teasdale and Barnard suggest that mood-incongruent memory becomes more likely because the implicational subsystem is freed to deal with any outstanding business of correcting informational discrepancies, such as conflicts between presently active goals and the current state of the environment (cf. Carver & Scheier, 1990).

Mood-state-dependent memory

A further possible effect of mood on memory relates to the correspondence of mood at the time of encoding and retrieval. Specifically, it has been suggested that material is better recalled when participants are in a similar mood state to the one they experienced at the time when this material was originally encountered (e.g. Bower, 1981). This predicted effect is known as *mood-state-dependent memory* and evidence for it is mixed.

According to Bower's (1981) associative network theory (see above), relations between stored items of information depend on the extent to which they have been experienced in conjunction with each other in the past. Thus, nodes representing moods may become associated with nodes representing material encountered while experiencing the corresponding mood. For example, if you are always in a good mood when you meet a certain friend, then good moods may come to activate thoughts of that friend (just as encountering that friend may come to activate good mood, cf. Watson & Rayner, 1920). The general implication of this associative principle is that mood may improve memory for material that was previously associated with a similar mood state, whether or not any semantic connection exists. In other words, we would expect better recall of material that was first presented in a similar mood to mood at time of recall. This proposed effect is analogous to the state-dependence often observed with respect to drug-induced states such as alcoholic intoxication (Eich, 1977). For example, it is a well-known phenomenon that people who have done something under the influence of alcohol can sometimes only remember what they have done when they again get drunk. Similarly, several investigators have argued that mood may set a distinctive context for learning so that reinstating this context improves memory.

Early research into mood-state-dependent memory appeared promising but not conclusive. For example, Henry, Weingartner, and Murphy (1973) found that patients with bipolar affective disorder (involving regular mood swings from depression to mania) were better able to recall previously generated free associations when their present mood matched mood at the time the associations were first generated. However, an alternative explanation for this effect is that patients who had shifted from mania to depression or depression to mania rather than remaining in the same mood state probably had also experienced more distinctive and memorable events in between the times of learning and recall and these intervening events may have interfered with recall of the initial associations.

Bower, Monteiro, and Gilligan (1978) attempted to demonstrate the phenomenon of mood-state-dependent memory in an experimental context. In their study, participants were put into a pleasant or an unpleasant mood using a hypnotic induction procedure (see Chapter 3) and then presented with a list of words to memorize. Memory for these words was tested on the following day after participants had been induced into either a similar or contrasting mood. According to predictions, participants who were trying to recall words while in a mood that was different to their mood when the words were originally learned should have shown worse memory performance than those whose mood was the same as at learning. However, no such effect was obtained. Similarly, Nasby and Yando (1982, see above) found no evidence of mood-state-dependent memory in their study.

In a further study, Bower and colleagues included a second distractor list of words in an attempt to manipulate the extent to which mood provided a distinctive context specific to the material to be recalled. Participants learned one word list while in a happy or sad mood, then learned another word list in a similar or different mood. After a delay, they were then asked to recall the first list while in either the same mood they were in when they had first learned it or in a contrasting mood. In addition, this second mood was either the same as or different from the mood in which the distractor list was memorized. Thus, in conditions where participants were asked to recall a word list in a different mood to that in which they had learned it, and this mood corresponded to the mood they had been in when learning the second list, there should be maximal interference of mood on memory.

The results of this study at last suggested the presence of mood-state-dependent memory. Specifically, memory was worst for participants in the maximal interference condition (different mood at recall from learning, but corresponding to the mood while learning the distractor list) and best for participants in the minimal interference condition (same mood at recall as learning, different mood at learning the distractor list).

A potential problem with this study concerns its within-subjects design which meant that each participant memorized two different word lists under similar or contrasting mood manipulations. This design feature may have alerted participants to the possibility that the experimenter intended mood differences to influence their memory performance, leading to deliberate or unconscious attempts to conform to these demand characteristics. For example, participants may have tried harder when attempting to recall words which they believed were supposed to be better remembered and been less thorough in their memory search when they believed that recall was intended to be weaker. This kind of alternative explanation becomes more plausible when it is noted that participants were preselected for suggestibility in order to facilitate the use of hypnosis in the experiment.

Subsequent attempts to replicate the mood-state-dependent memory effect have met with mixed results (e.g. Leight & Ellis, 1981; Nasby & Yando, 1982). Generally, it seems that supportive results require a design in which different things are learned under contrasting moods and there is potential for interference between the content of what is learned under the two conditions (e.g. Schare, Lisman, & Spear, 1984). However, even under these conditions, the effect does not always appear (Wetzler, 1985). Bower and Mayer (1989) concluded that they had failed to identify any crucial variable that might determine when mood-state-dependent memory would or would not occur and that the effect was an "unreliable, chance event" (p. 145).

On the other hand, Eich (1995) argued on the basis of his own research that mood-state-dependent memory was a reliable phenomenon that depended on the presence of a number of factors, including mood strength and quality, as well as active involvement in the generation of recall items. Again, there is a possibility that these factors may also enhance the demand characteristics of the mood-state-dependent design and directly encourage participants to provide supportive evidence. For example, all of Eich's reported positive evidence depended on explicit manipulations of mood that relied on participants' cooperation in generating and maintaining the required affect. In summary, the jury remains out on the reliability and validity of the mood-state-dependent memory effect.

Effects of mood on helping

Effects of mood on perception, reasoning, and memory are also likely to lead to indirect effects on the way people act. For example, people's behaviour may be determined by their mood-congruent perception of the object at which behaviour is directed. Further, affect-influenced evaluation of a particular goal will influence how vigorously it is pursued. Relatedly, mood may change people's attributions and judgements, which in turn influence actions. Finally, people's deliberate attempts to change their mood may involve them engaging in certain kinds of behaviour for the purposes of self-reward or distraction, for example (e.g. Morris & Reilly, 1987). In Chapter 6, we will focus specifically on this latter topic of deliberate affect regulation using action. In the present section, we look at the category of action that has been most commonly investigated in connection with mood, namely helping.

In general, people in a good mood seem more likely to be helpful towards other people. Once more, this observation conforms to our common-sense intuitions that happy people are usually more cooperative, as evidenced again by the fact that we are less willing to request favours when our potential benefactor is apparently in a bad mood. As with the effects of mood on persuasion, however, the findings concerning mood and helping paint a more complicated picture than usually envisaged by common sense.

Pleasant mood's basic tendency to enhance helping is illustrated in a study conducted by Isen and Levin (1972). These investigators found that participants who found a dime in the coin-return tray of a telephone kiosk were subsequently more likely to help a nearby stranger to pick up a pile of papers. However, subsequent research suggested that there are limits to the extent to which a person in a good mood will help someone else. Specifically, it has been proposed that people in a good mood are less likely to help when helping is likely to detract from their good mood in some way. In Isen and Simmonds' (1978) study, for example, good moods increased offers of help that involved reading and evaluating statements that participants believed would improve their mood, but decreased the likelihood of agreeing to read similar statements described as inducing bad mood. In other words, mood-maintenance motives may interfere with the desire to be helpful when in pleasant moods.

Cialdini, Baumann, and Kendrick's (1981) *negative-state-relief model* suggested that helping someone in trouble often depends on experiencing an unpleasant affective state of empathic distress. In their view, helping behaviour is not motivated by an altruistic desire to be of assistance, but rather by the need to alleviate one's own bad feelings about the other person's suffering. In support of this conclusion, Cialdini and colleagues (Cialdini, Schaller, Houlihan, Arps, Fultz, & Beaman, 1987) found that participants who were made to empathize with a victim were less inclined to help if they were given a cash reward (or praised) which dissipated their unpleasant affect before the opportunity to help arose, suggesting that their helping depended on the presence of bad feelings. According to this theory, then, helping a person who is in distress depends on the presence of unpleasant affect and may become less likely when pleasant affect is induced in the potential helper. Helping serves as a kind of affect-repair strategy that is triggered by a specific set of unpleasant feelings.

In addition to their effects on helping, good moods have been found to make people more likely to strike up a conversation, speak faster, take more risks, and generally express more liking and more positive attitudes towards others (see Isen, 1987 for a review). Clearly, many of these effects are related to the influences of pleasant mood on judgement reviewed above.

As with the case of judgement, the effects of unpleasant mood on behaviour are more complicated and less consistent than those of pleasant mood. Again, this is partly because unpleasant mood both distorts thinking in a mood-congruent manner and at the same time encourages people to try to improve their mood by looking on the bright side, and trying to do things that will make them feel better (mood-repair strategies). Thus, although unpleasant mood can increase aggressive behaviour towards other people (e.g. Berkowitz & Turner, 1974), it also, in certain circumstances, increases helping (Isen, Horn, & Rosenhan, 1973). Sometimes, mood-repair and mood-congruence pressures seem to cancel each other out and unpleasant mood fails to affect behaviour at all, even though the corresponding pleasant mood seems to make a big difference (e.g. Isen, 1970). In general, the evidence suggests that when people are able to counteract the mood-congruent effects of bad mood on behaviour, they will do so.

SUMMARY

Although moods have been found to exert many direct and obvious effects on psychological functioning in general accordance with the principle of mood congruence, they also show a less predictable pattern of influences. For example, under certain circumstances moods can result in mood-incongruent memory, and in general unpleasant moods have less consistent effects than pleasant moods. Thus, it seems that mood effects often depend on combinations and interactions of automatic and controlled processes. For example, being in a bad mood automatically attunes the person to negative aspects of the situation, but awareness of the bad mood may also lead either to attempts to change the mood, or attempts to understand what caused the mood, possibly with the ultimate intention of preventing similar occurrences in future. Whether the controlled processes activated as a result of mood awareness lead to direct mood regulation (emotion- or affect-focused coping) or attempts to deal with the situation (problem-focused coping) probably depends on the specific nature of the current transaction and the perceived level of resources available, but the appraisal of these considerations may also be affected by mood, making things seem generally less controllable in unpleasant moods.

If this analysis is correct, the effects of mood depend on variables relating to awareness, attributions about the causes of affect, and specific situational factors. Thus it may be that no single set of principles can account for the range of mood effects that might occur, and that investigators should therefore concentrate on clarifying distinctions and interactions between the kinds of process underlying the various findings (cf. Forgas, 1995). Alternatively, relatively non-specific models may be flexible enough to accommodate a wider variety of effects and to determine when and how these effects occur (e.g. Teasdale & Barnard, 1993).

In this chapter, we have specifically reviewed research that treats mood as an independent variable, and as a cause in a one-way cause–effect or input–output sequence. Clearly, such an approach reflects a restrictive perspective on a phenomenon which actually continually varies over time and which is in constant interaction with other aspects of psychological function. In the previous chapter, we argued that mood is best viewed as part of an ongoing transactional process, and the same argument also applies here. In the remaining chapters of the book, we will attempt to extend our understanding of the operation of mood as it changes over time, by considering its variations, how these variations may be regulated, and what implications failures of regulation may have on overall psychological function. In the final chapter, we will re-evaluate the research considered so far with specific reference to a process approach, and draw further attention to potential limitations of the investigations reviewed in the present chapter.

5

MOOD DYNAMICS

OVERVIEW

In previous chapters we examined some of the causes, correlates, and consequences of mood. In this chapter we concentrate on what is known about the ways in which moods unfold over time and what this tells us about underlying affective processes. In particular, this chapter examines the dynamics of mood from the perspective of three different conceptual models that were designed to account for more general processes of psychological change: the *dynamic equilibrium* model, the *social entrainment* model, and the *nonlinear dynamics* model. Limitations of these still relatively untested models are reviewed. In the final part of this chapter, we turn to a consideration of the kinds of methodology that might be appropriate for the investigation of mood dynamics. Many of the studies described in previous chapters used traditional survey or experimental methods which are not well suited for investigating changes that unfold in real time. For this reason, researchers have recently begun to apply an alternative *process approach* to psychological phenomena with temporal dimensions, which we describe briefly in the chapter's concluding section.

CHANGES IN MOOD

Everyone knows that moods change over time. Indeed, when describing one's own or someone else's moods in conversation, it is common to use time as a reference point. For example, people may say things like: "You're in a good mood today"; "He has been in a bad mood for weeks"; or "She is up one moment and down the next". It also seems obvious that some people's moods change more quickly or slowly than others, and that changes in mood can alter with age and circumstances. This raises the question of what, if anything, mood changes tell us about the affective processes that generate them. Unfortunately, psychology has generally shown a greater interest in mood stability than mood variability. For example, many psychological studies have used measures based on the average level of mood over extended periods. However, in recent years psychologists have shown an increasing interest in understanding the ways in which moods change over time.

In Chapter 3, we described a range of factors that have a causal influence on mood, including external factors, such as hassles and activities, and internal factors, such as physiology and personality. Chapter 4 reviewed a range of mental processes that are influenced by mood, including encoding, evaluation, and processing. Thus, like most researchers in this area, up to now we have treated causes of mood and mood's effects as separate topics. Although this separation is convenient for research purposes, in practice causes and effects are likely to combine to produce complex patterns of mood change over time. For example, a negative change in mood caused by an everyday hassle, such as an argument, could lead to a change in cognitive processing. This change might in turn influence the response to the precipitating situation resulting in the ultimate exacerbation or relief of the unpleasant mood, and so on.

It seems possible therefore to conceive of mood as an element in an interactive and articulated chain of events, in which mood constantly switches between modes of cause and effect. Alternatively, and more straightforwardly, we can make a basic assumption that mood is intrinsically a process that changes over time. This latter approach allows us to examine the development of unfolding mood states in order to find characteristic patterns of change. These patterns can then be related to internal and external factors. By considering how these factors change over time in relation to changes in mood, it should also be possible to specify likely causes and likely effects.

It will become apparent during this chapter that there are numerous ways of characterizing changes in mood. For example, the chapter will include discussion of mood variability, speed of mood change, mood swings, rhythms in mood, and non-linear changes in mood. Unfortunately, at present there are no specific theories or models of mood change that explain these different patterns of variation. We will therefore extract some principles from some general models of psychological change and use these to organize and examine our current knowledge of the various kinds of mood dynamics that commonly occur.

MOOD AS DYNAMIC EQUILIBRIUM

For well over a century, the processes of healthy living systems have generally been characterized in terms of *homeostasis* and related concepts, such as *stability* and *equilibrium* (Edlund, 1987). The homeostatic view presumes that a healthy system will always try to maintain a normal steady state. In a homeostatic model, then, factors that cause deviations from the equilibrium are conceived as threats to the health of the system. However, many researchers are beginning to challenge this view. Dynamic changes such as adaptive responses, developmental transitions, rhythms, and even instabilities are now seen as important characteristics of healthy systems. Indeed, some diseases can be identified by their abnormal temporal dynamics (Glass & Mackey, 1988). In many cases, the stability of a process has even become a sign of abnormality rather than normality (see Gottschalk, Bauer, & Whybrow, 1995).

The *dynamic equilibrium* model provides an alternative to the homeostatic model. A dynamic equilibrium model preserves the homeostatic view by still assuming that living systems try to preserve stability but also accommodates deviations from the equilibrium as part of the normal functioning of the system. This type of model has been used to explain changes in subjective well-being and psychological symptoms, both of which can clearly have an affective or mood-related component. For example, subjective well-being is usually conceptualized as having three components: positive affect, negative affect, and life satisfaction (Diener, 1984).

Headey and Wearing's (1989) dynamic equilibrium model of well-being was developed to address shortcomings in previous models that attempted to account for subjective well-being primarily in terms of personality characteristics or exogenous (environmental) variables such as life events. In a six-year longitudinal study, Headey and Wearing found that although personality characteristics may predispose people to experience relatively consistent life events and moderately stable levels of well-being, life events also have an additional independent influence on well-being over and above that exerted by personality. Their model accounts for these findings by proposing that each person is characterized by a normal pattern of life events and normal equilibrium level of well-being, both of which are predictable on the basis of stable person factors. Events only cause changes in well-being when they deviate from their equilibrium level, and deviations in well-being are eventually corrected because of the influence of the stable person characteristics. However, the return to equilibrium is slow enough for events to have a measurable impact on well-being in the short term. This last part of the model makes it different to simple adaptation models in which adaptation is so rapid that there are no measurable effects. One of the interesting predictions of Headey and Wearing's model is that history is likely to repeat itself in people's lives because their stable personal characteristics predispose them to experience repeatedly the same or similar favourable or unfavourable events (Headey & Wearing, 1991).

A related dynamic equilibrium model has been developed by Ormel and Schaufeli (1991) to account for changes in psychological symptoms or distress over time. The model assumes that each person has a characteristic level of symptoms that may be deflected by external events and then re-established by adaptive mechanisms. As in Headey and Wearing's model, it is further assumed that it takes time for the person to return to normal equilibrium and that there is therefore a measurable short-term impact on symptom levels. Again this model has obvious relevance to processes underlying affect variation especially since Ormel and Schaufeli's measures of distress included a scale for negative affect and a symptom scale that included items relating to nervous tension and depressive mood. In a test of their model, Ormel and Schaufeli found that two-thirds of people's variance in distress over time was attributable to differences between people's characteristic symptom levels, and that the remainder resulted from change agents in the environment. They also found that deviations from equilibrium were largely eliminated by adaptive mechanisms within one year of onset.

107

The adoption of a dynamic equilibrium approach to mood rests on the basic assumption that affect has both a stable and a changeable aspect. The stable aspect implies that people have a characteristic level of mood due to their enduring personal characteristics, and the changeable aspect assumes that this level of mood is influenced by deviations from normal events. Furthermore, such a model also implies that some kind of adaptive mechanism operates to return mood to its baseline. In the next two sections, the stable and changeable characteristics of mood will be examined. Mood swings will then be discussed as an example of a type of mood change that is difficult to reconcile within current dynamic equilibrium models.

Stability of mood

With respect to establishing a baseline or characteristic level for mood, current research suggests that moods are generally both continuous and mildly positive. For example, a study in which over 3,000 mood reports were collected from 133 respondents over a two-week period found that "no affect" was reported on only 20 occasions in all (Diener, Fujita, & Sandvik, 1994). Eighty-seven percent of the self-reports indicated generally pleasant affect but only 1 percent were at the highest possible level. Similarly, most of the hundreds of surveys of happiness that have been conducted around the world have also found that people generally report themselves to be mildly happy. However, this finding could partly reflect the fact that people prefer to present themselves in a positive or socially desirable way even when they are feeling less positive within themselves. Consistent with this argument, Schwarz and Strack (1991) found that public reports of well-being were significantly more favourable than supposedly private reports.

Despite the evidence that mood usually tends to stay at a stable and mildly pleasant level, it is also apparent that mood varies, both between people and over time. Personality models assume that mood level depends primarily on personality factors, whereas situational models stress the importance of life events. Diener and colleagues (1994) suggested that personality has a strong impact on long-term levels of mood but not on momentary mood, whereas situations exert a strong influence on momentary mood but not on long-term levels of mood.

Not only mood level but also mood variability seems to depend on stable personal characteristics. For example, Penner and colleagues (Penner, Shiffman, Paty, & Fritzsche, 1994) examined 75–100 mood reports collected from each of 54 respondents over a two-week period. They found that the amount of variability in a person's mood was consistent over time and across situations for the whole range of mood scale items. Similarly, Cooper and McConville (1990) found that individual differences accounted for 25 percent of the total variability in mood scores over time. In other words, variability in mood depends not only on the situations that people encounter but also on their personal characteristics.

A number of studies have shown that mood variability is related to specific personality traits. For example, Hepburn and Eysenck (1989) found that extraversion was related to greater variability of positive affect, and that neuroticism was related to greater variability of negative affect. However, the study by Penner and colleagues suggests that mood variability can be viewed as an individual trait or dispositional characteristic in its own right, rather than simply an expression of some other personality trait. Although it may be the case that mood variability simply represents the action of adaptive mechanisms returning mood to its baseline when events deviate from normal, as we shall see in the next section, mood also changes in response to events that are unlikely to represent substantial deviations from anyone's characteristic equilibrium level.

Although mood level and mood variability depend on stable personal characteristics, they are also influenced by a person's current state of well-being and can therefore change over time. For example, Slavney, Breitner, and Rabins (1977) showed that when women are in a temporary depressed state their mood tends to be more labile. Some studies have also found that daily mood is more variable during clinical depression (e.g. Hall, Sing, & Romanoski, 1991). In contrast, Cowdry and colleagues (Cowdry, Gardner, O'Leary, Leibenflut, & Rubinow, 1991) found that patients with major depression experienced less mood variability both within and across days than a non-depressed comparison group, but that patients with borderline personality disorder showed greater mood variability. These findings suggest that the relationship between affective disorders, mood level, and mood variability is complex, and depends on the type and severity of the problem. More importantly for the present purposes, the evidence suggests that mood deviates not only in response to unusual external events but also as a consequence of a complex dynamic relationship between personal characteristics and external events.

Changeability of mood

Although people's moods react strongly to some events, an adaptive process often rapidly counteracts these reactions. The baseline level of mood seems to be re-established quickly even following the experience of major life transitions (Costa, McCrae, & Zonderman, 1987) such as those resulting from severe injuries or lottery wins (Brickman, Coates, & Janoff-Bulman, 1978). Thus events apparently lose their power to evoke affect over time (see Diener, 1984). In other words, people adapt or habituate so that events bring less happiness or unhappiness with repeated exposure. Occurrences that deflect mood are thought to activate adaptive mechanisms that bring affect back to its baseline. However, it is unclear how this adaptation takes place. One possibility is that people's judgement of well-being is based on a standard derived from their own experiences and that it is this standard that is changed in order to bring levels of well-being back to normal after major events. For example, a person who suffers a severe limb injury may lower expectations of personal mobility and hence derive as much satisfaction from a short walk as he or she had previously done from a game of squash.

According to Solomon's (1980) opponent process theory, however, the loss of a pleasurable object to which a person has become habituated produces greater unhappiness than the unhappiness produced by losing the object prior to habituation. In other words, events have less influence on affect with repeated exposure but the loss of those events has greater and opposite influences on affect following repeated exposure. According to this account, it may take the loss of an object to reveal its importance for maintaining well-being. For example, winning the lottery may not have an enduring beneficial effect on states of well-being, such as mood, but once the person becomes accustomed to having the money then losing it is likely to have detrimental effects.

One way to look at mood's changeability is to investigate how it varies in relation to stressful events or daily hassles. Marco and Suls (1993) found that unpleasant mood was worse in response to a stressful event if the period prior to its occurrence had been problem-free. They also found that most stressful events had short-term effects on mood lasting no longer than 24 hours, but that they were more likely to spill over into the next day for people scoring high on dispositional negative affectivity (TNA). Other studies have also shown that the effects of daily events on mood rarely persist for more than a day (e.g. Stone & Neale, 1984) and that mood may actually show a contrast effect by being even better than usual the day after a bad event (e.g. DeLongis, Folkman, & Lazarus, 1988, and see Chapter 3). Such a contrast effect is clearly consistent with Solomon's opponent process theory.

When stressful events carry on for a number of days, emotional habituation seems to set in by the second day except in the case of interpersonal conflicts (Bolger, DeLongis, Kessler, & Schilling, 1989). Bolger and colleagues found that distressed mood continued to worsen over a number of days when people were involved in an ongoing argument, but that mood improved when the stressor was non-conflictual. One exception was that women's mood was better following the first day of a conflict when the conflict involved children. Bolger and colleagues believe that this greater speed of mood recovery may have occurred because women are more experienced at handling conflicts with children and are therefore able to resolve the problem more quickly. However, they also suggested that the results could be explained by the fact that mothers do not get involved in serious conflicts with their children as often as fathers do. Bolger and colleagues' study also showed that when a number of stressful events occurred on the same day this had less overall effect on mood than when comparable events were spread out over more than one day.

The changeability of mood can also be affected by a number of extrinsic factors. For example, Caspi, Bolger, and Eckenrode (1987) found that chronic ecologic stress, assessed in terms of people's perceptions of the quality of the neighbourhood where they live, increased the likelihood of daily events having an enduring effect on mood the next day, but that previous exposure to major life events decreased the impact of daily events. Their study also showed that social support, measured by the number of people who the person could turn to in times of need, diminished the enduring effects of events on next day mood. Other evidence suggests that undesirable events have a less enduring effect on mood than on physical symptoms, such as flu, headaches and back pain. For example, an increase in symptoms of infectious illness, such as colds and flu, has been found as much as four days after the occurrence of daily stressors (Stone, Reed, & Neale, 1987).

There is a commonly held belief that adolescents' moods are more volatile than those of adults. Larson, Csikszentmihalyi, and Graef (1980) used experience-sampling methodology to assess the validity of this generalization. They found that adolescents' moods generally *did* change more quickly than adults' moods: on average, atypically pleasant moods were reduced to two-thirds of their original strength within 30 minutes when experienced by adolescents but were still at half-strength two hours later when experienced by adults. Adolescents also tended to experience worse mood and wider mood swings but these appeared to be related to the types of activity that they engaged in rather than any inner turmoil or maladjustment. Indeed, there is some evidence that emotionally unstable people are more likely to spend longer rather than shorter amounts of time in an unpleasant or pleasant mood (Brandstätter, 1994).

The changeability of mood apparently depends on a range of factors including personality traits, gender, age, type of event, type of activity, previous exposure to stressors, and social support. Although a dynamic equilibrium model is useful for describing mood processes because it is capable of incorporating both personal and external influences of these various kinds, existing models would have to be modified in order to encompass changes in mood that depend on stable personal characteristics that operate within the realm of normal rather than extraordinary events. The final part of this section describes a very common type of mood change that has exactly these characteristics and therefore poses a problem for current dynamic equilibrium models.

Mood swings

A consistent change in mood working in either a negative or positive direction is known as a mood swing. The type of mood swing that has been the focus of most research interest operates over the course of a whole day, and is therefore sometimes referred to as *diurnal variation* in mood (DV). It is usually associated with worst mood in the morning and best mood in the evening but the reverse pattern is also possible. Wood and Magnello (1992) found that positive affect was significantly higher between 10 and 12 a.m. than on rising or retiring, but they also found that negative affect showed no diurnal variation. Some of our own results show a similar pattern. For example, Figure 5.1 shows ratings of good and bad mood at different times of day collected from 30 participants studied over a two-week period.

In a study of diurnal patterns of depressed mood, Robbins and Tanck (1987) asked 105 students to record daily changes in their mood for ten days. Depressed mood was reported on about one third of days and 84 percent of these days involved some type of mood swing. An increase in depressed mood over the

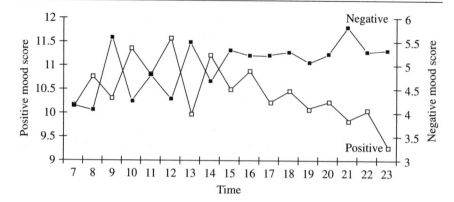

Figure 5.1   Self-ratings of positive and negative moods at different times of day

course of the day was the most common pattern. Those students who experienced days of constant depressed mood also exhibited higher levels of symptoms and showed less pleasure in social interactions than those whose days were always characterized by mood swings. These results imply that diurnal variation is not only common but also may be a sign of better mental health.

There is some evidence that diurnal variation changes with age. For example, Templer, Ruff, Ayers, and Beshai (1981) found that younger adults reported better mood toward the evening whereas older adults tended to report better mood in the morning. This could be due to a change in the underlying affective process or it could be due to differences in the pleasure derived from activities scheduled at different times of day. It seems plausible, for example, to imagine that younger adults derive greater pleasure from evening social events.

Diurnal variation in mood is also a well-known accompaniment of some types of depression. The usual pattern is that mood is worse in the morning during depressed periods. In our own research, we found that the mood of healthy individuals with higher scores on a standard depression inventory (BDI) became worse over the course of the day whereas the mood of individuals with lower scores remained relatively stable (Totterdell, 1995). However, Ede, Kravitz, and Templer (1976) found no association between diurnal variation and severity of depression in a clinical sample. Indeed, the fact that DV in mood is common in healthy people makes it doubtful that this pattern can be seen as a distinguishing symptom of a depressive disorder.

Evidence does suggest, however, that those depressed patients who experience DV are more likely to respond to certain types of therapy. For example, patients with bad mood in the morning seem to respond better to partial sleep deprivation and *photBotherapy* (timed exposure to bright light). Indeed, a tendency to develop mood swings may provide a general indication that depression is tractable because DV seems to disappear in severe depression. This would reinforce the view that dynamic systematic change rather than stability is sometimes the hallmark of a healthy system.

Diurnal variation in mood has also been associated with seasonal affective disorder (SAD) which usually takes the form of depression experienced specifically during the winter season. Graw and colleagues (Graw, Kräuchi, Wirz-Justice, & Pöldinger, 1991) found that about 75 percent of SAD patients showed worse mood in the morning. Although DV did not predict response to phototherapy, patients without DV were more likely to relapse within a week of treatment. It is now generally accepted that treatments such as phototherapy are successful partly because of their influence on circadian (about 24-hour) rhythms of various kinds (e.g. Volz, Mackert, Stieglitz, & Müller-Oerlinghausen, 1991).

Haug and Wirz-Justice (1993) argued that diurnal variation in mood reflects an underlying circadian rhythm that is normally masked by exogenous factors but that is unmasked by depression. By this, they mean that mood has a built-in rhythm of about 24 hours which is normally disguised by people's affective responses to external events during the day, but which resurfaces during depression due to changes in the environment or changes in affective reactivity to the environment. There is a wealth of research suggesting that the circadian system may have an important role in depression. However, the exact mechanisms are unknown. For example, different researchers have proposed that depression is a consequence of desynchronized, advanced, delayed, or unstable circadian rhythms (see Healy & Waterhouse, 1990).

The central conclusion to be drawn from the evidence reported in this section is that many types of mood swing seem to be based on *rhythmic* processes. Current dynamic equilibrium models are incapable of accounting for such processes. However, the next model to be described – the social entrainment model – assumes that all changes in mood are based on rhythms. These rhythms, which include circadian rhythms, are driven by internal and external processes.

MOOD AS SOCIALLY ENTRAINED RHYTHMS

The social entrainment model (McGrath & Kelly, 1986) was developed to conceptualize dynamic aspects of physiological, psychological, and social behaviour. The model was constructed around the basic observation that many biological processes display some form of rhythmicity. For example, there are rhythms in many physiological markers, such as body temperature and blood pressure. Moreover, there are psychological as well as physiological rhythms. For example, McGrath and Kelly describe how rhythms have also been detected in many personal behaviours (including the sleep–wake cycle, activity patterns, and expressivity) and in many interpersonal behaviours (including turn-taking in conversation and group interaction). Rhythms therefore seem to play an important role in the unfolding of many biological and psychological processes.

Rhythms can differ from each other depending on a number of characteristics such as periodicity, phase, and amplitude. The *period* of a rhythm is the time taken for the rhythm to return to the same point in its cycle. The *phase* of a rhythm is the time at which the rhythm reaches a particular point in its cycle (for

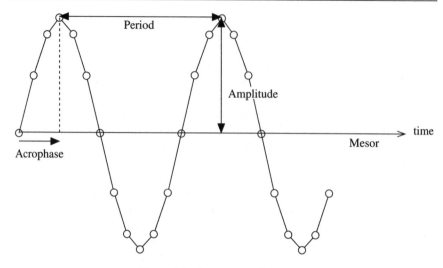

Figure 5.2 Parameters of a rhythm

example, the commonly reported *acrophase* refers to the time at which the rhythm reaches its peak). The *amplitude* of a rhythm indicates its strength and is measured by the distance between the midline (or *mesor*) and the peak of the rhythm. Figure 5.2 shows how these characteristics of a rhythm are measured.

At the heart of McGrath and Kelly's model is the notion that different rhythms are coordinated by a process known as *entrainment* in which one cyclic process is captured by, and set to oscillate in rhythm with, another cyclic process. The social entrainment model rests on five key propositions. The first of these is that much of human behaviour is temporal in nature and is regulated by processes that are cyclical or rhythmic. Second, these rhythms are endogenous, meaning that they are intrinsic to the individual. Third, internal rhythms become mutually entrained so that they act in synchrony within the individual. Fourth, the temporal patterns of behaviour of interacting individuals become mutually entrained. Fifth, the temporal patterns of behaviour become collectively entrained to certain external pacer events (also sometimes known as *zeitgebers*) and entraining cycles. Thus the theory has the potential for explaining how cultural and social processes might exert an indirect impact on internal rhythms, including those relating to mood.

McGrath and Kelly have incorporated their five propositions into a model which specifies four temporal components of functioning: rhythm, mesh, tempo, and pace. *Rhythm* refers to all endogenous rhythmic processes, whose periodicity may range from seconds to years. *Mesh* refers to the regulating processes that maintain the mutual entrainment of the rhythms and thus ensure that the rhythms have the same phase and periodicity. *Tempo* refers to the structure of the resulting temporal patterns of behaviour. Finally, *pace* refers to the external pacing events and entraining cycles that modify either the phase or periodicity of the rhythm.

Although nobody has specifically conceptualized mood dynamics in terms of the social entrainment model, it seems possible to interpret current research on certain aspects of variation in affect in terms of the components of the model. As we have seen, the social entrainment model specifies rhythmic processes, external *zeitgebers*, mutual entrainment, and tempo as key components contributing to the explanation of behaviour over time. In the next four sections, we consider these components in specific relation to mood dynamics.

Rhythms of mood

Most of the research on rhythms has concentrated on circadian rhythms, which are rhythms with a period of about 24 hours. Studies of circadian rhythms in mood have usually used subjective alertness as the main index of mood (e.g. Folkard, Hume, Minors, Waterhouse, & Watson, 1985), but a reliable circadian rhythm in global affect, which includes ratings of happiness and calmness, has also been found (Monk, Buysse, Reynolds, Jarrett, & Kupfer, 1992). Like other kinds of rhythm, circadian rhythms reflect the combined influence of an endogenous and an exogenous component. The endogenous component is generated by an internal pacemaker of some kind, whereas the exogenous component reflects the influence of a number of external factors including activity and lifestyle.

Circadian rhythms probably gave organisms an evolutionary advantage by allowing them to anticipate daily changes, in particular the change between light and darkness. Humans evolved as a diurnal species and hence their circadian rhythms prepare them for wakefulness during the day and sleep at night (e.g. Folkard, 1983). This fact helps to explain why human circadian rhythms usually reach their lowest ebb at about 4 a.m. and peak about twelve hours later.

The suprachiasmatic nucleus (SCN) of the human brain is thought to be responsible for generating endogenous circadian rhythms because lesioning the SCN and its projections to the limbic system has been found to have substantial disruptive effects on these rhythms (see Stephan & Zucker, 1972). However, there may be other endogenous oscillators. There is also evidence that endogenous circadian rhythms are generated by a genetic mechanism (Ashkenazi, Reinber, Bicakova-Rocher, & Ticher, 1993).

Circadian rhythms differ from one individual to another along a number of dimensions, including the phase, stability, and rate of adjustment of the rhythms. Several questionnaire measures have been developed to distinguish between people based on these dimensions. For example, scales are available to determine whether people are morning or evening types (e.g. Horne & Östberg, 1976; Smith, Reilly, & Midkiff, 1989). The circadian rhythms of morning types normally peak earlier in the day than those of evening types. This means that morning types are likely to be less alert in the evening but more alert in the morning than evening types.

There are also shorter (or quicker) and longer (or slower) rhythms than circadian rhythms. Rhythms of less than 20 hours are known as *ultradian* rhythms, and rhythms of more than 28 hours are known as *infradian* rhythms. Important physiological and behavioural ultradian rhythms include the approximately 90-minute cycle of non-rapid and rapid eye movement sleep and the approximately 90-minute cycle of basic rest and activity. Ultradian rhythms in mood have also been reported. For example, Tsuji, Fukuda, Okuno, and Kobayashi (1981) found rhythms in both pleasant and unpleasant moods of four to six hours in a group of healthy males. Similarly, Hall, Sing, and Romanoski (1991) found three to nine hour cycles in ratings of happy mood in both a non-depressed and a depressed group. The rhythms of the depressed group had greater amplitude. However, Cowdry (1992) called these findings into question by criticizing the method used in the study and its choice of sample. In our own research, we have also found some evidence for ultradian rhythms in cheerful and depressed mood and for a relation of rhythm amplitude with depressed affect, but it is difficult to rule out an artifactual explanation (Totterdell, 1995).

The infradian rhythm range includes *circaseptal* rhythms of about a week, *circatrigintan* rhythms of about a month, and *circannual* rhythms of about a year (see Reinberg, 1974). Infradian rhythms in mood between one and nine weeks in duration have been reported (e.g. Hersey, 1931; Whitton, 1978). However, the best known infradian rhythm in mood is that which is widely believed to accompany the approximately 28-day rhythm of the menstrual cycle in women. Unfortunately, many of the studies of menstrual-related changes have had conceptual and methodological shortcomings (see Sommer, 1973). In her review of the area, Patkai (1985) concluded that the pre-menstrual and menstrual phases of the cycle are associated with some unpleasant moods and somatic complaints in a majority of women but that results are conflicting regarding the pattern, incidence, and severity of symptoms.

McFarlane, Martin, and Williams (1988) collected prospective and retrospective mood reports, including estimates of mood stability, from a group of women and men. The only menstrual mood effect from the prospective reports was that normally cycling women reported more pleasant mood in the follicular and menstrual phases than men, or than women who were using a contraceptive pill. Fluctuations in women's mood were found to depend less on phase of the menstrual cycle than on day of week. Interestingly, *retrospective* reports exaggerated unpleasant moods in the premenstrual and menstrual phases and also exaggerated weekend highs and Monday blues. Other studies have also found that retrospective reports have generally revealed more effects than current reports, possibly because retrospective accounts are more likely to reflect stereotypic beliefs about menstruation. One study that found a menstrual-related cycle in mood and symptom ratings also demonstrated that it was usually within the range of variation reported by a male comparison group (Gallant, Hamilton, Popiel, Morokoff, & Chakraborty, 1991).

A number of studies have shown that people have a weekly rhythm in mood (e.g. Almagor & Ehrlich, 1990; Larsen & Kasimatis, 1990). For example, Larsen and Kasimatis found that a group of undergraduates had a strong weekly rhythm

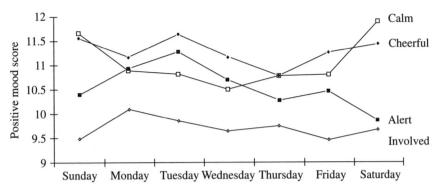

Figure 5.3   Self-ratings of positive mood adjectives on different days of the week

in pleasant mood. A sine wave with a period of seven days accounted for 40 percent of the variance in the daily mood data. Pleasant mood reached a peak around Friday or Saturday and a trough around Monday or Tuesday. However, Stone and colleagues (Stone, Hedges, Neale, & Satin, 1985) found no evidence for the widely held belief that mood is worst on Mondays – the so-called "Blue Monday" phenomenon. Instead they found that positive affect was highest and negative affect lowest at the weekend but that weekday mood did not vary depending on day of week.

Figure 5.3 shows good moods on different days of the week as reported by employed participants over a two-week period in one of our own studies. The figure shows that cheerfulness and calmness were highest at weekends and lowest during the middle of the week. However, alertness deteriorated over the course of the week, reaching its lowest level on Saturdays but then improving again on Sundays. This suggests that the participants used the weekend to recover from the fatiguing effect of their work week. Similar results for recovery in alertness on rest days have also been reported elsewhere (Totterdell, Spelten, Smith, Barton, & Folkard, 1995).

Zeitgebers of mood

It is possible that the weekly rhythm in mood has biological origins. For example, Larsen and Kasimatis (1990) demonstrated that extraverts' mood tends to be less entrained to a weekly cycle. One explanation is that extraverts attempt to elevate their arousal levels by seeking changes in routine that do not conform to their biological rhythms. However, it is most likely that the weekly rhythm has social origins and is entrained by our seven-day working week. The distinction between weekdays and weekends is significant for most people in relation to their activities and this probably accounts for the entrainment of their mood.

Other rhythms can also become socially entrained. It has been found, for example, that different temporal cues or *zeitgebers* can entrain mood provided that they have significance for the person. For example, Nelson (1971) found that students' mood was entrained to the academic term insofar as it changed in response to regular changes in work pressure and the arrival of deadlines. Thus, cheerfulness was normally highest at the start of term and lowest at the end. However, this kind of temporal patterning of mood probably represents a relatively weak form of entrainment because the mood cycle would probably have disappeared as soon as, or fairly soon after, the specific academic demand cues were removed.

Under normal circumstances, circadian rhythms are entrained to oscillate with a periodicity of 24 hours. Entrainment is enforced by *zeitgebers* such as light and dark, social cues such as meal times, and internal mechanisms such as those determining the sleep–activity cycle. However, studies in which humans have been isolated from all time cues for long periods of time have shown that the natural period of the body clock is closer to 25 than 24 hours (e.g. Wever, 1979). Participants in these isolation studies unknowingly tend to go to sleep one hour later each day, although the effect shows large individual differences. Other experiments in which the day has been artificially shortened or lengthened beyond the range of entrainment, have shown that the circadian rhythms of different psychophysiological functions begin to desynchronize from each other until they are free running at their own natural period (e.g. Folkard, Wever, & Wildgruber, 1983). Some rhythms, such as those underlying rectal temperature and serial reaction time in cognitive tasks, often turn out to be more strongly coupled to the body clock than others, such as those underlying alertness and memory-search speed (Folkard, Totterdell, Minors, & Waterhouse, 1993).

The timing of sleep exerts an important influence on circadian rhythms in mood. For example, two independent research groups have recently shown that reported happiness not only varies with circadian phase but is also influenced by an interaction between circadian phase and time since waking (Boivin et al. in press). This finding reinforces the results of one of our own studies (Totterdell, Reynolds, Parkinson, & Briner, 1994) in which we found that the timing of sleep influences mood the next day. In particular, we found that going to sleep earlier than usual was associated with greater alertness on the following morning and more cheerful mood throughout the next day.

Although human activity is normally aligned with the circadian system, there are occasions when humans are required to stay awake although their body clock requires them to sleep. When people's circadian rhythms are disturbed in this way, they usually report general feelings of malaise. For example, when people move suddenly into a different time zone this disruption is labelled jet lag. Jet lag occurs because people's circadian system is still set for the original time zone when they arrive at the new time zone. There is therefore a period during which people experience internal desynchronization while their rhythms adjust at different rates to the new time zone. However, this readjustment is facilitated by external cues such as those provided by light, activity, and local custom. Nightworkers are also required to displace their activities in time but adjustment may be more difficult for them because all the social cues encourage them to remain on a normal diurnal schedule.

Nightworkers are required to work when their circadian rhythms are at their lowest ebb and their resistance to sleep is at a minimum. Conversely, they are required to sleep when their rhythms are preparing them for wakefulness. Over a series of night shifts the circadian system begins to adjust to the changed schedule but different rhythms adjust at different rates. This means that nightworkers' rhythms not only run with different periods but are also out of phase with each other, so that they reach their peak at different times of day. The amplitude of the rhythms is normally also flattened during this period of desynchronization, meaning that the rhythms are weaker. Adjustment to nightwork can take several weeks and for many individuals the circadian system may never fully adjust (Knauth & Ilmarinen, 1975).

Desynchronization of rhythms during shiftwork may lead to mood disturbances. Most studies of the effects of nightwork on mood have concentrated on changes in fatigue and alertness. Folkard and Akerstedt (1989), for example, have developed a model that can predict shiftworkers' alertness at different times of day based on the combined effects of the body clock and the sleep–wake cycle. In one of the few studies to examine daily changes in mood across a series of night shifts, Bohle and Tilley (1993) found that nightwork affected measures of fatigue and activity but not tension, depression, anger, or confusion. However, higher than normal levels of depressed mood have been found among nurses working on a shift system that rotates between different shifts (Tasto, Colligan, Skjei, & Polly, 1978).

Therapeutic interventions that use artificial *zeitgebers* to shift the phase of circadian rhythms are currently being developed. The discovery that very bright light (about 2,500 lux) can suppress the pineal gland's natural secretion of melatonin at night (Lewy, Wehr, Goodwin, Newsome, & Markey, 1980) was instrumental to the development of these techniques. Subsequent research has shown that the appropriate timing and magnitude of bright light can advance, delay, and even suppress circadian rhythms (e.g. Jewett, Kronauer, & Czeisler, 1991). One potential use of these interventions would be to adjust shiftworkers' circadian rhythms to suit their work schedule better. Studies of bright light treatment during simulated night shifts have demonstrated large circadian phase shifts, and enhanced alertness and performance (e.g. Campbell & Dawson, 1990; Czeisler, Johnson, Duffy, Brown, Ronda, & Kronauer, 1990; Eastman, 1992). Oral ingestion of melatonin has also been found to induce phase shifts of the body's own natural rhythm in melatonin production. Shiftworkers who have taken melatonin prior to their altered bedtime have shown improved sleep and alertness (Folkard, Arendt, & Clark, 1993). Thus, some of the deleterious effects of external *zeitgebers* on mood-related variables may be remediated by carefully timed corrective action.

Mutual entrainment of mood

A number of studies have demonstrated that mutual entrainment or synchronicity of mood can develop between people who interact with one another over extended

119

periods. In other words, the moods of two individuals may become rhythmically attuned to one another over time. For example, Mansfield, Hood, and Henderson (1989) found that some couples show significant positive correlations in their daily mood reports, suggesting a process of contagion in which one person catches the mood of the other. By examining the associations between one partner's mood reports and the other partner's earlier mood reports, these investigators demonstrated that in some instances one partner was driving the mood of the other.

The amount of time that people spend together seems to influence the likelihood that they will show mutual entrainment. For example, roommates of depressed persons are more likely to become depressed over time themselves (Howes, Hokanson, & Loewenstein, 1985) and women who spend more time together are more likely to show menstrual cycle synchronization (McClintock, 1971).

Married couples usually spend a lot of time together and would therefore be expected to show a high degree of mutual entrainment of mood. In fact, the extent of entrainment between married partners seems to be a good predictor of their marital unhappiness. For example, Levenson and Gottman (1983) found that interpersonal interdependency between the physiological responding of partners while discussing a relationship problem was very strongly associated with rated dissatisfaction with their marriage. In other words, couples in which one partner's level of internal bodily upset tended to be associated with the other's during times of conflict generally functioned worse than couples whose reactions were not so mutually excitable. Levenson and Gottman also found that certain distinctive patterns of affect reciprocity were more likely when marital satisfaction was low. In particular, wives were more likely to reciprocate husbands' moods whether they were good or bad, but husbands were less likely to reciprocate wives' good moods. It therefore seems likely that couples in unsatisfying relationships become locked into a pattern of destructive mutual mood reciprocation. For example, a wife may start out in a good mood but if it fails to be reciprocated by her husband, she will then reciprocate his bad mood with her own bad mood, which he in turn reciprocates again. Thus a bad mood may reverberate back and forth between partners in a mutually exacerbative process.

The respective activation levels of partners may also have an impact on the course of their relationship. For example, Hoskins (1989) found that at times when partners showed greater desynchrony in activation they also experienced greater interactional-emotional needs. This finding clearly has implications for partners whose jobs require them to be active and alert at different times. A shiftworker, for example, may feel tired at a time when his or her partner is wide awake, which could lead to feelings of mutual frustration.

Although synchrony between people's affective rhythms is probably desirable and beneficial in most situations, there may also be occasions when it is better if rhythms are out of step. For example, Merten and Krause (1994) discovered that psychotherapy sessions were more successful when the facial affect between therapist and client was out of phase at the start but became mutually entrained over time. Retrospective analysis of the sessions suggested that in successful sessions

120

the therapist was regulating the client's affect, whereas in unsuccessful sessions the therapist was trying to please the client by reciprocating his or her affect from the outset and hence the therapist was being regulated by the client. Clearly, the relative effectiveness of these two kinds of therapeutic relationship may depend on the particular goals and purposes of the therapy in question (see Chapter 7) but Merten and Krause's study certainly presents a promising new approach to the investigation of interpersonal affect management. In the next chapter, we will discuss the specific topic of mood regulation in more detail.

The observation that therapists commonly find themselves in a corresponding mood to that of their clients during therapy sessions led Hatfield, Cacioppo, and Rapson (1994) to investigate the phenomenon of *emotional contagion*. According to their theory, one of the main reasons for emotional contagion is that people automatically tend to mimic the facial expressions, postures, and behaviours of others. Self-perceived feedback arising from these mimicked responses tends to lead in turn to the experience of a similar emotion to that being displayed by the other person (Laird & Bresler, 1992). In other words, people may feel themselves reacting in an emotional way when they copy someone else's emotional behaviour and come to perceive these feelings as part of their own emotional reaction. The evidence suggests that emotional contagion is usually very rapid and commonly occurs without a person's knowledge.

Hatfield and colleagues found that some people are consistently more likely to infect others with their emotions whereas other people are more susceptible to being emotionally infected. Emotionally infectious people are those who appear to feel strong emotions, can express those emotions, and are relatively unresponsive to the feelings of others. In contrast, people who are more vulnerable to contagion are those who attend closely to other people, define their identity in terms of their interrelatedness to others, mimic other people's expressions and are good at reading them, show awareness of their own emotions, and are generally emotionally reactive. In many situations it may be personally advantageous to bring other people's emotions into line with one's own using a contagion process, or alternatively to be empathically sensitive to the feelings of others in a direct and automatic way. Unfortunately, however, it seems unlikely that these capacities can be explicitly taught or developed because emotional contagion appears to be a highly complex and largely automatic process.

Tempo of mood

According to the social entrainment model, entrainment produces a characteristic structure or tempo in behaviour. Changes in mood therefore take place within the broader temporal structure of environmental and behavioural events, and the features of that temporal structure play an important role in influencing mood dynamics. In this section, we will examine two issues concerning tempo that have specific relevance to mood. The first issue concerns the relation of the structure and regularity of events to mood. The second issue concerns the relation of the order and pace of events to mood.

Bond and Feather (1988) found that the degree to which individuals perceive their time to be structured and purposive is positively associated with their self-esteem, optimism, reported health, and sense of purpose in life, and negatively associated with their depression, distress, anxiety, neuroticism, physical symptoms, hopelessness, and anomie. According to Hassard (1991), people's sense of time structure is largely socialized within formal organizations. Thus, family, school, and work all educate people about the rules of social time. More specifically, participation in organizational life provides people with a time structure that has the capacity to affect their well-being and hence their mood.

Just as belonging to an organization can provide a time-structure for everyday activities, ceasing to belong can take away this structure. For example, unemployment, which causes people to lose the regularity of their daily routines, can lead to increased depression (Feather & Bond, 1983). Another problem for the unemployed is filling time. In this regard, Warr, Banks, and Ullah (1985) found that the ability to fill time was negatively associated with psychological distress in an unemployed sample. Similarly, Kilpatrick and Trew (1985) showed that a decline in well-being among the unemployed was associated with decreased activity and withdrawal into the home.

A number of researchers have attempted to measure the regularity of people's daily routines and to relate changes in these routines to mental well-being. For example, Monk and colleagues (Monk, Petrie, Hayes, & Kupfer, 1994) found that regularity in daily lifestyle (as measured by the social rhythm metric) was associated with a number of variables including changes in alertness during the day.

Healy and Waterhouse (1995) argued that altered rhythms during depression are due to changes in lifestyle rather than disturbance of an endogenous circadian clock. In support of this view, it has been shown that social circadian rhythms are commonly disturbed during depression (e.g. Szuba, Yager, Guze, Allen, & Baxter, 1992). According to Healy and Waterhouse, depression, like shiftwork maladaptation, is triggered by environmental disruption. For example, isolation can sometimes lead to depression (see Kripke, Drennan, & Elliot, 1992). This may be due to disturbance of circadian rhythms or due to social factors such as loneliness.

The pace, as well as the regularity, of events can have dynamic effects on mood and satisfaction. Experiments have shown that satisfaction with an outcome depends not only on how positive the outcome is but also on the change, rate of change (velocity), and change of velocity (quasi-acceleration) in outcomes over time (Hsee, Salovey, & Abelson, 1994). For example, financial investments that increase in value slowly then speed up are preferred to those that continue to increase in value steadily. Similarly, people will often arrange events to obtain velocity effects of this kind (Salovey, Hsee, & Mayer, 1993). Experiments have shown, for example, that people not only prefer to open birthday gifts in order of ascending value but also that they prefer a more quickly ascending pattern. Moreover, it seems that people have preferences concerning the temporal contiguity of events. For instance, people prefer two events that are both positive or both negative to be separated in time, but prefer the events to occur simultaneously if one is positive and the other negative (Linville & Fischer, 1991).

According to Carver and Scheier's (1990) control process model, affect arises from discrepancies between expected and actual rates of movement towards goals. In particular, progress towards a goal that is faster than expected is associated with pleasant feeling, and progress towards a goal that is slower than expected is associated with unpleasant feeling. Consequently, a change in the rate of progress is experienced as a change of affect. For example, when acceleration towards a goal is great this results in a sense of exhilaration. One implication of Carver and Scheier's model is that people who have higher expectations of their rate of progress will tend to experience good moods less often. However, reference standards may also change in response to experienced success or failure in attaining goals at the expected rate, with the result that individuals experience roughly the same balance of pleasant and unpleasant moods over time. A similar process of goal adjustment would also be capable of explaining why people can adapt to severe life events, as discussed earlier in connection with the dynamic equilibrium model.

McGrath and Kelly (1986) also refer to changes in the steady state, or set points, of processes over time, suggesting that there may be common ground between the social entrainment model and the dynamic equilibrium model. Indeed, this connection was emphasized explicitly by McGrath and Kelly themselves in the following terms: "The particular usefulness of the Social Entrainment Model to the behavioural and the social sciences is the notion of dynamic equilibrium that underlies it; that is, the notion that much of human behaviour involves patterns of behaviour systems that fluctuate systematically over time" (p. 90). However, just as social entrainment and dynamic equilibrium models offer convergent accounts of many temporally articulated psychological processes, there are also phenomena that both accounts have difficulty in explaining. In the next section, we describe a form of mood change that is equally problematic for both theories.

MOOD AS NONLINEAR DYNAMICS

Most models have assumed that mood changes in proportion to event frequency or magnitude. According to this view, when these event characteristics are repeated they will exert equivalent effects on mood, and when they are altered their effects will also change in a way that is predictable on the basis of direct linear transformation rules. Indeed, the majority of the studies that we have described in this book so far have used statistical techniques that are based on linear equations. Linear equations are useful because they are additive and can therefore be combined to produce unique solutions. However, in practice, events do not always have simple additive effects on mood (for example, see Bolger et al., 1989). More generally, there is increasing evidence that many natural systems change in a non-linear rather than a linear fashion (see Barton (1994) for a review of the application of non-linear dynamics to psychological systems).

In a nonlinear system, a continuous change in one parameter can produce a mixture of continuous and discontinuous changes in the behaviour of another parameter. This means that jumps in behaviour can occur for no apparent reason. Non-linear systems can be described by non-linear equations which are not additive and do not necessarily produce unique solutions. These equations are also often *iterative*, which means that their solutions are fed back into the same equation. The implication of this is that the system's history of states is important in determining its behaviour. In other words, the system may react differently to the same event depending on its current status. For example, if we assume that mood is non-linear, a song that induces a sad mood on one occasion may have no affective impact at all on another occasion. Likewise, we may be surprised when a simple remark that was once greeted with laughter now results in a flood of tears.

The behaviour of non-linear systems can be understood by determining their *attractors* in *phase space*. This means that each state of the system is represented by a coordinate in an area or volume of space that encompasses all possible states of the system. Unless the process is random, these possible coordinates will converge on a fixed subset of the space known as the attractor. The shape or type of the attractor depends on the kind of non-linear system under consideration. One type of attractor, known as a *strange attractor*, is produced specifically by systems that are *chaotic*.

The behaviour of a chaotic system is highly irregular and therefore difficult to predict. However, chaotic behaviour arises from a deterministic or rule-based system and therefore although the behaviour is complex, it is not random. The behaviour of chaotic systems can diverge wildly from very similar starting points. For example, two stones released together into a river will usually end up at very different places. This is known as *sensitivity to initial conditions* and makes long-term point prediction all but impossible.

It is conceivable that mood processes, or at least some aspects of their operation, are chaotic. If this is so, then the implication is that it would be almost impossible to predict a person's state of mood at any given time. However, this does not rule out some more general characterization of the overall form of someone's mood dynamics.

Chaotic dynamics of mood

A number of researchers have begun to examine whether mood changes can be understood using the concepts and techniques of non-linear dynamics. For example, in our own research (Totterdell, Briner, Parkinson, & Reynolds, 1996) we have used a non-linear graphical technique known as a Poincaré plot to show that different mood variables exhibit different dynamic behaviour. Mood ratings were recorded at two-hourly intervals for two weeks by 30 participants. Figure 5.4 shows a Poincaré plot for depressed mood based on these data. The plot was constructed by plotting each participant's rating of depressed mood against the

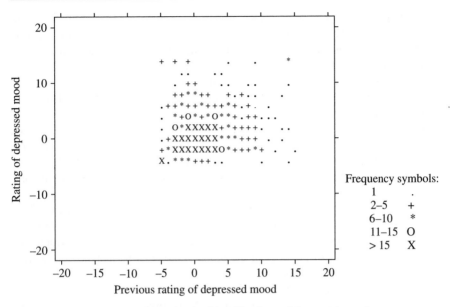

Figure 5.4   Poincaré plot for self-ratings of depressed mood

value of his or her rating two hours earlier. Ratings are expressed as differences from a participant's average so that all participants' data can be included on the same graph. The plot shows that lower ratings of mood tended to deviate more from the $x = y$ axis, indicating that there were greater changes in mood when the participants were more depressed. Similarly, Combs, Winkler, and Daley (1994) also found that mood oscillated more when people were less happy. These findings could reflect the fact that people are more likely to deploy mood-regulation strategies to get themselves out of bad moods than good moods (see Chapter 6).

It is possible that when regulation fails, mood shifts into a region of chaotic behaviour. For example, it has been suggested that clinically depressed mood shows chaotic characteristics (see Heiby, 1994). In order to substantiate this claim, Heiby has begun an ambitious study that will test for a chaotic pattern of mood during depression by collecting sadness ratings from a non-depressed and a depressed individual every 20 minutes for up to a year.

There is already evidence that mood has chaotic characteristics in people suffering from bipolar affective disorder. In a recent study, Gottschalk, Bauer, and Whybrow (1995) found that mood in bipolar patients can be characterized as a low-dimensional chaotic process. Their study showed that mood in this disorder is not cyclic over long periods, as had been previously assumed, but that it shows a higher degree of temporal organization than mood in individuals without a mood disorder.

A recent theory known as complexity theory (see Lewin, 1993) proposes that many natural systems operate at the boundary between order and chaos. This seems to give these systems emergent properties, such as increases in information-processing capacity. It is possible that mood processes also normally operate at this boundary but deviate from it during abnormal conditions such as those characterizing affective disorders. This deviation could either be towards highly ordered non-flexible dynamics or towards uncontrollable chaotic dynamics. However, these ideas are entirely hypothetical at present and would probably prove difficult to test in practice.

It would be wrong to assume that mood is only chaotic during mood disorders. For example, Combs and colleagues (1994) found that the mood of the five healthy participants in their study had a chaotic-like structure. Furthermore, Gottschalk and colleagues (1995) pointed out that the mood of their normal comparison group may have had a high chaotic dimension that was beyond their measurement range. It also seems likely that mood dynamics vary depending on the nature of the particular disorder in question. For example, Möller and Leitner (1987) have developed a non-linear model for analysing mood curves which they have used to identify differences in the mood changes of patients suffering from different types of affective disorder.

It is important to emphasize that the non-linear dynamic model of mood described in the present section does not preclude the rhythm-based model of mood proposed in the previous section. For example, Gottschalk and colleagues (1995) suggest that "an abnormally coupled or configured internal circadian oscillator involved in mood regulation could be driven to chaotic behavior by exogenous oscillations" (p. 957). In other words, chaos in mood may emerge from underlying cyclical processes. With respect to bipolar disorder, Gottschalk and colleagues speculate that psychosocial stressors may set up sustained pathologic dynamics that are responsible for subsequent bipolar episodes but that appear unlinked to the original stressors. In support of this view, Ehlers (1995) contends that patients with bipolar disorder may be particularly sensitive to social factors that disrupt their biological rhythms, and proposes the therapeutic use of behavioural and cognitive techniques to restabilize these rhythms (see Chapter 7 for a more detailed discussion of therapies for mood disorders).

In summary, the non-linear model offers hope for a unified view of dynamic processes, and in particular shows promise for a more complete understanding of mood dynamics. However, although the studies described in the present section represent an exciting new approach to the study of affective processes, there is still a great deal of research to be done before this or any of the other models can claim to explain the full range of mood changes. This research requires an improved strategy for investigating mood dynamics and it is to this strategy that we next turn our attention.

INVESTIGATING MOOD DYNAMICS: THE PROCESS APPROACH

Most psychologists have approached mood from an experimental angle, treating the phenomenon as a dependent or an independent variable in a simple and intact two-step causal sequence. There are three basic limitations to this approach. First, experimental investigation often involves taking people out of their usual environment, and this move can have obvious influences on mood. Second, as should already be clear from the discussion in the present and previous chapters, mood can in fact function as both cause and effect, and as an input as well as an output variable. Third and finally, experiments assessing mood effects usually only measure the dependent variable once at a single localized moment following the experimental manipulation, thus ignoring any possible effects of the passage of time.

To illustrate this final point, Sedikides (1994) has shown that some of the inconsistencies in the occurrence of mood congruency effects (see Chapter 4) may have arisen simply because the investigators failed to include time in the experimental design. In particular, Sedikides demonstrated that people describe themselves negatively immediately following the induction of a sad mood (mood-congruent effect) but describe themselves more positively (mood-incongruent effect) after a delay. The existence of rhythms in mood may also make time a decisive factor in determining findings. For example, investigations that only sample mood once or a few times run the risk of capturing only the low or the high point of its rhythm, thus biasing the results.

The limitations of the traditional experimental approach have led to the development of an alternative investigative strategy in recent studies of mood. These studies examine the ways in which mood unfolds over time in natural settings using a design that measures many variables on many occasions from many people. The use of this type of design for investigating patterns of change within individuals over time has been termed a *process approach* (Larsen, 1989). One basic advantage of this approach is that it enables stronger inferences to be made about causal relations.

The process approach integrates fixed and fluid approaches to personality. The *fixed* approach focuses on finding fundamental traits of personality based on averaged behavioural tendencies that individuals exhibit with some consistency. The *fluid* approach focuses on dynamic processes of personality by comparing individuals with themselves at different points in time, rather than with each other at the same point in time. The process approach combines these two approaches by focusing on stable but non-static processes of personality. In particular, temporal patterns are identified within individuals, and compared across individuals, to find consistent patterns of change. For example, different people may exhibit more or less overall variability in their moods (Larsen, 1987) or their mood might be more or less entrained to particular rhythms such as those relating to the menstrual cycle (Larsen & Kasimatis, 1990). These regular temporal patterns of variation that differentiate between individuals are referred to as second-order consistencies. The process approach acknowledges "that the subjects of our investigations are embedded within time, that time is fundamentally important to life as it is lived, and that personality processes take place over time" (Larsen, 1989, p. 179). Thus, the process approach also combines an *idiographic* (individual) and a *nomothetic* (population) approach.

The method of taking frequent repeated measurements of people's experiences has been called *intensive time-sampling*, and the studies employing these methods are sometimes referred to as *diary studies* or *daily experience studies* (even when measurements are recorded at frequencies other than once a day). The basic methodology involves collecting self-reports (and sometimes performance measures) relating to affect and other variables at fixed, event-contingent, or random intervals throughout the course of the day and/or week. It is then possible to chart the developing relationships between these variables over time.

The number of studies employing intensive time-sampling methods has increased rapidly in the last decade (Tennen, Suls, & Affleck, 1991) and shows no signs of deceleration as yet. It is our belief that the process approach has the potential to extend and deepen our general understanding of how psychological functions depend on time-related variables, and holds particular promise for the investigation of the dynamics of mood. (For a more detailed discussion of the specific methods and analysis techniques used in intensive time-sampling studies, see Appendix 1).

SUMMARY

In this chapter we have shown that studying the ways in which moods change over time not only helps psychologists understand the general characteristics of affective processes but also may reveal information about an individual's personality and mental state. We described mood dynamics in relation to three conceptual models. According to the dynamic equilibrium model, mood dynamics are the consequence of processes with a stable and a changeable aspect. Mood is maintained in a state of equilibrium by stable personal characteristics and recurring life events. Changes to the equilibrium have an impact on mood but the equilibrium is eventually restored by adaptive mechanisms. According to the social entrainment model, mood dynamics arise from internal rhythms that are entrained by the influence of external pacer events and other temporally structured factors including those relating to other people's moods. The most important rhythms in mood seem to be daily (circadian) and weekly (circaseptal) rhythms. Although there are links between the dynamic equilibrium and social entrainment models, some phenomena including certain types of non-linear change in mood are not yet explained by either model. However, the non-linear dynamic model of mood is able to account for such changes. According to this model, mood dynamics depend on deterministic processes that produce complex and sometimes apparently random or chaotic behaviour. This does not, however, preclude the possibility that these processes are based on rhythmic pacemakers that are influenced by psychosocial events. It is therefore feasible that the three models may eventually be synthesized within a more powerful explanatory framework of mood dynamics. With respect to methodology, we have suggested that the process approach is probably the most useful for studying mood dynamics. This approach studies individuals intensively over time to uncover consistent patterns of change between people.

6

MOOD REGULATION

OVERVIEW

Previous chapters have described some of the factors that can influence mood and the ways in which it changes over time. However, mood is not something that simply runs its own course in response to internal and external events outside our control. Instead, people often make evaluations of their moods which may in turn lead to active attempts at changing them in some way. The present chapter is concerned with this process of mood regulation. People use a range of cognitive and behavioural strategies to regulate their mood including distracting themselves, taking drugs or drinking alcohol, talking things over with someone else, and trying to deal directly with their current concern. In this chapter, we will review the range of available mood-regulation strategies, consider their relative effectiveness for different people in different circumstances, and examine the question of whether some people are generally better at mood regulation than others. Finally, we will discuss the processes that might underlie mood regulation and the factors that might influence their operation in order to pave the way for Chapter 7's discussion of how regulation might fail in clinical disorders of mood.

INTRODUCTION

One of the most obvious and uncontested facts about moods is that we are often aware of them at a conscious level. For example, we sometimes find ourselves feeling down for no good reason when we "get out of bed on the wrong side", or are suddenly overwhelmed by a definite wave of optimism and positivity. Occasionally, we may even ask ourselves whether there is any point or reason to these kinds of experiences, whether the intrusiveness of mood serves any particular purpose. According to many psychologists (e.g. Mandler, 1984), consciousness serves a control function and allows us to monitor what is happening more precisely in order that we can respond to the situation in a more focused and effective way. Similar reasoning may also be applied to our consciousness of moods: becoming aware of an affective state permits us to evaluate its significance and decide whether it is necessary to do something about it. This, in essence, constitutes the process of mood regulation that will be considered in detail in the present

129

chapter. Awareness of mood leads to its evaluation and appraisal, which may in turn lead to the implementation of deliberate strategies designed to maintain or modify the original affective state.

The most common application of this kind of process occurs when people find themselves in a bad mood, decide that this mood is undesirable, and therefore try to get themselves out of it for straightforward hedonistic reasons. However, there are also other possible varieties of mood regulation. For example, good or bad moods may be sometimes changed to neutral moods, and good moods may even occasionally be deliberately transformed into bad ones (e.g. Parrott, 1993). Furthermore, mood regulation does not always involve a *change* in mood, but may instead depend on its maintenance. For example, we may try to keep ourselves in good, bad, or neutral moods under certain circumstances. These different kinds of mood regulation may enable people to bring about some of the different effects of good and bad mood that were described in Chapter 4, such as when we need to make ourselves less excitable in order to settle down and work seriously on something. Later in the chapter we will elaborate on some of the other reasons why people might want to engage in different types of mood maintenance or change. However, most of the examples of mood regulation described in this chapter will involve the improvement of unpleasant moods, simply because this is the most heavily researched type of mood regulation.

Before we try to do something about our mood, we need to know what it is that we want to do, and only then can we decide what our strategic options are. Mood regulation therefore requires both some way of *evaluating* mood and some way of changing or maintaining mood for its operation. Below, we will examine each of these aspects of regulation in turn. With respect to mood evaluation, we will discuss processes relating to the monitoring of mood, and consider what sources of information about mood are available to these processes. We will also describe individual differences in people's ability to evaluate mood and the potential consequences of those differences. With respect to changing or maintaining mood, we will describe some alternative schemes for understanding and classifying mood-regulation strategies. We will examine the effectiveness of different types of strategy, and describe individual differences in the ability to influence mood. Some general issues relating to everyday mood regulation will then be considered, such as whether people can learn or be taught how to improve their happiness by regulating mood. The final part of this chapter will use our current understanding to map out the basic functions of a model of mood regulation. However, we will start by considering how mood regulation fits in with some of the phenomena described in previous chapters.

REGULATION IN RELATION TO OTHER ASPECTS OF THE MOOD PROCESS

Chapter 4 described how good and bad moods often have different effects. For example, it has been found that pleasant moods tend to bias perception, thinking, judgement, memory, and action towards evaluatively positive content, while un-pleasant moods often (but less consistently) show effects in the opposite direction. In other words, good moods are more likely to show mood-congruency effects than bad moods. One explanation of this asymmetry is that when people are in a bad mood they are more likely to use self-regulatory strategies to try to get themselves out of the mood, whereas people in a good mood are more likely to try to maintain it. Such processes could also prevent negative material from being consolidated in memory, hence making associative recall of unpleasant events less likely.

The previous chapter described various types of mood change. Some changes in mood may be of a sufficient size or intensity to automatically attract conscious attention. The person concerned may then decide on a course of action that involves instigating cognitive or behavioural strategies to correct, sustain, or change the mood. If this speculation is correct then we might expect unpleasant moods to be quickly repaired following stressful events. The fact that bad moods rarely seem to persist for very long, usually disappearing by the day following a stressful event (see Chapter 5), is consistent with this conclusion. Morris (1989) suggested three possible explanations for this lack of endurance of moods. First, it is possible that moods may decay spontaneously. Second, they may automatically instigate opponent processes which counteract the original affective state. Third and finally, moods may be changed by self-regulatory processes of some kind. The second opponent-process explanation could also be viewed as a type of mood regulation even though the processes are automatic and probably operate below the level of consciousness.

As well as causing mood regulation, mood changes may also arise as its direct consequence. Although many of the mood changes described in Chapter 5 probably occur in response to external events, some of them may depend instead (or in addition) on conscious and/or non-conscious mood regulation processes. For example, we described research suggesting that adolescents tend to have more changeable mood because of their peer-oriented lifestyle. However, it is also likely that adolescents deliberately engage in many of the activities that cause their moods to change. In other words, adolescents may be regulating their moods through their choice of activity, and causing it to be more volatile than it would otherwise be, even if they are not explicitly conscious of doing so.

Table 6.1 presents the basic distinctions between conscious and non-conscious mood regulation processes. In this chapter we will concentrate on conscious (in the sense of aware and deliberate) mood-regulation processes, but the boundary between conscious and non-conscious mood regulation is not always clear (see also Chapter 8). For example, helping another person can sometimes serve the function of alleviating one's bad mood by making the helper feel better about himself or herself. However, this does not necessarily mean that people help others with the explicit conscious intention of improving their mood, even though their helping clearly does fulfil that function. Indeed, this kind of mood regulation would probably fail if people were fully aware that their helping was done for

Table 6.1 Conscious and unconscious mood-regulation processes

	Evaluating Mood	*Changing Mood*
Conscious Processes	Conscious monitoring and appraisal of mood (e.g. mood awareness)	Deliberate selection and use of regulation strategies (e.g. positive thinking)
Non-conscious Processes	Non-conscious monitoring and appraisal of mood (e.g. ironic monitor)	Automatic selection and use of regulation strategies (e.g. opponent processes)

selfish rather than altruistic reasons. On the other hand, helping others clearly does represent a form of mood regulation to the extent that it seems to depend upon a need for mood improvement and a lack of alternative easier options for meeting this need. For example, Cialdini, Darby, and Vincent (1973) found that people are less likely to help if other means are available for alleviating their bad mood. Thus, mood regulation may be directed and partly intentional without being completely conscious or explicit.

EVALUATING MOOD

The ability to affect one's own psychological processes has been termed *mental control* (see Wegner & Pennebaker, 1993). One aspect of mental control concerns the monitoring and use of feelings to guide future thinking and actions: a capacity referred to by Salovey, Hsee, and Mayer (1993) as *emotional intelligence*. According to these investigators, three domains of emotional intelligence may be distinguished: the first of these concerns accurate appraisal and expression of emotion in oneself and in others; the second relates to adaptive regulation of emotion (again in both oneself and others); and the third involves the ability to utilize emotions. The first two of these domains encompass the general topic of mood regulation as defined in this chapter. In this section we will review the specific aspect of the first domain that is necessary for mood regulation, namely the ability to evaluate mood. Mood evaluation involves monitoring and appraising one's own, or other people's, moods. Any theory of mood regulation necessarily presupposes some process relating to mood evaluation of this kind because people must be able to detect on some level whether their mood is discrepant with their requirements and hence whether change is necessary.

Processes of mood monitoring

Mood monitoring occurs whenever information concerning mood is registered by, or provides input for, any psychological process or function. Thus, mood information must be represented somewhere in the cognitive system for mood monitoring to occur. In some cases, mood may be registered consciously, but in other cases mood provides an input for monitoring processes that operate below the level of awareness. For example, deliberate mood regulation probably depends on explicit conscious representation of mood information, whereas non-conscious mood regulation does not necessarily require conscious awareness. According to Morris (1992), mood states often go unnoticed although small fluctuations are registered and corrected by self-regulatory mechanisms. However, major changes in mood typically enter focal awareness and require explanation and often action.

Two modes of conscious affective experience have been distinguished. *Reflexive* experience implies awareness of the affect experience itself, whereas *irreflexive* experience involves feeling the affect "from the inside" (Frijda, 1986; Sartre, 1962). In other words, the irreflexive aspect of affect colours experience but is not necessarily itself the object of consciousness. For example, *knowing that* one is unhappy is a reflexive experience but simply *feeling* unhappy is an irreflexive experience. It is possible to experience a mood irreflexively without also having any reflexive experience of it: for example, during irreflexive experience a person may even deny being in a particular mood, as often happens when we are accused of being grumpy. However, many common experiences of mood have both reflexive and irreflexive aspects with the individual feeling the mood as well as knowing that he or she is feeling it. From the point of view of the monitoring process, it seems likely that mood must be experienced reflexively before it can be consciously monitored in an explicit way, but simple irreflexive experience may provide signals that are used in non-conscious monitoring.

One of the commonly accepted functions of consciousness is to allow more flexible control over cognitive processing (e.g. Mandler, 1984). It seems probable, therefore, that conscious reflexive mood monitoring involves controlled processing whereas non-conscious mood monitoring depends on automatic processing (see Shiffrin & Schneider, 1977). This should mean that competing cognitive demands will interfere more with conscious mood monitoring than with automatic monitoring. Wegner, Erber, and Zanakos (1993) have found some evidence to support this hypothesis.

Wegner and colleagues proposed that there is an ironic monitoring process which runs automatically whenever people engage in intentional mood regulation (see Chapter 4). This ironic process checks for the presence of information that would signal that the intentional process is not reaching its goal, making the person hypersensitive to the occurrence of that information. For example, when a person is trying to get into a good mood, the ironic process searches for evidence that good mood is not being achieved, and picks up the slightest indication of unpleasant affect. Therefore, when competing tasks interfere with the intentional process, the ironic monitor brings affective material into consciousness that has the opposite effect on mood to that intended. In the above example, negative material is brought into consciousness and the person ends up in a mood that is even more unpleasant than before. This reasoning might help to explain why our efforts to suppress our fear or depression often only seem to make things worse (e.g. Wegner, 1989; 1994, and see Chapter 7).

In support of their theory, Wegner and colleagues have shown that when people tried to get into a good or a bad mood at the same time as undertaking a cognitive task, they ended up in a mood opposite to the one intended. The study also found that words related to the non-intended rather than the intended mood produced greater semantic interference on a colour-naming task when participants were put under cognitive load. This suggests that there was greater cognitive accessibility to topics related to the non-intended or ironic mood.

There are differences of opinion concerning the way in which information about mood is represented and accessed. These differences have potential consequences for the form or structure of monitoring processes. The commonsense view is that mood is represented as a special kind of internal signal, akin to an energy level, that can be accessed directly using some form of simple readout (e.g. Buck, 1985). Other theories assume that reflexive judgements of affective state are inferences based on channels of relevant information arising from the body and environment (e.g. Valins, 1966). This means that mood monitoring may depend on relatively high-level cognitive decision processes. Another view is that affective experience is based not on reasoning but on a complex perceptual construct derived from multiple channels of information (e.g. Laird & Bresler, 1992). In the next section we consider the various kinds of internal and external information that could be used by mood-monitoring processes.

Sources of information about mood

Since the time of William James (e.g. James, 1898), it has commonly been assumed that affective experience depends, directly or indirectly, on feedback from bodily states, in particular from visceral changes including heart-rate, feelings of internal heat, and general arousal. The problem with accounts of monitoring based on internal sensations is that people seem to be poor at discriminating the relevant stimuli. For example, Pennebaker (1981) found that judgements about heart-rate were more responsive to external than internal stimuli. However, the fact that people believe that affect is connected with bodily reaction (e.g. Parkinson, 1990) suggests that they will rely on bodily signals as an indication of their affect in some circumstances.

Facial-feedback theory (e.g. Laird, 1974) assumes that people use information from their own facial expressions and facial movements to draw conclusions about their affective experience. Feedback from posture can also provide cues about affect. For example, people are more likely to characterize themselves as experiencing sadness when they are in a slumped seating position (Duclos et al., 1989). Research has shown that both facial and postural feedback can influence affective judgements irrespective of whether or not the feedback is explicitly represented in consciousness (e.g. Stepper & Strack, 1993; Zajonc, Murphy & Inglehart, 1989).

If mood is viewed as something distinct from its various bodily manifestations, then it is also possible that monitoring could directly access the intrinsic quality of mood. Zajonc and co-workers (1989), for example, have argued that specific neurotransmitters have direct effects on affective state which are immediately detected at the subjective level.

People can also infer that they are in a particular affective state from external cues such as their own behaviour and their situation. Indeed, Bem's (1972) self-perception theory suggests that people may infer their affect from observation of their own behaviour when internal cues are weak or ambiguous. As an example of an affective inference based on situational information, Kellerman, Lewis, and Laird (1989) found that self-reported feelings of passionate love were influenced by whether room lighting was soft and whether "romantic" music was playing.

Another important external source of information about affect is other people. Other people's responses can provide us with cues that our own mood requires monitoring. For example, we are more likely to pay attention to ourselves, and in particular to our moods and how we are expressing them, when other people react in a disturbed manner to something that we say or do. Such a process of self-attention can help us to work out what we are doing to bring about this interpersonal reaction. Relatedly, Buck (1989) has argued that a process of social biofeedback leads us to a better understanding of our own feelings. In his view, people receive signals about their expressions, and hence probably also their experiences, from the expressions of other people. Of course, sometimes people will also receive more direct verbal descriptions of their mood from other people, and this information too can be used in the mood-monitoring process.

So far, this discussion of the sources of affective information has worked from the familiar assumption that the relevant internal or external signals are registered at a single moment rather than over the course of more extended periods. However, people may have to generalize over time from these momentary experiences in order to infer their own mood. For example, if someone suggests to us that we have been in a bad mood all day, we may review our feelings and actions and their effects on other people since waking and conclude that we have been and indeed still are in a bad mood. Our own research (Parkinson, Briner, Reynolds, & Totterdell, 1995) suggests that generalized daily judgements of mood correspond quite closely to the average of momentary assessments made during the day. This finding suggests either that people can quite accurately aggregate internally sensed mood levels over time or that each separate assessment is already based on an extended period of time.

Individual differences in mood evaluation

According to Salovey and colleagues (1993), the precursors of emotional self-regulation are the predisposition to engage in regulation and the availability of strategies for regulation. In this section we will describe some of the factors that Salovey and colleagues have identified as affecting the predisposition for regulation, including level of emotional awareness and the meta-experience of mood.

As we have already described, mood regulation requires some form of mood monitoring, and mood monitoring at a conscious level requires some form of self-awareness. One aspect of self-awareness is *self-focused attention*, which refers to the allocation of attention towards internal thoughts and feelings rather than the external world. Self-focus can be brought about in a number of ways. For example, the presence of self-directing stimuli such as mirrors and cameras tends to increase self-focus. Mood itself, particularly negative affect, can also draw attention to the self (e.g. Ingram, 1990; Salovey, 1992). In addition, some individuals are dispositionally more self-focused than others. Self-focused individuals tend to score high on the personality dimension of private self-consciousness (Fenigstein, Scheier, & Buss, 1975).

Of specific relevance to the present discussion is the aspect of self-awareness known as *mood awareness* which refers to people's attention towards their own mood. Swinkels and Giuliano (1995) have identified two dimensions of mood awareness: *mood monitoring* and *mood labelling*. Individuals who score high on the mood monitoring dimension tend to scrutinize and focus on their moods across a wide range of situations, while individuals who score high on the mood labelling dimension have an ability to identify and categorize their moods. Compared with low mood monitors, high mood monitors tend to score higher on self-consciousness, be more neurotic, have lower self-esteem, and experience greater negative affect. Compared with low mood labellers, high mood labellers tend to be less socially anxious, less neurotic, more extravert, more non-verbally expressive, and experience greater positive affect. High mood labellers also score lower on a scale of *alexithymia*, which makes intuitive sense because this is a condition defined in terms of inability to identify feelings.

Individuals may also differ in their *meta-experience of mood*, which refers to the reflective experience of mood and involves the conscious evaluation and regulation of mood (Mayer & Gaschke, 1988). Meta-mood experiences include people's feelings about whether their moods are clear, acceptable, typical, under control, or about to change. Mayer and Gaschke have shown that the experience and meta-experience of mood are partially independent of each other. For example, at the meta-mood level, relaxed moods are evaluated as more acceptable and less out of control than moods that are characterized by positive affect.

Salovey and colleagues (1993) have distinguished between state and trait meta-mood experiences. The former are cognitions that individuals have while actually experiencing a mood, whereas the latter are more general longer-standing cognitions that individuals have about their moods. Salovey, Mayer, Goldman, Turvey, and Palfai (1995) have developed a questionnaire measure assessing trait meta-mood experience which contains three subscales relating to *attention* to moods, *clarity* in discriminating among feelings, and *beliefs* about maintaining good moods and repairing bad moods. Attention and clarity appear to be similar to the mood-awareness dimensions of monitoring and labelling in terms of their relationships with other variables. For example, people who typically allocate more attention to their moods tend to have greater self-consciousness, and people who display greater clarity about their moods are less likely to be depressed and have less ambivalence over their emotional expression.

Mayer and Stevens (1994) have attempted to synthesize and extend findings in this area using an approach which splits the meta-experience of mood into the two domains of evaluation and regulation. In their framework, evaluation of feelings includes clarity, acceptance, novelty, and influence over moods, and regulation of feelings includes repair, maintenance, and dampening of moods.

So far we have seen that there are different dimensions to the evaluation and regulation of mood and that individuals differ on these dimensions. However, it is also of interest to determine whether differences in the evaluation of mood affect people's ability to regulate their moods. Giuliano (1995) has shown that individual differences in mood awareness predicts mood regulation. In particular, high mood labellers reported greater positive moods following positive and negative mood inductions than low mood labellers, and high mood monitors reported greater negative moods following a negative mood induction than low mood monitors. In other words, people who are good at characterizing their moods also seem better able to get themselves out of a bad mood or maintain a good mood, while people who are chronically attentive to their mood states are also more sensitive to unpleasant events. In addition, Swinkels and Giuliano (1995) found that high mood monitors report less success at regulating their moods than low mood monitors.

High mood monitors are also more likely to report using regulation strategies that involved *rumination*, which is the tendency to dwell on, and mull over, the negative aspects of a situation. Salovey and colleagues (1995) found that individuals who reported being clear about their moods showed a greater decline in rumination and greater mood recovery following a negative mood induction than individuals with low clarity. People ruminate partly because they feel that it gives them an insight into their feelings (Lyubomirsky & Nolen-Hoeksema, 1993), whereas in practice rumination seems more likely to perpetuate depressed mood. Strategies that involve distracting attention away from the negative mood have been generally shown to be more effective than rumination (e.g. Nolen-Hoeskema, Morrow, & Fredrickson, 1993). More specifically, Lavallee and Campbell (1995) found that negative events that are related to people's current goals elicit greater regulatory responses such as rumination, and that it is these regulatory responses that are responsible for moods being more negative following goal-related negative events. However, it seems possible that rumination serves important functions other than those relating to immediate affect regulation and that these unrelated benefits may sometimes outweigh its short-term costs for mood.

We began this section on individual differences by describing the possible role of self-focused attention in the evaluation of mood. Some researchers believe that self-focused attention leads to unpleasant mood, and that unpleasant mood in turn leads to greater self-focused attention (see Lavallee and Campbell, 1995). The findings concerning rumination seem to support this view. However, as we shall see in the next section, self-focused attention arising in response to unpleasant moods can also lead to regulatory responses that alleviate the affect. Fortunately, this contradiction can probably be resolved by distinguishing between different dimensions of the evaluation of mood. For example, a high level of mood monitoring seems to initiate maladaptive regulation strategies such as rumination which lead to negative mood outcomes, whereas mood labelling seems to be associated with more productive strategies such as seeking social support (Swinkels & Giuliano, 1995). Of course, it is also likely that different strategies are differentially effective in different situations, and that even rumination may sometimes bring beneficial consequences for mood in the long term.

In summary, up to this point we have described what is currently known about the evaluation of mood. We have considered the various processes that may be involved in the monitoring and appraisal of mood, described the various sources of information about mood that are available to these processes, and examined how individuals differ in their ability to evaluate their mood. We have also discussed how these individual differences appear to influence the types of mood-regulation strategies that are implemented as well as predicting people's success in changing their moods. In the next section, we examine people's use of strategies for changing mood in further detail.

CHANGING MOOD

This section will consider the types of deliberate strategy that people use to bring about changes in their mood. In most instances, these strategies are intended to repair negative moods but, as we shall see later, other types of mood regulation are also possible. We will discuss what is known about the effectiveness of different types of mood-regulation strategy and briefly examine individual differences relating to their use. However, this research area is very much in its infancy and so the findings are as yet relatively sparse and the theories undeveloped. For example, most of the relevant conceptual and empirical work has either relied on clinical observations or borrowed from related areas such as coping. The relative paucity of work on this topic is reflected in the fact that at the time of writing we have found only three attempts to provide a reasonably comprehensive account of mood-regulation strategies. We shall describe these three models below.

Classifying mood regulation strategies

Morris and Reilly (1987; see also Morris, 1989) proposed a system for categorizing mood regulation strategies adapted from Pearlin and Schooler's (1978) system for classifying stress and coping strategies. They proposed three main categories of regulation. First, there are strategies that aim to manage mood directly, or work on the affect itself. These strategies include self-rewards, using alcohol, distraction, and the management of expressive behaviour. Second, there are strategies that aim to redefine the significance of the mood; in other words, the strategies change what the mood means to the person. These strategies include downward comparison (thinking of people who are worse off than oneself), attributional bias (internalizing success and externalizing failure), and cognitive reinterpretation. Third, there are strategies that aim to eliminate the cause of the mood by taking direct action on whatever produced the mood. These strategies include various types of problem-focused action such as engaging in increased effort to deal with the situation.

Morris and Reilly also identified affiliation as a fourth category of regulation. This category, which includes strategies of seeking social support, was identified as conceptually separate but related to the other three categories because the strategies that it contains can be used to implement each of the other categories. For example, social interaction can help manage the mood by being distracting, or it can reduce the significance of the mood, or it can eliminate the problem. We will consider the evidence for the use and effectiveness of some of the individual strategies from Morris and Reilly's four categories in the next section.

The theoretical basis for Thayer, Newman, and McClain's (1994) classification of mood-regulation strategies is Thayer's (1989) own two-dimensional biopsychological theory of mood. In this theory, the two dimensions of mood are associated with central states of bodily arousal and relate to *energy* (comparable to positive affect as defined in Chapter 2) and *tension* (related to negative affect). Self-regulatory behaviours are therefore designed either to raise energy or to reduce tension to optimal (but possibly changing) levels. Sometimes a mood-regulatory activity will affect only one dimension but many activities will affect both dimensions simultaneously. For example, exercise can simultaneously enhance energy and reduce tension. This, and the fact that exercise engages multiple physical and cognitive systems, is thought to make exercise a particularly effective strategy for affect regulation.

Thayer and colleagues identified 32 categories of mood-regulation behaviour by asking people how they usually changed a bad mood, how they increased their level of energy, and how they reduced tension. The categories of behaviour reported in connection with changing bad mood and those said to enhance energy and reduce tension were almost completely overlapping, which was taken as further evidence of the validity of the two-dimensional model. The strategies were then put into a fixed-response questionnaire and administered to a larger sample. Factor analysis of the responses produced six groups of strategy for changing a bad mood. These were identified as: active mood management; seeking pleasurable activities and distraction; passive mood management; support, ventilation and gratification; direct tension reduction; and withdrawal–avoidance. Similar analysis of the strategies used to raise energy yielded three factors: activity; reduced activity and rest; and use of stimulating substances (e.g. caffeine). Finally, the strategies for tension reduction were aligned with respect to three factors: emotional expression, food and drugs; muscle relaxation, cognitive control and stress management; and pleasant distraction. As Thayer and colleagues acknowledged, the structure of these factors was not as strong as desirable. This is probably because the factors combine independent behavioural categories. Active mood management, for example, includes strategies such as putting feelings into perspective, exercising, having a shower, self-gratification, and humour.

Westen (1994) has developed a rather different theoretical approach to understanding affect regulation. In his model, feelings are seen as mechanisms for selecting and retaining regulatory strategies, so that pleasant affective states reinforce the use of strategies and unpleasant affective states reduce their future probability. For example, if our experience teaches us that exercising generally makes us feel better, we will come to use exercise on other occasions with that specific purpose in mind. Thus, individuals develop a range of possible behavioural and mental strategies for regulating aversive affective states and maximizing pleasurable states. Strategies that have proved successful are more likely to be used again in similar situations.

Westen describes how his model can be used to interpret and integrate theory and research from a number of domains including behavioural, cognitive, evolutionary, and psychodynamic psychology. The model is also applicable to a range of social-cognitive phenomena relating to experienced discrepancies between reality and beliefs about the self. For instance, confrontation of another person who is obviously in need of assistance may lead to a mismatch between personal standards relating to the desirability of prosocial behaviour and the perception that no action has been taken by the self to meet these standards. This may cause a feeling of guilt that in turn activates a strategy such as helping behaviour. If helping successfully regulates the person's guilt then it is likely to be used again in similar circumstances in accordance with the principles stated above. However, if helping is not a viable option or has been previously unsuccessful then an alternative strategy such as denigrating the sufferer may be activated to alleviate the guilt (see Morris, 1989).

From an evolutionary perspective, Westen's model proposes that feelings are used to channel behaviour in adaptive directions. Some behavioural responses are biologically primitive and triggered automatically by psychophysiological states, such as the fight or flight response elicited by fear, whereas other responses involve more complex procedural skills that are learnt over time. According to Westen's view, people may also maintain and use responses that are no longer adaptive. For example, there is plenty of evidence from psychodynamic research that people frequently repress or distort information in order to avoid unpleasant feelings (see Chapter 7). These responses sometimes develop in childhood and persist into adulthood despite changes in circumstances which make them no longer appropriate. Psychodynamic accounts have also argued that people often hold multiple contradictory goals and therefore need to regulate multiple simultaneous affects.

The main distinguishing feature of Westen's model is that it assumes that regulatory responses are tailored to specific affects, whereas coping theories assume that responses are activated more generally by stressful circumstances. In a test of his model, Westen (1994) showed that different emotions evoke different kinds of regulatory responses. For example, anxiety was more likely to be associated with responses aimed at stifling the emotion, whereas guilt was more likely to be associated with responses aimed at making amends, such as apologizing or helping. However, Westen found that people who experience one unpleasant emotion are also more likely to experience other unpleasant emotions and hence are likely to use a range of regulatory strategies across the board.

Some of the work on the meta-experience of mood, which we described in the previous section, also suggests a way in which moods could select regulatory strategies. Mayer and Gaschke (1988) speculated that the co-occurrence of moods with meta-mood experiences over many situations could provide data allowing individuals to build theories about the situations that bring about specific moods. For example, a person may learn with experience to bring about situations that are associated with pleasant and understandable moods.

General impact of regulation strategies on affect

Although the three models of mood regulation described above adopt different theoretical stances and hence classify regulatory strategies differently, they all incorporate similar types of strategy. In this section we describe research that demonstrates that these strategies work in general, and in the next section we consider research assessing the relative effectiveness of different types of strategy.

We will begin by considering some cognitive strategies for alleviating a bad mood. One such strategy is to think about something pleasant such as a happy memory. This strategy probably works by triggering pleasant associations and priming other happy thoughts and feelings. Correspondingly, thinking about unpleasant events during a good mood should attenuate the pleasantness of this mood. Erber and Erber (1994) found exactly these effects of mood-incongruent recall following negative and positive mood inductions. The effects were greatest when people exerted more effort in recalling a mood-incongruent memory. This increased effort probably reduced participants' available cognitive capacity for processing mood-congruent thoughts.

Although mood-incongruent recall might have a beneficial impact on affect during unpleasant moods, in practice, mood-congruent recall seems to be a more common response in experiments assessing mood effects (see Chapter 4). However, Parrott and Sabini (1990) argued that one of the reasons for this is that participants recognize that the investigators are interested in how mood operates and therefore try to cooperate by maintaining rather than attempting to change mood. Consistent with this reasoning, these investigators found that mood-incongruent recall was more likely when people were not aware that their moods were relevant to the purposes of the study. Erber and Erber (1994) also found that mood-incongruent recall was more likely when people had a particular incentive to change their mood. For example, students were more likely to use mood-incongruent recall to alleviate a bad mood when they were about to participate in a class and therefore needed to be rid of any distractions in order to concentrate properly, whereas mood-congruent thoughts were more likely at the end of class.

Thinking about the future can also regulate mood. Persson and Sjöberg (1985) found that the negative aspects of anticipated events adversely affected current mood. Similarly, in our own research (Totterdell, Parkinson, Briner, & Reynolds, 1995) we have found that daily mood is more influenced by anticipated mood and subsequent events than by mood and events from the previous day. If people use thoughts about the future to alleviate bad moods, it would be expected that they would mostly imagine behaviours and circumstances that lead to pleasant affect. In support of this, Staats and Skowronski (1992) found that people perceived pleasant emotion terms as more applicable to their future experience than to their current experience. According to Tversky and Griffin (1991), expectations can have a hedonic impact whether or not the expected events actually happen. They suggest that expectations may influence mood in two opposing ways: first, the pleasantness or unpleasantness of the anticipated event may have direct and congruent consequences for mood, making people feel better, for example, when expectations are high (*endowment* effect). Second, expectations may exert a *contrast* effect by making what actually happens seem better or worse by comparison with what was anticipated. Although Tversky and Griffin suggest that these effects can both occur in response to the same expectation, one often outweighs the other, yielding a combined positive or negative impact on mood. The example that they give is that the dream of winning the lottery may enhance mood more than the disappointment of losing.

There is also evidence that positive thinking can improve mood. For example, if we assume that our affective reactions to events depend mainly on the way that these events are cognitively processed or evaluated (e.g. Lazarus, 1991), then selective attention to different aspects of these events is likely to make a difference to how they make us feel (e.g. Lazarus & Alfert, 1964). Thus, focusing on the positive aspects of an unpleasant event may reduce or even reverse its negative impact on mood. Goodhart (1985) found that positive thinking was associated with enhanced mood and that negative thinking was associated with worse mood when people evaluated a recent stressful event, but that only negative thinking predicted (worse) mood eight weeks later. Negative thinking also appeared to exacerbate the negative impact of subsequent events on positive affect. Further, positive and negative thoughts had a greater effect on mood when they concerned the self rather than external consequences. These findings suggest that the absence of negative thoughts, particularly self-relevant thoughts, may be more important in the long-term regulation of mood than positive thinking *per se*.

In their everyday reasoning about the causes of personal performance outcomes, people generally seem to show attributional biases that support positive views of themselves. In particular, they tend to attribute failures to external causes such as bad luck, and success to internal causes such as skill or effort (Zuckerman, 1979). These attributional biases also appear to influence mood (McFarlane & Ross, 1982), and their absence may be related to the development and maintenance of clinical depression (Alloy & Abramson, 1979). We might therefore conclude that certain interpretations of the causes of events serve the function of preventing bad moods and encouraging good ones.

Morris (1989) describes a number of other cognitive adjustments that people may make to modify the meaning or significance of a problem in order to reduce distress. One of these is downward comparison, in which people evaluate themselves in relation to others who are worse off. However, downward comparison may not be an effective strategy for everyone, and may have a different impact in different situations. For example, thinking about people who are relatively more deprived may lead to empathic concern and activate unpleasant associations as well as making one's own situation seem preferable by contrast. Aspinwall and Taylor (1993) found that only people with low self-esteem who had received a recent setback or who were put in a bad mood benefited from exposure to downward comparison information.

Various behavioural as well as cognitive strategies may be used to regulate mood. For example, just as people can think about pleasant things, they can also do pleasant things to make themselves feel better (*self-reward*). The technique of using rewards to improve affect is a common feature of many behavioural therapies which work from the general assumption that clinical depression is maintained by the lack of available reinforcing experiences (e.g. Lewinsohn & Graf, 1973). Consistent with this approach, Heiby (1983) has found that people who have a low frequency of self-reinforcement are likely to become more depressed following a decrease in external rewards. Under experimental conditions, non-depressed students who were instructed to increase the number of pleasant events that they experienced and to focus on the pleasantness of those events, showed a significant decrease in their level of depression (Dobson & Joffe, 1986). However, Morris (1989) describes similar studies that have found that instructing people to increase the frequency of their pleasurable activities can actually increase depressed mood, possibly because responding to instructions reduces people's sense of control. Although studies investigating everyday spontaneous behaviour have shown positive correlations between pleasurable activities and pleasant mood, it is not clear whether this reflects the impact of rewarding activity on mood, the effects of pleasant mood on activity, or both (see Morris, 1989).

Consumption of food, caffeine, nicotine, alcohol, and other drugs can all regulate mood. Intake of carbohydrates, in the form of sweets or starch, has been found to increase fatigue (e.g. Spring, Lieberman, Swope, & Garfield, 1986), but there is also evidence that spontaneous increased sweet consumption during a night shift reduces fatigue (Kräuchi, Nussbaum, & Wirz-Justice, 1990). Similarly, patients with seasonal affective disorder increase their intake of carbohydrates during winter depression, but no longer crave carbohydrates following phototherapy, which suggests that the increased intake represents a "self-healing attempt" (Kräuchi, Wirz-Justice, & Graw, 1990). There is also evidence that ingestion of psychostimulants such as tea, coffee, and nicotine are partly related to individual differences in people's level of activation at different times of day, implying that people may be attempting to modify this level in using these substances (Adan, 1994).

143

Alcohol is commonly reputed to act as a tension reducer. However, although there is some evidence that alcohol is used to moderate negative feelings (Marlatt, Kosturn, & Lang, 1975) and to improve mood (Hull & Bond, 1986), longer-term consumption of alcohol may actually increase depressed feelings (Anshensel & Huba, 1983). There is also evidence that the decision to consume alcohol bears little relation to current mood (DeCastro, 1990), which suggests that drinking is not spontaneously used for mood-regulation purposes. However, the recreational use of other drugs, such as cannabis and ecstasy, suggests that people can and do use them to achieve specific mood effects at particular times for particular activities.

Activity and exercise can also function as mood regulators. Taking moderate exercise, such as a five-minute walk, has been found to increase participants' arousal and reduce their desire to smoke or snack, suggesting that these alternative strategies may be interchangeable (Thayer, Peters, Takahashi, & Birkhead-Flight, 1992). Berger and Owen (1992) compared the impact of swimming (aerobic exercise) and yoga (non-aerobic exercise), and found that both activities resulted in decreases in tension, fatigue, and anger. High-intensity aerobic exercise, on the other hand, can lead to increases in tension and fatigue, even in people who are fit (Steptoe & Cox, 1988). These results suggest that moderate exercise is a better strategy for enhancing mood.

At the other end of the spectrum, strategies involving relaxation and rest can also enhance positive moods. However, there is some evidence that relaxation techniques can induce anxiety in some individuals (see Heide & Borkovec, 1984), although this probably only applies to a small number of people. Relaxation can include strategies involving sleep patterns and napping. Our own research suggests that going to sleep a little earlier than normal can enhance alertness and cheerfulness on the following day (Totterdell, Reynolds, Parkinson, & Briner, 1994). Napping can also be effective in some situations. For example, taking a nap before or during a night shift (e.g. Harma, Knauth, & Ilmarinen, 1989; Smith & Wilson, 1990) has been found to have beneficial effects for alertness; although negative effects have appeared in other studies (e.g. Rosa, 1993).

People can also change their mood by engaging in activities that divert attention away from their unpleasant feelings. For example, watching television (Zillmann, 1988) and listening to music (Locke & Keltner, 1993) are sometimes used for this purpose. Alternatively, people may regulate their mood by engaging in activities that eliminate the cause of the bad mood (Morris, 1989). For example, people might take steps to have their workload reduced. A wide range of activities can potentially fulfil distracting and problem-directed regulatory functions.

Earlier in the chapter we described how feedback from the face and from posture may provide a source of information about mood. It therefore seems possible that people learn to manage these expressive behaviours in order to regulate how they feel. Alternatively, people may control their expressions because of the effects that they have on other people's feelings. In other words, people may display an emotion without actually experiencing it, for social reasons (cf. Clark, Pataki, & Carver, 1995). Some jobs, such as that of flight attendant,

Table 6.2 Examples of different types of mood regulation strategy used to get out of a bad mood

Type of Strategy	Example of Strategy
Cognitive strategies	
Thinking of pleasant things	Think of things that make me happy
Anticipation	Think of a future event that I'm looking forward to
Positive thinking	Look on the bright side
Reinterpretation	Think about people who are worse off than me
Relaxation	Meditate
Rationalization	Try to understand my feelings
Acceptance	Let myself feel bad
Avoidance	Try to put it out of my mind
Behavioural strategies	
Doing pleasant things	Buy something for myself
Use of stimulants	Have a cup of coffee
Exercise	Go running
Relaxation	Take a break
Distraction	Keep busy
Problem-directed	Try to solve the problem
Sociotropic	Tell someone how I'm feeling
Expressive	Act happy
Venting feelings	Let off steam
Withdrawal	Spend some time alone

explicitly require and teach this type of surface acting (Hochschild, 1983). An alternative regulation strategy suggested by Hochschild is *deep* (or *method*) *acting*, which involves taking on the evaluations and thought patterns implied by the required affect and not just the associated overt expressions. Of course, expressive behaviour is not always intended to deceive and may in many circumstances be specifically used to convey genuine feelings. This kind of deliberate expression of real moods can also serve as a regulatory strategy. For example, signalling distress could indirectly alleviate unhappiness by triggering social support. However, the evidence suggests that people are just as likely to avoid as they are to seek the company of other people when they are in a bad mood (cf. Coyne, 1976, and see Morris, 1989).

In our own research we have collected examples of regulation strategies that people report using to get themselves out of bad moods. These reported regulation strategies were gathered from a number of sources, including questionnaire and interview studies. Even after eliminating identical and near-identical strategies, we were able to identify over 200 strategies. Although some of these strategies are similar in content, none of them are precisely the same. Undoubtedly, there are also strategies that we have not yet come across, or that have yet to be developed. In Table 6.2, we have picked out a few examples of strategies from our list that correspond to the types of mood-regulation considered in the preceding discussion.

Differential usage and effectiveness of regulation strategies

Having considered the range of available regulation strategies and how they might work in general terms, we now turn to questions relating to their relative frequency of use by people in everyday life, and more importantly their differential effectiveness across situations. The study by Thayer and colleagues (1994) mentioned above provides some information of this sort. The results of their study were based on people's *judgements* of which strategies they used the most and which they believed to be the most effective. Actual usage and actual effectiveness may therefore be different in practice. Disregarding this limitation, the study found that social interaction and cognitive techniques were rated as the most commonly used methods of mood regulation. The five most frequently used strategies for changing a bad mood were, in descending order: talking to or being with someone, controlling thoughts (e.g. by thinking positively), listening to music, avoiding the cause of the mood, and being alone. The five strategies rated as most effective were, in descending order: exercising, listening to music, talking to or being with someone, tending to chores, and resting, napping, or sleeping. Strategies that are used a lot but appear to be relatively less effective included avoiding the cause of a mood and trying to be alone. One of the problems with these descriptive findings, however, is that different strategies were represented at different generality. For example, "listening to music", "exercising" and "being alone" may in many circumstances be seen as subcategories of the more inclusive mood-regulation strategy of "avoiding the cause of a mood".

When the strategies were grouped into the six factors described earlier in this chapter, the strategies within active mood management and seeking pleasurable activities/distraction were first and second in rated effectiveness respectively. Direct tension reduction, which included using drugs, alcohol and sex, was least effective. "Expert ratings" by psychotherapists of the likely effectiveness of the six factors generally supported the order of these rankings. With respect to enhancing energy, controlling thoughts was rated as the single most effective strategy, and strategies involving activity were generally seen as more effective than those involving rest or stimulants. To reduce tension, religious or spritual activity was judged as the single most effective strategy, and strategies involving pleasant distraction were thought to be generally effective, although watching TV was not.

Individual differences in mood regulation

At the end of the section on evaluating mood, we saw that individual differences in people's ability to evaluate their mood had consequences for their ability to change mood. There may also be some individual differences that relate more directly to the deployment of regulation strategies. For example, some people may be more likely than others to use regulation strategies in general, and people may differ in the types of strategy that they are likely to use.

Catanzaro and Mearns (1990) developed a scale to measure people's generalized *negative mood regulation* expectancies (NMR). This refers to the extent to which people believe that their negative moods are controllable. They found that people with lower NMR scores reported higher levels of distress (Kirsch, Mearns, & Catanzaro, 1990). Lower NMR also seems to predict a slower rate of recovery from undesirable events such as the end of a romantic relationship (Mearns, 1991). Thus, people who believe that they can change an unpleasant mood also tend to be more successful at mood regulation in reality, although the particular aspects of regulation ability that lead to this effect are presently unknown.

People's level of self-esteem may also influence regulation-related behaviours and cognitions. Using a mood-induction procedure, Brown and Mankowski (1993) found that individuals with low self-esteem (LSE) shifted their self-evaluations in a downward direction while in an unpleasant mood. According to these investigators, this effect means that people suffering from LSE will find it more difficult to recover from unpleasant moods, because the consequent lowered self evaluations tend to sustain congruent affect. Similarly, Smith and Petty (1995) found that LSE participants exhibited mood-congruent recall when induced into a negative mood, whereas individuals with high self-esteem (HSE) showed mood-incongruent recall. In other words, only HSE individuals seemed to counteract bad moods by thinking about pleasant things. One possible explanation for this effect is that HSE individuals believe on the basis of previous experience that this strategy will work. Alternatively, people with HSE may simply be better at using regulation strategies in general. It is also possible that the relationship between self-esteem and regulation ability works in the opposite direction, with experience of successful mood regulation leading to enhanced self-esteem. There is certainly evidence that people use a number of cognitive strategies similar to those described above to regulate their esteem as well as their affect (see Westen, 1994). Research also suggests that LSE and high self-focus individuals are more likely to use alcohol as a mood regulator. Indeed, a number of studies have shown that increasing self-focus increases the use of self-regulatory strategies in general (see Morris, 1989).

Thayer and colleagues' study (1994) suggests that there may be gender differences in the use of regulation strategies. In particular, men were more likely to report seeking pleasurable activities combined with distraction, or to say that they used direct tension reduction (e.g. alcohol and drugs) to change bad moods, whereas women were more likely to report using passive mood management (e.g. watch TV, go shopping) or social support, ventilation, and gratification. Thayer and colleagues suggested that these differences may go some way towards explaining the common finding of higher depression levels in women than men. However, men and women were equally likely to report using active mood management strategies, which were rated as the most effective group of strategies.

There may also be other individual differences in mood-regulation style, meaning that some individuals are more likely to use particular strategies. For example, Westen (1994) found that people who tended to experience unpleasant emotions were more likely to use non-specific strategies, including disengagement (withdrawal of effort), denial, and venting (letting feelings out). He also found that people who feel emotions more intensely were more likely to use "hot" coping strategies, which alter feelings directly and quickly, than "cold" coping strategies, which are less direct and slower. Hot coping strategies included seeking social support and venting emotions, and cold coping strategies included planning and positive reinterpretation.

The distinction between *problem-focused* and *emotion-focused* coping (Folkman & Lazarus, 1980, and see Carver, Scheier, & Weintraub, 1989) may also have relevance for differences in mood regulation style. In problem-focused coping, individuals take steps to solve the problem that is causing them to feel threatened. In emotion-focused coping, individuals attempt to reduce their negative affect directly. According to Folkman and Lazarus (1985), emotion-focused coping can include wishful thinking, distancing, emphasizing the positive aspects of the situation, self-blame, tension-reduction, and self-isolation. These strategies clearly overlap with some of those used for mood regulation. It has also been found that situational factors have a strong influence on the coping strategies that individuals use (e.g. Mattlin, Wethington, & Kessler, 1990), which may also prove to be the case for mood-regulation strategies.

KEY ISSUES

This chapter has described some of the precursors of mood regulation and some of the strategies that people use to regulate their mood. The study of mood regulation represents a relatively new and exciting avenue of research but, as we pointed out earlier, it is immature at present and there are a number of important issues that still remain to be addressed.

Theoretical and methodological problems

One difficulty in classifying mood-regulation strategies is that the examples often have multiple purposes in general, or at least may serve different purposes on different occasions. For example, people sometimes go for a walk in order to cure a bad mood. This strategy could be construed as an example of behavioural withdrawal, or distraction, or seeking a pleasant activity, or exercise, or even relaxation. Alternatively, going for a walk could simply provide people with the opportunity to use cognitive strategies such as thinking of pleasant things, positive thinking, rationalization, or avoidance. The strategy may therefore be implemented with single or multiple aims. This fact obviously makes *a priori* classification of regulation strategies rather difficult. Determining people's specific regulatory intentions requires additional contextual information that is not available from simple strategy labels. However, as we shall see next, asking people what they had in mind when they used a strategy may not prove very helpful either.

Although people claim to use certain strategies, claim to understand why they

148

use them, and claim to know something about their respective relative effectiveness, the reality may be somewhat different. Evidence from related areas of research suggests that there is often good reason to doubt the validity of people's self-knowledge. For example, a study by Wilson, Laser, and Stone (1982) found that a group of participants who had recorded their own mood for five weeks were no more accurate than a group of "observers", who had no knowledge of the participants, in estimating the relations between their recorded moods and the potential predictors of mood. More generally, it has been suggested that people have little or no access to the operation of their own cognitive processes, and must therefore rely on *a priori* theories rather than use direct introspection to explain their behaviour (e.g. Nisbett & Wilson, 1977; see White, 1988 for a critical review of this thesis). However, it may be that explicitly intentional behaviour is not always subject to these same constraints on introspective access, and that people may often know what they are doing and why they are doing it when they are performing deliberate actions (e.g. Vallacher & Wegner, 1987). An issue that therefore requires further research is the extent to which people have an insight into their use of mood-regulation strategies under different circumstances, particularly those relating to degrees of conscious control.

Although most of this chapter has been concerned with deliberate mood regulation, there are times when it is unclear whether or not people are aware that they are deploying a mood-regulatory behaviour. For example, as we described earlier, although people may learn that helping someone else during a bad mood is sometimes a useful strategy, this does not mean that they deliberately choose to help someone simply in order to improve their own mood. Indeed, many people would be offended by the suggestion that they had helped someone just to make themselves feel better. The fact that mood does change after helping may be seen as reflecting the meeting of personal standards of altruism rather than being an anticipated self-serving reward. Furthermore, if people are not aware that helping serves affect regulation, then it seems to make little sense to say that their actions are motivated by selfish goals.

There are also times when people deploy a mood-regulation strategy through habit rather than with a specific affective goal in mind. For example, the generation of positive thoughts may become an automatic response to some adverse events. In fact it would be too burdensome to reflexively select every mood-regulatory response that was implemented.

Many people's everyday routine activities may also serve mood-regulatory functions. For example, many people probably automatically turn on the television when they get home from work. It is quite likely that people would not consider a habitual activity like this to be an instance of mood regulation. Yet this activity may change their mood for better or worse or it may prevent the occurrence of a worse or better mood. It is unclear whether we would wish to include or exclude such habitual activities from the study of mood regulation. If we include them, then almost all activities might be considered as mood regulatory to the extent that they are capable of exerting anticipated or unanticipated effects on affect, but if we exclude them then we may be imposing artificial boundaries that constrain or distort our general understanding of the processes involved.

A methodological concern is that parts of our current understanding of mood regulation are based on studies that were not explicitly designed to examine mood regulation. Morris (1989) highlighted two of the problems that result from this situation. First, many of the findings concerning regulation strategies are based on laboratory studies. Unfortunately, the results of these studies are not always reproduced in field studies. One reason for this could be that the laboratory studies encourage people to use strategies that they do not normally use in their everyday lives. For example, Morris, Reilly, and Englis (see Morris, 1989) found that the activities judged to have the greatest potential for improving mood are actually those that are used less often during bad moods. It is possible that being in a bad mood increases the effort required to engage in regulatory activities and hence makes them less likely. Indeed, if it were always an easy matter to get ourselves out of bad moods, then we would probably experience them less often (and for briefer periods) than we do. The second problem is that many of the relevant studies, particularly those concerned with the phenomenon of self-reward, have only considered half of the phenomenon in question. In particular, these investigations have shown that certain behaviours are more likely to occur during a bad mood but have failed to test whether mood actually improved as a consequence of performing these behaviours.

Motives for mood regulation

This chapter has primarily examined mood regulation that serves the purpose of changing a bad mood into a good mood. However, other forms of mood regulation are also possible. In other words, mood regulation does not always have a hedonic motive. For example, sometimes people want to change a good mood into a neutral or bad mood, and sometimes people want to prevent unpleasant or pleasant moods from changing (*mood maintenance*, Clark & Isen, 1982).

Parrott (1993) has described a dozen motives for inhibiting good moods and a dozen motives for maintaining bad moods, some of which are summarized here. One social motive for inhibiting good mood is the desire to behave appropriately in a social situation. For example, a person may feel that a neutral mood is more conducive to appearing serious at a formal occasion, such as an interview. Another social motive is the desire to influence other people's moods. For example, a teacher may wish to convey a neutral or bad mood in order to get students to work harder. A non-social motive for inhibiting a good mood is the desire to improve personal concentration on a task because good moods may make people more distractable (e.g. Schwarz & Bless, 1991). Another non-social motive is the desire to eliminate guilt about being in a good mood. For example, people sometimes feel that they are undeserving of pleasant feelings either because they have not earned them or because there are too many bad things in the world. Social motives for maintaining a bad mood include the desire to empathize with other people's misfortunes, and the need for sympathy. Non-social motives include facilitation of analytical thinking, preparation for bad times ahead, and the prevention of even worse moods.

Many social occasions require people to be in a mood that does not match their current mood. For example, funerals require people to be in a sad mood and yet if a person does not feel close to the deceased then he or she may actually be in a relatively good mood. This good mood requires inhibition in order to promote appropriate social behaviour. Of course in many circumstances several of these social demands may be met by simply simulating the *expression* of a sad mood, but often the control of affect itself is more convincing and easier to sustain.

Wegner and Erber (1993) described a number of studies showing that people regulate their moods in anticipation of social interaction. For example, in their own investigations they found that participants who were induced into sad or happy moods tried to neutralize their affect by choosing to read newspaper articles containing mood-incongruent material if they anticipated meeting someone. However, participants tried to maintain their mood by choosing congruent articles if they anticipated being alone. Another experiment showed that participants who were made to feel angry tried to maintain the mood if they believed that there would be an opportunity to retaliate, but tried to change the mood if they believed that no such opportunity would arise. It has also been demonstrated that people's mood tends to become more unpleasant before they convey bad news, presumably because they want their behaviour to be consistent with the negative emotional tone of the message.

Other non-social stimuli can also motivate people to minimize positive moods and maintain negative moods. For example, Mackie and Worth (1989) have argued that positive moods can disrupt systematic processing of persuasive messages by reducing available cognitive capacity, so people may deliberately put themselves in a negative mood to facilitate their cognitive performance.

Facilitating mood regulation

Some mood-regulation strategies may be very effective but very infrequently used because their effectiveness is not immediately obvious to people. Research could provide the means for uncovering these strategies so that people could then be taught to use them. An example of a strategy that is effective but not widely recognized as such is keeping a personal diary. In a series of studies, Pennebaker found that instructing people who had experienced a traumatic event to write about their associated thoughts and emotions produced enduring benefits to their well-being (Pennebaker & Beall, 1986), and immune system functioning (Pennebaker, Kiecolt-Glaser, & Glaser, 1988). Burt (1994) also found that diary-keeping was associated with reduced anxiety and fewer reported hassles among students. Diaries may regulate mood by helping people structure and assimilate emotional experiences. However, there is also a danger that diaries might encourage rumination, and hence maintenance of unpleasant affect, if used improperly.

151

It is also possible that people could be taught to use mood-regulation strategies that would increase their general happiness. In a series of studies by Fordyce (Fordyce, 1977; 1983), students were given a programme of instruction that taught them to modify their behaviours and attitudes to "approximate more closely the characteristics of happier people". Fordyce found that students who followed the programme showed increased happiness even after eighteen months compared to controls. The programme was based on fourteen principles of happiness, some of which clearly overlap with mood-regulation strategies. For example, the principles included: keep busy and be more active, spend more time socializing, get better organized and plan things out, stop worrying, develop positive and optimistic thinking, eliminate negative feelings and problems.

One potential problem with the explicit implementation of strategies to improve mood arises from the finding, reported in the previous chapter, that people's mood adapts or habituates over time to both very positive and very negative events. It therefore seems likely that people who wanted to maintain pleasant moods using mood-regulation principles would have to make a continual effort to do so, in order to counteract the tendency of dynamic mood equilibrium to restore affect to its usual level. According to this view, the most effective strategies would be those that reset the equilibrium level of the system in an upward direction. There may also be protective processes that would render a continual effort at mood regulation unsuccessful. Furthermore, given that moods are not purely hedonic in function, it is not even clear that perpetual pleasant moods are desirable.

TOWARDS A MODEL OF MOOD REGULATION

Although the study of mood regulation is still in its infancy, this chapter has highlighted a number of functions that appear to be basic to a model of the phenomenon. In practice, these functions could be arranged and implemented in any of a number of different ways and it is too early to know which is correct. However, these functions provide a means of organizing our understanding of mood regulation and, as we shall see in the next chapter, help us to think about the ways in which things can go wrong during mood regulation. The main functions of the mood regulation process are monitoring, appraisal, regulation, and reappraisal.

Monitoring

Some form of registration of mood information is a prerequisite to an evaluation of current mood. Mood monitoring involves conscious and non-conscious processes that make use of a range of internal and external sources of information about mood. Conscious monitoring of mood appears to be intermittent and may depend on some intensity (or change-based) threshold for attention being reached. There are also clear individual differences in the extent to which people are generally aware of their moods. These include differences in the amount of attention that is allocated to moods and in the ability to discriminate between different kinds of mood.

Appraisal

As well as monitoring mood, people must also be able to determine the meaning and personal significance of their moods. The outcome of this appraisal probably depends on how people are currently feeling, how their current feelings relate to their mood states in the past, what their affective goals are (in other words, what they want from their mood in the future), and their present situation. Although people's desired mood state is often based on hedonistic motivation (the desire to feel good), a range of other possible motives may make people prefer to be in a neutral or bad mood. It also seems likely that appraisal depends on relative rather than absolute judgements because standards of comparison change over time. Ultimately, the appraisal of mood leads either to a decision to change mood in a positive or negative direction or to a decision to maintain the current mood state.

Regulation

In order to bring about a change in mood or to maintain mood, people must have access to a repertoire of available regulation strategies and a means of choosing and selecting strategies. This repertoire is likely to include both cognitive and behavioural techniques. These techniques work by enabling people either to avoid, accept, engage, or distract themselves from their mood. In theory, any cognition or behaviour can potentially be used to change or maintain mood. However, it is clear that in practice some types of cognition and behaviour are used more often for mood regulation purposes, and that some of these are more effective, than others. The effectiveness of mood regulation strategies probably depends on which mood-related processes can be affected, the extent to which these processes are affected, and the relative importance of these processes to mood regulation as a whole. People's repertoire of strategies develops as a result of various learning processes, and the breadth and sophistication of their repertoire therefore depends on their life history. The selection of strategies will be influenced by what is feasible in the current situation and will be biased towards strategies that have been used in similar situations in the past, particularly if those strategies were successful (cf. Westen, 1994). Effective mood regulation probably depends on characteristics of the person, the situation, and the person's history of mood regulation experiences.

Reappraisal

Once a mood-regulation strategy has been implemented, it has to be evaluated in terms of its consequences for mood. This involves an appraisal of whether current mood is closer to, or further away from, the desired mood state than before. More precisely, proper evaluation involves a continuing reappraisal because the process of mood regulation is not instantaneous. Many of the strategies for regulating mood are indirect, meaning that they act on the situation rather than on the mood itself. It therefore usually takes time to bring about a deliberate change in mood. Furthermore, a chosen strategy may not be successful. According to Wegner and colleagues (1993), a background monitoring process runs continuously during the intentional control of mood and reinitiates the intentional process if it detects a failure to achieve the desired state. However, it would be pointless simply to keep on repeating the same strategy in the face of recurrent ineffectiveness. People therefore also require the ability to select another regulation strategy or to modify the original strategy if necessary.

Conclusions

Mood regulation apparently involves a highly iterative control process. Further complexity is added by the fact that people often have several simultaneous affective goals. Mood regulation therefore probably involves multiple parallel processes rather than a single serial process. However, it is unknown whether these processes are additive and continuous or non-additive and discontinuous.

Problems with mood regulation may arise at any point in this complex process. There are a number of different points at which judgements must be made and at which action may need to be taken. At each of these points, a faulty judgement or an ill-chosen action may conceivably impede mood regulation. Although it may be possible to correct the errors, in some instances corrective action can confound rather than rectify the difficulty. For example, Wegner and colleagues (1993) have hypothesized that depression may be the consequence of attempts to control sad moods under stressful conditions. In particular, they propose that failure of the intentional control process, resulting from the high load imposed by the stressors, enables a background monitoring process to produce an ironic effect in which the person becomes even more sad. Consequently the person may try even harder to improve his or her mood but this only produces even worse ironic effects. This "self-loading cyclic system might thus fuel ever-more serious ironic effects, such that trying not to be sad could over time engender severe sadness" (p. 1102). The next chapter will describe how other failures in the mood regulation process may give rise to a variety of mood disorders.

SUMMARY

This chapter has described how people regulate their moods using a variety of processes for a variety of purposes. In order to control mood in a purposeful way, it is necessary to be able to evaluate mood. This requires processes for dynamically monitoring mood and appraising its significance. In order to change or maintain mood, it is necessary to have a repertoire of cognitive and behavioural strategies that can affect mood. This chapter has examined some of these processes and strategies. We have shown that mood regulation is a complex control process and that there are significant individual differences in people's ability to regulate their moods. The next chapter considers whether mood disorders are the consequence of severe failures in the mood regulation process.

CLINICAL APPROACHES TO MOOD AND MOOD DISORDERS

OVERVIEW

In previous chapters, our main emphasis has been on everyday examples of mood and mood regulation. In the present chapter, we extend our discussion to the clinical conditions of depression and anxiety. The characteristics of these mood disorders present something of a challenge to our usual definition of moods as temporary, subject to spontaneous change, and variable in evaluative tone and intensity. This chapter specifically addresses this distinction between clinical disorders of anxiety and depression and normal, unpleasant mood states involving "depressed" or anxious "feelings". A variety of apparently incompatible psychological theories have been developed to explain the development and maintenance of mood disorders. These theoretical accounts have each suggested different methods of treating depression and anxiety, all of which appear to be of approximately equal efficacy in terms of clinical outcome. In this chapter, we will outline two of the most influential approaches to mood disorders (the *cognitive-behavioural* approach and the *psychodynamic-interpersonal* approach), describe the methods of psychotherapy associated with these approaches, and discuss some recent attempts to integrate ideas and methods from both approaches. Next, we consider the possible relevance of mood regulation to the explanation and treatment of mood disorders. In particular, we argue that the development and maintenance of phobias may be directly related to the use of faulty mood-regulation strategies. Failures of mood regulation may also play some role in specific varieties of depression, and we will review theoretical approaches that emphasize this aspect of the disorder. Finally, we will review evidence concerning the short-term effects of different forms of psychotherapy on mood within sessions, and the longer-term outcomes of clinical intervention for general well-being.

INTRODUCTION

Studies of mood change and regulation suggest that unpleasant moods are generally short-lived and subject to spontaneous variation as well as deliberate control. Against this background, the prevalence of psychological disorders of depression and anxiety may seem somewhat puzzling, because the associated mood states do not seem to be characterized by these features. For example, when they are clinically depressed, people describe their moods as persisting at a moderate or severe level of unpleasantness for relatively protracted periods. In the case of clinical depression, then, mood appears not to be a temporary state, does not change spontaneously, and is generally invariant in evaluative tone. Similarly people with certain types of anxiety disorders experience extreme feelings of dread, apprehension, and worry which do not diminish over time and are apparently unrelated to specific stimuli or events.

Despite the apparent abnormality of the mood states accompanying depression and anxiety, however, these disorders are relatively common in community samples of adults and children, and tend to follow a cyclical course. For example, Boyd and Weissman (1981) estimated that between 8 percent and 13 percent of men and between 20 percent and 26 percent of women experience at least one episode of clinical depression during their lifetime. The proportion of people who experience a relapse within one year of an episode of depression has been estimated to be as high as 50 percent (Evans et al., 1992). Less severe mood problems are even more common. For example, in a recent survey, one in seven adults in the UK reported experiencing psychological problems such as fatigue, worry, depression, obsessions, or phobias at some point during the previous week (Meltzer, Gill, & Petticrew, 1995).

Because such a clear distinction is often made between non-clinical mood disturbance and clinical (i.e. diagnosable) disorders, it is worth outlining the specific diagnostic criteria used to assess depression and anxiety. In the next two sections, we will therefore consider each of these clinical conditions in turn.

Characteristics of clinical depression

The key characteristic of clinical depression is a depressed mood, usually accompanied by lack of interest in, and inability to derive pleasure from, usual activities and pastimes. People who are depressed often describe themselves as "empty", "hopeless", "useless", and "helpless". Feeling isolated from others or cut off from others is also common. In this connection, Rowe (1983) suggests that people who are simply unhappy (e.g. those suffering a bereavement or similar negative event) can seek out and use help and support from other people and can comfort themselves, whereas clinically depressed people are unable either to make use of other peoples' sympathy, compassion, or concern, or to comfort themselves.

These subjective expressions of depression predominate in peoples' descriptions of what it is like to be depressed. However, self-reports of depressed mood are not in themselves sufficient indicators of clinical depression (Coyne, 1994), and diagnosis of depression therefore depends on the presence of a broader range of cognitive, motivational, and physical (biological) symptoms. Depression is diagnosed if and only if an individual has experienced depressed mood and/or loss of pleasure for at least two weeks, and reports at least four of the following symptoms: loss of, or increased, appetite; weight loss or weight gain; fatigue or loss of energy; lack of interest in sex; feelings of worthlessness or guilt; insomnia; early morning wakening; poor concentration or indecisiveness; recurrent thoughts of death or suicide; and psychomotor retardation or agitation (DSM-IV; APA, 1994). Individuals who report depressed mood or loss of interest for at least two years, but who do not have the additional problems necessary to meet the criteria for clinical depression are diagnosed as *dysphoric*.

The impact of depression on everyday functioning can be devastating. For example, depressed people report problems in concentration and motivation which often result in deterioration of their work performance (Mintz & Mintz, 1992). Severe depression may disrupt almost all normal daily activities including household duties (cleaning, cooking, shopping, child-care), self-care, relationships with friends, colleagues, spouse and children, and social activities (Lewinsohn, 1975). Depression is also linked with increased risk of suicide and suicide attempts (Hawton & Catalan, 1987). Perhaps most worryingly with regard to long-term effects, parental depression has been found to be associated with increased incidence of physical child-abuse, childhood behavioural problems, and depression in offspring (Chiariello & Orvaschel, 1995).

Characteristics of clinical anxiety

Depression and anxiety very often occur together (Barlow, 1988) and although the two disorders can be distinguished at conceptual level, their joint presentation may be difficult to unravel in practice (Goldberg, Bridges, Duncan-Jones, & Grayson, 1987). Diagnosis of anxiety is complicated by the fact that it may present itself in a number of different ways (e.g. as generalized anxiety disorder, panic disorder, obsessive compulsive disorder, or phobia). Some anxiety states such as *simple phobias* are characterized by variable levels of anxiety linked closely to a specific object or situation (e.g. dogs, spiders, travelling in lifts or aeroplanes). Exposure to this object or situation, either directly or in imagination, leads to extreme anxiety that often increases in relation to its physical or temporal proximity. Correspondingly, behavioural or cognitive avoidance of the object or situation is marked by relatively low levels of distress and anxiety. Other kinds of anxiety state are characterized by a much more diffuse presentation of distress. For example, *generalized anxiety disorder*, as the name implies, refers to a clinical state of chronic worry lasting for over six months, which is unrealistic or excessive, and which is focused on two or more concerns relating to life circumstances, physical health and safety, possible misfortunes and disasters, and/or financial difficulties. Unlike phobias or panic disorders, self-reported mood in generalized anxiety disorder shows a relatively stable and invariant pattern.

Relations and distinctions between normal and abnormal mood conditions

The relationship between normal (temporary) depressed or anxious mood states, mild mood disturbances, and diagnosable disorders of depression and anxiety presents some conceptual difficulties and has been the subject of much debate (e.g. Morris, 1989). One view of this relationship assumes that mood disorders are like normal moods only more so, depending on similar processes that simply manifest themselves in a more extreme way. In other words, normal and abnormal mood may be seen as both falling on the same conceptual continuum. This *continuity* model carries implications for the research and treatment of mood disorders. From a research perspective, it suggests that findings obtained from normal (i.e. non-clinical), or from mildly distressed populations can inform our understanding of the development and maintenance of clinical mood disorders. On this basis, much experimental research with non-depressed participants (such as that described in Chapter 4) has been used to try and understand the psychological processes underlying clinical depression. In other words, the impact of unpleasant moods on memory, information processing, and decision making is assumed to parallel some hypothesized cognitive processing deficits that have been observed in depressed patients (Haaga, Dyck, & Ernst, 1991). Similarly, it might be argued that mood disorders occur when normal controlled or automatic mood-regulation strategies fail. According to this perspective, then, clinical disorders of mood may be treated using predominantly psychological methods which enable the individual to implement effective mood-regulation strategies in order to achieve significant and lasting improvements in mood state.

An alternative position is to view everyday mood and clinical mood disorders as conditions that are qualitatively quite distinct. For example, Coyne (1994) argues that there are clear conceptual and empirical differences between self-reported distress, depressive symptoms, and diagnosable depression, and that research based on distressed people who have not been diagnosed as clinically depressed is often unhelpful in furthering our understanding and treatment of the disorder. In this connection, Fechner-Bates, Coyne, and Schwenk (1994) contend that self-reported symptoms of depression may often be due to problems in adjustment, bereavement, or transitory difficulties which would represent exclusion criteria for a clinical diagnosis. They argue that psychologists researching and treating clinical depression should take the lead from psychiatry, which specifically acknowledges the distinction between distress and depression. For example, biomedical psychiatrists generally assume that clinical mood disorders are primarily determined by genetic and biological factors that disrupt normal physiological functioning (and whose interactions with social conditions are secondary). Psychiatric research therefore attempts to isolate genetic, physiological, or other biological substrates of mood disorders, and to develop and evaluate treatment strategies that directly impact on this underlying pathology. For example, psychiatrists typically recommend the use of anti-depressant medication to correct clinical depression, and benzodiazepines (e.g. Valium, Librium) for anxiety disorders.

These two alternative views of mood disorders are sometimes characterized as mutually exclusive positions held by the opposing professional groups of psychologists and biomedical psychiatrists (e.g. Morris, 1989). From a pragmatic point of view, however, this polarization of the psychological and biomedical models of mood disorder is unhelpful. Etiological research suggests that genetic factors, social factors, and specific life experiences all play a significant role in the development of clinical mood disorders (Kendler, Kessler, Neale, Heath, & Eaves, 1993). Similarly, there are clear physiological as well as cognitive and behavioural correlates of both anxiety and depression (e.g. Anisman & Lapierre, 1981; Lader, 1975). Further, outcome studies suggest that both psychological and pharmacological treatments are effective in the treatment of mood disorders (Elkin et al., 1989). All these considerations suggest that psychological and biomedical approaches may be complementary rather than directly in conflict, and may simply address different aspects of the same multifaceted phenomenon. However, for reasons outlined in Chapter 1, the main focus of the present book is on psychological rather than physiological aspects of mood.

In this chapter, we take a compromise position falling between the twin extremes of absolute continuity or discontinuity. Specifically, we believe that it is likely that some of the processes underlying everyday mood phenomena also apply to some extent in some cases of clinical disorders of mood. For example, mood may become disordered when associated parameters reach extreme values, when regulatory mechanisms fail to operate effectively, or when combinations of processes interact in a chaotic way (see Chapter 6). However, it is also probable that mood disorders have some completely distinctive characteristics that are not found in everyday mood states. The degree to which continuity or discontinuity apply can only be determined by careful research assessing the relevance of normal mood processes to abnormal mood conditions. In the present chapter, we will specifically consider the extent to which mood disorders reflect failures in mood-regulation strategies, and examine the ways in which psychological treatments may help clients to regain effective control of their moods.

PSYCHOLOGICAL THEORIES OF MOOD DISORDERS

A great many different psychological models have been used as the basis of psychotherapeutic approaches to mood disorders. Most, however, fall into two broad categories. The first category includes *psychodynamic-interpersonal* models which emphasize the role of unconscious processes and interpersonal relationships in the development of disorders. The second category includes *cognitive-behavioural* theories which assume that mood and emotions are directly influenced by our thoughts and beliefs about the world. In this section, we will briefly describe the ways in which mood and disorders of mood are explained by both types of model, and then outline some of the treatment principles arising from each of them. Many previous descriptions of these therapeutic approaches have emphasized the differences between the two models and their apparent incompatibility. Recent clinical and theoretical developments, however, have involved an attempt to integrate concepts from both approaches. We will therefore conclude this section with a brief description of some *integrative models* of vulnerability to mood disorders, and of psychotherapy more generally.

160

Psychodynamic theories of mood disorder

Psychodynamic theories (e.g. Guntrip, 1971; Luborsky, 1981; Malan, 1979) have developed from Freudian ideas and principles to encompass a diverse range of models and ways of understanding human emotions and relationships. However, all psychodynamic theories have two important common components. The first is the assumption that interpersonal relationships play a key role in human experience. Because of biological and social demands, human beings are believed to be dependent on close personal relationships for personal survival. This dependency is at its most striking during infancy when relationships with caregivers are seen as critical in determining the development of both physical and emotional well-being. In Freud's early writings (e.g. 1910/1962), instinctive drives, including those relating to sex, hunger, and aggression, were viewed as primary causes of psychological problems. His later work (e.g. Freud, 1920/1950), however, explored the role of early relationships between infants and their carers in laying the foundations of mental health. This approach was further developed in clinical and academic contexts by neo-Freudians such as Donald Winnicott (1965) and Melanie Klein (Segal, 1964).

Structured observational research by Ainsworth (1967; 1989) and Bowlby (1980) provided clear illustrations of the important role of *attachment* and *separation* in infants and children. Based on studies of orphans, children in hospital, and observations of mothers with their children in North America, Africa, and Britain, Ainsworth, Bowlby and others described how early relationships with parent figures lay down strong patterns and expectations (of care and nurturance, of rejection, or of ambivalent feelings) which are then *projected* onto later adult relationships. These fundamental expectations about interpersonal relationships often become the focus of therapeutic attention in psychodynamic therapy.

The development of secure attachments to key caregivers is seen as a critical step in determining mental health. Through repeated positive interactions with carers, children are believed to internalize a positive image of self, to develop positive expectations of their social relationships with other people outside the immediate family, and to establish a secure base from which to explore the world beyond the family (Bowlby, 1980). Children for whom relationships with parental figures have been disrupted, for whom key parental figures were not available or were inconsistent, or for whom parental figures provided negative or punitive relationships develop insecure attachments (Ainsworth, Blehar, Waters, & Wall, 1978). Insecure attachments may take either of two forms. *Avoidant attachment* is marked particularly by the child's lack of distress and reluctance to approach the parent following separation, or by absence of attempts to seek comfort or solace when frightened or in pain. *Ambivalent attachment* is shown in inconsistent behaviours towards the parent, such as seeking help and comfort and then rejecting what is offered. Attachment appears to influence children's subsequent emotional and social development, and longitudinal observations have highlighted specific difficulties associated with both avoidant attachment (such as lack of

161

confidence, withdrawal, and exhibitionism) and ambivalent attachment (helplessness, low ego control, e.g. Erickson, Sroufe, & Egeland, 1985).

There has also been considerable interest in determining the impact of attachment styles on adult functioning. For example, Main, Kaplan, and Cassidy (1985) interviewed parents about their own experiences as children and their attitudes towards their own children and concluded that many of the parents' early attachment styles were transmitted to the next generation. Relatedly, Fonagy, Steele, and Steele (1991) examined attachment in pregnant women and later observed them interacting with their own children. In 75–80 percent of cases, the mother's attachment style, as rated during pregnancy, was found to be transmitted to her child. Thus mothers who reported experiencing anxiously attached relationships with their own parents were significantly more likely to have children who were anxiously attached to them.

There has also been some examination of the impact of attachment behaviours on work performance. For example, it has been argued that avoidance of close relationships in adults may be related to excessive concern with work and achievement. In this regard, some researchers have hypothesized that work and autonomy provide avoidantly attached individuals with a defence against close, intimate relationships in which they may expect to be rejected or abandoned. Autonomous success then becomes an alternative means of developing self-esteem and achieving social status (Hazan & Shaver, 1987; 1990).

The second core component of psychodynamic theories is the idea that uncomfortable, unacceptable, or painful thoughts and feelings (for example, about sexuality, loss, or aggression) which feel intolerable, overwhelming, or unmanageable are often consciously or unconsciously repressed through various defence mechanisms (such as *denial, projection, sublimation, displacement,* or *reaction formation*). In this connection, we have just described how angry, disappointed, or sad feelings about difficulties in forming interpersonal relationships may be *displaced* by channelling effort and energy into alternative areas such as work achievement. Another relevant defence mechanism is *transference*, which occurs when feelings, wishes, or expectations concerning one person (e.g. a parent or sibling) are projected or transferred onto other people. In general, individuals may embark upon future relationships with fears or hopes which determine the way in which these relationships develop and are maintained.

Psychodynamic therapy

A central concept in psychodynamic therapy is the therapeutic relationship between the client and the therapist. This relationship provides the security within which therapeutic work can occur and is also a fundamental means of bringing about change. Within the therapeutic relationship, transference is hypothesized to develop. As we have just mentioned, transference refers to the tendency to transfer one's past or present feelings for a salient person (e.g. one's father or mother) onto other people. These feelings may be pleasant or unpleasant: feelings of being let down, disappointed, or rejected may be transferred as easily as feelings of being supported, loved, and encouraged. As a key, neutral player in the client's life, the therapist often becomes the recipient of both pleasant and unpleasant transferred feelings. For example, clients who have had critical or rejecting parents may expect their therapist to be similarly critical or rejecting. This may lead to them trying various tactics to appease the therapist by adopting a compliant role or attempting to be a good client. Alternatively, therapy may be terminated prematurely by the client as a way of avoiding anticipated rejection from the therapist. Similarly, clients who have experienced repeated unresolved breaks in their relationships may be particularly vulnerable both to the therapist's absence (during holidays or illnesses, for example) and to the ultimate and inevitable ending of therapy. These events may evoke intense feelings of anger, abandonment, or loss which challenge the therapeutic relationship. The therapist's role is to help clients understand the links between their current emotions during therapy sessions and earlier feelings associated with separations, to enable them to explore these unresolved feelings, and to develop new patterns of relating and dealing with separations through the experience of coping with problems that emerge in the therapeutic relationship.

The general aim of psychodynamic therapy is to unravel the personal history of the client in such a way that connections between current difficulties and past experiences can be made explicit. This process of exploration and uncovering is facilitated by the therapist's use of transference. Close attention is given to the client's thoughts about, and feelings towards, the therapist, since these are believed to depend partly on thoughts and feelings experienced during previous relationships. These links and connections between the present and past are explicitly emphasized by the therapist during treatment sessions. In this way, the therapist enables the client to access hidden or unacknowledged feelings that have been successfully repressed since childhood. In the safety of the therapeutic relationship, these feelings can then be explored and resolved. It is this resolution of unacknowledged or repressed parts of the self that is seen as the key to bringing about changes in the client's depression or anxiety (Luborsky, 1981).

A number of methods are now available for assessing clients' main underlying problems and conflicts (Luborsky, Crits-Christoph, Mintz, & Auerbach, 1988; Malan, 1979). Application of these methods may help to validate psychodynamic treatment principles, to establish the reliability of therapists' clinical assessments, and to develop research into how therapeutic techniques bring about change. For example, Crits-Christoph, Cooper, and Luborsky (1988) measured the extent to which the accuracy of therapists' interpretations predicted outcome in psychodynamic therapy. Therapists' statements from transcripts of 86 treatment sessions were categorized as "interpretations" or "other responses" by two independent judges. Experienced clinicians then rated the accuracy of each of the identified interpretations. Finally, the outcome of therapy was assessed using general adjustment ratings made by each client and therapist (which were statistically corrected for initial levels of psychological distress). The investigators found that the accuracy of therapists' interpretations and the rated quality of the therapeutic relationship were both significant (and independent) predictors of judged outcome. Such research clearly goes some way towards scientifically demonstrating the potential clinical benefits of psychodynamic therapy.

Cognitive-behavioural theories of mood disorders

Cognitive theories of mood and mood disorder (e.g. Beck, 1976; Beck, Rush, Shaw, & Emery, 1979) are based on the premise that specific distorted ways of thinking about the world predispose people to have negative moods, which are maintained by automatic negative thoughts about the self, the world, and the future (the *cognitive triad*). In particular, the cognitive theory of depression states that the mental life of depressed people is characterized by almost exclusively negative thoughts that occur automatically and repetitively, and are difficult to control. The theory further assumes that depressed people are subject to systematic distortions in information processing which result in them selectively attending, perceiving, and remembering in ways that are congruent with, and therefore reinforce, their unpleasant moods (Haaga, Dyck, & Ernst, 1991). The effects of clinically depressed mood, in this view, are similar to (though more extreme than) the effects of more everyday unpleasant moods on processing, decision-making, and memory (see Chapter 4). Beck and his colleagues identified a number of cognitive distortions common to people with depression and anxiety. These include black-and-white thinking (i.e. the inability to see that events can be anything other than absolutely good or absolutely bad), selective abstraction (taking specific evidence out of context), minimization of positive events and magnification of negative events, and overgeneralizing.

Cognitive therapy works on the premise that individuals are vulnerable to depression and other mood disorders because they have characteristic inflexible, distorted, and automatic beliefs about the way the world operates. These beliefs are thought to be organized into coherent patterns or *schemas* that influence perception and interpretation. For example, if a person has a schema that is concerned primarily with being loved, dependency, and the need for closeness and intimacy, a resulting assumption that "If I am not loved unconditionally then I am worthless" may develop. Schemas are thought to encourage enhanced attention to information that either confirms or contradicts them. Thus, clients with a dependency schema might seek reassurance and objective evidence that they are loved, ruminate about times when they were loved, and keep mementoes of being loved (Valentine cards, love letters, photographs etc.). In general, evidence suggesting that they are not loved or that they are unlovable may be given more weight than evidence confirming lovability. Thus, depression may lead to an exaggerated sense of pessimism and hopelessness about the world.

Schemas linked with anxiety might revolve around negative judgements that others may make, or concern the client's personal vulnerability to physical disorders. Associated assumptions may include "If I don't perform perfectly in every

164

way then people will think that I'm useless", or "If I experience physical symptoms such as my heart beating fast, or breathlessness, then I am dangerously ill". As in the case of depression, these schemas and assumptions may lead to selective emphasis on negative aspects of the life situation, and unwarranted threatening inferences from the available evidence.

Cognitive-behaviour therapy

In contrast to the psychodynamic approach, which seeks to uncover and explore unacknowledged or hidden experiences and feelings, cognitive and behavioural therapies focus on resolving the client's current problems as they are presented by the client at the beginning of treatment. Within a cognitive-behavioural framework, the therapist's first task is to help clients understand how their current problems are maintained by the ways they think about their problems and by their habitual behaviours, and to demonstrate that changes in thinking and behaviour are possible. Using therapy sessions as a safe context in which to practise new ways of thinking and behaving, the therapist and client then work together to integrate these changes into the client's daily life.

In cognitive-behaviour therapy, the therapist–client relationship is characterized as collaborative. In particular, both parties agree on a goal, and on a procedure for moving toward it. Further, both therapist and client are actively involved in bringing about change. For example, self-management methods of therapy (e.g. Kanfer & Gaelick-Buys, 1991) emphasize the explicit engagement of clients as active participants in their own rehabilitation. The rationale for this emphasis is that strong motivation is the key to therapeutic change, that many behaviours are only accessible to the clients themselves, and that the process of recovery is often difficult and unpleasant. Within this behavioural approach, an early task in therapy is to increase the client's sense of self-efficacy and control as a necessary prerequisite of successful mood regulation.

Cognitive-behaviour therapy involves teaching clients to monitor their mood states, concurrent behaviours, and thoughts, and to identify negative thoughts and expectations. The therapist then encourages clients to evaluate the evidence for these thoughts and expectations by considering alternative explanations for events, and by conducting personal experiments to test these explanations. Following these interventions, clients who have claimed that they *always* felt terrible, that their days were *completely* devoid of pleasure, and that they were *absolutely* useless at everything they attempt to do, are often surprised to find that there is in fact some variation in their mood over time, that they do experience some small pleasures during the day, and that they do enjoy some limited success in their tasks. Cognitive-behaviour therapy can thus be helpful in inducing more realistic monitoring of mood, which in turn may lead to more effective and more focused mood regulation.

Therapy may also be directed toward changing clients' appraisals. Anxious clients tend to appraise their world as physically or psychologically threatening, and this appraisal is thought to mediate their anxious mood. Depressed clients tend to focus more generally on the negative aspects of their lives: they evaluate their self-worth to be minimal, their skills to be non-existent, and their lives to be devoid of pleasure. During therapy, clients are frequently encouraged to test out their negative beliefs. For example, a depressed person believing himself or herself to be unlikeable and boring might be asked to collect specific evidence both for and against this hypothesis. Distancing techniques are also used to help clients stand back from their problems, and evaluate their situation from another person's perspective. For instance, the therapist may ask clients to adopt the role of a friend or colleague, or to collect evidence comparing their own performance or abilities with those of colleagues and friends. This evidence would then be reviewed and discussed in detail at the next therapy session. To the extent that clients are persuaded that their appraisals of their problems are unduly negative, their affective reactions to these problems are likely to be reduced.

Therapists also encourage their clients to try out mood-regulation strategies, and to adopt an experimental approach to problem-solving in *homework assignments* that are completed between sessions. These assignments enable the client to practise and rehearse a wider range of techniques than is possible during the sessions themselves, as well as encouraging generalization of new skills and techniques to the client's normal life. For example, early in therapy, a priority may be to motivate clients to engage in some of the more active features of therapy. During sessions therefore, the client and therapist may agree on a series of behavioural exercises to be completed during the week. These exercises would be graded in difficulty so that the chances of the client experiencing success are maximized. Thus clients are encouraged to learn how to use effective strategies for dealing with unpleasant situations and negative feelings.

Integrative accounts of vulnerability

Cognitive-behavioural and psychodynamic-interpersonal therapies have evolved from quite separate theoretical backgrounds and involve distinctive training routes, models of supervision, and methods of assessing clinical outcomes. However, there have been increasing attempts to integrate the two theoretical perspectives and their associated therapeutic techniques. In this section and the next, we will discuss some of these efforts toward integration. A general consensus has begun to emerge concerning theories of vulnerability to depression and we will first briefly review the relevant literature. In the next section, we will describe how some therapists have begun to refine their therapeutic practice to incorporate concepts and techniques from other approaches. Finally, we will consider a meta-model that has been developed to explain psychological change occurring in both psychodynamic-interpersonal and cognitive-behavioural therapies.

A considerable amount of research has been concerned with establishing the role of specific vulnerability factors in the disruption of mood regulation and the development of mood disorders. A general assumption of this research is that mood disorders often develop following significant life events, and depend either on the characteristics of these events themselves, or on the individual's particular susceptibility to their effects (or some combination of the two). Kirschenbaum (1987) suggested that the usual self-regulatory strategies that we use to moderate our moods and our behaviours are most likely to fail following social stress, social pressures, physiological pressures, or a failure to reach some notional target. Many life events such as these can have a dramatic and protracted impact on our affective state.

Epidemiological evidence suggests that the distribution of depression and anxiety is not random across the population. For example, depression is more common in younger people than in older people, and women are more likely to be diagnosed with depression than are men. More precise understanding of vulnerability requires more focused and intensive investigation. For example, in a now classic study, Brown and Harris (1978) interviewed working-class women in an inner-city borough of London. As a group, this sample was generally expected to experience relatively high rates of depression. Brown and Harris established that there were also particular events that increased the risk of disorder. Three specific vulnerability factors were identified: the death of the woman's mother before the age of twelve years; caring for more than two children under five; and the lack of a close, confiding relationship with their male partner.

In the past decade, there has been a marked convergence of ideas about the factors underlying vulnerability to mood disorders. Specifically, both psychodynamic (e.g. Blatt, 1974; 1995) and cognitive-behavioural (e.g. Beck, 1983) theorists have suggested that preoccupation with either dependency or achievement needs increases the risk of depression. Although somewhat different terms are used to label the vulnerability factor in question, both perspectives suggest that people who have high levels of either dependency (or "sociotropy") or autonomy (or "self-criticism") are more susceptible to specific external stressors, have different presentations of disorders, use different regulation strategies when faced with difficult problems, and respond differently to treatment. Thus, dependent people are hypothesized to be vulnerable following interpersonal crises, to openly display their emotional distress, to actively seek out others to help them, and to respond well to therapy that focuses on interpersonal relationships and offers high levels of support. In contrast, autonomous people are hypothesized to be vulnerable to perceived or actual failures, to repress expressions of emotional disturbance, to avoid seeking help or admitting to their problems, and to respond best to collaborative treatment in which their own personal skills and abilities are acknowledged and in which they take responsibility for change.

Although these theoretical ideas have generated a considerable amount of research, empirical support for the role of autonomy and dependency in predisposing individuals to depression is still rather limited. However, the evidence does seem broadly consistent with the conclusion that dependency plays a part in the development of depression. For example, Hammen and colleagues (Hammen, Burge, Daley, Davila, Paley, & Rudolf, 1995) followed up 155 females for a year

167

after they graduated from high school (aged 17 and 18). The researchers monitored life events, depression, and other symptoms using regular interviews, and found that both negative thoughts and interpersonal crises, but not achievement-related crises, were significant predictors of depression and other psychological problems. Similarly, Gilbert and Reynolds (1990) found that *sociotropy* but not autonomy was significantly correlated with reported depressive symptoms and with neuroticism in a non-clinical population. Further, Hammen, Ellicott, Gitlin, and Jameson (1989) found from longitudinal data that the onset or exacerbation of depressive symptoms amongst depressed patients was associated with the occurrence of personally meaningful life events. In particular, sociotropic patients deteriorated following the experience of negative interpersonal events, and autonomous patients deteriorated following negative achievement events.

As well as affecting vulnerability to depression, it may be that dependence and autonomy moderate the efficacy of attempts to regulate mood. Some limited evidence for this was provided by Reynolds and Gilbert's (1991) investigation of the relationship between autonomy and dependency, coping strategies, and depressive symptoms in unemployed men. In general, unemployment is linked with high levels of depression amongst men (Warr, 1991). However, in Reynolds and Gilbert's sample, higher levels of activity appeared to protect autonomous men from depressive symptoms. Reported depression was markedly stronger among autonomous men who were high in social support and low in activity, and dependent men low in social support and high in activity, than among either dependent individuals high in social support or autonomous individuals high in activity. These results suggest that regulation strategies (e.g. the use of social support or activity) are only effective if they address the individual's specific vulnerability (i.e. based on dependency or autonomy needs). Within this population, autonomous men were vulnerable following unemployment because of the consequent loss of opportunities for achievement. High levels of social support not only failed to compensate for this loss, but may also have served to highlight the sense of failure and lack of autonomy experienced by these respondents. Correspondingly, dependent men were vulnerable because unemployment removed a source of social support, and their high levels of activity could not make up for this deficit.

Integrative models of psychotherapy

Many accounts of psychotherapy imply that different models of therapy are incompatible, and many therapists have vested interests in favouring one mode of therapy over all others. Increasingly, however, there have been attempts to develop models of psychotherapy and change which can integrate theoretical concepts from both psychodynamic and cognitive-behavioural approaches. A common approach to integration involves incorporating apparently valuable features of alternative models into one's preferred model in order to plug its gaps or correct its weaknesses. For example, Safran (1990a; 1990b) provided an account of cognitive therapy which was adapted to include aspects of psychodynamic-interpersonal therapies. In particular, Safran identified two important elements of psychodynamic-interpersonal therapies which had been underemphasized in standard cognitive-behavioural approaches. These were the central role of the therapeutic relationship, and the role of interpersonal relationships in maintaining psychological problems. Safran argued that cognitive therapists should use the therapeutic relationship both as a way of identifying patterns of dysfunctional interaction, and as a source of interpersonal experiences from which the client might learn new ways of relating to others. Essentially, this account provides a rationale for incorporating the concept of transference into cognitive therapy, and suggests ways in which cognitive therapists might use the therapeutic relationship as a vehicle for change.

The *assimilation model* (Stiles et al., 1990) is an example of an account which is integrative in the sense that it attempts to provide an overarching framework within which therapeutic change in different forms of therapy can be understood. The model views assimilation of problematic experiences by the client as a common component of successful psychotherapy. "Assimilation" in this context refers to the extent to which a problem is acknowledged, accepted, and ultimately mastered. Thus in all therapies clients initially present painful problems which they struggle with, and are unable to resolve. These problems may already be assimilated to different degrees, and the central goal of therapy is seen as one of helping clients to assimilate these problems further and ultimately to resolve them.

According to this framework, then, assimilation is viewed as a continuum. At one end of the continuum, some problems are completely unassimilated because they are repressed and therefore unconscious and unacknowledged. At the other end of the continuum, problems that have been overcome and mastered are viewed as completely assimilated and currently unproblematic. In between these two extremes, problems may be experienced as more or less assimilated. Initially, painful problems may enter awareness but be poorly understood. Understanding of these problems reduces unpleasant affect and promotes attempts to solve them. Problem solution is accompanied by pleasant affect leading finally to a sense of mastery and complete assimilation.

The process of assimilation is illustrated in Figure 7.1. Stages of assimilation are represented along the x axis of the graph. These stages are: (0) warded off, (1) unwanted thoughts, (2) vague awareness, (3) problem statement/clarification, (4) understanding/insight, (5) application/working through, (6) problem solution, and (7) mastery. The process of assimilation is marked by changes in both affect and attention to problems. Unpleasant mood increases with the emergence of problems as vaguely sensed and unwanted thoughts, then begins to decrease as problems are clarified and understood. Pleasant mood is experienced as problems are worked through and solutions are applied. Attention to the problem increases until the problems are understood then decreases as the problems become increasingly resolved.

According to the assimilation model, different psychotherapies focus on problems lying at differing points on the assimilation continuum (Stiles, Barkham,

salience/
valence

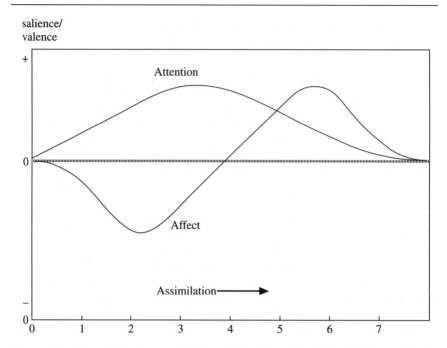

Figure 7.1 The assimilation model (adapted from Reynolds, Stiles, Barkham, Shapiro, Hardy and Rees, in press)

Shapiro, & Firth-Cozens, 1992). Psychodynamic-interpersonal therapies attend primarily to problems which are poorly assimilated, and painful feelings of which clients are only vaguely aware (stages 1 and 2). Through the use of exploration and insight, clients are helped to understand and clarify their problems. Once this clarification has been achieved, resolution of these problems is viewed as relatively unproblematic and beyond the immediate concern of therapy. Cognitive-behavioural therapies, in contrast, are primarily directed at problems which can be readily articulated by clients and of which they are already fully aware (partially assimilated at stage 3). Understanding is facilitated by providing an explanatory framework for these problems, and therapy then focuses on providing structured ways of solving them and maintaining positive changes.

The assimilation model provides a persuasive account of psychological change arising from divergent therapeutic approaches. Field, Barkham, Shapiro, and Stiles (1994) presented qualitative case material suggesting that the resolution of problems does follow the predicted stages and that clients' experiences in therapy can be reliably identified by observers. However, this work is as yet at a very early stage and a number of conceptual issues remain to be resolved. For example, it is still unclear how problems of which clients are only vaguely aware get dealt with in cognitive therapy. Correspondingly, the process whereby insights lead to problem resolution in psychodynamic therapies remains unspecified. Further, the assimilation model at present suggests a simple linear progression through stages of assimilation, whereas presumably clients may in fact present problems which cycle between stages, sometimes appearing clear and at other times being poorly understood or even "warded off".

Empirical support for the assimilation model is also rather limited at present. Although there is evidence that clients' mood differs in psychodynamic-interpersonal and cognitive-behavioural therapies (Reynolds et al., in press; Stiles, Shapiro, & Firth-Cozens, 1988), the extent to which mood change is related to level of assimilation has not been specifically examined. However, an important strength of the assimilation model from the perspective of mood disorders and mood regulation is its explicit inclusion of mood and mood change as core components of successful psychotherapy. In the next section, we will focus on mood disorders from the specific perspective of mood regulation.

MOOD DISORDERS AND MOOD REGULATION PROCESSES

From the perspective of the present volume, many cases of clinically disordered mood may be conceptualized as examples of problematic mood regulation. Similarly, Brewin (1989) suggested that affective disorders are experienced by people whose spontaneous attempts at self-regulation have been ineffective. In this section we will describe how two common mood disorders, phobias and depression, may arise from, and be maintained by, unsuccessfully implemented mood regulation.

The process of mood regulation we described in Chapter 6 includes at least four stages (monitoring, appraisal, regulation, and reappraisal) and problems may occur at any of these stages. We will begin by considering factors that may influence mood monitoring. As we have seen in earlier chapters, people differ considerably in the variability of their moods over time, their degree of mood awareness, and the extent to which they can discriminate and label different types of mood. These differences may each influence the outcome of the mood monitoring process. Presumably, people whose moods change slowly, who are relatively unaware of their moods, or who are unable to discriminate and label different gradations or kinds of mood, will find monitoring a more difficult task than those who are accustomed to mood variations, are generally aware of their moods, and have a rich linguistic and conceptual framework for labelling affect.

Mood monitoring leads to an appraisal of mood, or an attempt to determine the personal significance of mood. Meanings which people attribute to their mood states will in turn influence the extent to which they try to change or maintain the mood. For example, somebody who has recently been bereaved may view their depressed and hopeless mood as natural and inevitable and therefore not make any attempt to change the way they are feeling. In contrast, someone with an extreme fear of dogs or trains is likely to realize that similar feelings are not widely experienced by other people. Thus they may appraise the apparent abnormality of their affect in markedly negative terms, and explicitly try a number of ways of resolving their fears.

Processes of monitoring, appraising, regulating, and reappraising do not operate entirely independent of each other. For example, people who have a strong tendency to pay attention to their moods (i.e. high mood monitors) also tend to report low self-esteem and more unpleasant moods (Swinkels & Giuliano, 1995). As we have seen in Chapter 4, these unpleasant moods may in turn lead to mood-congruent effects, with the result that high mood monitors may also attend more to the negative aspects of their environment, remember negative rather than positive events, and make more negative judgements about their circumstances. These processes of selective attention, memory, and decision-making may thus reinforce and sustain unpleasant mood states, making spontaneous mood change less likely. Moreover, highly self-conscious people apparently also tend to try to regulate their moods by thinking and ruminating about their mood state and problems: a strategy which generally appears to be rather less effective than using distraction to draw attention away from unpleasant moods (e.g. Nolen-Hoeksema, Morrow, & Fredrickson, 1993).

In our discussion so far, we have implied that differences in the regulation of normal affective reaction to life events can lead to clinically disordered mood. However, as we have already discussed, the distinction between clinical mood disorders and normal, unpleasant mood states is contentious. Many individuals experience protracted periods of negative affect and it is unclear if these individuals are at greater risk of developing clinical depression and anxiety than other people, or indeed how normal reactions to life events such as bereavement, trauma, or business failures become of clinical significance. Direct support for the mood-regulation explanation apparently requires longitudinal studies of the natural history of mood disorders. Unfortunately prior detection of suitable participants for such investigations is problematic because individuals typically only come to the notice of clinicians and researchers after the onset of their mood disorder. Correspondingly, the majority of people who report chronic unpleasant mood states never develop diagnosable mood disorders and so do not provide a suitably vulnerable sample for studying how clinical conditions arise. However, as Brewin (1989) suggests, *retrospective* accounts do indicate that many mood disorders are triggered by unsuccessful mood-regulation strategies. In the following sections, we will specifically consider the role of problems of mood regulation in the development and maintenance of the contrasting mood disorders of phobias and depression.

Phobias

Phobias are characterized by exaggerated fear of a specific type of object or situation. From the present perspective, phobias provide a good example of a problem that appears to be maintained by mood-regulation strategies that bring short-term relief but which actually increase and maintain the problem in the longer term. People suffering from phobias typically make use of *avoidance* strategies that minimize exposure to a feared object or situation (e.g. dogs, public speaking, travelling in enclosed spaces such as lifts or aeroplanes, social interactions) so as to avert their anticipated affective impact. For example, someone with a phobia about flying may go to extreme lengths to avoid the need for foreign travel or seek out other less anxiety-provoking means of transport.

Phobic anxiety may initially arise in a number of ways. First, fear may develop simply because of a specific aversive experience. For example, after having been bitten by a dog, a child may show fear and try to avoid physical proximity to other dogs. Second, fears may develop through a process of classical conditioning where a relatively neutral activity (e.g. shopping, walking alone) becomes associated with a very aversive and distressing physical experience such as fainting, feeling sick, or becoming breathless (Rachman, 1991; Watson & Rayner, 1920). This is hypothesized to be a common pathway to the development of agoraphobia. Typically, clients report having experienced frightening and inexplicable physical symptoms during an innocuous shopping trip or other outing. Subsequently the memory of this experience and the distress it evoked become linked or associated with all similar activities. In order to avoid further frightening experiences and/or the anxiety that these experiences produce, the agoraphobic client may eventually refuse to leave the house alone. A third way in which fears may develop depends on a process of social or vicarious learning, where the client observes fearful behaviour in other people (Ost & Hugdahl, 1981). For example, many people develop fears of spiders and mice not because they have ever been bitten by a spider or a mouse but because they see that other people behave as if they were frightened of spiders and mice.

Phobias are not only characterized by a specific fear (*phobic anxiety*) but also by a system of avoidance. The purpose of avoidance is to minimize exposure to the feared object or situation. In other words, avoidance reflects an attempt to regulate fear and anxiety. In the short term, avoidance strategies may work very effectively in reducing the chance of encountering the feared object or situation. For example, if you were afraid of space travel, you might very effectively control your fear simply by avoiding all opportunities to train as an astronaut. Unfortunately, however, most phobias concern commonly experienced objects or situations, making it far more difficult to maintain successful avoidance without considerable disruption to daily life. Thus, phobic clients' avoidance systems generally tend to become more complex over time. A person with a phobia about dogs, for example, may begin to avoid public parks and open spaces where dogs are exercised. This initial avoidance will reduce exposure to dogs but probably not eliminate contact entirely, and increasingly more complex strategies will often be implemented including not going out alone and not visiting people or places where dogs may be present.

In addition to this behavioural avoidance, people with phobias will often develop *cognitive* strategies involving hypervigilance and a continual scanning of the environment for evidence of the feared stimulus (Clark, 1986; Clark et al., 1988; Mathews & MacLeod, 1986). Phobic individuals also usually develop beliefs about what would happen if they did have to confront a dog at close quarters (e.g. "I'll get bitten" or "I'll lose control of myself and panic"), or about what other people would think of them under these circumstances ("If I lose control, everyone will think I'm completely stupid"). Alternatively, elaborate strategies may be constructed for avoiding thinking about dogs. These strategies may include not looking at pictures of dogs, not watching television programmes which feature dogs, avoiding conversations about dogs, and using distraction techniques. Unfortunately, these very efforts to suppress dog-related thoughts in order to avoid feeling anxious may in fact paradoxically strengthen the association between dogs and anxiety (Wegner, Shortt, Blake, & Page, 1990).

Not only does phobic avoidance often become a source of anxiety and worry itself, but it also ensures that the individual is never exposed to corrective experiences. In other words, avoiding the phobic object specifically prevents sufferers from learning through experience that dogs are not in fact usually dangerous, and stops them from getting any practice at tolerating elevated levels of anxiety. For these reasons, exposure to the feared object and to the resulting feelings of anxiety and fear is a central focus of treatments for anxiety states in general and phobias in particular (Marks, 1987).

In therapy, patients are taught how their avoidance has exacerbated and maintained the problem and are helped to expose themselves to the feared object either *in vivo* (in real life) or using imagination (Butler, 1989; Marks, 1987). Therapists attempt to provide patients with coping strategies that will compete with the physiological symptoms (e.g. sweating, feeling sick, heart thumping), cognitive aspects (e.g. beliefs about fainting or looking stupid), and behavioural effects (e.g. avoidance, running away) of anxiety during increasing degrees of exposure to the feared object. These strategies may include relaxation exercises focused on the physiological component of anxiety, the use of distraction or positive coping statements to counter negative, anxiety-linked thoughts, and role play, rehearsal, or modelling by the therapist to encourage behavioural change. An important component of treatment is the assignment of tasks which the client completes between sessions and which complement the strategies used during treatment itself. One rationale for using these "homework" tasks is to encourage generalization of any achieved changes to the client's life outside therapy sessions, so that treatment gains can be maintained after the therapy is over.

Depression

There are a number of pathways to depression. For some people, the disorder arises suddenly with no obvious external cause; in other cases, the problem appears to develop as a response to specific negative life events (such as a series of bereavements); and for a third group, depression emerges only after a long period of unhappiness and discontent. Investigation of these various developmental routes has mainly been retrospective, however. This is because clinicians are usually only able to identify relevant cases after the onset of the condition. In other words, when people present themselves to clinics and mental health services for help they are already depressed and therefore their account of how their problems began will inevitably be from memory. Thus our understanding of the development of depression is likely to be incomplete.

The clinical presentation of somebody who is depressed is often marked by a sense of being "stuck". Depressed mood seems unremitting and tactics for improving it all appear to be ineffectual. A range of cognitive deficits are also exhibited by depressed people: they remember more negative events than positive events; they attend more to negative aspects of their situation; and, given specific evidence, they reach more gloomy conclusions than non-depressed people (Haaga, Dyck, & Ernst, 1991). In addition, depressed people tend to have lowered levels of activity, and experience fewer rewarding and positive events (Lewinsohn, 1975). Cognitively and behaviourally then, the strategies used by depressed people seem more likely to maintain or exacerbate their unpleasant moods than to improve them.

A number of integrative psychological theories have been developed which imply that regulation processes play a central part in the development and maintenance of depressed moods. These theories tend to assume that depressed feelings first arise from the disruption of important roles or the failure to meet significant personal goals, and that these feelings are then maintained because these roles or goals can neither be fulfilled nor abandoned. For example, Oatley and Bolton (1985) suggested that certain social roles provide the individual with a sense of personal identity and self-worth. These roles may be interpersonal (e.g. the role of parent, spouse, friend, or lover), or may relate to work and achievement (e.g. effective employee, manager, or colleague). However, maintenance of these social roles may be threatened either because of the loss of a person or situation essential to the role's enactment, or because other factors make it impossible to sustain convincing or satisfactory performance of the role. These threats to the social role may elicit unpleasant emotions which will continue until an alternative replacement role can be found.

Other theorists suggest that it is the failure to achieve highly valued goals which leads to feelings of depression (Carver & Scheier, 1982; 1990, and see Chapters 3 and 6). These goals may be interpersonal (e.g. concerning intimacy or social integration), or they may be orientated toward status and power. Each individual has multiple goals, some of which may conflict with each other, leading to potential problems. Internal monitoring processes assess the extent to which the individual is making progress towards meeting the goals, and generate affective experiences in accordance with this assessment. In particular, rapid progress results in pleasant mood states, whereas slow progress results in unpleasant mood states. According to this theory, sustained unpleasant mood arises in situations where progress towards goals remains slow or non-existent, and where the individual is unable to abandon or change goals, or to focus on alternative goals.

Pyszczynski and Greenberg (1987) argued that when important social roles or personal goals are lost or thwarted, this brings about a state of self-focus directed at the perceived discrepancy between the desired state of affairs specified in the goal and the actual situation at the time. Perception of this discrepancy typically leads to an initial attempt to repair or recover the situation. In circumstances where the goals still cannot be attained, they are sometimes abandoned without great difficulty, either by derogating and denying the importance and significance of the original goal, or by substituting another replacement goal. Each of these strategies allows the individual to withdraw from the regulatory cycle of self-focus and goal orientation. In some circumstances, however, the unattainable goal may be too central or too important to abandon or devalue. When such a situation arises, continued self-focus on the unattainable goal and the current inability to attain it results in persistent unpleasant mood. This unpleasant mood may in turn lead to further negative thoughts and attributions, self-blame, and a more negative self-image, all of which reciprocally serve to maintain the negative self-focus and unpleasant mood.

Theories such as Pyszczynski and Greenberg's help to account for depression arising from the loss of social attachments. A common interpersonal goal is to establish and maintain a long-term intimate relationship with a romantic partner. This goal of intimacy can be thwarted in a number of ways, including divorce or separation, or the death of a partner. After experiencing a loss of intimacy, people may respond in a number of ways (Hays, Kasl, & Jacobs, 1994). Some people refuse to relinquish their emotional attachment. For example, Murray-Parkes (1972) described the characteristic process of "searching" which occurs among widows and widowers, and involves immersing themselves in memories and souvenirs of their dead spouse, sensing the presence of the absent partner in the house or garden, and holding imaginary conversations and discussions as if the other person was still with them. This focusing of attention on the past, on shared experiences, mementoes and memories appears to be a common phase of grieving and may represent a necessary step towards coming to terms with the abandonment of important social goals.

Most people do report a gradual reduction in the levels of distress they experience following bereavement or other loss (Hays, Kasl, & Jacobs, 1994). Some establish new relationships; some invest more in other relationships (e.g. with their children or grandchildren), and others simply accept that their goal of life-long intimacy and companionship has been irrevocably disrupted. Each of these strategies involves making some kind of adjustment concerning the valued goal of intimacy. For some individuals, however, these initially adaptive coping strategies may eventually become a means of perpetuating and elaborating the original distress. Persistent focus on the situation in which one has lost the means of achieving an important life goal, and on the associated experience of personal loss may determine the extent to which normal processes of grief develop into enduring symptoms of clinical depression. Maintaining a sense of intimacy with a partner who has died or otherwise left never to return not only involves working towards a goal that is irretrievably unattainable, but also usually interferes with the attainment of other potentially compensating goals. Such an extended period of grief appears to have similar effects to other kinds of rumination and self-focus

(Nolen-Hoeksema, Parker, & Larson, 1994). Rather than resolving the cause of current difficulties or problems or reducing their emotional impact, it only serves to increase awareness of unpleasant mood and to impede the implementation of more effective mood-regulation strategies.

Psychological treatment of depression involves helping individual clients to develop a wider repertoire of strategies for dealing with emotional disruptions. For example, in cases where depression has been precipitated by loss or bereavement, therapy might initially focus on encouraging clients to acknowledge and express their grief within the therapy session. This may involve structured techniques such as helping clients to write down their thoughts and feelings about their grief (Pennebaker, Colder, & Sharp, 1990), using photographs and mementoes of the lost person to evoke memories and emotions, or encouraging clients to imagine that their lost loved one is occupying an empty chair in the consulting room, thus providing them with the opportunity to say the things that they had left unsaid (the "empty chair technique", Greenberg & Rice, 1981). Although these procedures appear to increase self-focus, an important aspect of such clinically guided grief is that the experiences are shared with another person (i.e. the therapist) who can help the client to take a new perspective on their loss and to place it in the wider context of their life. For example, the recent death may have re-evoked memories and feelings from other earlier separations or deaths which have never been satisfactorily resolved and which now serve to perpetuate the current problems. In addition, the developing relationship with the therapist provides the client with evidence that new relationships are possible and may help to replace some of the intimacy that has been lost.

In addition to providing support and assisting in the expression of feelings, therapy may also involve encouraging clients to develop alternative behaviours which are incompatible with self-focus and rumination. This might simply involve structuring daily activities around practical tasks. Often these daily tasks specifically include some interpersonal component as a potential means of reducing the client's social isolation. For example, simple tasks might include visiting the library or taking exercise, and more complex tasks might include attending social events or taking on a role in a voluntary organization. It may also be necessary to help the client to identify alternative goals. These alternative goals are not intended to replace feelings of loss, or to remove the need for intimacy, but rather to establish a broader range of concerns which may provide different sources of satisfaction. In general terms, then, therapy may help to alleviate maladaptive affective reactions to loss by encouraging acknowledgement of the problem (including affect monitoring and appraisal), and assisting in the development of affect-regulation strategies such as finding new sources of pleasure and satisfaction.

PSYCHOLOGICAL INTERVENTIONS FOR MOOD DISORDERS

People who present themselves as clients to psychotherapy services typically do not believe that they can regulate their moods. Indeed, their current experience is often that their mood is relatively stable, very negative, and beyond their control. They usually have a sense of being "stuck". More specifically, clients may have little explicit understanding of their current difficulties; they may have selected strategies that have failed to change their mood; and they may have developed an incomplete, externalized interpretation of their problems within which they see themselves as passive victims.

According to our model of mood regulation, effective psychotherapy should enable clients to gain a sense of control over their emotional states, to attend to and label their moods, and to engage in more successful, self-generated mood-regulation strategies. Ideally, psychotherapy should also prevent further episodes of depression or anxiety by helping clients to avoid using unsuccessful mood-regulation strategies in future, and by ensuring that appropriate strategies are redeployed during the early stages of negative mood changes.

Although different types of psychotherapy are based on quite distinctive theoretical models of personality and emotional development, a number of factors are common to each of their treatment programmes. All therapies offer the following: an expectation that change is possible; a model and a rationale for explaining the client's current problems; a supportive and secure helping relationship; the opportunity to try out new ways of behaving, thinking and feeling; and an explicit contract between the therapist and client to explore ways of changing (Frank, 1971).

Over and above these common features, different modes of psychotherapy use a variety of specific techniques to bring about change in affect. Jones and Pulos (1993) suggested that therapies differ markedly in their treatment of affective material. In particular, they argued that cognitive-behavioural therapies encourage clients to control negative affect through the mobilization of explicit self-regulation skills, whereas psychodynamic-interpersonal therapies encourage clients to explore and experience negative affect in order to uncover, understand, and overcome intrapersonal and interpersonal blocks to mood regulation. Although changing mood is clearly a major aim of psychotherapy, very little research has directly examined what happens to mood during treatment, or tried to predict recovery from mood disorders and its maintenance on the basis of mood and mood change within sessions. However, some substantial controlled trials of psychotherapy have included evaluation of relatively short-term clinical outcomes. Unfortunately, though, many of these investigations have failed to consider potential problems arising from subsequent relapse and remission. In the following sections, we will review research concerning the impact of psychotherapy sessions on mood states, the outcomes of psychotherapy for mood disorders, and the maintenance of psychotherapeutic change in psychodynamic-interpersonal and cognitive-behavioural therapy.

Affective impact of psychotherapy sessions

Differences between the processes of psychodynamic therapy and cognitive-behaviour therapy and their respective impacts on clients have been illustrated in a handful of psychotherapy process studies. For example, Elliott and colleagues (1994) provided a detailed qualitative analysis of insight events occurring during cognitive-behavioural and psychodynamic-interpersonal psychotherapy. Immediately after a treatment session, clients were asked to identify the most helpful event that had happened during that session. For the psychodynamic insight event, the client selected a part of the session in which the therapist had identified an important theme in his life, that of "seducing" other people. The theme of seduction is clearly emotionally loaded; for this client, it evoked specific memories and feelings which concerned early childhood experiences involving his relationship with his mother. Instead of allowing the client to use his typical strategy of suppressing these painful thoughts and feelings about seduction, the therapist encouraged him to experience and elaborate the emotionally charged material. Such confrontation of painful feelings may have similar effects to the use of exposure to feared objects during cognitive-behavioural treatment of anxiety (see above). Experiencing these feelings more fully in the supportive environment of the therapy session allowed the client to address fears that might otherwise have been overwhelming. The therapist was then able to help the client to make links between these uncomfortable, unresolved feelings and some of his current difficulties with other people (including the therapist). In addition, the novelty of the affective experience enabled the client to rework some of his other thoughts and feelings that had become associated with the general notion of seduction. Two weeks after the identified event, the client reported that he had experienced insight into his ambivalent feelings about his mother, and that he had managed to tolerate these uncomfortable feelings rather than pushing them away.

The insight event selected by a female client in cognitive-behavioural therapy presented a contrasting account. This client described an experience at work where she had felt humiliated by a male colleague with whom she had a long-standing conflict. At the beginning of the insight event, the client had attributed responsibility for her humiliation to her own failures and shortcomings. By using humour, her female therapist then helped her see the incident in a rather different light. Specifically, the therapist suggested that the male colleague in question had behaved in a somewhat ridiculous way. The client's insight into this experience was to see that she need not take total responsibility for the colleague's behaviours, that he had been behaving like "a pain", and that there may have been other motivations for his behaviour towards her, such as jealousy. In reporting the impact of this event, the client indicated that she felt relieved and held less negative views of herself as a consequence of the insight. Two weeks after the session, the client stated that she still valued this insight, and that other colleagues with whom she had decided to discuss the problem had confirmed its validity.

Elliott and colleagues' qualitative analysis of significant events in psychotherapy confirms Jones and Pulos's (1993) suggestions about the differences between the two approaches. In particular, psychodynamic-interpersonal therapy genuinely does appear to involve therapists and clients working together to heighten mood states and to evoke a complex network of negative emotions and associations, while

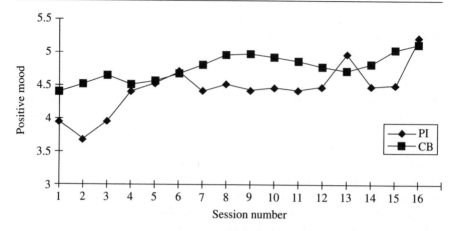

Figure 7.2 Ratings of positive mood in cognitive-behavioural and psychodynamic-interpersonal therapy

cognitive behaviour therapy works by minimizing clients' negative emotions and by shifting their personal attributions of responsibility to some external source such as another person or circumstances.

Additional support for these distinctions comes from a recent study by Reynolds and colleagues (Reynolds, Stiles, Barkham, Shapiro, Hardy, & Rees, in press). These investigators examined post-session mood ratings completed by a sample of 117 clients who had been randomly assigned to either cognitive-behavioural or interpersonal-psychodynamic psychotherapy. Averaging across all sessions of therapy, cognitive-behaviour therapy clients rated their sessions as smoother, and their moods immediately after sessions as more positive, than did clients who received psychodynamic-interpersonal therapy. Differences relating to whether the character of sessions changed as therapy progressed were also found. In particular, early sessions of psychodynamic-interpersonal therapy were much less smooth and less positive but became increasingly smooth and positive over later sessions. In contrast, sessions of cognitive behaviour therapy were uniformly smooth and positive throughout the course of treatment. By the end of therapy, clients in both types of therapy reported equally smooth sessions and equally positive moods. Differences in ratings of positive mood in the two therapies can be seen in Figure 7.2. The graph shows averaged ratings of positive mood made by 30 clients following each of sixteen sessions of psychodynamic-interpersonal therapy and corresponding ratings made by another 30 clients following each of sixteen sessions of cognitive-behaviour therapy. These findings strongly suggest systematic differences in the processes underlying the effectiveness of different forms of therapy. As might be expected on the basis of the theoretical considerations discussed above, cognitive-behaviour therapy occurs in a relatively calm environment in which the therapist and client systematically approach the presented problems in a planned and collaborative way. In contrast, psychodynamic-interpersonal therapy is delivered in a more intense atmosphere in which early sessions in particular are characterized by emotional turbulence.

Wiser and Goldfried (1993) examined single sessions of these two kinds of psychotherapy conducted by established practitioners who had been identified as being respected and competent by expert judges. Each therapist provided a tape recording of a session which they felt included a clinically significant change in the client, and indicated the moment at which this change had occurred. Independent researchers then rated the client's maximum and average level of emotional experiencing for each minute of the session. Taking sessions as a whole, the researchers found no overall differences between cognitive-behavioural and psychodynamic therapy in levels of emotional experiencing. However, interesting distinctions between the two treatment modes were apparent when the identified periods of important clinical change were specifically analysed. In the psychodynamic-interpersonal therapy, clients exhibited significantly higher levels of experiencing during these clinical-change segments than in other parts of the sessions, whereas in the cognitive-behavioural therapy, clients showed *lower* emotional experiencing during corresponding segments. Further, psychodynamic-interpersonal therapists spoke for the same proportion of time in the change and non-change segments, but cognitive-behaviour therapists spoke more in the clinical change segments than in the non-change segments. These findings provide additional support for our earlier conclusions about the differences between the two forms of psychotherapy. As anticipated, cognitive-behaviour therapists help clients to be objective and realistic, and use therapeutic techniques such as questioning, disputation, restructuring, and behavioural assignments as ways of reducing negative affect within and outside the therapeutic session. In contrast, psychodynamic-interpersonal therapists use affective experiences to provide clues about intrapsychic issues, and encourage the elaboration of feelings and beliefs.

Outcomes of psychotherapy for affective disorders

The available research findings strongly suggest that psychotherapy sessions have clear and immediate effects on clients' moods. However, some of these effects may be rather ephemeral, and may fail to meet the longer-term needs of clients, who are generally seeking lasting changes in their mood states and enduring relief from the disabling symptoms of depression and anxiety. Although there is little direct evidence that the beneficial short-term impact of sessions is causally related to the overall long-term outcomes of therapy, psychological therapies for the affective disorders are still probably some of the most systematically evaluated therapeutic methods in the health-care field. The reassuring common conclusion of all existing reviews of psychotherapy outcome research is that the benefits of psychotherapy are substantial compared to other methods of intervention, and significantly greater than those of no treatment at all (e.g. Lambert & Bergin, 1994; Smith, Glass, & Miller, 1980). For example, Dobson (1989) reviewed ten outcome studies assessing the treatment of depression using cognitive-behaviour therapy and concluded that the clinical outcome of the average client treated with cognitive-behaviour therapy surpassed 98 percent of non-treated control patients. The outcomes of psychological treatments for anxiety disorders have been less extensively evaluated but a number of case studies (e.g. Salkovskis, Jones, & Clark, 1986) and controlled clinical trials (e.g. Butler, Fennell, Robson, & Gelder, 1990) have demonstrated that cognitive and behavioural interventions bring about significant improvements in clinical state which are maintained up to six months after treatment.

Outcome studies also suggest that the changes resulting from psychotherapy occur relatively rapidly. For example, Howard, Kopta, Krause, and Orlinsky (1986) reviewed data from fifteen samples comprising 2,431 clients who had received individual, weekly psychotherapy. They observed that over 50 percent of patients had improved after eight sessions of therapy and that 68 percent had improved after sixteen sessions. After sixteen sessions, this rate of improvement slowed down, so that at 26 sessions approximately 75 percent of patients had improved, and after 52 sessions approximately 80 percent had improved. These data indicate the operation of a "law of diminishing returns" such that increases in the length of treatment bring less improvement the longer therapy continues.

As evidence for the efficacy of psychotherapy has accumulated, a new and somewhat puzzling problem has emerged. On the one hand, different methods of psychotherapy vary dramatically in terms of their theoretical rationales, therapist behaviours and techniques, and in the impacts and focus of therapy sessions (as discussed above). On the other hand, however, reviews of the literature suggest that these contrasting methods bring about broadly *similar* results when compared in controlled experimental conditions (the *equivalence paradox*: Luborsky, Singer, & Luborksy, 1975; Stiles, Shapiro, & Elliott, 1987).

Two alternative explanations for this apparent paradox have been proposed. First, it may be that many "active ingredients" are common to all kinds of psychotherapy (including support, encouragement, a positive therapeutic alliance, a system of understanding problems, and an expectation of beneficial change). The presence of these common factors alone, it is suggested, may be sufficient to bring about change. Correspondingly, the absence of the same factors may effectively rule out the possibility of improvement.

The second explanation also accepts the essential role played by common ingredients of different therapies in effecting change. However, this alternative account further suggests that particular technical interventions (e.g. interpretations, challenging dysfunctional beliefs) have additional specific effectiveness for subgroups of clients, over and above the impact of any factors common to all therapies. In other words, certain characteristic features of psychodynamic-interpersonal therapy may provide benefit only to clients who are specifically suited to this kind of therapy, or whose particular problems turn out to be correctable using the associated techniques. Similarly, different clients and different problems may be more amenable to treatment using cognitive-behavioural therapy. According to this account, the standard practice of random allocation of clients to therapy conditions in outcome research may average out specific interactions between individual clients and the treatments they receive. In effect, each treatment group may contain clients who are suited to the allocated form of therapy together with clients who would respond better to an alternative regime. If this conclusion is correct, an important goal of research is to identify what factors determine whether cognitive-behavioural or psychodynamic-interpersonal therapy is more appropriate to the case in question.

As we have seen from studies of session impact, mood responds relatively quickly to therapy. In this regard, Howard and colleagues (Howard, Leuger, Maling, and Martinovich, 1993) proposed that the results of psychotherapy become apparent in three stages. The first stage is *remoralization* and involves improvements in subjectively experienced well-being including mood. These mood changes are then followed by *remediation* (reduction in symptoms), and finally by *rehabilitation* (general enhancement of functioning at work, in family life, and during social interaction). Remoralization may be an essential first step in any therapeutic work because clients who do not experience some rapid subjective improvement may lose the motivation to participate actively in their therapy, or may even discharge themselves from treatment. In support of the conclusion that remoralization is the first stage of therapeutic change, Kopta, Howard, Lowry, and Beutler (1994) found that acute distress symptoms responded most rapidly to treatment. In particular, reports of "crying easily" were significantly reduced in 50 percent of clients after five sessions. Reports of chronic distress symptoms (e.g. "blaming yourself", "feeling no interest") also responded well to therapy but took between eleven and seventeen sessions. The problems most resistant to change were those involving relationships with other people and those apparently related to long-term personality problems, of which fewer than 50 percent had improved after 52 sessions. Similar findings have also been reported by Barkham and colleagues (Barkham, Rees, Stiles, Shapiro, Hardy, & Reynolds, in press) who examined the rate of change reported by 212 depressed clients in time-limited psychotherapy. These investigators also found that subjective distress (mood) changed more quickly than problems in interpersonal relationships.

Maintenance of therapeutic change

An important criterion for evaluating any therapeutic intervention concerns the extent to which it reduces the probability of occurrence of future disorders. As we have seen earlier in this chapter, mood disorders are typically chronic and cyclical; that is, untreated they tend to last for approximately six months to a year, and up to 50 percent of clients will experience some recurrence of their problems within a year. It is in this context that consideration of the duration and maintenance of therapeutic effects have become of considerable practical importance.

As argued above, some irrevocable life experiences such as poor relationships with parents or early separations may make people specifically vulnerable to mood disorders such as depression and anxiety. In addition, characteristic patterns of thinking about the world also appear to predispose people to these clinical conditions. Unless psychotherapy is able to provide permanent resolution for both these kinds of vulnerability factors, clients may remain at risk of future difficulties, particularly when faced with future crises.

Psychological treatments of depression offer a promise of sustained improvement because they deal with both the interpersonal and situational vulnerabilities in an individual's history (psychodynamic-interpersonal therapy) and the distorted cognitive and behavioural styles that contribute to the development and maintenance of depression and anxiety (cognitive-behavioural therapy). The goal of maintaining improvement when treatment is over is made explicit in cognitive-behaviour therapy, which encourages clients to plan strategies for coping with future difficulties. The idea is that clients who receive therapy will be able to apply some of the techniques and insights picked up during therapy to their subsequent lives. In particular, clients should be able to anticipate likely problems and crises, select from a wide range of strategies for dealing with them, and have the skills to evaluate and modify their responses if their strategies prove ineffective (Evans et al., 1992; Simons, Murphy, Levine, & Wetzel, 1986). In contrast, the administration of medication is believed to provide no lasting protective function; patients given this kind of treatment will inevitably attribute their mood changes to their medication rather than to themselves, and will gain no new skills that may be applied to future difficulties. Recent recommendations therefore suggest that drug therapies need to be administered indefinitely for individual patients who have a history of recurrent depression (Greden, 1993; Montgomery, 1994).

Clinical outcome studies have typically included only brief follow-up periods which include only one or two measures of clinical state. Nicholson and Berman (1983) calculated the mean follow-up period to be around eight-and-a-half months and called the need for longer follow-ups into question on the basis that improvement immediately after treatment and at follow-up was very highly correlated. Their interpretation of this latter finding was that therapeutic change was stable and that follow-up data were therefore largely redundant. With hindsight, it is apparent that these conclusions are based on an inadequate concept of mood which assumes that isolated assessments of mood are representative of longer-term variations and trends in affect. In this regard, it is clearly important that relapse and remission of symptoms in mood disorders should be investigated using methods which allow for repeated measurement of moods and symptoms, and which acknowledge the relevance of mood-change processes. Since Nicholson and Berman's review, there has been an increasing awareness of the vulnerability of depressed clients to relapse and a corresponding interest in evaluating longer-term therapy outcomes more stringently and in developing treatment packages which maximize the possibility of maintaining change (Shea et al., 1992).

Shapiro and colleagues (Shapiro, Rees, Barkham, Hardy, Reynolds, & Startup, 1995) examined the extent to which cognitive-behaviour therapy and psychodynamic-interpersonal therapy protected depressed clients from relapse. More than a hundred clients were followed up for one year after therapy. Their initial response to treatment and their status at a three-month follow up suggested a slight but non-significant advantage for clients in cognitive-behaviour therapy. Taking the sample as a whole it seemed that the short-term effects of treatment were very largely maintained one year after the end of therapy. Monitoring the outcomes and follow-up scores of individual clients presented a somewhat different picture, however. Although over 50 percent did remain symptom-free and had sought no further psychological or psychiatric help during the follow-up period, almost half of the clients reported an unstable pattern over the year, characterized either by partial remission at one or more assessment points or by the clients seeking further help for their psychological problems (therapy or medication).

The recent focus on maintaining therapeutic benefits presents a more realistic orientation to the treatment of psychological problems. As we have seen, a significant number of individuals may be more vulnerable to mood disorders because of their adverse life experiences or chronic deprivation. Brief methods of psychological treatments apparently have quite dramatic impacts on their subjective sense of well-being and seem to help individuals regain a sense of control over their mood states. Increasingly, however, it appears that for many individuals with chronic problems these changes cannot be sustained without the ongoing support of a structured therapeutic environment. For these clients, the idea that a limited number of therapy sessions can provide life-long protection against future problems seems somewhat overoptimistic. An important direction at the interface of mood research and psychotherapy research is to establish how the remoralizing effects of therapies on mood and perceived mood-regulation skills can be provided in less costly and more accessible services which are capable of supporting vulnerable individuals on a longer-term basis.

SUMMARY

In this chapter, we have covered a considerable amount of ground. We have highlighted some of the conceptual difficulties in differentiating between normal mood states and clinical mood disorders, outlined two major approaches to the theory and therapy of mood disorders, considered how phobias and depression may each be conceptualized as arising from problems with mood regulation, and reviewed the impacts of therapy on mood within sessions, at the end of therapy, and following therapy. Each of these topics has illustrated how the failure to consider mood as a process hinders our understanding of mood disorders.

Adopting a process perspective to mood disorder appears to have considerable practical and theoretical potential. First, principles relating to mood regulation may help to provide a framework for integrating theoretical accounts of mood disorders and their treatment. Second, intensive, longitudinal studies of mood change may help to clarify why some people develop mood disorders while others do not, why some people but not others recover spontaneously from the impact of negative life events such as bereavement and unemployment, and why some individuals seem prone to frequent episodes of depression. This kind of study may

8

CONCLUSIONS AND
FUTURE DIRECTIONS

OVERVIEW

So far in this book, we have reviewed psychological theory and research into mood and drawn attention to the potential benefits of adopting a real-time approach that emphasizes the regulatory processes underlying mood variation. In this final chapter, we summarize our conclusions from previous chapters, and apply these conclusions to some of the basic topics considered earlier in the book. In particular, we consider some of the consequences of a process approach for theory and research into mood structure and the causes and effects of mood and mood change. In addition, we sketch out a provisional model of mood variation and regulation that we hope will help to orient research in this area, and highlight some of the important issues which we believe still need to be addressed. The psychological investigation of moods as changing and regulated processes is still at a relatively early stage of development and we will indicate what we believe to be its most exciting future directions and applications. Finally, we present a revised definition of mood based on our current state of knowledge.

IMPLICATIONS OF A PROCESS APPROACH TO MOOD

Most current psychological approaches treat moods as momentary mental states with simple perceived qualities (Chapter 2). Research typically focuses on either the factors leading to these states (Chapter 3), or the consequences of being in these states for other aspects of psychological functioning (Chapter 4). In this book, we have reviewed theory and research that adopts a more dynamic perspective on mood. In particular, we have considered the ways in which mood changes over time (Chapter 5), the processes underlying active regulation of mood (Chapter 6), and how such regulatory processes might be implicated in clinical disorders of mood (Chapter 7). Our central argument has been that attention to these changing and changeable aspects of mood can open up a more realistic outlook on this research area. In this chapter, we review our conclusions so far and speculate some more about the nature and potential of a process approach to mood. In this section, we return specifically to some of the basic issues about mood that were raised in the earlier chapters and show how application of a more dynamic perspective helps to clarify them.

Mood structure

In Chapter 2, we reviewed research examining the similarities and differences between mood states as they are represented conceptually and as they arise in everyday experience. It is apparently possible to characterize the quality of mood by specifying its value along semantic dimensions of pleasantness and activation. Further, certain combinations of pleasantness and activation seem to be experienced more commonly than others. However, we also concluded that pleasantness and activation are not the only meaningful dimensions that may be applied to different mood states, but rather represent the most basic internal characteristics of the momentary perception of affect. For example, if you suddenly surfaced into consciousness and immediately wanted to define your current affective state then its pleasantness and activational aspects might be the only kinds of information that would register in the first instance. In other words, introspection without reference to historical or situational context (cf. Wundt, 1897), may only permit awareness of a general attraction or repulsion at some level (or an approach or avoidance tendency) and a degree of activity associated with this attraction or repulsion (rate of approach or avoidance). To extend these possible distinctions, it is necessary to make reference to the relational setting or to the unfolding of the psychological state over time.

With respect to the situational context of affect, distinctions between mood states, apart from those based on pleasantness and activation, are often based on *extrinsic* as well as intrinsic features (Russell, 1978). In other words, it is not only affect's internal characteristics that are important but also how these characteristics bear on current personal or environmental concerns. For example, particular emotions may be characterized as combinations of pleasantness and activation values that are attributed to particular causes in the life situation. Guilt is an unpleasant emotion that is seen as resulting from your own misdemeanour whereas anger is an unpleasant activated state apparently arising from another person's misdemeanour against you, for example (cf. Ortony, Clore, & Collins, 1988; Reisenzein, 1994). Similarly, we might characterize different kinds of unfolding mood according to the way they are related to whatever else is happening in the person's life. Thus, an unpleasant mood that persists despite relatively undemanding conditions is qualitatively different from an unpleasant mood that is sustained by continuing negative circumstances or pressures. In clinical terms, the former example might be similar to endogenous depression while the latter case represents a reactive and potentially more tractable condition. Similarly, Teasdale and Barnard (1993) argued that moods with similar evaluative tone may be maintained by different kinds of intrapsychic or situational processes, whose specific nature may determine their consequences for general cognitive functioning (see Chapter 4). On the basis of this discussion, it seems possible to characterize affective states according to their general degree of relationship to the currently unfolding situational context, as well as by reference to the specific nature of that relationship. Failure to address these extrinsic aspects of affective states is bound to restrict our current understanding of mood structure and operation.

Another way of extending our appreciation of the variety of possible moods is to consider affect as a process that unfolds over time rather than as a simple and intact momentary state. For example, there are several possible distinctions that can be drawn between different mood experiences on the basis of their temporal characteristics. In particular, a rapid decline or increase in pleasantness or activation would obviously feel very different from a gradual one. Similarly, contrast effects are likely to influence the perception of pleasant moods depending on whether they follow more or less pleasant moods as well as on how quickly the respective changes occur. One implication of this analysis is that the developing history of any mood variation makes a difference to the perception and interpretation of current momentary mood (cf. Parkinson, Briner, Reynolds, & Totterdell, 1995), so that the same mental state attains a different meaning as a function of its temporal context, much in the same way as cold water feels even colder on a hot day.

From the present perspective, the unfolding development of the mood process is not important simply because it changes the perceptual experience of momentary mood. Rather, we believe that the true character of mood only reveals itself when the process is continually tracked over time. In other words, we want to argue that moods have inherent temporal structure, which is difficult to discern from consideration of momentary samples. In much the same way, a single movie frame can conceal aspects of the ongoing action that only become apparent when it is viewed as part of an extended and ongoing sequence of footage. Information about character and plot in sequence is relatively less available from a still than a moving picture. Correspondingly, moods by their very nature have temporal extension and are patterned according to their dynamic characteristics as well as in terms of their momentary internal constitution.

Paradoxically, it seems that trying to understand the structure of mood by focusing on a single elementary moment of experience adds complications that disappear when the phenomenon is addressed as part of an unfolding psychological process embedded in the real-time situational context. For example, we often know what mood we are in by picking up its changes on-line as we interact with the environment.

A basic implication of this analysis is that the focus on momentary mood qualities of pleasantness and activation gives an impoverished picture of the phenomenon. Systematic investigation is needed of different kinds of mood change over time and their implications for conscious experience and for other aspects of psychological function (see below). As a first step in this task, fundamental descriptive research should address people's everyday distinctions between different kinds of temporally defined mood states, such as exhilaration, deflation, and disappointment (cf. Carver & Scheier, 1990).

189

Predictors of mood

Approaching mood as a momentary state also restricts our understanding of the variables that determine its onset. In Chapter 3, we looked at the various personal, situational, and transactional factors that might contribute to the causation of moods. Clearly, a wide range of psychologically relevant processes can make a difference to the way we feel at any given moment. However, seeing mood as a simple outcome, or as the response in a one-way stimulus–response chain, tends to draw attention away from the real-time attunement of moods to ongoing projects and concerns. In everyday life, moods are not always simply triggered by separate events that happen inside or outside the person (or somewhere between). Rather, mood state contributes to all encounters from the outset and the route taken towards any goal is partly shaped by the affective aspects of what is happening. To put this in another way, moods precede as well as follow transactions and are typically part of what happens during those transactions rather than extraneous variables. When people win a contest or achieve some honour, for example, their success does not simply influence mood in a one-way causal sequence, but rather the anticipations of the outcome impact on prior mood as it develops, and the fulfilment of the goal feeds into this already ongoing mood process. If success is sudden and unanticipated, the change in affect will be more dramatic, perhaps giving the illusion of having arisen purely in direct reaction to an intact event. However, if the build up of expectations occurs over a more extended period and the outcome is perceived as more or less inevitable, affective change will be more gradual and self-sustaining (cf. Carver & Scheier, 1990).

Rather than focusing on how localized environmental events or stable personal dispositions lead to one-shot mood outcomes, research into mood predictors needs to look more closely at how changing situational and personal factors and their interactions contribute to different kinds of mood variations over time. For example, Larsen and Kasimatis (1990) showed that people scoring higher on a questionnaire measure of extraversion showed less of a regular weekly rhythm in mood changes (see also Chapter 5). In order to extend this promising approach, it is necessary to consider the situational and personal predictors as well as the affective outcomes in dynamic terms. Further, rather than seeing causality as unidirectional, it is important to recognize that mood is part of a broader unfolding process and has effects as well as causes.

Mood effects

Research into mood effects tends to treat the variable as a momentary input rather than a momentary output. In Chapter 4, we reviewed studies investigating how pleasant and unpleasant moods affect other aspects of psychological functioning. The present process approach calls attention to two basic limitations of this kind of research. The first of these arises from operationally defining mood in terms of its momentary internal structure which is usually characterized in terms of degrees of pleasantness and activation (see above). In practice, most studies in this area make simple and direct comparisons between the effects of good and bad moods (or good, bad, and neutral moods). Not only does this focus specifically exclude more specific varieties of momentary affect (e.g. Keltner, Ellsworth, & Edwards, 1993; Westen, 1994), but also it fails to address the importance of more temporally articulated mood qualities (as outlined above). One simple example of how mood's effects depend on time-related variables is provided by Sedikides (1994) who showed that unpleasant moods produce mood-congruence in the short term but incongruence after a brief time delay.

A second limitation of mood effects research concerns its treatment of the independent variable as divorced from its unfolding transactional context. As we have argued in connection with research into mood predictors, mood is typically part of the transactional process, not something that goes on entirely outside it. One of the most obvious research implications of this argument is that mood manipulations may have differential impact on people depending on their concurrent and recent mood. Not only might mood induction be more or less effective depending on whether prior mood contrasts or is consistent with the intended mood (as discussed above), but also the achievement of comparable moods may have different effects for people with different mood histories (or indeed different anticipated mood futures). For example, a change from mildly pleasant to moderately pleasant mood may seem more "natural" to the person experiencing it than a change from mildly unpleasant to moderately pleasant mood. Because the latter change may be seen as more surprising, it is also more likely to lead to explicit monitoring of mood and possible attempts at regulation. These indirect consequences of mood-change might in turn bring their own effects on judgement and behaviour. More generally, it is not sufficient to establish mood equivalence at a momentary level in order to predict similar mood effects.

Of course, if temporal factors are crucial to understanding the operation of mood, experimental approaches that rely on one-shot measures and before-and-after designs can only ever provide a restricted window on the big picture of the process under investigation. The best way to understand what mood does in this view is to investigate the way it unfolds over time and how its variations relate to other aspects of developing psychological transactions. Thus, in Chapter 5, we addressed the temporal signatures of various kinds of changing moods, and in Chapter 6, we considered some of the psychological systems underlying these patterns of mood over time.

ASPECTS OF MOOD REGULATION

Seeing moods as continuous and continuously changing phenomena leads to an emphasis on the real-time dynamic processes underlying mood variation. In Chapter 6 we suggested that automatic and controlled regulatory processes underlie many changes in mood and discussed Wegner's (1994) theory of how these kinds of process might interact. In the next two sections of the present chapter, we take this analysis further and start to develop our own model of mood regulation. First, however, two disclaimers: first, given that research in this area is still at a relatively early stage of development, our model will be correspondingly lacking in precise specification; second, although we believe that our theoretical position captures many important aspects of changing moods as discussed in previous chapters, we are not yet in a position to offer direct or definitive empirical support for the model. However, we believe that it is worthwhile to sketch out the basic shape of a theory that may be capable of accounting for dynamic features of mood processes as they relate to real-time transactional encounters in the social world, if only to encourage more focused research on these issues and further development of theoretical understanding.

Any control-based model of affect regulation necessarily incorporates at least four kinds of process (see also Chapter 6). The first and most basic process is the unfolding of affect itself (insofar as it can meaningfully be separated from its transactional context). The second is a monitoring process which registers information relating to the affective process to check that regulation is working effectively. The third process involves some kind of appraisal (however basic) which assesses whether current monitored mood (or recent mood-change) conforms to goals (which are either preset or generated on-line by a further intentional process). The fourth and final process concerns the regulation operation proper which is intended to bring mood into line with goals of one kind or another.

In reality, the separation between these four kinds of process might not be as absolute as implied by the preceding discussion. For example, awareness of mood may contribute directly to mood itself, and regulation may sometimes seem to be an intrinsic part of the affective process rather than something that operates independently on mood at a different level of functioning (cf. Mayer, Salovey, Gomberg-Kaufman, & Blainey, 1991). However, for the purposes of elaborating a theory it is worth maintaining these broadly defined distinctions. Bearing this in mind, the model should specify how the four aspects of the affect regulation process can operate independently and how they may interact with each other in different circumstances. In the sections that follow, we will first consider the specific characteristics of affect, affect monitoring, affect appraisal, and affect regulation processes, and then illustrate some possible sequences of events characterizing affect-regulation episodes across the four levels, in order to give a general idea of what an integrative model of the overall system might look like. As we have already conceded, we are not yet in a position to specify a formal theory of mood regulation, but we can at least sketch out a rough outline of the shape such a model might take.

Mood process

The prevalent conception of mood in contemporary psychology is that it is a kind of internal signal carrying evaluative information, and also perhaps a motivational state supplying (or withholding) activation. In this view, mood is an indication of whether we are favourably or unfavourably disposed towards what is happening in our lives, and provides a source of (or a drain on) "energy" or "drive" for engaging or disengaging with the situation. In this section, we will consider the informational and motivational aspects of mood separately, drawing attention to some of the limitations of many current approaches.

The present position contrasts with prevailing ideas about mood in a number of ways: first, we believe that mood is not just a simple signal but rather a potential source of many kinds of relatively complex information involving temporal articulation as well as internal momentary structure. Second, we contend that registration of this mood-related information can happen in a number of direct and indirect, non-conscious as well as conscious ways (see section on mood monitoring below). Third, we do not think that all of the possible effects of mood depend on registration of the information that it contains, but may also reflect more direct, motivational factors. Fourth, our view is that the motivational aspects of mood involve *direction* as well as general activation or the provision of non-specific "energy" or "drive" (cf. Duffy, 1962), and that they predispose individuals to engage in particular varieties of developing action. Each of these points is developed further in the discussion that follows.

1. *Mood as information*

According to many contemporary theories of mood and emotion, one of the key adaptive purposes of the affective system is to inform individuals about their current state of relations with the environment (e.g. Buck, 1985; Frijda, 1988; Morris, 1992; Thayer, 1989). For example, Schwarz (1990) argued as follows:

> At a general level, one may assume that a positive affective state informs the individual that the world is a safe place, one that does not threaten the person's current goals. . . . Negative affective states, on the other hand, inform the individual that the current situation is problematic . . . If this is so, one's affective state can serve as a simple but highly salient indicator of the nature of the situation one is in. (p. 543)

According to this view, unpleasant affective states serve as warnings that something is going wrong, and pleasant affective states are safety signals which encourage taking a breather, adopting a more relaxed attitude, or exploring new possibilities. In other words, the registration of affective information is believed to provide the individual with a global assessment of the relevance of the current life situation for personal concerns.

Again, one of the main limitations of this account is that it focuses almost exclusively on the pleasantness dimension of affect. Moods are thought to provide information that is generally evaluative but nothing more. In our view, the kinds of information supplied by mood are more complex and more varied than implied by such an account. For example, moods contain information with internal temporal structure and can therefore register rates of change in psychological adjustment as well as providing a static readout of the current situation. In this connection, Carver and Scheier (1990, see Chapter 3) have suggested that affect conveys

193

internal feedback about how rapidly goals are being approached rather than simply signalling how far away these goals presently are. Thus, pleasant affect signals more rapid movement towards success than anticipated and unpleasant affect signals unexpectedly slower progress. However, even in Carver and Scheier's model, affect registers temporally integrated information about transactions on a moment-by-moment basis, summarizing an unspecified time period in an instantaneous single value. In contrast, we believe that affect is continually attuned on-line to rate of progress and changes in rate of progress. For example, a feeling of exhilaration corresponds to accelerating approach towards a valued goal. In addition, our view is that the specific quality of mood not only depends on a general-purpose readout of some abstractly defined goal-approach parameters but also on the particular nature of the current transaction, the specific character of the associated goal and so on. For instance, an irritable mood not only implies frustration of minor goals but also a mode of relating to the people who are around you at the time. At the informational level, then, mood is not just a non-specific evaluative signal, but also carries more direct implications for action *and* interpretation. Additionally, as we have made clear in previous chapters, these goal-related determinants of mood do not represent the only relevant input variables that shape the course of affective states over time.

A second limitation of most informational theories of affect is that they fail to address the process (or processes) whereby mood signals are picked up by the cognitive system. In our view, affective information of various kinds may be registered in a number of different ways depending on the specific monitoring processes that are in operation at the time (see next section), but in some circumstances may remain as only a *potential* source of data that is not actually consulted by any monitoring process. In other words, the fact that mood contains information does not mean that this information is always used by the individual, or that the central function of the mood process is to provide such information.

2. Mood as motivation

Many current theories of mood attribute most or all of its effects to its signal value (e.g. Schwarz, 1990) or to its related influences on cognitive processing (Forgas, 1995). This emphasis is in line with the contemporary prevalence of cognitive approaches to psychology in general. However, part of the distinctiveness of affective phenomena derives from the fact that they relate to "energy", "drive", and incentive in addition to information: indeed this is one of the reasons why affect and cognition have often been treated as independent categories of psychological functioning (cf. Zajonc, 1980). In our view, not all of the impact of mood depends on its signal value, because being in particular moods also directly predisposes people to engage in certain kinds of action.

Several theories of mood have emphasized its motivational or drive properties. For example, theories that focus on the activation components of affective experience often imply that various forms of physiological arousal may provide metabolic energy that supports certain kinds of activity (cf. Thayer, 1989). Other models have emphasized the activating properties of central nervous system processes supporting positive affect and the inhibitory centres that are implicated in the production of negative affect (e.g. Gray, 1987; Larsen & Ketelaar, 1991). Similarly, some investigators have drawn attention to the possible reward and punishment properties of pleasant and unpleasant affective states.

More relevant to the concerns of the present book are theories emphasizing the different kinds of regulatory behaviour that different kinds of mood state tend to encourage. For example, Clark and Isen (1982) argue that pleasant moods tend to invoke maintenance activities while unpleasant moods are often followed by the use of mood-repair strategies. Although this account seems to imply that the particular quality of mood states partly determines their differential motivational impact, in fact the basic assumption is that human behaviour is hedonistically motivated whatever mood is being experienced (so that pleasant states are desired and unpleasant states unwanted). More recently, Parrott (1993) has suggested that some kinds of mood regulation may depend on intentions that are not motivated by a desire for immediate gratification. According to both these accounts, it is not moods themselves that carry motivational properties; instead, more general principles of psychological functioning determine what kinds of mood are required.

In our view, moods reflect changing dispositions towards certain modes of action and interpretation and are thus tightly bound up with motivational as well as informational processes from the outset. For example, being in an irritable mood implies that you are ready to react with annoyance to minor interpersonal impediments, and that you are inclined to interpret other people's behaviour as personally insulting. A mood of excitement similarly bears direct relation to action and interpretation. Specifically, when excited, you are attuned to aspects of the situation indicating impending success, and motivated to keep on trying to attain the imminent goal. Rapid increases in excitement of this kind produce a dynamically different state of exhilaration which may provide information that the need for effort is almost over, and may motivate a final push to reach the end of your striving. Although some of these specific motivational properties of different moods clearly relate to the notion of activation in some way, its different manifestations in different kinds of developing situation strongly suggest that no unitary dimension is involved. Similarly, different mood states are not simply characterized by positive or negative reinforcement but rather represent different and changing patterns of allocating attraction and aversion to different aspects of the ongoing situation. A final point illustrated by the example of exhilaration is that motivational processes seem to be selective with respect to their temporal as well as spatial allocation of resources.

Mood-monitoring processes

Mood monitoring occurs whenever information concerning mood is registered by, or provides direct input to, any other cognitive process. In Chapter 6, we discussed some of the controlled and automatic processes underlying monitoring of different kinds. In the present section, it is only necessary to summarize our earlier conclusions about how monitoring operates in the context of more general mood-regulation processes.

In our view, mood is not necessarily consciously registered and not always monitored even by implicit and automatic processes. We believe that mood can occur at a relatively non-conscious level, be felt but not characterized, or be explicitly recognized as a particular kind of mood state. For example, we can be in a bad mood without realizing it, we can feel bad without being explicitly focused on the state, or we can know that we are feeling bad. We may also register different aspects of mood in different ways, and through different information channels, including social feedback, proprioception, feelings of flow and so on. In short, there are many possible kinds of monitoring, all of which are distinguishable in principle from the mood process itself although they may have relatively intricate interactions with it.

The importance of mood monitoring in the regulation process is that it ensures that activities undertaken to modify or maintain mood do not run on blindly when they are either having no effect or have already met their requirements. According to Wegner (1994), monitoring can be achieved using a simple and automatic matching process which checks for prespecified mood values. Although such a mechanism might be adequate for registering simple informational aspects of mood, such as its general level of intensity and activation, more sophisticated monitoring is clearly required in the implementation of more particular and more strategic mood-regulation intentions. For example, a mood-regulation goal might be to stay affectively attuned to your partner in an ongoing interaction, which would require continual assessment of the quality of the other person's as well as your own affective state and the way each changes (qualitatively and quantatively) over time. A monitoring process such as that proposed by Wegner would require continual resetting to new values of required affect under these circumstances, effectively removing any advantages it might allow in terms of conservation of cognitive capacity. In our view, monitoring may involve relatively intricate tracking processes which are attuned to complex attributes of multifaceted and temporally articulated mood states.

Mood appraisal processes

The interaction of mood processes with mood-monitoring processes leads to registration of affective information at some level. Although this will often carry intrinsic implications about whether the state is concordant or conflicts with current motivational concerns, some form of appraisal is usually necessary before these implications are worked through and appropriate strategies for action can be selected. For example, although registration of an unpleasant mood often already implies that the state is unwanted, there may be other overriding concerns which moderate the conclusion that it should be removed as quickly as possible, depending on how the mood relates to other aspects of the current life situation. Further, the mood needs to be evaluated in the context of available resources before any decision about what action is required can be made (cf. Lazarus, 1991).

As with monitoring, there are probably a wide variety of processes that may contribute to appraisal in different circumstances. Some of these may be fairly basic pattern-matching procedures similar to, and possibly continuous with, monitoring itself. For example, in the case of automatic regulatory processes relating to mood, appraisal and monitoring are simultaneous and co-extensive, with detection of deflections from preset values leading directly to preprogrammed corrective responses. However, deliberate mood regulation often requires a more flexible assessment of the mood in context and of currently available resources that may be allocated to any activity that the implications of the mood might encourage.

In more controlled instances of regulation, mood-appraisal processes assess the relevance of present mood for currently active projects and concerns, determine whether any action needs to be taken, and if it does, specify the kind of action that is necessary, and whether currently available regulatory resources are capable of supporting such action. For example, mood will be appraised in more negative terms to the extent that it is seen as impeding progress towards current goals and to the extent that the opportunities for correcting the unwanted mood are limited. Thus, mood appraisal may lead to meta-mood experiences whereby individuals come to approve or disapprove of their own feelings (cf. Mayer & Stevens, 1994). The basic function of mood appraisal is to mediate between mood monitoring and mood regulation itself, determining whether regulation is required and what form it should take, as well as whether that kind of regulation is feasible.

Of course, mood appraisal is not necessarily a separate stage of the mood regulation process that must be completed before any attempt at regulation is made. Rather, monitoring may lead to immediate regulation attempts which take place in parallel with appraisal of the implications of the mood in its overall context (including these same already ongoing regulation attempts). Like monitoring, appraisal may occur continuously or periodically over the course of mood-regulation episodes, though its main roles are in the initial decision to regulate, selection of appropriate regulation responses, and evaluation of the success of these responses with reference to their impact on monitored mood.

Mood regulation processes

Mood regulation refers to any process directed at changing or maintaining mood, whose operation depends specifically on monitored values of mood. As suggested above, some forms of mood regulation may be conscious, controlled, deliberate, and explicit, whereas others may be non-conscious, automatic, involuntary, and implicit, although in practice many forms of mood regulation involve both of these varieties of process to differing degrees.

Mood regulation is defined by its *function* rather than its *content* or structure. In other words, it includes all kinds of activities that are directed towards changing

197

or maintaining mood, and we cannot specify the nature of these activities independently of their intended affective impact. Generally speaking, any kind of stimulus, process, or activity that can influence mood may be used as part of a mood-regulation process. Thus, the range of possible mood-regulation strategies is almost limitless (see Chapter 6). Furthermore, a particular episode of mood regulation may incorporate a number of subprocesses or combined strategies, so the process itself cannot always be seen as a unitary one.

To give some idea of the range of mood regulation strategies that are available, in our own research, we have distinguished self-reported *deliberate* strategies based on the following criteria, though these are obviously not exhaustive:

1 *Implementation medium*: Some strategies are implemented at the *cognitive* level and others involve *behavioural* interventions. Essentially, this distinction hinges on whether the attempt to improve affect is conducted by thinking or by doing something, although clearly many strategies (e.g. use of relaxation tapes) involve a mixture of cognition and behaviour.
2 *Strategic intention*: A second basic distinction between kinds of strategy concerns whether they are intended as ways of avoiding, or ways of addressing, the problem at hand (or the current affect). *Diversionary* strategies involve redirecting cognition or action away from the present concern (e.g. avoidance, withdrawal, or distraction), whereas *non-diversionary* strategies involve sustained attention to the problem or the associated affect (e.g. acceptance or engagement).
3 *Resource deployment focus*: Among the strategies that address rather than avoid the concern, some are directed at the situation that seems to have occasioned the unpleasant feelings (*situation-directed*), while others are directed at the feelings themselves (*affect-directed*).

In addition to the categories arising from these basic distinctions, there are also further meaningful subcategories depending on the medium, intention, focus, and specific content of each strategy. It is worth noting that many strategies do not fit neatly into any single category because they are apparently capable of fulfilling a number of different affect-regulatory functions (multipurpose strategies). See Table 8.1 for a provisional summary of the range of mood regulation strategies that people report using in their everyday lives.

On the basis of this classification of mood-regulation strategies, we can conclude that different strategies for regulating different moods serve different functions for the individual trying to change or maintain mood. Correspondingly the effectiveness of the various techniques is mediated by different kinds of process. For example, some strategies work by generating new inputs for processing which may lead to affective consequences, others by making a difference to the situation that is thought to have occasioned or to be maintaining the affective condition. Different strategies are probably differentially effective in regulating mood in different situations and for different people, depending also on the specific nature of the affect being experienced. Selection of suitable strategies across a range of

Table 8.1 A typology of mood-regulation strategies

			Cognitive	Behavioural
DIVERSIONARY STRATEGIES	**Avoidance**		• Mentally switch off • Try to put it out of my mind	• Remove myself from the situation • Avoid doing chores
	Distraction	Relaxation-oriented	• Meditate • Think of what I'll do when I get free time	• Lie in the sun • Take a bath/shower
		Pleasure-oriented	• Think about things that make me happy • Fantasize about pleasant things	• Do the things that I enjoy • Engage in comfort eating
		Mastery-oriented	• Think about work • Plan things to do	• Do something I've been putting off doing • Tidy up
NON-DIVERSIONARY STRATEGIES	**Engagement**	Affect-directed	• Think about why I'm in a bad mood • Work out if my feelings are justified	• Get it out of my system • Seek sympathy
		Situation-directed	• Evaluate why things aren't going well • Make plans about solving the problem	• Confront the problem head-on • Seek practical advice
	Acceptance	Affect-directed	• Let myself feel bad • Try not to force myself to cheer up	• Let the down feeling flow out of me • Cry
		Situation-directed	• Try to accept the situation • Put it down to experience	• Get on with things • Wait for things to pick up

circumstances as a result of realistic appraisal is likely therefore to facilitate well-being and affective control (see Chapter 7).

There is little point in trying to catalogue the entire range of mechanisms underlying the impact of mood regulation strategies because it overlaps almost entirely with the processes that control mood in general. As mentioned above, any factor that has an effect on mood may be used as part of a regulation strategy in the right circumstances. This means that the specific regulatory aspect of mood-regulation episodes is even more variable and indeterminate than the monitoring and affective aspects considered above.

MOOD-REGULATION EPISODES

In the previous section, we considered four aspects of the mood-regulation process: mood itself; monitoring; appraisal; and regulation proper. Any particular example of mood regulation involves these four kinds of interacting process to differing degrees and in different ways. Before outlining a general model of how mood regulation works, it is worth considering some specific examples to illustrate the variety and complexity of the processes involved.

Deliberate upward regulation of mood

The prototypical instance of mood regulation occurs when people register the fact that they are feeling bad and decide to do something about it. How are the various processes distinguished above involved in such an episode?

The first stage involves the recognition that current mood is unpleasant. This may happen in a number of ways. For example, mood may cross a preset threshold of unpleasantness which automatically brings the state into explicit consciousness (cf. Morris, 1992). It seems likely that more intense mood states are attention-demanding without the need for any controlled monitoring to take place. Similarly, sudden *changes* in mood may be intrinsically salient, triggering a kind of internal orienting reaction (cf. Sokolov, 1963). According to this second principle, relatively less intensely unpleasant moods may be registered automatically if they contrast dramatically with previous ongoing mood.

Another way in which mood might enter awareness is as a result of situational attunement. For example, self-attention may occur relatively automatically when you are sitting down in front of a mirror or when a camera is pointed at you (e.g. Beaman, Klentz, Diener, & Svanum, 1979; Carver & Scheier, 1982). Similarly, certain familiar social situations may be strongly associated with particular affective experiences leading to a habitual tendency to focus on feelings. For example, at a wedding you may notice mildly unpleasant feelings simply because they do not match the usual reaction to such occasions. Such situationally induced affect attunement may be spontaneous or may occur in a more controlled manner when explicit anticipations or prescriptions about feelings are brought into play (e.g. Hochschild, 1983).

200

A related way in which unpleasant moods may enter consciousness depends on directed monitoring. For example, a deliberate affect-regulatory goal may already be in place which attunes the monitoring system to particular values or changes in affect, as might happen after making a decision not to allow yourself to get too upset by whatever you are expecting to happen. According to Wegner's (1994) model, once such a mood-regulation intention has been implemented, an automatic monitoring process that checks for the presence of intention-discrepant affect continues to operate until the regulatory attempt is explicitly terminated. Thus, in Wegner's view, the person becomes sensitized to relevant affect information as a function of a controlled process, but the sensitization itself is automatic and imposes few demands on cognitive resources.

Affect may also be recognized as unpleasant as a function of the deliberate interrogation of feelings. For example, some people seem to be chronically attentive to the affective implications of what happens to them (e.g. Swinkels & Giuliano, 1995) and habitually monitor their mood at frequent intervals. Alternatively, someone else might draw attention to your apparent mood, for example, by saying that you seem depressed or unusually cheerful, leading to focused introspection on your part. In either of these cases, the monitoring process may detect an unpleasant mood that is already present, or the act of self-attention itself may influence mood in a negative direction (cf. Ingram, 1990; Salovey, 1992) by enhancing perception of existing discrepancies between actual and ideal self (e.g. Duval & Wicklund, 1972).

The way in which mood information is registered during monitoring makes a difference to the nature and extent of additional appraisal that is necessary. In the case of directed monitoring resulting from deliberate affect-regulatory goals, registration of the unwanted mood information already carries negative appraisal implications. Thus, no further explicit appraisal may be necessary before a decision is made to implement a mood-regulation strategy from the available repertoire. However, if time and opportunity are available for weighing up available options, and if no particular strategy has been selected in advance, appraisal may still mediate the specific choice of activity. Similarly, automatic appraisal conclusions may accompany the spontaneous registration of unpleasant moods that pass preset intensity or change thresholds. Indeed, the simple presence of unpleasant mood is seen by some theorists as a warning signal to the conscious system that things are not going well (cf. Frijda, 1986; Schwarz, 1990). On the other hand, if mood information is consulted either capriciously or because some relatively trivial occurrence draws attention to it, the level and nature of unpleasant affect will usually need to be appraised before any decision about suitable action is taken.

Even in cases where mood is already recognized as carrying negative implications, it is likely that activation of conscious processing leads to additional more elaborative appraising, which may alter the initial predefined interpretation and evaluation of what is happening. Of course, in all of these cases, unpleasant affect is usually going to be appraised in negative terms anyway, but the important point

201

is that the degree and significance of this negative appraisal are not fully determined by the intrinsic qualities of the affective state itself. For example, if you are at a funeral and find yourself feeling appropriately bad, then this realization may be appraised in positive terms. In other words, although feeling bad is always bad in one way, you can also feel good about feeling bad. The resulting composite of evaluative state based on the affect itself together with its monitoring and appraisal does not carry a single and simple value on any pleasantness dimension but rather conveys a multilevel form of ambivalence (cf. Mayer & Gaschke, 1988, and see Chapter 2).

Regardless of how unpleasant mood is registered or otherwise intrudes into consciousness, appraisal of the condition as unwanted tends to encourage the implementation of some kind of mood-regulation attempt. However, before such a decision is finally made, a number of other relevant transactional factors may also require appraisal. One of the most important of these relates to the anticipated success of regulation. For example, some people have relatively low *generalized negative mood regulation expectancies* (Catanzaro & Mearns, 1990), believing that there is usually little that can be done to avert their unpleasant feelings. Correspondingly, there may be more specific circumstances which lead to the interpretation of unpleasant mood as uncontrollable, such as when mood change is thought to arise from "natural" or hormonal factors in conditions like the premenstrual syndrome. In these cases, the appraisal of an unpleasant mood as unwanted may not lead to active mood-regulation attempts intended to change one's feelings, but rather may invoke acceptance of what is happening or feelings of helplessness.

In general, different instances of mood regulation may be more or less considered, and more or less attuned to the specific nature of the current concern. For example, people probably have habitual strategies for improving their mood which are deployed in a relatively automatized way when dealing with a wide range of minor negative deflections in mood. Further, some people characteristically react to moods with helplessness or acceptance, whereas others have favourite techniques of distraction such as engaging in a familiar and well-liked leisure activity such as listening to music or reading. However, for many people, when mood regulation is conducted for explicit and well-considered reasons, there may be more careful consideration of appropriate strategies based on further appraisal. For example, people may choose to listen to different kinds of music depending on what kind of mood they are in and on precisely how they would like it to change. Thus, when depressed, you may decide to wallow in your feelings and listen to some suitably downbeat songs, or you may try to fight against your lethargy or despair with something more upbeat and exhilarating. Skilled mood regulators are able to tailor their use of strategies to the particular nature of the mood experienced depending on appraised availability of personal and situational regulation resources (at least on those occasions when they feel like doing so).

Another important component of adaptive mood regulation is sensitivity to likely failures of regulation attempts at the earliest possible stage. This seems to imply continuous or recurrent attention to mood during regulation. However, it may be that one successful mode of mood regulation is to become so deeply involved in a distraction activity that little cognitive capacity remains for explicit monitoring. In such cases, Wegner's idea of an implicit and automatic monitoring process helps to explain why such strategies do not bring about unwanted affective consequences without there being any explicit checks of their continuing effectiveness. Of course, if the system is already attuned to high levels of, and dramatic increases in, unpleasant affect independently of any intentionally initiated checks, additional directed monitoring may be unnecessary.

Making sure that the current affect-regulation strategy is working effectively and is still necessary for maintaining or improving mood depends on more than a non-conscious monitoring process, however. Attention also needs to be devoted to appraising whether the current situation still necessitates mood regulation, for example. Often in explicit and focused mood regulation attempts, explicit monitoring and appraisal processes will continue to operate intermittently after the regulation operation has been initiated. At some point, the whole set of processes may be terminated when appraisal determines either that the affect and situation are no longer problematic or that none of the deployed processes are serving mood-regulation goals effectively. In these cases, some form of reappraisal may lead to a cessation of active mood-regulation efforts. For example, when things get really bad, people may simply decide to give in to their feelings. In fact, even this might be seen as mood regulation of a kind, since the expression of unpleasant affect often serves as a call for help which may effectively enlist social support. Further, many theorists consider that venting of feelings has direct benefits due to the supposed "hydraulic" properties of the affective system (e.g. Freud, 1910). Such ideas underlie the popular notion that bottling up your feelings is generally a bad thing.

People do not only try to put themselves into a better mood when they are feeling bad, but may also attempt to improve ongoing pleasant feelings. Many of the processes and interactions considered above will apply similarly in this second related case of mood regulation. However, it may be that the monitoring task is relatively more demanding of cognitive resources when mood is already pleasant. Specifically, enhancement of pleasant mood requires some check that mood is not simply remaining at previous levels of pleasantness, and default monitoring processes that automatically register strong moods or sudden mood-changes are incapable of fulfilling this function. The demands of the monitoring task are likely to be less pronounced when the mood-regulation goal is simply to maintain rather than improve pleasant mood.

Deliberate downward regulation of mood

Although the most common kind of deliberate mood regulation occurs when people try to make themselves feel better or try to stay in an existing pleasant mood (Clark & Isen, 1982), Parrott (1993) proposed a number of motives for sustaining unpleasant moods or for making feelings less rather than more pleasant. For example, people may try to stop themselves from getting too excited about an anticipated pleasant event, in order to ward off potential disappointment should things actually not turn out as well as expected. Similarly, people may attempt to contain their excitement when a protracted and difficult task is nearly finished in case their joy should distract them from what still needs to be done. Another mood-depression motive is suggested by the idea that unpleasant mood states are characterized by careful analytic processing of information (e.g. Mackie & Worth, 1991; Schwarz & Bless, 1991, see Chapter 4), so that maintenance of the unpleasant mood may facilitate performance on tasks where this kind of cognitive work is necessary. Finally, and from a more social perspective, people may try to keep their moods in tune with those of others in order to maintain affective solidarity, even when the other people are feeling worse than themselves (cf. Hochschild, 1983).

Investigation of these non-hedonistic forms of mood regulation is still at an early stage, but it seems likely that some of the same mechanisms that are involved in alleviation of unpleasant mood are implicated in many cases. As in the examples of regulation motivated by pleasant mood maintenance or enhancement considered above, however, an important potential difference relates to the explicitness of monitoring that is required. Maintenance of unpleasant mood requires a monitoring process capable of detecting intrusions of pleasant mood, however mild. It seems unlikely that the mental system would be automatically attuned to such states under normal circumstances, given that people's usual mood tends to fall within this range (e.g. Diener, 1984), and given that pleasant moods seem to imply that nothing in the current life situation requires attention (e.g. Schwarz & Bless, 1991).

Although monitoring may be more difficult in the case of downward mood regulation, the regulation process itself may be easier to implement and sustain. The reason for this is contained in Frijda's (1988) *law of hedonic asymmetry* which argues as follows: "*Pleasure is always contingent upon change and disappears with continuous satisfaction. Pain may persist under persisting adverse conditions*" (italics in original, p. 353). According to Frijda, hedonic asymmetry arises from the signal function of affect. Unpleasant affect informs the cognitive system that something needs attention in the current situation and therefore tends to endure until all concerns have been met, whereas pleasant affect is a signal that "no more action is needed" (p. 354), which immediately serves its function without any need for persistence (see also Wegener & Petty, 1994, and Chapter 4). If these generalizations are valid then pleasant affect is, by its very nature, more fragile and more evanescent than unpleasant affect, and thus may be more easily disposed of, simply by thinking of something unpleasant, for example. Indeed, if getting out of unpleasant moods was easy, then according to simple hedonistic principles, we might expect that such conditions would be more rare and more short-lived than they actually are.

Automatic mood regulation

Automatic as well as consciously controlled processes play a role in mood regulation of various kinds. For example, it may be that physiological systems maintain a psychological equilibrium using negative feedback principles, implicitly detecting any deviations from preset parameters relating to affect and implementing homeostatic processes to correct them (cf. Headey & Wearing, 1989). The standard values specified in such systems may vary over time, partly underlying consistent fluctuations in mood over the course of the day, week, or month (see Chapter 5, above). Such an analysis seems particularly applicable to (general or patterned) activation of the autonomic nervous system which must automatically adjust to the changing energy demands associated with various activities (e.g. Duffy, 1962). Thus the metabolic requirements of vigorous exercise are met by increases in autonomic arousal which usually returns to baseline soon after exertion is over without any need for conscious intervention. Clearly, such changes in activation may also influence or reflect affective differences at some level (e.g. Zillmann, 1978).

Although some variables relevant to affect are dependent on these kinds of equilibrating mechanisms, we think it unlikely that mood states themselves are ever automatically monitored in precisely this way. This is because mood does not in our view consist of any unitary signal that could in principle be registered in a simply defined feedback loop. Indeed, we have suggested above that mood is an integrated cognitive-motivational condition that also carries intrinsic temporal structure. It is hard to conceive of any automatic feedback mechanism that would be capable of reading off simple enough parameters based on such a phenomenon to allow effective regulation. In short, our view is that only some of the variables contributing to mood are regulated in this homeostatic way.

Nevertheless, mood regulation may go on at a largely automatic level when the person has developed certain habitual strategies of mood regulation which can then be implemented without thought in relevant situations. However, in these cases there is always the possibility that values of mood falling above some preset threshold will result in conscious override of the automatized function. In general, most real-life instances of mood regulation probably depend on variable combinations of automatic and controlled processes.

Anticipatory mood regulation

All the episodes of mood regulation considered so far begin with the registration of mood information as a result of implicit or explicit monitoring processes. In this section, we will consider the possibility that mood regulation may be implemented to avert anticipated affective consequences in a proactive rather than reactive way.

A simple example of anticipatory mood regulation occurs when people know that a situation is likely to make them feel bad and make active efforts to resist its influence. For example, when an examination or interview is approaching, people may plan their activities and organize their environment to allow them to deal with any nervousness they expect to experience. In some circumstances, this preparatory activity may even circumvent the occurrence of any affective reaction completely.

In many situations, cultural, institutional, or relationship-based norms may prescribe what mood is appropriate (e.g. Hochschild, 1983), and to the extent that these situations are predictable, some of the relevant affective work may be done in advance. For example, people often try to get themselves in the mood for going out to a party, pub, or nightclub by playing certain kinds of music or by engaging in other preparatory rituals, such as getting dressed up in appropriate clothes. Indeed, UK television programming implicitly acknowledges some of the most common anticipatory affect-regulation goals by scheduling shows promoting an excitable and lively atmosphere (e.g. *Blind Date* or *Noel's House Party*) early on Saturday evening, thus setting the agenda for certain kinds of social interaction. Similarly, institutional environments are often explicitly designed in a way that encourages appropriate kinds of affective response, as illustrated by the conventional layout of a courtroom or a church, which positions important people to whom respect is due in physically higher positions and so on. These examples show that a lot of the work contributing to mood regulation goes on behind the scenes before any specific interaction begins, and not all of it depends on people's individual efforts to control their own affect.

In a related way, other people's anticipatory efforts towards mood regulation in less formal social settings are also likely to contribute to our own reactions, such as when friends are making obvious efforts to be upbeat and we respond accordingly. In addition to these various effects of norms about appropriate affective conduct (cf. Hochschild, 1983), our anticipatory mood regulation is also shaped by more specific impression-management goals, such as when we know we are going to meet someone who we want to respond favourably to us. Of course, similar impression-management goals may also contribute to more reactive regulation of affect that is already ongoing (e.g. Clark, Pataki, & Carver, 1995).

Processes of anticipatory mood regulation clearly do not begin with any registration or monitoring of goal-incongruent mood information. Instead the origin of regulatory activity depends directly on broader intentional goals. However, mood monitoring may still be necessary once the regulation attempt is underway in these cases, in order to ensure that selected strategies are being successfully implemented.

Reconciling regulation with the functionality of mood

In the preceding discussion, we have implied that mood presents a pattern of information and energy that is subject to various kinds of control process designed to change or maintain it. For example, we have assumed that feeling bad may

206

provoke attempts to make oneself feel better, thus transforming or removing the original state. Such an analysis might be seen as suggesting that mood is something that generally interferes with our goals and needs to be modified for the purpose of more effective psychological functioning.

However, we have also acknowledged that mood serves the function of informing the cognitive system about the status of current concerns, thus facilitating adaptive encounters with the environment. Correspondingly, mood can help to provide motivation for ongoing tasks and projects. If mood works in these ways to help us deal with our problems and successes, why would we be motivated to modify or control it in any way?

The answer is that moods may be more or less adaptive and more or less appropriate to the ongoing situation (see Chapter 7), and they may reflect situations that are more or less controllable. Correspondingly, in some cases, we may act in direct accordance with the implications of our mood (situation-directed regulation), while in others we may attempt to deal with the mood itself (affect-directed regulation, cf. Lazarus, 1991). Which of these options is taken depends on how we appraise the implications of our mood, and on whether the available resources seem capable of addressing any identified concern (cf. Lazarus, 1991).

Situation-directed regulation usually occurs when moods signal concerns that are obvious and easy to address. For example, when we are in a bad mood, we often try to determine what is wrong with our current life situation in order to do something about it (directly following the mood's informational and motivational functions considered above). If successful, this activity is itself likely to lead indirectly to an improvement in mood. In general, the default action taken in response to registration of mood information is probably to deal with the situation that occasioned the mood. However, as argued earlier, one of the characteristics of mood is that it often has no specific cause or object, so this task may not always be as simple as it might seem. When no obvious mood-relevant concern is identified, the person may engage in more general modes of activity intended to address a wide range of aspects of the current life situation in order to remove the unpleasant affective state. This latter kind of activity begins to seem more like mood regulation than action directly induced by mood.

Even when the object or focus of the mood is obvious, it may be that addressing this concern is impractical for any of a variety of reasons. In these cases, mood's functionality stops being beneficial when its informational and motivational aspects begin to interfere with other aspects of performance. For example, feeling continually bad about your career performance when no other viable openings are available may demotivate you in your current work, distract you from what you are doing, and generally undermine your chances of being in a position to capitalize on any future opportunity that may eventually arise. If the situation is appraised in terms such as these, then direct mood-regulation attempts would certainly seem to represent an adaptive option.

The bottom line is that mood regulation takes its place in wider control systems which motivate action more generally and which themselves sometimes incorporate mood as part of their function. Because everyday life actually involves striving towards a wide range of goals at different levels, some of which are related and compatible, others of which may be irreconcilable, it is perfectly conceivable for processes that are functional and adaptive within certain contexts to produce dysfunctional consequences in other circumstances (see Chapter 7).

SKETCH FOR A THEORY OF MOOD REGULATION

In the preceding section, we have outlined a number of ways in which mood-regulation episodes might unfold. Different cases may begin from different start points, involve different subprocesses in different ways, and assign different priorities to these subprocesses. Furthermore, each subprocess may be mediated by different kinds of operation at an automatic or a controlled level. In view of these observations, it seems clear that any inclusive model of mood regulation needs to be relatively flexible in its specifications. In this section, we will attempt to draw some general conclusions on the basis of some of the commonalities among the examples of mood regulation considered above in order to help pave the way towards development of such a theory. We will begin by treating mood regulation as a simple sequential process and consider each of its stages in turn, then consider some of the possible limitations of such a view.

Entry points to the mood regulation system

Episodes of mood regulation can start in a number of ways, as indicated above. The impetus for mood regulation may come from mood itself (as in the case of extreme values or salient deflections in affect intruding into consciousness), from more explicit mood-monitoring processes (when consultation of feelings results in a decision to adjust them), or from transactional factors leading directly to a mood-regulation intention. Although mood monitoring at some level is clearly the most common start point for affect regulation, there are cases where this factor is not primary, such as when anticipatory mood-regulation attempts are initiated as a result of predicted situational requirements. However, as soon as mood begins to be regulated explicitly there needs to be some check on its current status in order to determine the extent and nature of the modification required. In other words, one of the first things that needs to happen when mood is to be regulated is that some kind of reference needs to be made to its present condition.

In conjunction with this early monitoring process, there is also likely to be some kind of mood appraisal that evaluates mood in its transactional context and assesses what needs to be done. Appraisal sets the priorities for the operations designed actually to regulate the mood. Once mood has been monitored and appraised in some way, the system is in a position to initiate the regulation attempt itself.

208

Regulation in operation

Appraisal typically facilitates the selection of regulation strategies perceived as suitable to current personal and situational constraints. However, it is also possible that default regulation strategies may kick in as a result of simple detection of preset values or changes in affect registered by automatic monitoring processes carrying predefined appraisal implications. In these cases, appraisal probably runs in parallel with regulation proper in order to allow subsequent adjustment of the selected strategy.

The process of regulation itself is hard to specify except in terms of its intentions as determined by appraisal (see above). Although most previous accounts have concentrated mainly on regulation goals relating to simple values along pleasantness and activation dimensions, we believe that regulation may involve maintenance of mood, upward changes, downward changes or more precisely prespecified trajectories. The goal specification may even incorporate temporal parameters, such as when we tell ourselves to slow down the rate at which our excitement is building so that it better matches the actual estimated time of arrival of a desired outcome (e.g. children lying awake in eager anticipation of Christmas Day). Any of these mood-regulation intentions may be implemented using a wide variety of strategies or combinations of strategies which work in a number of different ways and are mediated by very different processes.

Different regulation intentions require different kinds of monitoring process which in turn may draw on different kinds of mental resources. For example, as argued above, monitoring probably proceeds automatically when the current task of regulation is simply to reduce or remove an unpleasant mood. In some cases, it may be sufficient to rely on pattern-matching mechanisms whose function is simply to register high values of unpleasant affect or sudden downward deflections (cf. Wegner, 1989). At the other extreme, however, an intention to coordinate mood over time with the anticipated development of the ongoing situation necessitates much closer attunement to several parameters relating to mood and thus probably draws on more cognitive resources. Information about mood of this latter variety is unlikely to be directly accessible to any simple readout function. Instead, mood monitoring in these cases may involve various kinds of attentional process directed at many different aspects or concomitants of mood states, including personal, situational, and transactional factors (see Chapter 6).

Termination of mood regulation attempts

Mood regulation does not always terminate as such, rather new priorities for action may emerge when mood itself ceases to be a specific problem. On other occasions a deliberate mood-regulation attempt may be specifically abandoned in response to prespecified changes in monitored mood, or when monitoring processes reveal that regulation is ineffective. In general, mood regulation ceases when reappraisal of mood after regulation suggests either that further use of strategies would be futile or when monitoring registers the attainment of a prespecified affective goal state. A final alternative reason for cessation of mood regulation is when some other independent concern arises which requires immediate action and reallocation of resources away from mood regulation.

Limitations of the simple sequential model

One way of characterizing the course of mood regulation would be to say that it begins with some change in affect which is then monitored and appraised and these mediating processes finally lead to the output of a regulation operation. However, much of the discussion above has implied that this four-stage model represents something of an oversimplification. In this section, we review some of the limitations of the sequential account of the mood-regulation process.

A general problem concerns the proposed fixed sequence of stages. As we have argued above, a number of different routes to regulation are possible, with different start points, different implementations of regulation operations, and different modes of termination. Furthermore, many of the subprocesses involved in regulation can clearly operate in parallel rather than in series, making them overlapping rather than genuinely sequential. Similarly, the close interactions between subprocesses often makes it difficult to treat them separately. In terms of ordering of stages, failed regulation may lead to reappraisal which starts the process up again at a different point, raising the possibility that the overall process is often cyclical and involves repeated iterations of subprocesses or combinations of subprocesses. Finally, the regulation process may take a different course at almost any stage as a result of changing circumstances registered by monitoring or appraisal or some interaction of these subprocesses.

Another limitation of the simple sequential model is that it considers mood regulation in isolation from the wider context of action control. A more realistic approach might involve treating mood regulation as part of a broader hierarchical goal structure, and seeing its operation as dependent on processes at higher and lower levels (cf. Carver & Scheier, 1982). For example, a specific mood-regulation attempt may itself be motivated by more general impression-management goals, whose attainment by means other than mood regulation may remove the need for continuation of the process. Correspondingly, concerns from separate motivational systems may intrude into the mood-regulation process when resources are urgently required for other tasks (cf. Oatley & Johnson-Laird, 1987).

Mood regulation itself is also probably organized hierarchically rather than as a simple one-level series of subprocesses. For example, automatic monitoring processes probably support and interact with controlled monitoring, which may also contribute directly to higher level appraisal processes. The subprocesses each have their own internal structure which accounts for their characteristic mode of operation, but also there are interactions between subprocesses at a number of different levels which give the overall system emergent properties which are not obvious simply from consideration of the separate mechanisms.

For all the above reasons, we might better view mood regulation as a *system* of operations rather than as a chain of subprocesses. The above discussion has drawn attention to a number of basic operating characteristics of such a system. To be more precise at this stage would be premature speculation, but we hope that the rough sketch we have outlined will provide the basis for a fuller picture as the details are filled in by more focused research.

FUTURE OF MOOD RESEARCH

Mood, and affect more generally, has become an increasingly popular topic within psychology over recent decades (see Chapter 1). The research reviewed in this book offers testament to this development and gives some indication of how far our understanding has advanced. However, a great many unanswered questions concerning mood and mood regulation still remain. In this section, we will draw attention to what we consider to be the most important of these outstanding issues in order to signpost some likely directions for future exploration.

Mood theory

Despite recent advances, it is apparent that existing theories of mood are still relatively undeveloped and generally incapable of capturing the complexity and flexibility of the many processes involved. In our view, progress in this regard does not only depend on the continuing accumulation of empirical data about mood, but also on basic conceptual work. Mood researchers lack a guiding theory which could provide direction for their investigations and help in the interpretation of the mass of evidence that is already available.

One of the consequences of the weakness of mood theory relative to empirical mood research is that methodologies often develop in response to practical rather than theoretical pressures. For example, although operationalizing mood in terms of two basic self-report dimensions or two dozen adjectives may be highly convenient, it does little to facilitate our understanding of the fundamental nature of the phenomenon. More generally, the separation of research topics relating to mood structure, mood predictors, mood effects, mood dynamics, and mood regulation serves obvious simplifying functions, but may prevent researchers from catching sight of the broader picture. When a dynamic process approach to mood is adopted, it becomes clear that many of the taken-for-granted distinctions between areas of investigation are artificial (e.g. mood does not have simple causes and effects, and its structure overlaps with that of regulation). Future theory should therefore direct itself to developing more integrative analyses of mood phenomena.

Mood methodology

One of the greatest methodological challenges facing mood research is to find ways of exploring what is, by definition, a transitory and experiential phenomenon

211

without unduly distorting or influencing the processes involved. For example, the use of very frequent self-reports may allow better consideration of mood's temporal dimension but unfortunately brings the disadvantage of continually drawing respondents' attention to mood, leading to the possibility of explicit regulation attempts. Thus the measurement process itself may influence what it is intended to assess in a neutral way. Future methodological advances may help researchers to minimize or better take account of these reactive aspects of mood measurement. For example, the use of peer or observer ratings and certain kinds of cued retrospective reports (e.g. using video replay of the original action, Gottman & Levenson, 1985) may avoid some of these problems. While extended mood-adjective checklists may be suitable for use in some cross-sectional designs, intensive mood sampling clearly requires development of other approaches.

A related methodological goal is to find ways of studying and analysing moods which are practicable but still capable of reflecting the richness, complexity, and variability of mood. While Chapter 2 suggested that different methods of measuring mood have produced a reasonable degree of consensus concerning the dimensions of mood, this certainly does not mean that the measurement of mood is no longer problematic. For example, the generally accepted structure of mood has been discerned from studies that have usually used single measurement points or averaged data. However, it may be that when mood is considered as a temporally articulated condition, a different or more changeable structure may emerge. Study of such temporal structure requires new statistical techniques that are capable of tracing the influence of previous mood on current mood, such as dynamic factor analysis (Molenaar, 1985; Molenaar, Degooijer, & Schmitz, 1992). Recent evidence that the structure of mood differs between people (Feldman, 1995b, see Chapter 2) also indicates the need for improved measurement and analysis techniques.

Mood research

Although we know a great deal about the structure and operation of mood, there are still a great number of basic descriptive issues that remain to be addressed before we are able to accurately map out the landscape of the terrain to be explored. For example, we still do not know how quickly or how often moods typically change, or how wide are the individual differences in patterns of change. Without answers to these apparently simple questions about patterns of temporal variation in mood, it is often difficult to interpret or contextualize existing research findings.

Tracking of day-by-day and moment-by-moment changes in mood should be supplemented by investigations encompassing wider time frames. Indeed, it seems important to investigate how moods may change year by year over the life span and to explore the connections between long-term and short-term variations. For example, charting the natural history of the development of some kinds of clinical depression requires extensive longitudinal investigation of a kind that is currently rarely undertaken for obvious practical reasons, but which may be crucial to our understanding of such disorders (see Chapter 7).

A social as well as a temporal dimension is missing from most current mood research, and investigation of interpersonal and organizational factors may extend and elaborate our understanding of mood. For example, recent research has revealed that people may catch other people's mood by a process of *emotional contagion* (e.g. Hatfield, Cacioppo, & Rapson, 1994). Sometimes, this kind of contagion process can lead to mood states spreading rapidly throughout a group of people. For example, it is often possible to characterize the general mood of a crowd at a sporting event. However, current research still treats mood as if it were something that resided purely and simply within the individual. Another direction for the future, therefore, is to investigate whether mood can be described and measured at a group rather than an individual level (cf. George, 1990). Indeed, it may be possible to specify a whole hierarchy of embedded group moods, ranging from mood in a family or work group to the mood of a whole country (e.g. de Rivera, 1992). For example, it is currently common to refer to the presence or absence of a "feel good" factor among the nation's population. If such a factor exists, it seems worth considering how it might be measured and determining whether it reflects anything more than the sum of individual people's moods. Further, we might profitably track changes in *affective climate* (de Rivera, 1992) over time and examine the institutional and intergroup processes that determine its regulation.

Summary

The general recommendation of this book is that research should orient itself towards the dynamic aspects of mood and the regulatory processes contributing to mood variation. As we have argued in this section, such an orientation requires theoretical and methodological development as well as basic descriptive and exploratory investigation. Although much of the future of mood research remains unpredictable, we hope that we have been able to give some indications of possible ways forward.

MOOD ACROSS THE SUBDISCIPLINES OF PSYCHOLOGY

Mood research clearly has an impact on a number of psychological domains, including clinical, personality, biological, health, consumer, educational, and occupational psychology. While each of these areas already deals with mood in some degree, its importance is often underestimated. In this section, we consider how a process approach to mood, together with a focus on regulation and variation, might clarify mood's role in these different subdisciplines.

Clinical psychology

Chapter 7 described how the development and maintenance of some mood disorders can be explained partly by reference to failures of mood regulation. Some of the empirical work on regulation strategies described above could help fill out this perspective. In terms of therapy, there may be potential for improving people's ability to evaluate their moods and for teaching people to modify or change their regulation strategies. Chapter 5's discussion of mood dynamics highlighted connections between certain types of change in mood and mood disorders. There is also evidence that changes in mood during depression resemble mood changes in some individuals during shiftwork, and may therefore have a similar aetiology (Healy & Waterhouse, 1995). Connections such as these represent a potential bridge between the understanding of normal and abnormal states of mood.

Personality psychology

Consideration of mood dynamics may also help to change our view of personality. At present, personality psychology is largely dominated by the quest to find a fundamental set of personality characteristics which apply generally and consistently to all people (e.g. Block, 1995). Such an approach tends to encourage a very static view of personality. In contrast, the study of moods over time encourages a dynamic perspective from which personality is seen as reflecting people's ongoing adjustment to the environment and their anticipation of changes in the environment. From such a standpoint, changes tell us something fundamental about the person, rather than being mere noise in the data. Similarly, the mainly descriptive analysis of associations between personality and mood discussed in Chapter 3 (e.g. if people tend generally to feel happy they are more likely to feel happy today) could be developed by looking at patterns of mood change rather than aggregated mood levels.

Biological psychology

The emergence of mood as a highly organized, complex, and purposeful process in human psychology may also cause biological psychology to reconsider the neuropsychology of mood. The emotion centres of the brain, which are thought to reside mainly in the limbic system, have generally been considered as governing more primitive, lower neurological functions than the higher functions of the cortex. A number of neuropsychologists now believe that this view is wrong (e.g. Cytowic, 1994; Rosenfield, 1995). For example, in Rosenfield's view, affect is an integral part of a system that dynamically generates consciousness of the self. Such a thesis is clearly more compatible with the present book's dynamic and regulational perspective on mood.

Health and consumer psychology

Another challenge for the future will be to improve our understanding of the relation between mood and physical health. For example, we currently know very little about the relation between mood and the immune system (e.g. Cohen & Williamson, 1991; O'Leary, 1990). Knowledge is also lacking concerning the relation between lifestyle choices, including what people eat and drink, and their effects on mood and physiology. Research into these areas of relative ignorance would seem capable of addressing important concerns in both health and consumer psychology. For example, health promotion activities may come to focus more on the benefits of particular behaviours for mood and well-being. Similarly, consumer products may be designed and marketed in future with mood-enhancing benefits in mind.

Educational and occupational psychology

From an educational perspective, new concepts emerging from research on mood and emotion could update our view of the goals of education. For example, the concept of emotional intelligence, which is now attracting both academic (e.g. Salovey, Mayer, Goldman, Turvey, & Palfal, 1992) and more popular attention (e.g. Goleman, 1996), acknowledges that people have abilities for understanding and using their feelings in purposeful ways. This recognition of the importance of this kind of affective ability may lead educationalists to place increased emphasis on emotional, interpersonal, and intrapersonal skills to supplement the more conventional problem-solving capacities.

This issue also has relevance for occupational psychology. For example, many jobs require emotional skills more than problem-solving skills, particularly those that require high levels of communication and where the display and management of emotion is an intrinsic part of the work role (e.g. Hochschild, 1983; Rafaeli & Sutton, 1987). At present, many of these jobs are undervalued, partly because of gender bias but also, relatedly, because of the devaluation of emotion. There may, therefore, be a shift towards job selection based on emotional skills. It is too early to say whether this will bring similar problems to job selection based on other more conventional forms of personality and skill assessment.

Popular psychology

What effect will research dedicated to the study of affect have on the wider population? As with behavioural and cognitive psychology and other areas of social science, new concepts and ways of thinking about people will slowly disseminate from academic practices. For example, people may become more attuned to the fact that moods serve multiple functions and to the fact that they can exert and enhance control over their own and other people's moods. Rather than seeing ourselves as simply information processors, as suggested by cognitive approaches, we may begin to regard ourselves also as affect regulators. Of course, this may in turn lead to us employing different patterns of monitoring and regulation to those we used before, thus transforming the psychological phenomenon itself. If such a *double hermeneutic*, whereby social scientists help to create and construct the phenomena they investigate (cf. Barley & Knight, 1992; Gergen, 1973), does indeed develop, an understanding of its operation will need to be incorporated into future research into mood and mood regulation.

Conclusions

In this section and the previous one, our speculations about the future of mood research and its implications for other areas of psychology have been generally optimistic. However, long-term prediction of what might happen is always a hazardous business and, according to the non-linear model of change described in Chapter 5, often likely to be wrong. We also know from research reviewed in this book that optimism is not the same as realism, but that optimism may get us in the right mood for approaching what has to be done today. So it is from within this upbeat and perhaps biased frame of mind that the future of mood and mood regulation research looks positive to us.

REFORMULATION OF MOOD

In the first chapter of this book, we presented a provisional definition of mood based on common-sense understanding of the phenomenon. Having reviewed psychological research into the structure and operation of mood, and considered the processes regulating mood's variations over time, we are now in a position to reformulate and extend this definition as follows: *Mood reflects changing non-specific psychological dispositions to evaluate, interpret, and act on past, current, or future concerns in certain patterned ways.* In addition, we are able to flesh out this revised definition by making some more substantive descriptive observations about how mood is constituted and how it works:

- The quality of mood depends on its temporally defined internal characteristics and their mode of relation to the ongoing situation. Although moods always carry values relating to pleasantness and activation dimensions, these values do not provide a complete specification of the status of mood (although they may characterize the conscious experience of mood at any given moment).
- Mood is controlled by processes that are attuned to the developing status of ongoing transactions in the context of currently available metabolic, mental, situational, and social resources.
- Mood arising from one set of concerns may have interactive impacts on other aspects of functioning in a variety of ways that depend both on the quality of the mood, the processes sustaining it, and its mode of regulation.

216

- Mood may be registered by the cognitive system in a number of different ways but does not require such registration to affect functioning. In particular, mood is not always a conscious phenomenon, though the imposition of consciousness may moderate its operation.
- Mood itself is continuous but its conscious registration may be episodic.
- Mood is part of a broader system of action control and is itself subject to regulation in accordance with the broader concerns relating to biology, culture, relationships, and social and personal identity.

The central conclusion of this book is that mood is a much more complex phenomenon than had previously been assumed. It is clear that the hedonistic and perceptual view, in which moods are reduced to a simple matter of feeling good or bad, does not do justice to a construct (or set of interrelated constructs) that is turning out to be sophisticated in function and wide-ranging in its effects. Proper understanding of mood in these terms can only help to clarify our appreciation of the general operation of the psychological system within which mood processes play a vital role.

Appendix

METHODS FOR IMPLEMENTING A PROCESS APPROACH TO MOOD

This appendix provides basic information about the techniques used in intensive time-sampling studies of mood. In particular we discuss the different methods available and their potential drawbacks so that the reader who is interested in taking the process approach to mood further is better equipped to make appropriate methodological decisions. In the first section we discuss the intensive time-sampling methods themselves; in the second section, we consider how mood-changes might be operationalized and parameterized; and in the final section, we review the options for analysis of the data that are produced in this kind of study.

INTENSIVE TIME-SAMPLING METHODS

Three main techniques are used for intensive time-sampling: interval-contingent, signal-contingent, and event-contingent recording (Wheeler & Reiss, 1991). *Interval-contingent* recording requires participants to report their experiences at fixed and pre-determined time intervals. The advantages of this method are that all events and experiences can be sampled and the data are amenable to time-series analysis. Its main disadvantage is that the time of recording may be some time after the events or experiences have occurred and hence participants' responses may be susceptible to distortions of memory. *Signal-contingent* recording requires participants to report their current experiences whenever prompted by a signal, such as an alarm (this method is also known as *experience sampling*, e.g. Csikszentmihalyi & Larson, 1987). Signals are usually presented at quasi-random intervals but can also be given at fixed intervals as in interval-contingent recording. The advantages of the signal-contingent method are that participants report their current experiences rather than relying on memory, and specific rather than aggregated events are sampled. The disadvantage is that some events may be missed. *Event-contingent* recording requires participants to report their experiences when prespecified events, such as arguments, hassles, or uplifts (see Chapter 3), occur. This method is less intrusive than the other two under most circumstances but it is also less suitable for studying the unfolding of processes.

A number of different instruments are available for signalling participants and recording data. For example, radiopagers, programmable watches and calculators, and pocket computers may be used for giving signals, and paper diaries, computer diaries, and telephone interviews may be used for recording responses (see Totterdell & Folkard, 1992).

Several different formats are also possible for the collection of self-reported mood measures. These include open-ended questions, event checklists, and response scales. Open-ended questions allow participants to use their own words to describe their mood experiences. Event checklists provide a list of mood adjectives that enable participants to indicate which moods they have experienced. Response scales require participants to indicate the frequency or intensity with which they have experienced particular moods using some form of graded scale. The disadvantages of event checklists and response scales are that they may focus on events that are not salient for the participant and that they are often open to misinterpretation. However, open-ended responses are usually more difficult to categorize and compare. Alternatives to self-reports include informant reports in which information about a target person's mood are made by someone who spends a lot of time in his or her company, such as a spouse or work colleague. Less direct measures of mood, such as physiological and performance responses, are also sometimes used.

Intensive time-sampling studies generally require a lot of time and effort from participants. Missing data are therefore a common problem. Standard deletion procedures for dealing with missing data are unfortunately not feasible with diary data because they would drastically reduce the dataset. For this reason, it is necessary to use analysis techniques that allow for missing data. However, a cut-off point for data inclusion may also be necessary if response rates begin to decay rapidly. Issues surrounding the design and conduct of intensive time-sampling studies are discussed in further detail by Stone, Kessler, and Haythornthwaite (1991).

PARAMETERS OF MOOD DYNAMICS

Chapter 5 described a number of features of mood dynamics including variability, speed of change, swings, and rhythms. Clearly the parameters of mood that we have considered in previous chapters do not completely capture these dynamics. However, researchers have developed a number of ways of measuring these features.

Most studies of mood variability have used the *standard deviation* (a commonly used statistical measure of variability in a distribution) of a person's mood scores over time as an index of variability. In a recent refinement of this measure, Penner and colleagues (1994) used the standard deviation divided by the mean in order to control for score magnitude (producing an index which they referred to as the *coefficient of variation*). However, Larsen (1987) pointed out that standard deviation measures average extremity of change but not frequency of change. For example, he was able to demonstrate that individuals can have very different patterns of change in mood over time yet still have the same standard deviation.

219

Larsen therefore recommends using a *spectral analytic* approach, which fits sine-cosine waves of different periods to time-series in mood to provide an index of frequency of change.

Another way of summarizing rate of change in mood is to use a measure of *autocorrelation*. Autocorrelation measures the association between each score in a time-series and its immediately preceding score. A higher autocorrelation therefore indicates less changeability over time. However, the relation between rate of change and variability in mood is not always obvious. For example, in Larson and colleagues' (1980) study of mood change in adolescents and adults (discussed in Chapter 5), a negative correlation between the autocorrelation and the standard deviation of mood was obtained. In other words, those persons with greater variation in mood also tended to experience *slower* mood changes. An alternative to these measures is to record the length of time it takes for a good or bad mood to subside. However, this technique requires the use of reference points for defining extreme and normal moods, which can often seem rather arbitrary.

Mood swings can be parameterized in a number of ways. Diurnal variation, for example, is usually measured in terms of the difference between a morning and an evening measure of mood (Cowdry et al., 1991). Another way of parameterizing mood swings is to take an average of all positive changes in mood and all negative changes in mood, or to take an average of all absolute changes.

There are also several methods for detecting and parameterizing rhythms. However, a common problem with many of the widely used techniques, such as spectral analysis and cosinor analysis, is that they assume that the rhythm is sinusoidal (shaped like a sine wave). In Chapter 5, we described some of the parameters of rhythms such as period, phase, and amplitude. Readers who are interested in pursuing rhythm analysis further should refer to one of the more specialized texts from chronobiology, for example, Minors and Waterhouse (1988).

ANALYSING TEMPORAL DATA

Analysing temporal data can be a complex but rewarding affair. For those interested in the details of analysing temporal data we recommend the review by West and Hepworth (1991). However, we will briefly describe some of the main issues and techniques in the present section.

The main problem in analysing within-subject temporal data is that the observations in the time-series from each participant are not independent and therefore do not conform to the assumptions of standard statistical techniques such as analysis of variance and multiple regression. There are three types of non-independence: trend, cycle, and serial dependency. *Trend* refers to systematic change over time due to factors such as response habituation and practice. *Cycle* refers to a rhythm or subcycle within the time series, for example due to circadian or day-of-week effects. *Serial dependency*, also known as *autocorrelation*, refers to the fact that adjacent observations are more likely to be correlated than observations at greater time intervals. In some cases these three temporal effects will

220

be of interest but otherwise they need to be removed from the data before the analysis starts. Fortunately, there are standard techniques available for removing trend, cycle, and serial dependency (see West & Hepworth, 1991).

The simplest method of analysing the data, and one that avoids the problems of non-independence, is to summarize the time-series from each participant using a parameter that can be used to compare participants. Some of these parameters were described in the previous section. However, such procedures fail to take full advantage of the rich temporal nature of the data.

Alternatives to summary statistics include *structural equation modelling* and *time-series methods*. Structural equation models are suitable when there are few time points but many participants, whereas time-series methods are suitable when there are many time points but few participants. Unfortunately, many intensive time-sampling studies have fewer time points than required by conventional time-series analysis but more than is practical for structural equation modelling. Pooled time-series methods are suitable for this type of dataset.

Another alternative is to analyse the time-series from each participant separately and then combine the results. For example, within-subject correlations may be calculated for each participant and then used as data for further between-subjects analysis. See Larsen (1989) for examples of other types of within-subject analysis.

As outlined in this section, investigators may choose from a wide range of available options for analysing mood dynamics. The choice of option depends primarily on the specific nature of the research question being addressed and secondarily on the quality of data. Unfortunately most of the current options are based on linear rather than non-linear models, and mood researchers may therefore also need to become more familiar with developments in non-linear analysis.

REFERENCES

Abelson, R. P., & Sermat, V. (1962). Multidimensional scaling of facial expressions. *Journal of Experimental Psychology, 63,* 546–564.

Adan, A. (1994). Chronotype and personality factors in the daily consumption of alcohol and psychostimulants. *Addiction, 89,* 455–462.

Ainsworth, M. (1967). *Infancy in Uganda: Infant care and the growth of love.* Baltimore: John Hopkins University Press.

Ainsworth, M. (1989). Attachments beyond infancy. *American Psychologist, 44,* 709–716.

Ainsworth, M., Blehar, M., Waters, E., & Wall, S. (1978). *Patterns of attachment: A psychological study of the strange situation.* Hillsdale, NJ: Erlbaum.

Alloy, L. B., & Abramson, L. Y. (1979). Judgement of contingency in depressed and non-depressed students. *Journal of Experimental Psychology: General, 108,* 441–485.

Alloy, L. B., Abramson, L. Y., & Viscusi, D. (1981). Induced mood and the illusion of control. *Journal of Personality and Social Psychology, 41,* 1129–1140.

Almagor, M., & Ehrlich, S. (1990). Personality correlates and cyclicity in positive and negative affect. *Psychological Reports, 66,* 1159–1169.

American Psychological Association (APA) (1994). *Diagnostic and statistical manual: IV.* Washington DC: APA.

Anisman, H., & Lapierre, Y. D. (1981). Stress and depression: Formulations and caveats. In S. Burchfield (Ed.) *Physiological and psychological interactions in response to stress* (pp. 67–88). New York: Hemisphere.

Anshensel, C. S., & Huba, G. J. (1983). Depression, alcohol use, and smoking over one year: A four wave longitudinal causal model. *Journal of Abnormal Psychology, 92,* 119–133.

Appley, M. H., & Trumbull, R. (1986). Development of the stress concept. In M. H. Appley & R. Trumbull (Eds) *Dynamics of stress: Physiological, psychological and social perspectives* (pp. 3–10). New York: Plenum Press.

Arnold, M. B. (1960). *Emotion and personality: vol. 1. Psychological aspects.* New York: Columbia University Press.

Ashkenazi, I. E., Reinberg, A., Bicakova-Rocher, A., & Ticher, A. (1993). The genetic background of individual variations of circadian-rhythm periods in healthy human adults. *American Journal of Human Genetics, 52,* 1250–1259.

Aspinwall, L. G., & Taylor, S. E. (1993). Effects of social comparison direction, threat, and self-esteem on affect, self-evaluation, and expected success. *Journal of Personality and Social Psychology, 64,* 708–722.

Averill, J. R. (1975). A semantic atlas of emotional concepts. *JSAS Catalog of Selected Documents in Psychology, 5,* 330 (Ms. No. 421).

Barkham, M., Rees, A., Stiles, W. B., Shapiro, D. A., Hardy, G. E., & Reynolds, S. A. (in press). Dose-effect relations in time-limited psychotherapy for depression. *Journal of Consulting and Clinical Psychology.*

Barley, S. R., & Knight, D. B. (1992). Toward a cultural theory of stress complaints. *Research in Organizational Behaviour, 14,* 1–48.

Barlow, D. H. (1988). *Anxiety and its disorders: The nature and treatment of anxiety and panic.* New York: Guildford Press.

Baron, R. A. (1987). Interviewer's mood and reactions to job applicants: The influence of affective states on applied social judgements. *Journal of Applied Social Psychology, 17,* 911–926.

Barton, S. (1994). Chaos, self-organization, and psychology. *American Psychologist, 49,* 5–14.

Batson, C. D., Shaw, L. L., & Oleson, K. C. (1992). Distinguishing affect, mood, and emotion: Toward functionally based conceptual distinctions. In M. S. Clark (Ed.) *Review of personality and social psychology 13: Emotion* (pp. 294–326). Newbury Park, CA: Sage.

Baumgardner, A. H., Kaufman, C. M., & Levy, P. E. (1989). Regulating affect interpersonally: When low self-esteem leads to greater enhancement. *Journal of Personality and Social Psychology, 56,* 450–467.

Beaman, A. L., Klentz, B., Diener, E., & Svanum, S. (1979). Self-awareness and transgression in children: Two field studies. *Journal of Personality and Social Psychology, 37,* 1835–1846.

Beck, A. T. (1976). *Cognitive therapy and the emotional disorders.* New York: International Universities Press.

Beck, A. T. (1983). Cognitive therapy of depression: New perspectives. In P. J. Clayton & J. E. Barrett (Eds) *Treatment of depression: Old controversies and new approaches* (pp. 265–284). New York: Raven Press.

Beck, A. T., Rush, A. J., Shaw, B. F., & Emery, G. (1979). *Cognitive therapy of depression.* New York: Guildford Press.

Becker, H. S. (1953). Becoming a marihuana user. *American Journal of Sociology, 59,* 235–242.

Bem, D. J. (1972). Self-perception theory. In L. Festinger (Ed.) *Advances in experimental social psychology* (vol. 5, pp. 1–62). New York: Academic Press.

Bentler, P. M. (1969). Semantic space is (approximately) bipolar. *Journal of Psychology, 71,* 33–40.

Berger, B. G., & Owen, D. R. (1992). Mood alteration with yoga and swimming: Aerobic exercise may not be necessary. *Perceptual and Motor Skills, 75,* 1331–1343.

Berkowitz, L., & Turner, C. W. (1974). Perceived anger level, instigating agent, and aggression. In H. London & R. E. Nisbett (Eds) *Thought and feeling: Cognitive alteration of feeling states* (pp. 174–189). Chicago, IL: Aldine.

Berlyne, D. E. (1960). *Conflict, arousal and curiosity.* New York: McGraw-Hill.

Blaney, P. H. (1986). Affect and memory: A review. *Psychological Bulletin, 99,* 229–246.

Blatt, S. J. (1974). Levels of object representation in anaclitic and introjective depression. *Psychoanalytic Study of the Child, 29,* 107–157.

Blatt, S. J. (1995). The destructiveness of perfectionism: Implications for the study of depression. *American Psychologist, 50,* 1003–1020.

Bless, H., Bohner, G., Schwarz, N., & Strack, F. (1990). Mood and persuasion: A cognitive response analysis. *Personality and Social Psychology Bulletin, 16,* 331–345.

Bless, H., Mackie, D. M., & Schwarz, N. (1992). Mood effects on attitude judgements: Independent effects of mood before and after message elaboration. *Journal of Personality and Social Psychology, 63,* 585–595.

Block, J. (1957). Studies in the phenomenology of emotions. *Journal of Abnormal and Social Psychology, 54,* 358–363.

Block, J. (1995). A contrarian view of the five-factor approach to personality description. *Psychological Bulletin, 117,* 187–215.

Bohle, P., & Tilley, A. J. (1993). Predicting mood change on night shift. *Ergonomics, 36,* 125–134.

Boivin, D. B., Czeisler, C. A., Dijk, D. J., Duffy, J. F., Folkard, S., Minors, D., Totterdell, P., & Waterhouse, J. (in press) Coincidence of the sleep–wake cycle and endogenous circadian phase regulates mood in healthy young subjects. *Archives of General Psychiatry.*

Bolger, N., DeLongis, A., Kessler, R. C., & Schilling, E. A. (1989). Effects of daily stress on negative mood. *Journal of Personality and Social Psychology, 57,* 808–818.

Bolger, N., & Schilling, E. A. (1991). Personality and the problems of everyday life: The role of neuroticism in exposure and reactivity to daily stressors. *Journal of Personality, 59,* 355–386.

Bond, M. J., & Feather, N. T. (1988). Some correlates of structure and purpose in the use of time. *Journal of Personality and Social Psychology, 55,* 321–329.

Bower, G. H. (1981). Mood and memory. *American Psychologist, 36,* 129–148.

Bower, G. H. (1983). Affect and cognition. *Philosophical Transactions of the Royal Society of London, Series B, 302,* 387–402.

Bower, G. H., & Cohen, P. R. (1982). Emotional influences in memory and thinking: Data and theory. In M. S. Clark & S. T. Fiske (Eds) *Affect and cognition* (pp. 291–333). Hillsdale, NJ: Lawrence Erlbaum Associates.

Bower, G. H., & Mayer, J. D. (1985). Failure to replicate mood-dependent retrieval. *Bulletin of the Psychonomic Society, 23,* 39–42.

Bower, G. H., Monteiro, K. P., & Gilligan, S. G. (1978). Emotional mood as a context for learning and recall. *Journal of Verbal Learning and Verbal Behavior, 17,* 573–585.

Bowlby, J. (1980). *Loss, sadness and depression. Attachment and loss* (vol. 3). London: Hogarth Press.

Boyd, J. H., & Weissman, M. M. (1981). Epidemiology of affective disorders. *Archives of General Psychiatry, 38,* 1039–1046.

Bradburn, N. M. (1969). *The structure of psychological well-being.* Chicago, IL: Aldine.

Brandstätter, H. (1991). Emotions in everyday life situations: Time sampling of subjective experience. In F. Strack, M. Argyle, & N. Schwarz (Eds) *Subjective well-being: An interdisciplinary approach* (pp. 173–192). Oxford: Pergamon Press.

Brandstätter, H. (1994). Changeability of mood. *Proceedings of the 8th conference of the International Society for Research on Emotions* (pp. 183–187). Storrs, CT: ISRE Publications.

Brewin, C. (1989). Cognitive change processes in psychotherapy. *Psychological Review, 96,* 379–394.

Brickman, P., Coates, D., & Janoff-Bulman, R. (1978). Lottery winners and accident victims: Is happiness relative? *Journal of Personality and Social Psychology, 36,* 917–927.

Briner, R. B., Reynolds, S., Totterdell, P., & Parkinson, B. (1994). Putting work in its place: The contribution of work and leisure activities to daily mood. Paper presented at the British Psychological Society Occupational Psychology Conference, Birmingham.

Broadbent, D. E. (1954). The role of auditory localization in attention and memory span. *Journal of Experimental Psychology, 47,* 191–196.

Brown, G. W., & Harris, T. O. (1978). *The social origins of depression.* London: Tavistock.

Brown, J. D., & Mankowski, T. A. (1993). Self-esteem, mood, and self-evaluation: Changes in mood and the way you see you. *Journal of Personality and Social Psychology, 64,* 421–430.

Bruner, J. S., Goodnow, J., & Austin, G. (1956). *A study of thinking.* New York: John Wiley.

Bruner, J. S., & Postman, L. (1947). Emotional selectivity in perception and reaction. *Journal of Personality, 16,* 69–77.

Buck, R. (1985). Prime theory: An integrated view of motivation and emotion. *Psychological Review, 92,* 389–413.

Buck, R. (1989). Emotional communication in personal relationships: A developmental-interactionist view. In C. Hendrick (Ed.) *Review of personality and social psychology 10: Close relationships* (pp. 144–163). Newbury Park, CA: Sage.

Burns, D. D. (1980). *Feeling good: The new mood therapy*. New York: Signet.

Burt, C. D. B. (1994). Prospective and retrospective account-making in diary entries: A model of anxiety reduction and avoidance. *Anxiety, Stress and Coping*, 6, 127–140.

Butler, G. (1989). Issues in the application of cognitive and behavioural strategies to the treatment of social phobia. *Clinical Psychology Review*, 9, 91–107.

Butler, G., Fennell, M., Robson, P., & Gelder, M. (1990). Comparison of behavior therapy and cognitive behavior therapy in the treatment of generalized anxiety disorder. *Journal of Consulting and Clinical Psychology*, 59, 167–175.

Byrne, D. (1971). *The attraction paradigm*. New York: Academic Press.

Cacioppo, J. T., Klein, D. J., Berntson, G. G., & Hatfield, E. (1993). The psychophysiology of emotion. In M. Lewis & J. Haviland (Eds) *Handbook of emotions* (pp. 119–142). New York: Guilford.

Campbell, J. D., & Fehr, B. (1990). Self-esteem and perceptions of conveyed impressions: Is negative affectivity associated with greater realism? *Journal of Personality and Social Psychology*, 58, 122–133.

Campbell, S. S., & Dawson, D. (1990). Enhancement of nighttime alertness and performance with bright ambient light. *Physiology and Behaviour*, 48, 317–320.

Carlson, R. (1992). *You can be happy no matter what*. San Rafael, CA: New World Library.

Carver, C. S., & Scheier, M. F. (1982). Control theory: A useful conceptual framework for personality, social, clinical and health psychology. *Psychological Bulletin*, 92, 111–135.

Carver, C. S., & Scheier, M. F. (1990). Origins and functions of positive and negative affect: A control process view. *Psychological Review*, 97, 19–35.

Carver, C. S., Scheier, M. F., & Weintraub, J. K. (1989). Assessing coping strategies: A theoretically based approach. *Journal of Personality and Social Psychology*, 56, 267–283.

Caspi, A., Bolger, N., & Eckenrode, J. (1987). Linking person and context in the daily stress process. *Journal of Personality and Social Psychology*, 52, 184–195.

Catanzaro, S. J., & Mearns, J. (1990). Measuring generalized expectancies for negative mood regulation: Initial scale development and implications. *Journal of Personality Assessment*, 54, 546–563.

Chaiken, S. (1980). Heuristic versus systematic information processing and the use of source versus message cues in persuasion. *Journal of Personality and Social Psychology*, 39, 752–766.

Chiariello, M. A., & Orvaschel, H. (1995). Patterns of parent–child communication: Relationship to depression. *Clinical Psychology Review*, 15, 395–407.

Cialdini, R. B., Baumann, D. J., & Kendrick, D. T. (1981). Insights from sadness: A three step model of the development of altruism as hedonism. *Developmental Review*, 1, 207–223.

Cialdini, R. B., Darby, B., & Vincent, J. (1973). Transgression and altruism: A case for hedonism. *Journal of Experimental Social Psychology*, 9, 502–516.

Cialdini, R. B., Schaller, M., Houlihan, D., Arps, K., Fultz, J., & Beaman, A. L. (1987). Empathy-based helping: Is it selflessly or selfishly motivated? *Journal of Personality and Social Psychology*, 52, 749–758.

Clark, D. M. (1986). Cognitive therapy of anxiety. *Behavioural Psychotherapy*, 14, 283–294.

Clark, D. M., Salkovskis, P., Gelder, M., Koehler, J., Martin, M., Anastasiades, P., Hackman, A., Middleton, H., & Jeavons, A. (1988). Tests of a cognitive theory of panic. In I. Hand and H. Wittchen (Eds) *Panic and phobias II* (pp. 149–158). Heidelberg: Springer.

Clark, D. M., & Teasdale, J. D. (1985). Constraints on the effects of mood on memory. *Journal of Personality and Social Psychology*, 48, 1595–1608.

Clark, D. M., Teasdale, J. D., Broadbent, D. E., & Martin, M. (1983). Effects of mood on lexical decisions. *Bulletin of the Psychonomic Society, 21,* 175–178.

Clark, L. A., & Watson, D. (1988). Mood and the mundane: Relations between daily life events and self-reported mood. *Journal of Personality and Social Psychology, 54,* 296–308.

Clark, L. A., & Watson, D. (1991). Tripartite model of anxiety and depression: Psychometric evidence and taxonomic implications. *Journal of Personality and Social Psychology, 100,* 316–336.

Clark, M. S., & Isen, A. M. (1982). Toward understanding the relationship between feeling states and social behavior. In A. H. Hastorf & A. M. Isen (Eds) *Cognitive social psychology* (pp. 73–108). New York: Elsevier.

Clark, M. S., Pataki, S. P., & Carver, V. H. (1996). Some thoughts and findings on self-presentation of emotions in relationships. In G. Fletcher & J. Fitness (Eds) *Knowledge structures in close relationships* (pp. 247–274). Mahwah, NJ: Lawrence Erlbaum Associates.

Cohen, S., & Williamson, G. M. (1991). Stress and infectious disease in humans. *Psychological Bulletin, 109,* 5–24.

Colvin, C. R., & Block, J. (1994). Do positive illusions foster mental health? An examination of the Taylor and Brown formulation. *Psychological Bulletin, 116,* 3–20.

Colvin, C. R., Block, J., & Funder, D. C. (1995). Overly positive self-evaluations and personality: Negative implications for mental health. *Journal of Personality and Social Psychology, 68,* 1152–1162.

Combs, A., Winkler, M., & Daley, C. (1994). A chaotic systems analysis of rhythms in feeling states. *Psychological Record, 44,* 359–368.

Cooper, C., & McConville, C. (1990). Interpreting mood scores: Clinical implications of individual differences in mood variability. *British Journal of Medical Psychology, 63,* 215–225.

Cooper, M. L., Frone, M. R., Russell, M., & Mudar, P. (1995). Drinking to regulate positive and negative emotions: A motivational model of alcohol use. *Journal of Personality and Social Psychology, 69,* 990–1005.

Costa, P. T., & McCrae, R. R. (1980). Influence of extraversion and neuroticism on subjective well-being: Happy and unhappy people. *Journal of Personality and Social Psychology, 38,* 668–678.

Costa, P. T., McCrae, R. R., & Zonderman, A. B. (1987). Environmental and dispositional influences on well-being: Longitudinal follow-up of an American national sample. *British Journal of Psychology, 78,* 299–306.

Cowdry, R. W. (1992). Identification of mood variance in depression. *American Journal of Psychiatry, 149,* 1121.

Cowdry, R. W., Gardner, D. L., O'Leary, K. M., Leibenflut, E., & Rubinow, D. R. (1991). Mood variability: A study of four groups. *American Journal of Psychiatry, 148,* 1505–1511.

Coyne, J. C. (1976). Depression and the response of others. *Journal of Abnormal Psychology, 85,* 186–193.

Coyne, J. C. (1994). Self-reported distress: Analog or ersatz depression? *Psychological Bulletin, 116,* 29–45.

Crits-Christoph, P., Cooper, A., & Luborsky, L. (1988). The accuracy of therapists' interpretations and the outcome of dynamic psychotherapy. *Journal of Consulting and Clinical Psychology, 56,* 490–495.

Csikszentmihalyi, M. (1992). *Flow: The psychology of happiness.* London: Rider.

Csikszentmihalyi, M., & Csikszentmihalyi, I. S. (1988). *Optimal experience: Psychological studies of flow in consciousness.* Cambridge: Cambridge University Press.

Csikszentmihalyi, M., & Larson, R. E. (1987). Validity and reliability of the experience sampling method. *Journal of Nervous and Mental Diseases, 175,* 526–536.

Csikszentmihalyi, M., & LeFevre, J. (1989). Optimal experience in work and leisure. *Journal of Personality and Social Psychology*, 56, 815–822.

Cunningham, M. R. (1979). Weather, mood, and helping behaviour: Quasi-experiments with the sunshine samaritan. *Journal of Personality and Social Psychology*, 37, 1947–1956.

Cytowic, R. (1994). *The man who tasted shapes*. London: Abacus.

Czeisler, C. A., Johnson, M. P., Duffy, J. F., Brown, E. N., Ronda, J. M., & Kronauer, R. E. (1990). Exposure to bright light and darkness to treat physiologic maladaptation to night work. *New England Journal of Medicine*, 322, 1253–1259.

Daly, E. M., Lancee, W. J., & Polivy, J. (1983). A conical model for the taxonomy of emotional experience. *Journal of Personality and Social Psychology*, 45, 443–457.

Dan, A. J., & Monagle, L. (1994). Sociocultural influences on women's experiences of premenstrual symptoms. In J. H. Gold & S. K. Severino (Eds) *Premenstrual dysphoria: Myths and realities* (pp. 201–211). Washington, DC: American Psychiatric Press.

DeCastro, J. M. (1990). Social, circadian, nutritional, and subjective correlates of the spontaneous pattern of moderate alcohol intake in humans. *Pharmacology, Biochemistry, and Behavior*, 35, 922–931.

DeLongis, A., Coyne, J. C., Dakof, G., Folkman, S., & Lazarus, R. S. (1982). Relationship of daily hassles, uplifts and major life events to health status. *Health Psychology*, 1, 119–136.

DeLongis, A., Folkman, S., & Lazarus, R. S. (1988). The impact of daily stress on health and mood: Psychological and social resources as mediators. *Journal of Personality and Social Psychology*, 54, 486–495.

de Rivera, J. H. (1992). Emotional climate: Social structure and emotional dynamics. In K. T. Strongman (Ed.) *International review of studies on emotions* (vol. 2, pp. 197–218). Chichester: Wiley.

Diener, E. (1984). Subjective well-being. *Psychological Bulletin*, 95, 542–575.

Diener, E., & Emmons, R. A. (1984). The independence of positive and negative affect. *Journal of Personality and Social Psychology*, 47, 1105–1117.

Diener, E., Fujita, F., & Sandvik, E. (1994). What subjective well-being researchers can tell emotion researchers about affect. *Proceedings of the 8th conference of the International Society for Research on Emotion* (pp. 30–42). Storrs, CT: ISRE Publications.

Diener, E., & Iran-Nejad, A. (1986). The relationship in experience between various types of affect. *Journal of Personality and Social Psychology*, 50, 1031–1038.

Diener, E., Larsen, R. J., Levine, S., & Emmons, R. A. (1985). Intensity and frequency: Dimensions underlying positive and negative affect. *Journal of Personality and Social Psychology*, 48, 1253–1265.

Dittmann, A. T. (1972). *Interpersonal messages of emotion*. New York: Springer.

Dobson, K. S. (1989). A meta-analysis of the efficacy of cognitive therapy for depression. *Journal of Consulting and Clinical Psychology*, 57, 414–419.

Dobson, K. S., & Joffe, R. (1986). The role of activity level and cognition in depressed mood in a university sample. *Journal of Clinical Psychology*, 42, 264–271.

Dohrenwend, B. S., & Dohrenwend, B. P. (1981). *Stressful life events and their contexts*. New York: Prodist.

Dohrenwend, B. S., Dohrenwend, B. P., Dodson, M., & Shrout, P. E. (1984). Symptoms, hassles, social supports, and life events: Problems of confounding measures. *Journal of Abnormal Psychology*, 93, 222–230.

Dohrenwend, B. P., & Shrout, P. E. (1985). "Hassles" in the conceptualization and measurement of life stress variables. *American Psychologist*, 40, 780–785.

Duclos, S. E., Laird, J. D., Schneider, E., Sexter, M., Stern, L., & Van Lighten, O. (1989). Emotion-specific effects of facial expressions and postures on emotional experience. *Journal of Personality and Social Psychology*, 57, 100–108.

Duffy, E. (1962). *Activation and behavior*. New York: Wiley.

Duval, S., & Wicklund, R. A. (1972). *A theory of objective self-awareness*. New York: Academic Press.

Eastman, C. I. (1992). High intensity light for circadian adaptation to a 12-h shift of the sleep schedule. *American Journal of Physiology, 263*, 428–436.

Ede, A., Kravitz, H., & Templer, D. (1976). Diurnal variation and endogenous component of depression. *British Journal of Psychiatry, 128*, 508–512.

Edlund, M. (1987). *Psychological time and mental illness*. New York: Gardner Press.

Ehlers, C. L. (1995). Chaos and complexity. Can it help us to understand mood and behavior? *Archives of General Psychiatry, 52*, 960–964.

Ehrlichman, H., & Halpern, J. N. (1988). Affect and memory: Effects of pleasant and unpleasant odours on retrieval of happy and unhappy memories. *Journal of Personality and Social Psychology, 55*, 769–779.

Eich, J. E. (1977). State-dependent retrieval of information in human episodic memory. In I. M. Birnbaum & E. S. Parker (Eds) *Alcohol and human memory* (pp. 141–157). Hillsdale, NJ: Lawrence Erlbaum Associates.

Eich, J. E. (1995). Searching for mood dependent memory. *Psychological Science, 6*, 67–75.

Ekman, P. (1994). Moods, emotions, and traits. In P. Ekman & R. J. Davidson (Eds) *The nature of emotion* (pp. 56–58). New York: Oxford University Press.

Ekman, P., & Davidson, R. J. (Eds) (1994). *The nature of emotion*. New York: Oxford University Press.

Ekman, P., & Friesen, W. V. (1975). *Unmasking the face*. Englewood Cliffs, NJ: Prentice-Hall.

Elkin, I., Shea, T., Watkins, J. T., Imber, S. D., Sotsky, S. M., Collins, J. F., Glats, D. R., Pilkonis, P. A., Leber, W. R., Docherty, J. P., Fresker, S. J., & Parloff, M. B. (1989). National Institute for Mental Health treatment of depression collaborative research program: General effectiveness of treatments. *Archives of General Psychiatry, 46*, 971–982.

Elliott, R., Shapiro, D. A., Firth-Cozens, J., Stiles, W. B., Hardy, G. E., Llewelyn, S. P., & Margison, F. R. (1994). Comprehensive process analysis of insight events in cognitive-behavioral and psychodynamic-interpersonal psychotherapies. *Journal of Counseling Psychology, 41*, 449–463.

Epstein, S. (1983). A research paradigm for the study of personality and emotions. In M. M. Page (Ed.) *Nebraska Symposium on Motivation 1982: Personality – Current Theory and Research* (pp. 91–154). Lincoln, NE: University of Nebraska Press.

Erber, R., & Erber, M. W. (1994). Beyond mood and social judgement: Mood incongruent recall and mood regulation. *European Journal of Social Psychology, 24*, 79–88.

Erickson, M. F., Sroufe, L. A., & Egeland, B. (1985). The relationship between quality of attachment and behaviour problems in preschool in a high-risk sample. *Monographs of the Society for Research in Child Development, 50*, 147–166.

Evans, M. D., Hollon, S. D., DeRubeis, R. J., Piasecki, J. M., Grove, W. M., Garvey, M. J., & Tuason, V. B. (1992). Differential relapse following cognitive therapy and pharmaco-therapy for depression. *Archives of General Psychiatry, 49*, 802–808.

Eysenck, H. J. (1967). *The biological basis of personality*. Springfield, IL: Charles C. Thomas.

Feather, N. T., & Bond, M. J. (1983). Time structure and purposeful activity among employed and unemployed university graduates. *Journal of Occupational Psychology, 56*, 241–254.

Fechner-Bates, S., Coyne, J. C., & Schwenk, T. L. (1994). The relationship of self-reported distress to depressive disorders and other psychopathology. *Journal of Consulting and Clinical Psychology, 62*, 550–559.

Feldman, L. A. (1995a). Variations in the circumplex structure of mood. *Personality and Social Psychology Bulletin, 21*, 806–817.

Feldman, L. A. (1995b). Valence focus and arousal focus: Individual differences in the structure of affective experience. *Journal of Personality and Social Psychology, 69,* 153–166.

Fenigstein, A., Scheier, M. F., & Buss, A. H. (1975). Public and private self-consciousness: Assessment and theory. *Journal of Consulting and Clinical Psychology, 43,* 522–527.

Field, S., Barkham, M., Shapiro, D. A., & Stiles, W. B. (1994). Assessment of assimilation in psychotherapy: A qualitative case study of problematic experiences with a significant other. *Journal of Counseling Psychology, 41,* 397–406.

Flapan, D. (1968). *Children's understanding of social interaction.* New York: Teachers College Press.

Folkard, S. (1983). Diurnal variation. In G. R. J. Hockey (Ed.) *Stress and fatigue in human performance* (pp. 245–271). Chichester: Wiley.

Folkard, S., & Akerstedt, T. (1989). Towards the prediction of alertness on abnormal sleep/ wake schedules. In A. Coblentz (Ed.) *Vigilance and performance in automatized systems* (pp. 287–296). Dordrecht: Kluwer.

Folkard, S., Arendt, J., & Clark, M. (1993). Can melatonin improve shift workers' tolerance of the night shift? Some preliminary findings. *Chronobiology International, 10,* 315–320.

Folkard, S., Hume, K. I., Minors, D. S., Waterhouse, J. M., & Watson, F. L. (1985). Independence of the circadian rhythm in alertness from the sleep/wake cycle. *Nature, 313,* 678–679.

Folkard, S., Totterdell, P., Minors, D., & Waterhouse, J. (1993). Dissecting circadian performance rhythms: Implications for shiftwork. *Ergonomics, 36,* 283–288.

Folkard, S., Wever, R., & Wildgruber, C. M. (1983). Multi-oscillatory control of circadian rhythms in human performance. *Nature, 305,* 223–226.

Folkman, S., & Lazarus, R. S. (1980). An analysis of coping in a middle-aged community sample. *Journal of Health and Social Behavior, 21,* 219–239.

Folkman, S. & Lazarus, R. S. (1985). If it changes it must be a process: Study of emotion and coping during three stages of a college examination. *Journal of Personality and Social Psychology, 48,* 150–170.

Fonagy, P., Steele, M., & Steele, H. (1991). Intergenerational patterns of attachment: Maternal representations during pregnancy and subsequent infant–mother attachments. *Child Development, 62,* 891–905.

Fordyce, M. W. (1977). Development of a program to increase personal happiness. *Journal of Counseling Psychology, 24,* 511–521.

Fordyce, M. W. (1983). A program to increase happiness: Further studies. *Journal of Counseling Psychology, 30,* 483–498.

Forgas, J. P. (1991). Affective influences on partner choice: Role of mood in social decisions. *Journal of Personality and Social Psychology, 61,* 708–720.

Forgas, J. P. (1992). Affect in social judgements and decisions: A multiprocess model. *Advances in Experimental Social Psychology, 25,* 227–275.

Forgas, J. P. (1993). On making sense of odd couples: Mood effects on the perception of atypical relationships. *Personality and Social Psychology Bulletin, 19,* 59–70.

Forgas, J. P. (1995). Mood and judgement: The Affect Infusion Model (AIM). *Psychological Bulletin, 117,* 39–66.

Forgas, J. P., & Bower, G. H. (1987). Mood effects on person perception judgements. *Journal of Personality and Social Psychology, 53,* 53–60.

Forgas, J. P., Bower, G. H., & Krantz, S. (1984). The influence of mood on perceptions of social interactions. *Journal of Experimental Social Psychology, 20,* 497–513.

Forgas, J. P., Bower, G. H., & Moylan, S. J. (1990). Praise or blame? Affective influences on attributions for achievement. *Journal of Personality and Social Psychology, 59,* 809–819.

Frank, J. D. (1971). Therapeutic factors in psychotherapy. *American Journal of Psychotherapy, 25,* 350–361.

Freud, S. (1910/1962). *Two short accounts of psycho-analysis*. Harmondsworth: Pelican.

Freud, S. (1920/1950). *Beyond the pleasure principle*. London: Hogarth Press.

Frijda, N. H. (1986). *The emotions*. Cambridge: Cambridge University Press.

Frijda, N. H. (1988). The laws of emotion. *American Psychologist*, *43*, 349–358.

Frijda, N. H. (1994). Varieties of affect: Emotions and episodes, moods, and sentiments. In P. Ekman & R. J. Davidson (Eds) *The nature of emotion* (pp. 59–67). New York: Oxford University Press.

Frijda, N. H., Kuipers, P., & ter Schure, E. (1989). Relations among emotion, appraisal, and emotional action readiness. *Journal of Personality and Social Psychology*, *57*, 212–228.

Frijda, N. H., Mesquita, B., Sonnemans, J., & van Goozen, S. (1991). The duration of affective phenomena or emotions, sentiments, and passions. In K. T. Strongman (Ed.) *International review of studies on emotion* (vol. 1, pp. 187–225). Chichester: Wiley.

Gallant, S. J., Hamilton, J. A., Popiel, D. A., Morokoff, P. J., & Chakraborty, P. K. (1991). Daily mood and symptoms: Effects of awareness of study focus, gender, menstrual-cycle phase, and day of the week. *Health Psychology*, *10*, 180–189.

Gardner, H. (1985). *The mind's new science: A history of the cognitive revolution*. New York: Basic Books.

George, J. M. (1990). Personality, affect, and behaviour in groups. *Journal of Applied Psychology*, *75*, 107–116.

Gergen, K. T. (1973). Social psychology as history. *Journal of Personality and Social Psychology*, *26*, 309–320.

Gilbert, P., & Reynolds, S. (1990). The relationship between the Eysenck personality questionnaire and Beck's concepts of sociotropy and autonomy. *British Journal of Clinical Psychology*, *29*, 319–325.

Giuliano, T. A. (1995). Mood awareness predicts mood change over time. Poster presented at the 103rd Annual Convention of the American Psychological Association, New York.

Gladstones, W. H. (1962). A multidimensional scaling study of facial expression of emotion. *Australian Journal of Psychology*, *14*, 95–100.

Glass, L., & Mackey, M. C. (1988). *From clocks to chaos – The rhythms of life*. Princeton, NJ: Princeton University Press.

Gold, A. E., MacLeod, K. M., Frier, B. M., & Deary, I. J. (1995). Changes in mood during acute hypoglycemia in healthy participants. *Journal of Personality and Social Psychology*, *68*, 498–504.

Goldberg, D. P., Bridges, K., Duncan-Jones, P. & Grayson, D. (1987). Dimensions of neurosis seen in primary care settings. *Psychological Medicine*, *17*, 461–470.

Goldberg, L. R. (1990). An alternative "description of personality": The Big Five factor structure. *Journal of Personality and Social Psychology*, *59*, 1216–1229.

Goleman, D. (1996). *Emotional intelligence: Why it can matter more than IQ*. London: Bloomsbury.

Goodhart, D. E. (1985). Some psychological effects associated with positive and negative thinking about stressful outcomes: Was Pollyanna right? *Journal of Personality and Social Psychology*, *48*, 216–232.

Gottman, J. M., & Levenson, R. W. (1985). A valid procedure for obtaining self-report of affect in marital interaction. *Journal of Consulting and Clinical Psychology*, *53*, 151–160.

Gottschalk, A., Bauer, M. S., & Whybrow, P. C. (1995). Evidence of chaotic mood variation in bipolar disorder. *Archives of General Psychiatry*, *52*, 947–959.

Graw, P., Kräuchi, K., Wirz-Justice, A., & Pöldinger, W. (1991). Diurnal variation of symptoms in seasonal affective disorder. *Psychiatry Research*, *37*, 105–111.

Gray, J. A. (1987). Perspectives on anxiety and impulsivity: A commentary. *Journal of Research in Personality*, *21*, 493–509.

Greden, J. F. (1993). Anti-depressant maintenance medications: When to discontinue and how to stop. *Journal of Clinical Psychiatry*, *54*, 39–47.

Green, D. P., Goldman, S. L., & Salovey, P. (1993). Measurement error masks bipolarity in affect ratings. *Journal of Personality and Social Psychology, 64*, 1029–1041.

Greenberg, L. S., & Rice, L. N. (1981). The specific effects of a Gestalt intervention. *Psychotherapy: Theory, Research and Practice, 18*, 31–37.

Guntrip, H. (1971). *Psychoanalytic theory, therapy and the self.* London: Basic Books.

Haaga, D. A. F., Dyck, M. J. & Ernst, D. (1991). Empirical status of cognitive theory of depression. *Psychological Bulletin, 110*, 215–236.

Hall, D. P., Sing, H. C., & Romanoski, A. J. (1991). Identification and characterization of greater mood variance in depression. *American Journal of Psychiatry, 148*, 1341–1345.

Hammen, C. L., Burge, G., Daley, S. E., Davila, J., Paley, B., & Rudolf, K. D. (1995). Interpersonal attachment cognitions and prediction of symptomatic response to interpersonal stress. *Journal of Abnormal Psychology, 104*, 436–443.

Hammen, C., Ellicott, A., Gitlin, M. & Jameson, K. R. (1989). Sociotropy/autonomy and vulnerability to specific life events in patients with unipolar depression and bipolar depression. *Journal of Abnormal Psychology, 98*, 154–160.

Harlow, H. F. (1958). The nature of love. *American Psychologist, 13*, 673–685.

Harma, M., Knauth, P., & Ilmarinen, J. (1989). Daytime napping and its effects on alertness and short-term memory performance in shiftworkers. *International Archives of Occupational and Environmental Health, 61*, 341–345.

Hart, H. (1957). *Self-conditioning: The new way to a successful life.* London: Oldbourne Press.

Hassard, J. (1991). Aspects of time in organization. *Human Relations, 44*, 105–125.

Hatfield, E., Cacioppo, J. T., & Rapson, R. L. (1994). *Emotional contagion.* Cambridge: Cambridge University Press.

Haug, H., & Wirz-Justice, A. (1993). Diurnal variation of mood in depression: Important or irrelevant? *Biological Psychiatry, 34*, 201–203.

Hawton, K., & Catalan, J. (1987). *Attempted suicide: A practical guide to its nature and management* (2nd edn). Oxford: Oxford University Press.

Hays, J. C., Kasl, S. V., & Jacobs, S. C. (1994). The course of psychological distress following threatened and actual conjugal bereavement. *Psychological Medicine, 24*, 917–927.

Hazan, C., & Shaver, P. (1987). Romantic love conceptualized as an attachment process. *Journal of Personality and Social Psychology, 52*, 511–524.

Hazan, C., & Shaver, P. (1990). Love and work: An attachment theoretical perspective. *Journal of Personality and Social Psychology, 59*, 270–280.

Headey, B., & Wearing, A. (1989). Personality, life events, and subjective well-being: Toward a dynamic equilibrium model. *Journal of Personality and Social Psychology, 57*, 731–739.

Headey, B., & Wearing, A. (1991). Subjective well-being: A stocks and flows framework. In F. Strack, M. Argyle, & N. Schwarz (Eds) *Subjective well-being* (pp. 49–73). Oxford: Pergamon Press.

Healy, D., & Waterhouse, J. M. (1990). The circadian system and affective disorders: Clocks or rhythms? *Chronobiology International, 7*, 5–10.

Healy, D., & Waterhouse, J. M. (1995). The circadian system and the therapeutics of the affective disorders. *Pharmacology and Therapeutics, 65*, 241–263.

Hebb, D. O. (1946). On the nature of fear. *Psychological Review, 53*, 259–276.

Heiby, E. M. (1983). Toward the prediction of mood change. *Behavior Therapy, 14*, 110–115.

Heiby, E. M. (1994). Implications of chaos theory for time-series assessment of depression. *23rd International Congess of Applied Psychology*, July 17–22, Madrid.

Heide, F. J., & Borkovec, T. D. (1984). Relaxation-induced anxiety: Mechanisms and theoretical implications. *Behavior Research and Therapy, 22*, 1–12.

Heider, F. (1958). *The psychology of interpersonal relations.* New York: John Wiley.

231

Henry, G., Weingartner, H., & Murphy, D. L. (1973). Influence of affective states and psycho-active drugs on verbal learning and memory. *American Journal of Psychiatry*, *130*, 966–971.

Hepburn, L., & Eysenck, M. W. (1989). Personality, average mood and mood variability. *Personality and Individual Differences*, *10*, 975–983.

Hersey, R. B. (1931). Emotional cycles in man. *Journal of Mental Science*, *77*, 151–169.

Hilgard, E. R. (1980). The trilogy of mind. *Journal of the History of the Behavioral Sciences*, *16*, 107–117.

Hochschild, A. R. (1983). *The managed heart: Commercialization of human feeling.* Berkeley, CA: University of California Press.

Holmes, T. H., & Rahe, R. H. (1967). The social readjustment rating scale. *Journal of Psychosomatic Research*, *11*, 213–218.

Horne, J., & Östberg, O. (1976). A self-assessment questionnaire to determine morningness–eveningness in human circadian rhythms. *International Journal of Chronobiology*, *4*, 97–110.

Hoskins, C. N. (1989). Activation – A predictor of need fulfillment in couples. *Research in Nursing and Health*, *12*, 365–372.

Howard, K. I., Kopta, S. M., Krause, M. S., & Orlinsky, D. E. (1986). The dose-effect relationship in psychotherapy. *American Psychologist*, *41*, 159–164.

Howard, K. I., Leuger, R. J., Maling, M. S., & Marinovich, Z. (1993). A phase model of psychotherapy outcome: Causal mediation of change. *Journal of Consulting and Clinical Psychology*, *61*, 678–685.

Howes, M. J., Hokanson, J. E., & Loewenstein, D. A. (1985). Induction of depressive affect after prolonged exposure to a mildly depressed individual. *Journal of Personality and Social Psychology*, *49*, 1110–1113.

Hsee, C. K., & Abelson, R. P. (1991). The velocity relation: Satisfaction as a function of the first derivative of outcome over time. *Journal of Personality and Social Psychology*, *60*, 341–347.

Hsee, C. K., Salovey, P., & Abelson, R. P. (1994). The quasi-acceleration relation: Satisfaction as a function of the change of velocity of outcome over time. *Journal of Experimental Social Psychology*, *30*, 96–111.

Hull, J. G., & Bond, C. F. Jr. (1986). Social and behavioral consequences of alcohol consumption and expectancy: A meta-analysis. *Psychological Bulletin*, *99*, 347–360.

Ingram, R. E. (1990). Self-focused attention in clinical disorders: Review and a conceptual model. *Psychological Bulletin*, *107*, 156–176.

Ingram, R. E., & Smith, T. W. (1984). Depression and internal versus external focus of attention. *Cognitive Therapy and Research*, *8*, 139–152.

Ingram, R. E., Smith, T. W., & Brehm, S. S. (1983). Depression and information processing: Self-schemata and the encoding of self-referent information. *Journal of Personality and Social Psychology*, *45*, 412–420.

Isen, A. M. (1970). Success, failure, attention and reactions to others: The warm glow of success. *Journal of Personality and Social Psychology*, *15*, 294–301.

Isen, A. M. (1984). Toward understanding the role of affect in cognition. In R. S. Wyer & T. K. Srull (Eds) *Handbook of social cognition* (vol. 3, pp. 179–236). Hillsdale, NJ: Lawrence Erlbaum Associates.

Isen, A. M. (1987). Positive affect, cognitive processes, and social behavior. *Advances in Experimental Social Psychology*, *20*, 203–253.

Isen, A. M., Clark, M., & Schwartz, M. F. (1976). Duration of the effect of good mood on helping: "Footprints on the sands of time". *Journal of Personality and Social Psychology*, *34*, 385–393.

Isen, A. M., & Daubman, K. A. (1984). The influence of affect on categorization. *Journal of Personality and Social Psychology*, *47*, 1206–1217.

Isen, A. M., Horn, N., & Rosenhan, D. (1973). Effects of success and failure on children's generosity. *Journal of Personality and Social Psychology, 27,* 239–247.

Isen, A. M., & Levin, P. F. (1972). The effect of feeling good on helping: Cookies and kindness. *Journal of Personality and Social Psychology, 34,* 384–388.

Isen, A. M., & Simmonds, S. F. (1978). The effect of feeling good on a helping task that is incompatible with good mood. *Social Psychology, 41,* 345–349.

Izard, C. E. (1972). *Patterns of emotions: A new analysis of anxiety and depression.* San Diego, CA: Academic Press.

Izard, C. E., Wehmer, G. M., Livsey, W., & Jennings, J. R. (1965). Affect, awareness, and performance. In S. S. Tomkins & C. E. Izard (Eds) *Affect, cognition, and personality* (pp. 2–41). New York: Springer.

Jacobsen, E. (1957). Normal and pathological moods: Their nature and functions. In R. S. Eisler, A. F. Freud, H. Hartman, & E. Kris (Eds) *The psychoanalytic study of the child* (pp. 73–113). New York: International Universities Press.

James, W. (1898). *The principles of psychology* (vol. 2). London: Macmillan.

Jersild, A., & Holmes, F. (1935). Children's fears. *Child Development Monographs, 20.*

Jewett, M. E., Kronauer, R. E., & Czeisler, C. A. (1991). Light-induced suppression of endogenous circadian amplitude in humans. *Nature, 350,* 59–62.

Johnson, E. J., & Tversky, A. (1983). Affect, generalization, and the perception of risk. *Journal of Personality and Social Psychology, 45,* 20–31.

Johnson, T. J., Feigenbaum, R., & Weiby, M. (1964). Some determinants and consequences of the teacher's perception of causation. *Journal of Experimental Psychology, 55,* 237–246.

Johnston, D. W., & Anastasiades, P. (1990). The relationship between heart rate and mood in real life. *Journal of Psychosomatic Research, 34,* 21–27.

Jones, E. E., & Pulos, S. M. (1993). Comparing the process in psychodynamic and cognitive-behavioral therapies. *Journal of Consulting and Clinical Psychology, 61,* 306–316.

Kaminer, W. (1993). *I'm dysfunctional, you're dysfunctional: The recovery movement and other self-help fashions.* New York: Vintage Books.

Kanfer, F. H., & Gaelick-Buys, L. (1991). Self-management methods. In F. H. Kanfer & A. P. Goldstein (Eds) *Helping people change: A textbook of methods* (4th edn, pp. 305–360). New York: Pergamon Press.

Kanner, A. D., Coyne, J. C., Schaefer, C., & Lazarus, R. S. (1981). Comparison of two models of stress measurements: Daily hassles and uplifts versus major life events. *Journal of Behavioral Medicine, 4,* 1–29.

Kavanagh, D. J., & Bower, G. H. (1985). Mood and self-efficacy: Impact of joy and sadness on perceived capabilities. *Cognitive Therapy and Research, 9,* 507–525.

Kellerman, J., Lewis, J., & Laird, J. D. (1989). Looking and loving: The effects of mutual gaze on feelings of romantic love. *Journal of Research in Personality, 23,* 145–161.

Keltner, D., Ellsworth, P. C., & Edwards, K. (1993). Beyond simple pessimism: Effects of sadness and anger on social perception. *Journal of Personality and Social Psychology, 64,* 740–752.

Kendler, K. S., Kessler, R. C., Neale, M. C., Heath, A. C., & Eaves, L. J. (1993). The prediction of major depression in women: Towards an integrated etiologic model. *American Journal of Psychiatry, 150,* 1139–1148.

Kenny, A. (1963). *Action, emotion, and will.* London: Routledge and Kegan Paul.

Kilpatrick, R., & Trew, K. (1985). Life-styles and psychological well-being among unemployed men in Northern Ireland. *Journal of Occupational Psychology, 58,* 207–216.

Kirsch, I., Mearns, J., & Catanzaro, S. J. (1990). Mood-regulation expectancies as determinants of dysphoria in college students. *Journal of Counseling Psychology, 37,* 306–312.

Kirschenbaum, D. S. (1987). Self-regulatory failure: A review with clinical implications. *Clinical Psychology Review*, 7, 77–104.

Knauth, P., & Ilmarinen, J. (1975). Continuous measurement of body temperature during a 3-week experiment with inverted working and sleeping hours. In P. Colquhohn, S. Folkard, P. Knauth, & J. Rutenfranz (Eds) *Proceedings of the 3rd International Symposium on Night and Shiftwork* (pp. 66–74). Opladen: Westdeutscher Verlag.

Kopta, S. M., Howard, K. I., Lowry, J. L., & Beutler, L. E. (1994). Patterns of symptomatic recovery in psychotherapy. *Journal of Consulting and Clinical Psychology*, 62, 1009–1016.

Kräuchi, K., Nussbaum, P., & Wirz-Justice, A. (1990). Consumption of sweets and caffeine in the night shift: Relation to fatigue. In J. Horne (Ed.) *Sleep '90* (pp. 62–64). Bochum: Pontenagel Press.

Kräuchi, K., Wirz-Justice, A., & Graw, P. (1990). The relationship of affective state to dietary preference: Winter depression and light therapy as a model. *Journal of Affective Disorders*, 20, 43–53.

Kraut, R. E. (1982). Social presence, facial feedback, and emotion. *Journal of Personality and Social Psychology*, 42, 853–863.

Kripke, D. F., Drennan, M. D., & Elliott, J. A. (1992). The complex circadian pacemaker in affective disorders. In Y. Touitou and E. Haus (Eds) *Biologic rhythms in clinical and laboratory medicine* (pp. 265–276). Berlin: Springer-Verlag.

Kuhn, T. S. (1962). *The structure of scientific revolutions*. Chicago, IL: University of Chicago Press.

Kuykendall, D., & Keating, J. (1990). Mood and persuasion: Evidence for the differential influence of positive and negative states. *Psychology and Marketing*, 7, 1–9.

Lacey, J. I., & Lacey, B. C. (1958). Verification and extension of the principle of autonomic response stereotypy. *American Journal of Psychology*, 71, 50–78.

Lader, M. (1975). *The psychophysiology of mental illness*. London: Routledge and Kegan Paul.

Laird, J. D. (1974). Self-attribution of emotion: The effects of expressive behavior on the quality of emotional experience. *Journal of Personality and Social Psychology*, 29, 473–486.

Laird, J. D., & Bresler, C. (1992). The process of emotional experience: A self-perception theory. In M. S. Clark (Ed.) *Review of personality and social psychology 13: Emotion* (pp. 213–234). Newbury Park, CA: Sage.

Lambert, M., & Bergin, A. E. (1994). The effectiveness of psychotherapy. In A. E. Bergin & S. L. Garfield (Eds) *Handbook of psychotherapy and behavior change* (4th edn, pp. 143–189). New York: Wiley.

Langer, E. J. (1975). The illusion of control. *Journal of Personality and Social Psychology*, 32, 311–328.

Langston, C. A. (1994). Capitalizing on and coping with daily-life events: Expressive responses to positive events. *Journal of Personality and Social Psychology*, 67, 1112–1125.

Larsen, R. J. (1987). The stability of mood variability: A spectral analytic approach to daily mood assessments. *Journal of Personality and Social Psychology*, 52, 1195–1204.

Larsen, R. J. (1989). A process approach to personality psychology: Utilizing time as a facet of data. In D. M. Buss & N. Cantor (Eds) *Personality psychology: Recent trends and emerging directions* (pp. 177–193). New York: Springer-Verlag.

Larsen, R. J. (1992). Neuroticism and selective encoding and recall of symptoms: Evidence from a combined concurrent–retrospective study. *Journal of Personality and Social Psychology*, 62, 480–488.

Larsen, R. J., & Diener, E. (1987). Affect intensity as an individual difference characteristic: A review. *Journal of Research in Personality*, 21, 1–39.

Larsen, R. J., & Diener, E. (1992). Promises and problems with the circumplex model of emotion. In M. S. Clark, (Ed.) *Review of personality and social psychology 13: Emotion* (pp. 25–59). Newbury Park, CA: Sage.

Larsen, R. J., Diener, E., & Emmons, R. A. (1986). Affect intensity and reactions to daily life events. *Journal of Personality and Social Psychology, 51*, 803–814.

Larsen, R. J., & Kasimatis, M. (1990). Individual differences in entrainment of mood to the weekly calendar. *Journal of Personality and Social Psychology, 58*, 164–171.

Larsen, R. J., & Ketelaar, T. (1991). Personality and susceptibility to positive and negative emotional states. *Journal of Personality and Social Psychology, 61*, 132–140.

Larson, R., Csikszentmihalyi, M., & Graef, R. (1980). Mood variability and the psychosocial adjustment of adolescents. *Journal of Youth and Adolescence, 9*, 469–490.

Lavallee, L. F., & Campbell, J. D. (1995). Impact of personal goals on self-regulation processes elicited by daily negative events. *Journal of Personality and Social Psychology, 69*, 341–352.

Lazarus, R. S. (1984). Puzzles in the study of daily hassles. *Journal of Behavioural Medicine, 7*, 375–389.

Lazarus, R. S. (1991). *Emotion and adaptation.* New York: Oxford University Press.

Lazarus, R. S. (1994). The stable and the unstable in emotion. In P. Ekman & R. J. Davidson (Eds) *The nature of emotion* (pp. 79–85). New York: Oxford University Press.

Lazarus, R. S., & Alfert, E. (1964). Short circuiting of threat by experimentally altering cognitive appraisal. *Journal of Abnormal and Social Psychology, 69*, 195–205.

Lazarus, R. S., DeLongis, A., Folkman, S. & Gruen, R. (1985). Stress and adaptational outcomes: The problem of confounded measures. *American Psychologist, 40*, 770–779.

Lazarus, R. S. & Folkman, S. (1984). *Stress, appraisal, and coping.* New York: Springer.

Leight, K. A., & Ellis, H. C. (1981). Emotional mood states, strategies, and state-dependency in memory. *Journal of Verbal Learning and Verbal Behavior, 20*, 251–266.

Levenson, R. W., & Gottman, J. M. (1983). Marital interaction: Physiological linkage and affective exchange. *Journal of Personality and Social Psychology, 45*, 587–597.

Lewin, R. (1993). *Complexity, Life at the edge of chaos.* London: Dent.

Lewinsohn, P. M. (1975). The behavioural study and the treatment of depression. In M. Hersen, R. Eisler & P. Miller (Eds) *Progress in behavior modification* (vol. 1, pp. 19–65). New York: Academic Press.

Lewinsohn, P. M., & Graf, M. (1973). Pleasant activities and depression. *Journal of Consulting and Clinical Psychology, 41*, 261–268.

Lewy, A. J., Wehr, T. A., Goodwin, F. K., Newsome, D. A., & Markey, S. P. (1980). Light suppresses melatonin secretion in humans. *Science, 210*, 1267–1269.

Linville, P. W., & Fischer, G. W. (1991). Preferences for separating or combining events. *Journal of Personality and Social Psychology, 60*, 5–23.

Locke, K. D., & Keltner, D. (1993). Using art for comparison and distraction: Effects on negative emotions and judgements of satisfaction. *Cognition and Emotion, 7*, 443–460.

Luborsky, L. (1981). *Principles of psychoanalytic psychotherapy.* New York: Basic Books.

Luborsky, L., Crits-Christoph, P., Mintz, J., & Auerbach, A. (1988). *Who will benefit from psychotherapy? Predicting therapeutic outcomes.* New York: Basic Books.

Luborsky, L., Singer, B., & Luborksy, L. (1975). Comparative studies of psychotherapies: Is it true that "Everyone has won and all must have prizes"? *Archives of General Psychiatry, 32*, 995–1008.

Lutz, C. A. (1988). *Unnatural emotions: Everyday sentiments on a Micronesian atoll and their challenge to western theory.* Chicago, IL: University of Chicago Press.

Lyubomirsky, S., & Nolen-Hoeksema, S. (1993). Self-perpetuating properties of dysphoric rumination. *Journal of Personality and Social Psychology, 65*, 339–349.

Mackie, D. M., & Worth, L. T. (1989). Processing deficits and the mediation of positive affect in persuasion. *Journal of Personality and Social Psychology, 57*, 27–40.

Mackie, D. M., & Worth, L. T. (1991). Feeling good, but not thinking straight: The impact of positive mood on persuasion. In J. P. Forgas (Ed.) *Emotion and social judgements* (pp. 201–219). Oxford: Pergamon Press.

Main, M., Kaplan, K., & Cassidy, J. (1985). Security in infancy, childhood and adulthood: A move to the level of representation. In I. Bretherton & E. Waters (Eds) Growing points of attachment theory and research. *Monographs for the Society for Research in Child Development, 50* (1–2 Serial No. 209), 66–104.

Malan, D. (1979). *Individual psychotherapy and the science of psychodynamics.* London: Butterworths.

Mandler, G. (1984). *Mind and body: The psychology of emotion and stress.* New York: Norton.

Mansfield, P. K., Hood, K. E., & Henderson, J. (1989). Women and their husbands: Mood and arousal fluctuations across the menstrual cycle and days of the week. *Psychosomatic Medicine, 51,* 66–80.

Manstead, A. S. R., & Tetlock, P. E. (1989). Cognitive appraisals and emotional experience: Further evidence. *Cognition and Emotion, 3,* 225–240.

Marangoni, C., Garcia, S., Ickes, W., & Teng, G. (1995). Empathic accuracy in a clinically relevant setting. *Journal of Personality and Social Psychology, 68,* 854–869.

Marco, C. A., & Suls, J. (1993). Daily stress and the trajectory of mood: Spillover, response assimilation, contrast, and chronic negative affectivity. *Journal of Personality and Social Psychology, 64,* 1053–1063.

Marks, I. (1987). *Fears, phobias, and rituals: Panic, anxiety and their disorders.* Oxford: Oxford University Press.

Marlatt, G. A., Kosturn, C. F., & Lang, A. R. (1975). Provocation to anger and opportunity for retaliation as determinants of alcohol consumption in social drinkers. *Journal of Abnormal Psychology, 84,* 652–659.

Martin, D. J., Abramson, L. Y., & Alloy, L. B. (1984). The illusion of control for self and others in depressed and nondepressed college students. *Journal of Personality and Social Psychology, 46,* 125–136.

Martin, L. L., Ward, D. W., Achee, J. W., & Wyer, Jr. R. S. (1993). Mood as input: People have to interpret the motivational implications of their moods. *Journal of Personality and Social Psychology, 64,* 317–326.

Mathews, A. M., & MacLeod, C. (1986). Discrimination without awareness in anxiety states. *Journal of Abnormal Psychology, 95,* 131–138.

Matlin, M. W., & Stang, D. (1979). *The Polyanna principle: Selectivity in language, memory and thought.* Cambridge, MA: Shenkman.

Matthews, G. (1992). Mood. In A. P. Smith & D. M. Jones (Eds) *Handbook of human performance* (vol. 3, pp. 161–193). London: Academic Press.

Mattlin, J. A., Wethington, E., & Kessler, R. C. (1990). Situational determinants of coping and coping effectiveness. *Journal of Health and Social Behaviour, 31,* 103–122.

Mayer, J. D., Gayle, M., Meehan, M. E., & Haarman, A-K. (1990). Toward a better specification of the mood-congruency effect in recall. *Journal of Experimental Social Psychology, 26,* 465–480.

Mayer, J. D., & Bremer, D. (1985). Assessing mood with affect-sensitive tasks. *Journal of Personality Assessment, 49,* 95–99.

Mayer, J. D., & Gaschke, Y. N. (1988). The experience and meta-experience of mood. *Journal of Personality and Social Psychology, 55,* 102–111.

Mayer, J. D., Salovey, P., Gomberg-Kaufman, S., & Blainey, K. (1991). A broader conception of mood experience. *Journal of Personality and Social Psychology, 60,* 100–111.

Mayer, J. D., & Stevens, A. A. (1994). An emerging understanding of the reflective (meta-) experience of mood. *Journal of Research in Personality, 28,* 351–373.

McClintock, M. K. (1971). Menstrual synchrony and suppression. *Nature, 229,* 244–245.

McCrae, R. R., & Costa, P. T. (1987). Validation of the five-factor model across instruments and observers. *Journal of Personality and Social Psychology, 52*, 81–90.

McCrae, R. R., & Costa, P. T. (1991). Adding *liebe und arbeit*: The full five-factor model and well-being. *Personality and Social Psychology Bulletin, 17*, 227–232.

McFarlane, C., & Ross, M. (1982). The impact of causal attributions on affective reactions to success and failure. *Journal of Personality and Social Psychology, 43*, 937–946.

McFarlane, J., Martin, C. L., Williams, T. M. (1988). Mood fluctuations: Women versus men and menstrual versus other cycles. *Psychology of Women Quarterly, 12*, 201–223.

McFatter, R. M. (1994). Interactions in predicting mood from extraversion and neuroticism. *Journal of Personality and Social Psychology, 66*, 570–578.

McGrath, J. E., & Kelly, J. R. (1986). *Time and human interaction. Toward a social psychology of time*. New York: Guilford Press.

Mearns, J. (1991). Coping with a breakup: Negative mood regulation expectancies and depression following the end of a romantic relationship. *Journal of Personality and Social Psychology, 60*, 327–334.

Meltzer, H., Gill, B., & Petticrew, M. (1995). *The prevalence of psychiatric morbidity among adults aged 16–64 living in private households in Great Britain*. London: OPCS, Bulletin No. 1.

Merten, J., & Krause, R. (1994). Longitudinal studies of emotional development within psychotherapy. *Proceedings of the 8th conference of the International Society for Research on Emotions* (pp. 162–166). CT: ISRE Publications.

Meyer, G. J., & Shack, J. R. (1989). The structural convergence of mood and personality: Evidence for old and new "directions". *Journal of Personality and Social Psychology, 57*, 691–706.

Miller, D. T., & Ross, M. (1975). Self-serving biases in the attribution of causality: Fact or fiction? *Psychological Bulletin, 82*, 213–225.

Miller, G. A. (1956). The magical number seven, plus or minus two: Some limits on our capacity for processing information. *Psychological Review, 63*, 81–97.

Miller, G. A., & Johnson-Laird, P. N. (1976). *Language and perception*. Cambridge, MA: Harvard University Press.

Minors, D. S., & Waterhouse, J. M. (1988). Mathematical and statistical analysis of circadian rhythms. *Psychoneuroendocrinology, 13*, 443–464.

Mintz, J. & Mintz, L. I. (1992). Treatment of depression and the functional capacity to work. *Archives of General Psychiatry, 49*, 761–768.

Molenaar, P. C. M. (1985). A dynamic factor model for the analysis of multivariate time-series. *Psychometrika, 50*, 181–202.

Molenaar, P. C. M., Degooijer, J. G., & Schmitz, B. (1992). Dynamic factor analysis of nonstationary multivariate time-series. *Psychometrika, 57*, 333–349.

Möller, H. J., & Leitner, M. (1987). Optimizing a nonlinear mathematical approach for the computerized analysis of mood curves. *Psychopathology, 20*, 255–267.

Monk, T. H., Buysse, D. J., Reynolds III, C. F., Jarrett, D. B., & Kupfer, D. J. (1992). Rhythmic vs homeostatic influences on mood, activation, and performance in young and old men. *Journal of Gerontology, 47*, 221–227.

Monk, T. H., Petrie, S. R., Hayes, A. J., & Kupfer, D. J. (1994). Regularity of daily life in relation to age, gender, sleep quality and circadian rhythms. *Journal of Sleep Research, 3*, 196–205.

Montgomery, S. A. (1994). Antidepressants in long-term treatment. *Annual Review of Medicine, 45*, 447–457.

Morris, W. N. (1989). *Mood: The frame of mind*. New York: Springer-Verlag.

Morris, W. N. (1992). A functional analysis of the role of mood in affective systems. In M. S. Clark (Ed.) *Review of personality and social psychology 13: Emotion* (pp. 256–293). Newbury Park, CA: Sage.

237

Morris, W. N., & Reilly, N. P. (1987). Toward the self-regulation of mood: Theory and Research. *Motivation and Emotion*, *11*, 215–249.

Murray, N., Sujan, H., Hirt, E. R., & Sujan, M. (1990). The influence of mood on categorization: A cognitive flexibility interpretation. *Journal of Personality and Social Psychology*, *59*, 411–425.

Murray-Parkes, C. (1972). *Bereavement: Studies of grief in adult life*. Harmondsworth: Penguin.

Nasby, W., & Yando, R. (1982). Selective encoding and retrieval of affectively valent information: Two cognitive consequences of children's mood states. *Journal of Personality and Social Psychology*, *43*, 1244–1253.

Neale, J. M., Hooley, J. M., Jandorf, L., & Stone, A. A. (1987). Daily life events and mood. In C. R. Snyder & C. E. Ford (Eds) *Coping with negative life events: Clinical and social perspectives* (pp. 161–189). New York: Plenum.

Neisser, U. (1976). *Cognition and reality*. San Francisco, CA: W. H. Freeman.

Nelson, T. M. (1971). Student mood during a full academic year. *Journal of Psychosomatic Research*, *15*, 113–122.

Nicholson, R. A., & Berman, J. S. (1983). Is follow-up necessary in evaluating psychotherapy? *Psychological Bulletin*, *93*, 261–278.

Niedenthal, P. M., & Setterland, M. B. (1994). Emotion congruence in perception. *Personality and Social Psychology Bulletin*, *20*, 401–411.

Nisbett, R. E., & Wilson, T. D. (1977). Telling more than we can know: Verbal reports on mental processes. *Psychological Review*, *84*, 231–259.

Nolen-Hoeksema, S., Morrow, J., & Fredrickson, B. L. (1993). Response styles and the duration of episodes of depressed mood. *Journal of Abnormal Psychology*, *102*, 20–28.

Nolen-Hoeksema, S., Parker, L. E., & Larson, J. (1994). Ruminative coping with depressed mood following loss. *Journal of Personality and Social Psychology*, *67*, 92–104.

Nowlis, V., & Nowlis, H. H. (1956). The description and analysis of moods. *Annals of the New York Academy of Science*, *65*, 345–355.

Oatley, K. (1992). *Best laid schemes: The psychology of emotions*. Cambridge: Cambridge University Press.

Oatley, K., & Bolton, W. (1985). A social-cognitive theory of depression in reaction to life events. *Psychological Review*, *92*, 372–388.

Oatley, K., & Johnson-Laird, P. N. (1987). Towards a cognitive theory of emotions. *Cognition and Emotion*, *1*, 29–50.

O'Leary, A. (1990). Stress, emotion, and human immune function. *Psychological Bulletin*, *108*, 363–382.

Ormel, J., & Schaufeli, W. B. (1991). Stability and change in psychological distress and their relationship with self-esteem and locus of control: A dynamic equilibrium model. *Journal of Personality and Social Psychology*, *60*, 288–299.

Ortony, A., Clore, G. L., & Collins, A. (1988). *The cognitive structure of emotions*. New York: Cambridge University Press.

Osgood, C. E. (1962). Studies on the generality of affective meaning systems. *American Psychologist*, *17*, 10–28.

Osgood, C. E., May, W. H., & Miron, M. S. (1975). *Cross-cultural universals of affective meaning*. Urbana, IL: University of Illinois Press.

Osgood, C. E., Suci, G. J., & Tannebaum, P. H. (1957). *The measurement of meaning*. Urbana, IL: University of Illinois Press.

Ost, L. G., & Hugdahl, K. (1981). Acquisition of phobias and anxiety response patterns in clinical patients. *Behaviour Research and Therapy*, *21*, 623–631.

Parkinson, B. (1990). Interrogating emotions. A dyadic task for exploring the common sense of feeling states. *European Journal of Social Psychology*, *60*, 327–334.

Parkinson, B. (1995). *Ideas and realities of emotion*. London: Routledge.

Parkinson, B., Briner, R. B., Reynolds, S., & Totterdell, P. (1995). Time frames for affect: Relations between momentary and generalized mood reports. *Personality and Social Psychology Bulletin, 21*, 331–339.

Parkinson, B., & Lea, M. (1991). Investigating personal constructs of emotions. *British Journal of Psychology, 82*, 73–86.

Parrott, W. G. (1993). Beyond hedonism: Motives for inhibiting good moods and for maintaining bad moods. In D. M. Wegner & J. W. Pennebaker (Eds) *Handbook of mental control* (pp. 278–305). Englewood Cliffs, NJ: Prentice Hall.

Parrott, W. G., & Sabini, J. (1990). Mood and memory under natural conditions: Evidence for mood incongruent recall. *Journal of Personality and Social Psychology, 59*, 321–336.

Patkai, P. (1985). The menstrual cycle. In S. Folkard & T. H. Monk (Eds) *Hours of work – Temporal factors in work scheduling* (pp. 87–96). New York: Wiley.

Pavlov, I. P. (1927). *Conditioned reflexes.* London: Oxford University Press.

Pearlin, L. I., & Schooler, C. (1978). The structure of coping. *Journal of Health and Social Behaviour, 19*, 2–21.

Pennebaker, J. W. (1981). Stimulus characteristics influencing estimation of heart rate. *Psychophysiology, 18*, 540–548.

Pennebaker, J. W., & Beall, S. K. (1986). Confronting a traumatic event: Toward an understanding of inhibition and disease. *Journal of Abnormal Psychology, 95*, 274–281.

Pennebaker, J. W., Colder, M., & Sharp, L. K. (1990). Accelerating the coping process. *Journal of Personality and Social Psychology, 58*, 528–537.

Pennebaker, J. W., Kiecolt-Glaser, J. K., & Glaser, R. (1988). Disclosure of traumas and immune function: Health implications for psychotherapy. *Journal of Consulting and Clinical Psychology, 56*, 239–245.

Penner, L. A., Shiffman, S., Paty, J. A., & Fritzsche, B. A. (1994). Individual differences in intraperson variability in mood. *Journal of Personality and Social Psychology, 66*, 712–721.

Persson, L., & Sjöberg, L. (1985). Mood and positive expectations. *Social Behaviour and Personality, 13*, 171–181.

Petty, R. E., & Cacioppo, J. T. (1986). The elaboration likelihood model of persuasion. *Advances in Experimental Social Psychology, 19*, 123–205.

Pignatiello, M. F., Camp, C. J., & Rasar, L. A. (1986). Musical mood induction: An alternative to the Velten technique. *Journal of Abnormal Psychology, 95*, 295–297.

Pollock, K. (1988). On the nature of social stress: Production of a modern mythology. *Social Science and Medicine, 26*, 381–392.

Postman, L., & Brown, D. R. (1952). Perceptual consequences of success and failure. *Journal of Abnormal and Social Psychology, 47*, 213–221.

Pyszczynski, T., & Greenberg, J. (1987). Self-regulatory perseveration and the depressive self-focusing style: A self-awareness theory of reactive depression. *Psychological Bulletin, 102*, 122–138.

Rachman, S. J. (1991). Neo-conditioning and the classical theory of fear acquisition. *Clinical Psychology Review, 11*, 155–174.

Rafaeli, A., & Sutton, R. I. (1987). Expression of emotion as part of the work role. *Academy of Management Review, 12*, 23–37.

Reinberg, A. (1974). Aspects of circannual rhythms in man. In E. T. Pengelley (Ed.) *Circannual clocks* (pp. 423–505). London: Academic Press.

Reisenzein, R. (1994). Pleasure-arousal theory and the intensity of emotions. *Journal of Personality and Social Psychology, 67*, 525–539.

Reynolds, S., & Gilbert, P. (1991). Psychological impact of unemployment: Interacting effects of individual vulnerability and protective factors. *Journal of Counseling Psychology, 38*, 76–84.

Reynolds, S., Stiles, W. B., Barkham, M., Shapiro, D. A., Hardy, G. E., & Rees, A. (in press). Acceleration of changes in session impact during contrasted time-limited psychotherapies. *Journal of Consulting and Clinical Psychology.*

Robbins, P. R., & Tanck, R. H. (1987). A study of diurnal patterns of depressed mood. *Motivation and Emotion, 11,* 37–49.

Rosa, R. (1993). Napping at home and alertness on the job in rotating shift workers. *Sleep, 16,* 727–735.

Rosaldo, M. Z. (1984). Toward an anthropology of self and feeling. In R. A. Shweder & R. A. LeVine (Eds) *Culture theory: Essays on mind, self, and emotion* (pp. 137–157). Cambridge: Cambridge University Press.

Roseman, I. J. (1991). Appraisal determinants of discrete emotions. *Cognition and Emotion, 5,* 161–200.

Rosenfield, I. (1995). *The strange, familiar and forgotten. An anatomy of consciousness.* London: Picador.

Ross, L., & Nisbett, R. E. (1991). *The person and the situation: Perspectives of social psychology.* New York: McGraw-Hill.

Rowe, D. (1983). *Depression: The way out of your prison.* London: Routledge and Kegan Paul.

Ruckmick, C. A. (1936). *The psychology of feeling and emotion.* New York: McGraw-Hill.

Russell, J. A. (1978). Evidence of convergent validity on the dimensions of affect. *Journal of Personality and Social Psychology, 36,* 1152–1168.

Russell, J. A. (1979). Affective space is bipolar. *Journal of Personality and Social Psychology, 37,* 345–356.

Russell, J. A. (1980). A circumplex model of affect. *Journal of Personality and Social Psychology, 39,* 1161–1178.

Russell, J. A. (1983). Pancultural aspects of the human conceptual organization of emotions. *Journal of Personality and Social Psychology, 45,* 1281–1288.

Russell, J. A., & Bullock, M. (1985). Multidimensional scaling of emotional facial expressions: Similarity from preschoolers to adults. *Journal of Personality and Social Psychology, 48,* 1290–1298.

Russell, J. A., Lewicka, M., & Niit, T. (1989). A cross-cultural study of a circumplex model of affect. *Journal of Personality and Social Psychology, 57,* 848–856.

Russell, J. A., & Mehrabian, A. (1977). Evidence for a three-factor theory of emotions. *Journal of Research in Personality, 11,* 273–294.

Russell, J. A., Weiss, A., & Mendelsohn, G. A. (1989). Affect grid: A single-item scale of pleasure and arousal. *Journal of Personality and Social Psychology, 57,* 493–502.

Safran, J. D. (1990a). Towards a refinement of cognitive therapy in light of interpersonal theory: 1. Theory. *Clinical Psychology Review, 10,* 87–105.

Safran, J. D. (1990b). Towards a refinement of cognitive therapy in light of interpersonal theory: 2. Practice. *Clinical Psychology Review, 10,* 107–121.

Salkovskis, P. M., Jones, D. R. O., & Clark, D. M. (1986). Respiratory control in the treatment of panic attacks: Replication and extention with concurrent measurement of behaviour and pCO_2. *British Journal of Psychiatry, 148,* 526–532.

Salovey, P. (1992). Mood-induced self-focused attention. *Journal of Personality and Social Psychology, 62,* 699–707.

Salovey, P., Hsee, C. K., & Mayer, J. D. (1993). Emotional intelligence and the self-regulation of affect. In D. M. Wegner, & J. W. Pennebaker (Eds) *Handbook of mental control* (pp. 258–277). Englewood Cliffs, NJ: Prentice Hall.

Salovey, P., Mayer, J. D., Goldman, S., Turvey, C., & Palfai, T. P. (1995). Emotional attention, clarity, and repair. Exploring emotional intelligence using the trait meta-mood scale. In J. W. Pennebaker (Ed.) *Emotion, disclosure, and health* (pp. 125–154). Washington, DC: American Psychological Association.

Salovey, P., O'Leary, A., Stretton, M. S., Fishkin, S. A., & Drake, C. A. (1991). Influence of mood on judgements about health and illness. In J. P. Forgas (Ed.) *Emotion and social judgements* (pp. 241–262). Oxford: Pergamon Press.

Sartre, J.-P. (1962). *Sketch for a theory of the emotions.* London: Methuen.

Schachter, S. (1959). *The psychology of affiliation.* Stanford, CA: Stanford University Press.

Schachter, S. (1964). The interaction of cognitive and physiological determinants of emotional state. In L. Festinger (Ed.) *Advances in experimental social psychology* (vol. 1, pp. 49–80). New York: Academic Press.

Schachter, S., & Singer, J. E. (1962). Cognitive, social, and physiological determinants of emotional state. *Psychological Review, 69,* 379–399.

Schare, M. L., Lisman, S. A., & Spear, N. E. (1984). The effects of mood variation on state-dependent retention. *Cognitive Therapy and Research, 8,* 387–408.

Schiffenbauer, A. (1974). Effect of observer's emotional state on judgements of the emotional state of others. *Journal of Personality and Social Psychology, 30,* 31–35.

Schlosberg, H. (1952). The description of facial expression in terms of two dimensions. *Journal of Experimental Psychology, 44,* 229–237.

Schlosberg, H. (1954). Three dimensions of emotion. *Psychological Review, 61,* 81–88.

Schnurr, P. P. (1989). Endogenous factors associated with mood. In W. N. Morris, *Mood: The frame of mind* (pp. 35–69). New York: Springer-Verlag.

Schwarz, N. (1990). Feelings as information: Informational and motivational functions of affective states. In E. T. Higgins & R. M. Sorrentino (Eds) *Handbook of motivation and cognition* (vol. 2, pp. 527–561). New York: Guilford Press.

Schwarz, N., & Bless, H. (1991). Happy and mindless, but sad and smart? The impact of affective states on analytic reasoning. In J. P. Forgas (Ed.) *Emotion and social judgements* (pp. 55–71). Oxford: Pergamon.

Schwarz, N., & Clore, G. L. (1983). Mood, misattribution, and judgements of well-being: Informative and directive functions of affective states. *Journal of Personality and Social Psychology, 45,* 513–523.

Schwarz, N., & Clore, G. L. (1988). How do I feel about it? Informative functions of affective states. In K. Fiedler & J. P. Forgas (Eds) *Affect, cognition, and social behavior* (pp. 44–62). Toronto: Hogrefe.

Schwarz, N., & Strack, F. (1991). Evaluating one's life: A judgement model of subjective well-being. In F. Strack, M. Argyle, & N. Schwarz (Eds) *Subjective well-being* (pp. 27–47). Oxford: Pergamon Press.

Schwarz, N., Strack, F., Kommer, D., & Wagner, D. (1987). Soccer, rooms, and the quality of your life: Mood effects on judgements of satisfaction with life in general and with specific life-domains. *European Journal of Social Psychology, 17,* 69–79.

Sedikides, C. (1994). Incongruent effects of sad mood on self-conception valence: It's a matter of time. *European Journal of Social Psychology, 24,* 161–172.

Segal, H. (1964). *Introduction to the work of Melanie Klein.* New York: Basic Books.

Shapiro, D., Rees, A., Barkham, M., Hardy, G. E., Reynolds, S., & Startup, M. (1995). Effects of treatment duration and severity of depression on the maintenance of gains after cognitive-behavioral and psychodynamic-interpersonal psychotherapy. *Journal of Consulting and Clinical Psychology, 63,* 378–387.

Shea, M. T., Elkin, I., Imber, S. D., Sotsky, S. D., Watkins, J. T., Collins, J. F., Pilkonis, P. A., Leber, W. R., Krupnick, J., Dolan, R. T., & Parloff, M. (1992). Course of depressive symptoms over follow-up: Findings from the National Institute of Mental Health Treatment of Depression Collaborative Research Program. *Archives of General Psychiatry, 49,* 782–787.

Shiffrin, R. M., & Schneider, W. (1977). Controlled and automatic information processing II: Perceptual learning, automatic attending, and a general theory. *Psychological Review, 84,* 127–190.

Simon, H. A. (1982). Comments. In M. S. Clark & S. T. Fiske (Eds) *Affect and cognition* (pp. 333–342). Hillsdale, NJ: Lawrence Erlbaum Associates.

Simons, A. D., Murphy, G. E., Levine, J. L., & Wetzel, R. D. (1986). Cognitive therapy and pharmacotherapy for depression: Sustained improvement over one year. *Archives of General Psychiatry, 43,* 43–49.

Singer, J. A., & Salovey, P. (1988). Mood and memory: Evaluating the network theory of affect. *Clinical Psychology Review, 8,* 211–251.

Slavney, P. R., Breitner, J. C., & Rabins, P. V. (1977). Variability of mood and hysterical traits in normal women. *Journal of Psychiatric Research, 13,* 155–160.

Smith, A. P., & Wilson, M. (1990). The effects of naps during night duty on the performance and mood of female nurses working in an intensive care unit. In G. Costa, G. Cesana, K. Kogi, & A. Wedderburn (Eds) *Shiftwork: Health, sleep and performance* (pp. 147–153). FrankfurtMain: Peter Lang.

Smith, C. A., & Ellsworth, P. C. (1985). Patterns of cognitive appraisal in emotion. *Journal of Personality and Social Psychology, 48,* 813–838.

Smith, C. A., Haynes, K. N., Lazarus, R. S., & Pope, L. K. (1993). In search of the "hot" cognitions: Attributions, appraisals, and their relation to emotion. *Journal of Personality and Social Psychology, 65,* 916–929.

Smith, C. S., Reilly, C., & Midkiff, K. (1989). Evaluation of three circadian rhythm questionnaires with suggestions for an improved measure of morningness. *Journal of Applied Psychology, 74,* 728–738.

Smith, M. L., Glass, G. V., & Miller, T. I. (1980). *The benefits of psychotherapy.* Baltimore, MD: The John Hopkins University Press.

Smith, S. M., & Petty, R. E. (1995). Personality moderators of mood congruency effects on cognition: The role of self-esteem and negative mood regulation. *Journal of Personality and Social Psychology, 68,* 1092–1107.

Snowden, R., & Christian, B. (Eds) (1983). *Patterns and perceptions of menstruation: A World Health Organization international study.* London: Croom Helm.

Sokolov, E. N. (1963). *Perception and the conditioned reflex.* New York: Macmillan.

Solomon, R. L. (1980). The opponent-process theory of acquired motivation: The costs of pleasure and the benefits of pain. *American Psychologist, 35,* 691–712.

Sommer, B. (1973). The effect of menstruation on cognitive and perceptual-motor behaviour: A review. *Psychosomatic Medicine, 35,* 513–534.

Spring, B. J., Lieberman, H. R., Swope, G., & Garfield, G. S. (1986). Effects of carbohydrate on mood and behavior. *Nutrition Reviews, 44,* 51–60.

Staats, S., & Skowronski, J. (1992). Perceptions of self-affect: Now and in the future. *Social Cognition, 10,* 415–431.

Stearns, C. Z., & Stearns, P. N. (1986). *Anger: The struggle for emotional control in America's history.* Chicago, IL: University of Chicago Press.

Stephan, F., & Zucker, I. (1972). Circadian rhythms in drinking behaviour and locomotor activity of rats are eliminated by hypothalamic lesions. *Proceedings of the National Academy of Science, USA, 69,* 1583–1586.

Stepper, S., & Strack, F. (1993). Proprioceptive determinants of emotional and nonemotional feelings. *Journal of Personality and Social Psychology, 64,* 211–220.

Steptoe, A., & Cox, S. (1988). Acute effects of aerobic exercise on mood. *Health Psychology, 7,* 329–340.

Stiles, W. B., Barkham, M., Shapiro, D. A., & Firth-Cozens, J. (1992). Treatment order and thematic continuity between contrasting psychotherapies: Exploring an implication of the assimilation model. *Psychotherapy Research, 2,* 112–124.

Stiles, W. B., Elliott, R., Llewelyn, S. P., Firth-Cozens, J. A., Margison, F. R., Shapiro, D. A., & Hardy, G. (1990). Assimilation of problematic experiences by clients in psychotherapy. *Psychotherapy, 27,* 411–420.

Stiles, W. B., Shapiro, D. A., & Elliott, R. (1987). Are all psychotherapies equivalent? *American Psychologist, 41*, 165–180.

Stiles, W. B., Shapiro, D. A., & Firth-Cozens, J. A. (1988). Do sessions of different treatments have different impacts? *Journal of Counseling Psychology, 35*, 391–396.

Stone, A. A., Hedges, S. M., Neale, J. M., & Satin, M. S. (1985). Prospective and cross-sectional mood reports offer no evidence of a "Blue Monday" phenomenon. *Journal of Personality and Social Psychology, 49*, 129–134.

Stone, A. A., Kessler, R. C., & Haythornthwaite, J. A. (1991). Measuring daily events and experiences: Decisions for the researcher. *Journal of Personality, 59*, 575–607.

Stone, A. A., & Neale, J. M. (1984). Effects of severe daily events on mood. *Journal of Personality and Social Psychology, 46*, 137–144.

Stone, A. A., Reed, B. R., & Neale, J. M. (1987). Changes in daily event frequency precede episodes of physical symptoms. *Journal of Human Stress, 13*, 70–74.

Stretton, M. S. (1990). Predicting health concerns. Unpublished doctoral dissertation, Yale University, New Haven, CT.

Swann, W. B. Jr., Wenzlaff, R. M., Krull, D. S., & Pelham, B. W. (1992). Allure of negative feedback: Self-verification strategies among depressed persons. *Journal of Abnormal Psychology, 101*, 293–306.

Swinkels, A., & Giuliano, T. A. (1995). The measurement and conceptualization of mood awareness: Attention directed towards one's mood states. *Personality and Social Psychology Bulletin, 21*, 934–949.

Szuba, M. P., Yager, A., Guze, B. H., Allen, E. M., & Baxter, L. R. (1992). Disruption of social circadian rhythms in major depression: A preliminary report. *Psychiatry Research, 42*, 221–230.

Tajfel, H. (1957). Value and the perceptual judgement of magnitude. *Psychological Bulletin, 64*, 192–204.

Tasto, D. L., Colligan, M. J., Skjei, E. W., & Polly, S. J. (1978). The health consequences of shiftwork. *DHEW (NIOSH) Publication*, no. 178–154.

Taylor, S. E., & Brown, J. D. (1988). Illusion and well-being: A social psychological perspective on mental health. *Psychological Bulletin, 103*, 193–210.

Taylor, S. E., & Brown, J. D. (1994). Positive illusions and well-being revisited: Separating fact from fiction. *Psychological Bulletin, 116*, 21–27.

Teasdale, J. D., & Barnard, P. J. (1993). *Affect, cognition, and change.* Hove: Lawrence Erlbaum Associates.

Teasdale, J. D., & Fogarty, S. J. (1979). Differential effects of induced mood on retrieval of pleasant and unpleasant events from episodic memory. *Journal of Abnormal Psychology, 88*, 248–257.

Templer, D. I., Ruff, C. F., Ayers, J. L., & Beshai, J. A. (1981). Diurnal mood fluctuation and age. *International Journal of Aging and Human Development, 14*, 189–193.

Tennen, H., Suls, J., & Affleck, G. (1991). Personality and daily experience: The promise and the daily challenge. *Journal of Personality, 59*, 313–338.

Tetlock, P. E., & Levi, A. (1982). Attribution bias: On the inconclusiveness of the cognition-motivation debate. *Journal of Experimental Social Psychology, 18*, 68–88.

Thayer, R. E. (1989). *The biopsychology of mood and arousal.* New York: Oxford University Press.

Thayer, R. E., Newman, J. R., & McClain, T. M. (1994). Self-regulation of mood: Strategies for changing a bad mood, raising energy, and reducing tension. *Journal of Personality and Social Psychology, 67*, 910–925.

Thayer, R. E., Peters, D. P., Takahashi, P. J., & Birkhead-Flight, A. M. (1992). Mood and behavior (smoking and sugar snacking) following moderate exercise: A partial test of self-regulation theory. *Personality and Individual Differences, 14*, 97–104.

243

Tomkins, S. S. (1962). *Affect, imagery and consciousness: vol. 1. The positive affects.* New York: Springer.

Tomkins, S. S. (1963). *Affect, imagery and consciousness: vol. 2. The negative affects.* New York: Springer.

Totterdell, P. (1995). Effects of depressed affect on diurnal and ultradian variations in mood in a healthy sample. *Chronobiology International, 12,* 278–289.

Totterdell, P., Briner, R. B., Parkinson, B., & Reynolds, S. (1996). Fingerprinting time series: Dynamic patterns in self-report and performance measures uncovered by a graphical nonlinear method. *British Journal of Psychology, 87,* 43–60.

Totterdell, P., & Folkard, S. (1992). In situ repeated measures of affect and cognitive performance facilitated by use of a hand-held computer. *Behavior Research Methods, Instruments, and Computers, 24,* 545–553.

Totterdell, P., Parkinson, B., Briner, R., & Reynolds, S. (1995). Forecasting feelings: Determinants and effects of self-predictions of mood. Manuscript submitted for publication, University of Leicester.

Totterdell, P., Reynolds, S., Parkinson, B., & Briner, R. B. (1994). Associations of sleep with everyday mood, minor symptoms and social interaction experience. *Sleep, 17,* 466–475.

Totterdell, P., Spelten, E., Smith, L., Barton, J., & Folkard, S. (1995). Recovery from work shifts: How long does it take? *Journal of Applied Psychology, 80,* 43–57.

Tsuji, Y., Fukuda, H., Okuno, H., Kobayashi, T. (1981). Diurnal rhythm of alpha wave activity and mood. *Electroencephalogr. Clinical Neurophysiology, 52* (suppl.), 43.

Tversky, A., & Griffin, D. (1991). Endowment and contrast in judgements of well-being. In F. Strack, M. Argyle, & N. Schwarz (Eds) *Subjective well-being* (pp. 101–118). Oxford: Pergamon Press.

Tversky, A., & Kahneman, D. (1973). Availability: A heuristic for judging frequency and probability. *Cognitive Psychology, 5,* 207–232.

Valins, S. (1966). Cognitive effects of false heart rate feedback. *Journal of Personality and Social Psychology, 4,* 400–408.

Vallacher, R. R., & Wegner, D. M. (1987). What do people think they're doing? Action identification and human behavior. *Psychological Review, 94,* 3–15.

Velten, E. Jr., (1968). A laboratory task for induction of mood states. *Behavior Research and Therapy, 6,* 473–482.

Volz, H. P., Mackert, A., Stieglitz, R. D., & Müller-Oerlinghausen, B. (1991). Diurnal variations of mood and sleep disturbance during phototherapy in major depressive disorder. *Psychopathology, 24,* 238–246.

Wagner, H. L., MacDonald, C. J., & Manstead, A. S. R. (1986). Communication of individual emotions by spontaneous facial expression. *Journal of Personality and Social Psychology, 50,* 737–743.

Warr, P. B. (1987). *Work, unemployment and mental health.* Oxford: Oxford University Press.

Warr, P., Banks, M., & Ullah, P. (1985). The experience of unemployment among black and white urban teenagers. *British Journal of Psychology, 76,* 75–87.

Warr, P., Barter, J., & Brownbridge, G. (1983). On the independence of positive and negative affect. *Journal of Personality and Social Psychology, 44,* 644–651.

Watson, D. (1988a). The vicissitudes of mood measurement: Effects of varying descriptors, time frames, and response formats on measures of positive and negative affect. *Journal of Personality and Social Psychology, 55,* 128–141.

Watson, D. (1988b). Intraindividual and interindividual analyses of positive and negative affect: Their relation to health complaints, perceived stress, and daily activities. *Journal of Personality and Social Psychology, 54,* 1020–1030.

Watson, D., & Clark, L. A. (1984). Negative affectivity: The disposition to experience aversive emotional states. *Psychological Bulletin, 96,* 465–490.

Watson, D., & Clark, L. A. (1994). Emotions, moods, traits, and temperaments: Conceptual distinctions and empirical findings. In P. Ekman & R. J. Davidson (Eds) *The nature of emotion* (pp. 89–93). New York: Oxford University Press.

Watson, D., Clark, L. A., & Tellegen, A. (1988). Development and validation of brief measures of positive and negative affect: The PANAS scales. *Journal of Personality and Social Psychology, 54*, 1063–1070.

Watson, D., & Pennebaker, J. W. (1989). Health complaints, stress, and distress: Exploring the central role of negative affectivity. *Psychological Review, 96*, 234–254.

Watson, D., & Tellegen, A. (1985). Toward a consensual structure of mood. *Psychological Bulletin, 98*, 219–235.

Watson, J. B. (1929). *Psychology from the standpoint of a behaviorist* (3rd edn). Philadelphia, PA: Lippincott.

Watson, J. B., & Rayner, R. (1920). Conditioned emotional reactions. *Journal of Genetic Psychology, 37*, 394–419.

Wegener, D. T., & Petty, R. E. (1994). Mood management across affective states: The hedonic contingency hypothesis. *Journal of Personality and Social Psychology, 66*, 1034–1048.

Wegener, D. T., Petty, R. E., & Smith, S. M. (1995). Positive mood can increase or decrease message scrutiny: The hedonic contingency view of mood and message processing. *Journal of Personality and Social Psychology, 69*, 5–15.

Wegner, D. M. (1989). *White bears and other unwanted thoughts: Suppression, obsession, and the psychology of mental control*. New York: Guilford Press.

Wegner, D. M. (1994). Ironic processes of mental control. *Psychological Review, 101*, 34–52.

Wegner, D. M., & Erber, R. (1993). Social foundations of mental control. In D. M. Wegner & J. W. Pennebaker (Eds) *Handbook of mental control* (pp. 36–56). Englewood Cliffs, NJ: Prentice Hall.

Wegner, D. M., Erber, R., & Zanakos, S. (1993). Ironic processes in the mental control of mood and mood-related thought. *Journal of Personality and Social Psychology, 65*, 1093–1104.

Wegner, D. M., & Pennebaker, J. W. (1993). Changing our minds: An introduction to mental control. In D. M. Wegner & J. W. Pennebaker (Eds) *Handbook of Mental Control*. Englewood Cliffs, NJ: Prentice Hall.

Wegner, D. M., Shortt, J. W., Blake, A. W., & Page, M. S. (1990). The suppression of exciting thoughts. *Journal of Personality and Social Psychology, 58*, 409–418.

Weiner, B. (1986). *An attributional theory of motivation and emotion*. New York: Springer-Verlag.

Wertheimer, M. (1925). Gestalt theory. In W. D. Ellis (Ed.) (1938) *A sourcebook of Gestalt psychology* (pp. 1–11). London: Routledge and Kegan Paul.

West, S. G., & Hepworth, J. T. (1991). Statistical issues in the study of temporal data. *Journal of Personality, 59*, 609–662.

Westen, D. (1994). Toward an integrative model of affect regulation: Applications to social-psychological research. *Journal of Personality, 62*, 641–667.

Wetzler, S. (1985). Mood state-dependent retrieval: A failure to replicate. *Psychological Reports, 56*, 759–765.

Wever, R. A. (1979). *The circadian system of man: Results of experiments under temporal isolation*. New York: Springer.

Wheeler, L., & Reiss, H. T. (1991). Self-recording of everyday life events: Origins, types and uses. *Journal of Personality, 59*, 339–354.

White, P. A. (1988). Knowing more about what we can tell: "Introspective access" and causal report accuracy 10 years later. *British Journal of Psychology, 79*, 13–45.

Whitton, J. L. (1978). Periodicities in self-reports of health, sleep and mood variables. *Journal of Psychosomatic Research, 22*, 111–115.

Williams, K. J., & Alliger, G. M. (1994). Role stressors, mood spillover, and perceptions of work–family conflict. *Academy of Management Journal, 37,* 837–868.

Williams, K. J., Suls, J., Alliger, G. M., Learner, S. M., & Wan, C. K. (1991). Multiple role juggling and daily mood states in working mothers: An experience sampling study. *Journal of Applied Psychology, 76,* 664–674.

Wilson, P. (1995). *Instant calm: Over 100 successful techniques for relaxing mind and body.* London: Penguin Books.

Wilson, T. D., Laser, P. S., & Stone, J. I. (1982). Judging the predictors of one's own mood: Accuracy and the use of shared theories. *Journal of Experimental Social Psychology, 18,* 537–556.

Winnicott, D. W. (1965). *The family and individual development.* New York: Basic Books.

Wiser, S., & Goldfried, M. R. (1993). A comparative study of emotional experiencing in psychodynamic-interpersonal and cognitive-behavioural therapies. *Journal of Consulting and Clinical Psychology, 61,* 892–895.

Wittgenstein, L. (1953). *Philosophical investigations.* Oxford: Blackwell.

Wolfe, T. (1983). *The purple decades.* London: Jonathan Cape.

Wood, C., & Magnello, M. E. (1992). Diurnal changes in perceptions of energy and mood. *Journal of the Royal Society of Medicine, 85,* 191–194.

Wood, J. V., Saltzberg, J. A., & Goldsamt, L. A. (1990). Does affect induce self-focused attention? *Journal of Personality and Social Psychology, 58,* 899–908.

Worth, L. T., & Mackie, D. M. (1987). Cognitive mediation of positive affect in persuasion. *Social Cognition, 5,* 76–94.

Wundt, W. (1897). *Outlines of psychology.* Leipzig: Wilhelm Engelmann.

Young, S. N. (1991). The 1989 Borden Award Lecture: Some effects of dietary components (amino acids, carbohydrate, folic acid) on brain serotonin synthesis, mood, and behaviour. *Canadian Journal of Physiology and Pharmacology, 69,* 893–903.

Zajonc, R. B. (1980). Feeling and thinking: Preferences need no inferences. *American Psychologist, 35,* 151–175.

Zajonc, R. B., Murphy, S. T., & Inglehart, M. (1989). Feeling and facial efference: Implications of the vascular theory of emotion. *Psychological Review, 96,* 395–416.

Zautra, A. J., Guarnaccia, C. A., Reich, J. W., & Dohrenwend, B. P. (1988). The contribution of small events to stress and distress. In L. H. Cohen (Ed.) *Life events and psychological functioning* (pp. 123–148). Beverly Hills, CA: Sage.

Zillmann, D. (1978). Attribution and misattribution of excitatory reactions. In J. H. Harvey, W. Ickes, & R. F. Kidd (Eds) *New directions in attribution research* (vol. 2, pp. 335–368). Hillsdale, NJ: Lawrence Erlbaum Associates.

Zillmann, D. (1988). Mood management: Using entertainment to full advantage. In L. Donohew, H. E. Sypher, & E. T. Higgins (Eds) *Communication, social cognition, and affect* (pp. 147–171). Hillsdale, NJ: Erlbaum.

Zuckerman, M. (1979). Attribution of success and failure revisited, or: The motivational bias is alive and well in attribution theory. *Journal of Personality, 47,* 245–287.

INDEX

Abelson, R. P. 20, 47, 122
Abramson, L. Y. 93–4, 142
acceptance 130, 150–1, 153, 198–9
acquiescence response bias 35
action tendency 8, 40–1
activation 17–42, 117, 120, 143, 144, 188, 194–5, 205
activities (as predictors of mood) 48–51
activity 22, 111, 118, 122, 131, 143–4, 146, 149–50, 152
Adan, A. 143
adaptation 107–9, 132, 140, 152
adolescents 111, 131
affect 4
affect grid 36–7
affect infusion model 84–5
affect intensity measure (AIM) 60–1
affect priming 77–80, 92, 99–100
affective climate 213
affective impact of psychotherapy 178–81
Ainsworth, M. 161
Akerstedt, T. 119
alcohol 138, 143, 146, 147
alertness 115, 117, 118, 119, 122, 143, 144
alexithymia 136
Alfert, E. 142
Alliger, G. M. 66
Alloy, L. B. 93–4, 142
Almagor, M. 116
ambivalence 32, 137, 202
American Psychological Association 158
analytic processing 74, 82, 151, 204
Anastasiades, P. 12, 59
Anisman, H. 160
Anshensel, C. S. 144
anticipation 142, 205–6
anxiety 16, 144, 156, 157, 158, 164–5, 167, 172–4
Appley, M. H. 47
appraisal 6, 40, 66, 130, 132, 152–3, 165–6, 196–7, 201, 203, 207
Arnold, M. B. 59
arousal *see* activation
Ashkenazi, I. E. 115

Aspinwall, L. G. 143
assimilation model 169–71
associative network 77–80, 99–100
attachment 161–2
attributional bias 94, 139, 142
autocorrelation *see* serial dependency
automatic processes 73–4, 77, 84, 88, 92, 103, 131–3, 149, 191, 196, 197, 200, 201, 205
autonomy 167–8
Averill, J. R. 22, 23, 39
avoidance 139, 145, 146, 153, 172–4, 198–9
awareness 37, 73, 129–30, 133, 135–7, 149, 152, 192

Barkham, M. 169–71, 180, 183, 184–5
Barley, S. R. 216
Barlow, D. H. 158
Barnard, P. J. 11, 56, 79, 80, 82, 84, 85–8, 98, 99, 104, 188
Baron, R. A. 90
Barton, S. 123
baseline 108–9
Batson, C. D. 5
Baumgardner, A. H. 54
Beall, S. K. 151
Beaman, A. L. 200
Beck, A. T. 164, 167
Becker, H. S. 12
behavioural tasks 165, 174, 177
Bem, D. J. 135
Bentler, P. M. 35
bereavement 159, 176–7, 185
Berger, B. G. 144
Bergin, A. E. 181
Berkowitz, L. 103
Berlyne, D. E. 28
Berman, J. S. 184
biopsychological theory 139, 214
bipolar affective disorder 100, 125–6
Blaney, P. H. 97, 98
Blatt, S. J. 167
Bless, H. 74–5, 76, 82, 83, 85, 96, 150, 204
Block, J. 23, 61, 93, 214
blood-glucose level 58

247

body clock 115, 118, 119, 122, 126
Bohle, P. 119
Boivin, D. B. 118
Bolger, N. 44, 45, 62, 110, 123
Bolton, W. 175
Bond, C. F. Jr. 144
Bond, M. J. 122
Borkovec, T. D. 144
Bower, G. H. 52, 53, 54, 72, 77–8, 79, 80, 82, 90, 93, 94, 99–101
Bowlby, J. 161
Boyd, J. H. 157
Bradburn, N. M. 32
Brandstätter, H. 48, 111
Bremer, D. 39
Bresler, C. 121, 134
Brewin, C. 171, 172
Brickman, P. 109
bright light 112, 113, 119, 143
Briner, R. B. 49, 118, 124–5, 135, 142, 144, 189
Broadbent, D. E. 10
Brown, D. R. 92
Brown, G. W. 167
Brown, J. D. 93, 147
Bruner, J. S. 10, 89
Buck, R. 134, 135, 193
Bullock, M. 21
Burns, D. D. 3
Burt, C. D. B. 151
Butler, G. 174, 182
Byrne, D. 76

Cacioppo, J. T. 38, 95, 121, 213
caffeine 139, 143
Campbell, J. D. 46, 67, 93, 137
Campbell, S. S. 119
carbohydrates 58, 143
Carlson, R. 3
Carver, C. S. 66, 99, 123, 148, 175, 189, 190, 193–4, 200, 210
Caspi, A. 44, 45, 110
Catalan, J. 158
Catanzaro, S. J. 147, 202
Chaiken, S. 95
changeability 109–11, 220
chaos 124–6
Chiariello, M. A. 158
Christian, B. 12
Cialdini, R. B. 102, 132
circumplex models 25–32
Clark, D. M. 53, 79, 173, 182
Clark, L. A. 5, 6, 32, 36, 44, 45, 50–1, 61, 91
Clark, M. S. 8, 54, 144, 150, 195, 204, 206
clinical approach 156–86, 214
Clore, G. L. 6, 7, 27, 30, 73, 77, 80–2, 85, 88, 89, 97, 188
cognitive behaviour therapy 160, 164–6, 168–9, 170, 171, 174, 178–82, 184–5

cognitive deficits 175
cognitive triad 164
Cohen, P. R. 80
Cohen, S. 215
Colvin, C. R. 93
Combs, A. 125, 126
complexity theory 125–6
concept of mood 1–8
congruence 15, 70–104, 127, 131, 141, 147, 151, 172, 191
conscious processes 73, 77, 80–2, 89, 129, 131–3, 136, 149, 152
contagion 120–1, 213
continuity model 159–60
contrast effect 110, 142, 189
control process model 66–7, 123, 192, 193–4, 207–8, 210
controlled processes 73–4, 81, 83, 84, 88, 92, 103, 191, 196, 197, 200, 201
Cooper, C. 108
Cooper, M. L. 12
coping 67, 103, 138, 140, 148
Costa, P. T. 59, 61, 109
Cowdry, R. W. 109, 116
Cox, S. 144
Coyne, J. C. 45, 46, 47, 65, 145, 157, 159
Crits-Christoph, P. 163
cross-cultural evidence 26–7
Csikszentmihalyi, I. S. 50, 65
Csikszentmihalyi, M. 50, 65–6, 111, 218, 220
Cunningham, M. R. 50
Cytowic, R. 214
Czeisler, C. A. 118, 119

daily (life) events see events, hassles, uplifts
Daly, E. M. 39
Dan, A. J. 12
Daubman, K. A. 94
Davidson, R. J. 5
Dawson, D. 119
day of week see rhythm: weekly
de Rivera, J. H. 213
DeCastro, J. M. 144
decay 110, 111, 131, 220
defence mechanisms 162
definition 2, 9–10, 216–17
DeLongis, A. 45, 46, 65, 110, 123
dependency 164, 167–8
depression 16, 93, 100, 109, 111–13, 116, 119, 120, 122, 125, 137, 142, 143, 147, 154, 156, 157–8, 159, 164, 166, 167–8, 174–8, 183–4, 188
depressive realism 93
desynchrony 118–19, 120
diary keeping 151
diary study 128
Diener, E. 29, 30, 33, 34, 38, 44, 60–1, 62, 78, 107, 108, 109, 200

dimensions (of affect) 14, 19–32, 188
distraction 137, 138, 144, 146, 153, 199
Dittmann, A. T. 20
diurnal variation 111–13, 220
Dobson, K. S. 143, 181–2
Dohrenwend, B. P. 44, 46, 47, 65
Dohrenwend, B. S. 44, 46, 65
downward comparison 138–9, 143
drugs 58, 139, 143, 146, 147 *see also* alcohol,
    caffeine, nicotine
Duclos, S. E. 134
Duffy, E. 56, 193, 205
duration 5, 110–11, 131
Duval, S. 201
dynamic equilibrium 105, 106–13, 123, 152,
    205
dynamic factor analysis 212

Eastman, C. I. 119
Ede, A. 112
Edlund, M. 106
Ehlers, C. L. 126
Ehrlich, S. 116
Ehrlichman, H. 53
Eich, J. E. 100, 101
Ekman, P. 5, 6, 22, 38
elaboration likelihood model (ELM) 95
Elkin, I. 160, 184
Elliott, R. 169, 179
Ellis, H. C. 101
Ellsworth, P. C. 40, 191
Emmons, R. A. 33, 34, 44, 62
emotion 4–9, 87, 188
emotion-focused coping 67, 103, 148, 198
emotional intelligence 132, 215
endowment effect 142
energy 139, 146, 193
entrainment 114, 117–20, 127
    mutual 114, 119–20
    social 105, 113–15, 121, 123
Epstein, S. 13
equilibrium *see* dynamic equilibrium
equivalence paradox 182–3
Erber, M. W. 141
Erber, R. 133, 134, 141, 151, 154
Erickson, M. F. 162
evaluation 22, 129, 130, 131, 132–8, 153
Evans, M. D. 157, 184
evening type 115
events 107, 108, 109, 110, 111, 113, 114, 121,
    123, 142
exercise 57, 139, 144, 146
expectations *see* anticipation
experience sampling 48, 218
experimental mood manipulations 51–5
expressive behaviour 138, 144–5, 151
extraversion 35, 108, 117, 136, 190
Eysenck, H. J. 35, 59
Eysenck, M. W. 108–9

facial expression 20–2, 38
facial-feedback theory 134, 144
fatigue *see* alertness
Feather, N. T. 122
Fechner-Bates, S. 159
Fehr, B. 93
Feldman, L. A. 31, 34, 212
Fenigstein, A. 136
Field, S. 170–1
Fischer, G. W. 123
Flapan, D. 11
flow 50
Fogarty, S. J. 72
Folkard, S. 115, 117, 118, 119, 219
Folkman, S. 43, 45, 46, 47, 48, 64, 65, 110,
    148
Fonagy, P. 162
food 58, 139, 143 *see also* carbohydrates
Fordyce, M. W. 152
Forgas, J. P. 53, 54, 72, 76, 77, 81, 83, 84–5,
    88, 90, 94, 97, 103, 194
Frank, J. D. 178
frequency 33
Freud, S. 161, 203
Friesen, W. V. 38
Frijda, N. H. 5, 7, 8, 9, 41, 73, 133, 193, 201,
    204

Gaelick-Buys, L. 165
Gallant, S. J. 116
Gardner, D. L. 109, 220
Gardner, H. 10
Gaschke, Y. N. 136, 141, 202
generalized anxiety disorder 158
generalized mood 135
George, J. M. 213
Gergen, K. T. 216
Gilbert, P. 168
Giuliano, T. A. 37, 136, 137, 138, 172,
    201
Gladstones, W. H. 21
Glass, L. 106
Gold, A. E. 58–9
Goldberg, D. P. 158
Goldberg, L. R. 61
Goldfried, M. R. 181
Goleman, D. 215
Goodhart, D. E. 142
Gottman, J. M. 120, 212
Gottschalk, A. 106, 125, 126
Graf, M. 143
Graw, P. 113
Gray, J. A. 195
Greden, J. F. 184
Green, D. P. 35
Greenberg, J. 175–6
Greenberg, L. S. 177
Griffin, D. 142
Guntrip, H. 161

Haaga, D. A. F. 159, 164, 175
Hall, D. P. 109, 116
Halpern, J. N. 53
Hammen, C. L. 167–8
happiness 108, 109, 118, 152
Harlow, H. F. 11
Harma, M. 144
Harris, T. O. 167
Hart, H. 3
Hassard, J. 122
hassles 44–6, 65 see also events
Hatfield, E. 121, 213
Haug, H. 113
Hawton, K. 158
Hays, J. C. 176
Hazan, C. 162
Headey, B. 107, 205
Healy, D. 113, 122, 214
heart rate 59
Hebb, D. O. 11
hedonic contingency 96–7, 204
hedonism 130, 142, 150, 152, 153, 195, 203–4
Heiby, E. M. 125, 143
Heide, F. J. 144
Heider, F. 63
helping 101–2, 131–2, 140, 149
Henry, G. 100
Hepburn, L. 108–9
Hepworth, J. T. 220, 221
Hersey, R. B. 116
heuristic processing 74, 78, 85, 96
Hilgard, E. R. 4
Hochschild, A. R. 145, 200, 206, 215
Holmes, F. 11
Holmes, T. H. 44
homeostasis 106–7, 205
homework assignments 235, 247
Horne, J. 115
Hoskins, C. N. 120
"how do I feel about it?" heuristic 80, 85
Howard, K. I. 182, 183
Howes, M. J. 120
Hsee, C. K. 47, 122, 132, 135, 136
Huba, G. J. 144
Hugdahl, K. 173
Hull, J. G. 144

ICS see interacting cognitive subsystems
illusion of control 93, 94
Ilmarinen, J. 119
implicational processing 87, 88, 99
incongruence 70, 72, 73, 84, 97, 98, 99, 103, 127, 141, 147, 151, 191
independence of PA and NA 32–5
individual differences 3, 31, 34, 35, 59–63, 107, 108, 109, 111, 127, 135–8, 143, 146–8, 214
informational theories 76–82

Ingram, R. E. 75, 98–9, 136, 201
integrative models of psychotherapy 160, 168–71
intensity 2, 6, 33, 73
intensive time-sampling 128, 218–19, 212, 221
interacting cognitive subsystems (ICS) 85–8, 99
interpersonal psychodynamic therapy 161–4, 166, 170, 178, 179–81, 184–5
Iran-Nejad, A. 34
ironic monitor 133, 154, 196
irreflexive experience 133
Isen, A. M. 6, 8, 9, 54, 72, 74, 75, 77, 78, 83, 94, 98, 102, 103, 150, 195, 204
Izard, C. E. 22, 24, 90

Jacobsen, E. 11, 76
James, W. 134
Jersild, A. 11
jet lag 118
Jewett, M. E. 119
Joffe, R. 143
Johnson, E. J. 92–3
Johnson, T. J. 94
Johnson-Laird, P. N. 10, 66, 210
Johnston, D. W. 12, 59
Jones, E. E. 178, 179
judgement (effects of mood on) 92–4, 109, 146, 153, 154

Kahneman, D. 92
Kaminer, W. 11
Kanfer, F. H. 165
Kanner, A. D. 45, 46, 47, 65
Kasimatis, M. 116–17, 127, 190
Kavanagh, D. J. 79
Keating, J. 53
Kellerman, J. 135
Kelly, J. R. 113–14, 123
Keltner, D. 40, 144, 191
Kendler, K. S. 160
Kenny, A. 7
Ketelaar, T. 62, 195
Kilpatrick, R. 122
Kirsch, I. 147
Kirschenbaum, D. S. 167
Klein, M. 161
Knauth, P. 119, 144
Knight, D. B. 216
Kopta, S. M. 182, 183
Kräuchi, K. 113, 143
Krause, R. 120–1
Kraut, R. E. 53
Kripke, D. F. 122
Kuhn, T. S. 11
Kuykendall, D. 53

Lacey, B. C. 56
Lacey, J. I. 56

Lader, M. 160
Laird, J. D. 121, 134, 135
Lambert, M. 181
Langer, E. J. 93
Langston, C. A. 47
Lapierre, Y. D. 160
Larsen, R. J. 13, 29, 30, 33, 44, 60–1, 62, 91,
    116–17, 127, 190, 195, 219–20, 221
Larson, R. 111, 218, 220
Lavallee, L. F. 46, 67, 137
Lazarus, R. S. 7, 14, 40, 43, 45, 46, 47, 48,
    64, 65, 67, 110, 142, 148, 197, 207
Lea, M. 39
LeFevre, J. 50, 65–6
Leight, K. A. 101
Leitner, M. 126
Levenson, R. W. 120, 212
Levi, A. 94
Levin, P. F. 54, 72, 102
Lewin, R. 125
Lewinsohn, P. M. 143, 158, 175
Lewy, A. J. 119
life events 167, 168, 172, 174
Linville, P. W. 123
Locke, K. D. 144
Luborsky, L. 161, 163, 182
Lutz, C. A. 27
Lyubomirsky, S. 137

Mackey, M. C. 106
Mackie, D. M. 74, 78–9, 95–6, 151, 204
MacLeod, C. 173
Magnello, M. E. 111
Main, M. 162
maintenance of therapeutic effects 183–5
Malan, D. 161
Mandler, G. 11, 129, 133
Mankowski, T. A. 147
Mansfield, P. K. 120
Manstead, A. S. R. 40, 53
Marangoni, C. 39
Marco, C. A. 110
Marks, I. 174
Marlatt, G. A. 144
Martin, D. J. 93–4
Martin, L. L. 82, 96, 97
Mathews, A. M. 173
Matlin, M. W. 78
Matthews, G. 57, 58
Mattlin, J. A. 148
Mayer, J. D. 39, 53, 98, 101, 122, 132, 135,
    136, 137, 141, 192, 197, 202, 215
McClintock, M. K. 120
McConville, C. 108
McCrae, R. R. 59, 61, 109
McFarlane, C. 142
McFarlane, J. 116
McFatter, R. M. 62

McGrath, J. E. 113–14, 123
Mearns, J. 147, 202
measurement (of mood) 35–9, 127, 211–12
Mehrabian, A. 23
melatonin 119
Meltzer, H. 157
memory (effects of mood on) 97–101
menstrual cycle 15, 116, 120, 127
mental control 132
Merten, J. 120–1
meta-mood 135, 136, 141, 197
Meyer, G. J. 29, 61
Miller, D. T. 94
Miller, G. A. 10
Minors, D. S. 115, 118, 220
Mintz, J. 158
Mintz, L. I. 158
misattribution 80–1
Molenaar, P. C. M. 212
Möller, H. J. 126
Monagle, L. 12
monitoring 130, 132–4, 136–8, 152, 154, 165,
    171–2, 195–6, 201, 203
Monk, T. H. 115, 122
Montgomery, S. A. 184
mood as information 73, 80–2, 85, 193–4, 201
mood awareness see awareness
mood congruence see congruence
mood disorders 15–16, 109, 126, 154, 156–86
mood incongruence see incongruence
mood labelling 136, 137, 138, 171
mood maintenance 75, 83, 102, 103, 130, 150,
    153, 195
mood monitoring see monitoring
mood regulation see regulation
mood repair 74, 75, 83, 98, 102, 103, 136–7,
    195
mood swing see swing
mood-state-dependent memory see
    state-dependent memory
morning type 115
Morris, W. N. 6, 7, 38, 73, 102, 131, 133,
    138–9, 143, 144, 145, 147, 150, 159, 193,
    200
motivation 85, 95–7, 193, 194–5
motives 150–1
multiple role juggling 66
Murray, N. 94
Murray-Parkes, C. 176
music 144, 146

NA see negative affect
naps 144, 146
Nasby, W. 97–8, 100, 101
Neale, J. M. 44, 45, 110, 111, 117
negative affect (NA) 29–35, 107, 109, 111,
    117, 136
negative affectivity see trait negative affect

negative mood regulation (NMR) 147, 202
Neisser, U. 11
Nelson, T. M. 118
neuroticism 35, 109, 136
Nicholson, R. A. 184
nicotine 143
Niedenthal, P. M. 92
nightwork see shiftwork
Nisbett, R. E. 53, 63, 149
Nolen-Hoeksema, S. 137, 172, 176–7
non-conscious processes 131–3, 152
nonlinear dynamics 105, 123–6
Nowlis, H. H. 5, 6, 11
Nowlis, V. 5, 6, 11

O'Leary, A. 91, 215
Oatley, K. 9, 66, 175, 210
opponent process 109, 131
Ormel, J. 107
Ortony, A. 6, 27, 30, 188
Orvaschel, H. 158
Osgood, C. E. 22, 23, 27, 28
Ost, L. G. 173
Östberg, O. 115
Owen, D. R. 144

PA see positive affect
PANAS (Positive And Negative Affect Scale) 36
Parkinson, B. 8, 9, 39, 49, 56, 118, 124–5, 134, 135, 142, 144, 189
Parrott, W. G. 72, 84, 98, 130, 141, 150–1, 195, 204
Patkai, P. 116
Pavlov, I. P. 76
Pearlin, L. I. 138–9
Pennebaker, J. W. 61, 75, 132, 134, 151, 177
Penner, L. A. 108, 109, 219
perception (effects of mood on) 89–92
personality characteristics see individual differences
Persson, L. 142
persuasion (effects of mood on) 95–7
Petty, R. E. 53, 77, 79, 95, 96–7, 147, 204
phobia 16, 156, 172–4
phototherapy see bright light
physiological approach 12–13, 159, 160, 214
physiological precursors 56–9
Pignatiello, M. F. 53
pleasantness 2, 17–42, 110, 116, 117, 141, 142, 152, 188, 193
pleasure 139, 146
Poincaré plot 124
Pollock, K. 47
positive affect (PA) 29–35, 107, 109, 111, 117
positive affectivity see trait positive affect
positive thinking 142, 146, 152
Postman, L. 89, 92

predictors (of mood) 14, 43–69, 190
problem-focused coping 67, 103, 139, 144, 148, 152, 198
process approach 13, 105, 126–8, 187–91, 218
processing style 74–5, 78, 82, 95–7
projection 161, 162
psychodynamic theories 161–2, 168–71
psychopharmacology 159, 184
psychotherapy 16, 120–1, 126, 156–86
Pulos, S. M. 178, 179
Pyszczynski, T. 175–6

Rachman, S. J. 173
Rafaeli, A. 215
Rahe, R. H. 44
Rayner, R. 76, 100, 173
reasoning (effects of mood on) 92–4
recording method (signal, interval, event) 128, 218–19
recovery 117, 137, 147
reflexive experience 133, 134
regulation 3, 13, 15, 75, 83–4, 102, 121, 191–211
regulation strategies 74, 75, 125, 129, 130, 138–48, 149–54, 166, 168, 172, 174, 175–7, 178, 184, 195, 198–200, 202
Reilly, N. P. 102, 138–9
Reinberg, A. 115, 116
Reisenzein, R. 6, 23, 31, 188
Reiss, H. T. 218
relapse 221, 262
relaxation 139, 144, 174, 198–9
representation 23, 31, 38, 73, 134
Reynolds, S. 49, 118, 124–5, 135, 142, 144, 168, 170, 171, 180, 183, 184–5, 189
rhythm 15, 113–17, 127, 220
  circadian 113, 115, 118, 119, 122, 126
  infradian 116
  social 122
  ultradian 115–16
  weekly 116–17, 190
Rice, L. N. 177
Robbins, P. R. 111–12
Rosa, R. 144
Rosaldo, M. Z. 27
Roseman, I. J. 40
Rosenfield, I. 214
Ross, L. 63
Ross, M. 94, 142
Rowe, D. 157
Ruckmick, C. A. 9, 55
rumination 137–8, 151
Russell, J. A. 21, 23, 24–9, 30, 36–7, 39, 188

Sabini, J. 72, 84, 98, 141
Safran, J. D. 168–9
Salkovskis, P. M. 173, 182

Salovey, P. 35, 47, 52, 91, 98, 122, 132, 135, 136, 137, 192, 201, 215
Sartre, J.-P. 133
Schachter, S. 11, 12, 56
Schare, M. L. 101
Schaufeli, W. B. 107
Scheier, M. F. 66, 99, 123, 136, 148, 175, 189, 190, 193–4, 200, 210
Schiffenbauer, A. 90
Schilling, E. A. 44, 45, 62, 110, 123
Schlosberg, H. 20, 21, 25, 26
Schneider, W. 73, 133
Schnurr, P. P. 50, 57
Schooler, C. 138–9
Schwarz, N. 7, 73, 74–5, 76, 77, 80–2, 83, 85, 88, 89, 96, 97, 108, 150, 193, 194, 201, 204
seasonal affective disorder (SAD) 113, 143
Sedikides, C. 52, 127, 191
Segal, H. 161
self-esteem 136, 143, 147
self-focused attention 75, 90–1, 94, 98–9, 135, 136–7, 147, 175–6, 200, 201
self-perception theory 135
self-report 24, 36–9, 128, 212, 219
self-reward 138, 143, 150
self-serving attributional bias 94
semantic differential 22, 27, 28
semantic network 77–80
serial dependency 220–1
Sermat, V. 20
Setterland, M. B. 92
Shack, J. R. 29, 61
Shapiro, D. A. 169–71, 179, 180, 182, 183, 184–5
Shaver, P. 162
Shea, M. T. 160, 184
Shiffrin, R. M. 73, 133
shiftwork 118–19, 120, 122, 144
Shrout, P. E. 46, 65
signal function 7, 193
Simmonds, S. F. 102
Simon, H. A. 79
Simons, A. D. 184
simple phobia see phobia
Singer, J. A. 98
Singer, J. E. 56
situations (as predictors of mood) 48–51
Sjöberg, L. 142
Skowronski, J. 142
Slavney, P. R. 109
sleep 118, 119, 144, 146 see also naps
sleep deprivation 112
Smith, A. P. 144
Smith, C. A. 40
Smith, C. S. 115
Smith, M. L. 181
Smith, S. M. 53, 147

Smith, T. W. 75, 98–9
Snowden, R. 12
social roles 175–7
social support 110, 111, 138, 139, 145, 146, 147, 148
sociotropy 167
Sokolov, E. N. 200
Solomon, R. L. 109–10
Sommer, B. 116
spectral analysis 220
spreading activation 77–80, 92, 93
Spring, B. J. 143
Staats, S. 142
stability 105, 106, 107, 108–9, 112, 116
Stang, D. 78
state-dependent memory 99–101
Stearns, C. Z. 24
Stearns, P. N. 24
Stephan, F. 115
Stepper, S. 134
Steptoe, A. 144
Stevens, A. A. 137, 197
Stiles, W. B. 169–71, 180, 182, 183
Stone, A. A. 44, 45, 110, 111, 117, 219
Strack, F. 81, 108, 134
stress 47–8
stressors see hassles
Stretton, M. S. 91
structure (of mood) 17–42, 188–9, 212
Suls, J. 66, 110, 128
suprachiasmatic nucleus 115
Sutton, R. I. 215
Swann, W. B. Jr. 91
swing 100, 108, 111–13, 220
Swinkels, A. 37, 136, 137, 138, 172, 201
symptoms 91, 107, 111, 116
Szuba, M. P. 122

Tajfel, H. 89
Tanck, R. H. 111–12
Tasto, D. L. 119
Taylor, S. E. 93, 143
Teasdale, J. D. 11, 53, 56, 72, 79, 80, 82, 84, 85–8, 98, 99, 104, 188
television 144, 146, 147, 206
Tellegen, A. 24, 29–32, 35, 36
Templer, D. I. 112
tempo 121–2
Tennen, H. 128
tension 107, 119, 139, 144, 146, 147
Tetlock, P. E. 40, 94
Thayer, R. E. 50, 57, 58, 63, 139–40, 144, 146, 147, 193, 195
therapeutic alliance/relationship 163, 164, 165, 169, 177, 182
therapy outcome 160, 164, 181–4
Tilley, A. J. 119
time of day see diurnal variation

time structure 3, 5, 6, 121–2, 189, 191
time-frame 32, 33, 34, 35, 135, 212
time-series 218, 221
Tomkins, S. S. 75
Totterdell, P. 49, 112, 116, 117, 118, 124–5,
    135, 142, 144, 189, 219
trait negative affect 60–2
trait positive affect 61–2
transactional theory 63–8
transactions 7, 14, 63–8, 190, 191
transference 162–3, 169
Trew, K. 122
tridimensional model 19–20
Trumbull, R. 47
Tsuji, Y. 116
Turner, C. W. 103
Tversky, A. 92–3, 142

unemployment 122, 168, 185
uplifts 46–7 see also events

Valins, S. 134
Vallacher, R. R. 149
variability 3, 13, 15, 105, 107, 108, 109–11,
    115, 116, 127, 171, 219
Velten, E. Jr. 51–2
Volz, H. P. 113
vulnerability 166–8, 184

Wagner, H. L. 53
Warr, P. B. 32–3, 122, 168
Waterhouse, J. 113, 115, 118, 122, 214, 220
Watson, D. 5, 6, 24, 29–32, 34, 35, 36, 44, 45,
    49, 50–1, 61, 75, 91
Watson, J. B. 10, 76, 100, 173
Wearing, A. 107, 205
weather 50–1, 81
Wegener, D. T. 53, 77, 79, 96–7, 204

Wegner, D. M. 132, 133, 134, 149, 151, 154,
    174, 191, 196, 201, 203, 209
Weiner, B. 66
Weissman, M. M. 157
well-being 32, 107, 108, 109, 110, 122, 151
Wertheimer, M. 64
West, S. G. 220, 221
Westen, D. 140–1, 147–8, 153, 191
Wetzler, S. 101
Wever, R. A. 118
Wheeler, L. 218
White, P. A. 149
Whitton, J. L. 116
Wicklund, R. A. 201
Williams, K. J. 66
Williamson, G. M. 215
Wilson, M. 144
Wilson, P. 3
Wilson, T. D. 53, 149
Winnicott, D. W. 161
Wirz-Justice, A. 113, 143
Wiser, S. 181
Wittgenstein, L. 7
Wolfe, T. 11
Wood, C. 111
Wood, J. V. 53, 75
Worth, L. T. 78–9, 95–6, 151, 204
Wundt, W. 10, 19, 20, 188

Yando, R. 97–8, 100, 101
Young, S. N. 58

Zajonc, R. B. 11, 134, 135, 194
Zautra, A. J. 47
zeitgeber 114, 115, 117–19
Zillmann, D. 144, 205
Zucker, I. 115
Zuckerman, M. 142